The Sociology of
Health and Medicine

In memory of my grandmother
Ellen F. Harrison

The Sociology of Health and Medicine

A Critical Introduction

ELLEN ANNANDALE

Polity Press

Copyright © Ellen Annandale 1998

The right of Ellen Annandale to be identified as author of this work has been
asserted in accordance with the Copyright, Designs and Patents Act 1988.

First published in 1998 by Polity Press in association with Blackwell Publishers
Ltd.

Reprinted 1999, 2001, 2002, 2003, 2005, 2007 (twice), 2009, 2010 (twice)

Polity Press
65 Bridge Street
Cambridge CB2 1UR, UK

Polity Press
350 Main Street
Malden, MA 02148, USA

ISBN 978-0-7456-1357-4
ISBN 978-0-7456-1358-1 (pb)

A catalogue record for this book is available from the British Library and has been
applied for from the Library of Congress.

Typeset in 10 on 12 pt Palatino
by Ace Filmsetting Ltd, Frome, Somerset
Printed and bound in Great Britain by the MPG Books Group

This book is printed on acid-free paper.

For further information on Polity, visit our website: www.politybooks.com

Contents

Contents

Preface

The study of health and medicine is now well established within many sociology departments at both undergraduate and Master's level, and students of the discipline have been able to draw upon a number of excellent textbooks from the 1970s, 1980s and the early 1990s. However, in the course of my own teaching it has become increasingly apparent that the content of these texts has been superseded by the swift pace of change in the wider discipline in sociology, particularly in sociological theory, and by the implications of wide-scale changes in the delivery of health care for research in the field. These changes invite reconsideration of established issues in the discipline and throw up new areas for debate. It is for this reason that this text has been written.

The Sociology of Health and Medicine has been written for advanced undergraduates and students beginning Master's level courses and, therefore, assumes an undergraduate knowledge of sociology. The intention throughout is to draw attention to the ways in which considerations of health, illness and health care are fundamental to an understanding of contemporary society. Historically, wider sociology has paid relatively little attention to the sociology of health and medicine, yet the shifting terrain of sociological theory itself now provides the opportunity for its concerns to assume centre stage. As sociologists take ever more account of embodied experience and the risks to health thrown up by rapid social change and the emergence of new axes of experience no longer easily subsumed under traditional divisions such as class, 'race', age and gender, issues of long-standing interest such as the relationship between social structure and health, and the experience of illness, take on an added significance and enter into the wider remit of the discipline.

Two themes in particular run through the book which are integral not only to the sociology of health and illness, but also to the parent discipline. The first of these is the question of how we can understand inequality in an intellectual and political climate which increasingly stresses the death of social class, the shifting boundaries of gender and 'race', and the emergence of new forms of social division. The second theme, which relates to the first, concerns the claim that we are reaching, or have reached, the 'end of modernity' and attempts to theorize a new social order. The book does not argue directly for one way of understanding inequality and the new social order over others, but rather threads each through the discussion of various issues and attempts to evaluate the relative merits of different theoretical positions, notably as they help us to understand issues of illness and health care.

The book begins by considering the theoretical landscape of the discipline. Chapter 1 reflects on the origins of the sociology of health and illness and the large body of research that has emerged from the theoretical traditions of political economy and symbolic interactionism, as well as revisions to these traditions during the 1990s. Chapter 2 covers the spectrum of contemporary social theories which are contesting the modernist thrust in the social sciences. It begins with a consideration of Foucauldian social constructionism and moves on to debate the potential of postmodern social theories to enliven our understanding of health-related concerns. Finally, chapter 3 reviews the insights of feminism, taking as its central point the internal fragmentation of feminist thought during the 1980s and 1990s, and the implications that this has for attempts to theorize not only women's health, but also social relations of gender.

The theoretical foundation set in the first part of the book is taken forward into the second section, which addresses contemporary social inequalities as they relate to social class, gender and 'race'. As already mentioned, one of the most crucial issues that faces the discipline is how inequality can be signified in an era of rapid social change that appears to be imploding the social divisions that have been axiomatic to sociologists. Chapter 4 explores the large and well-established body of research on class inequalities in health, considering the lack of fit that seems to be emerging between concepts that are employed in the research literature within the sociology of health and illness, and wider theoretical debates on class in the social sciences. Chapter 5 continues this theme in the context of gender. It reviews historical and contemporary data on mortality and morbidity and reflects critically upon the assumptions of gender difference that have traditionally animated research in the field. The final chapter in this section explores 'race', inequality and health status. As is well known, research on 'race' and health is limited and much of that which does exist is problematic for a number of reasons. In the chapter I argue that research on health, illness and health care has much to gain from engaging with lively debates on 'race' and ethnicity in the wider social science literature.

The third section of the book turns to contemporary health care, beginning with a consideration of the structure of health-care provision in chapter 7. The crisis of modernity is nowhere more evident than in the breakdown of post-war health-care systems. The British National Health Service (NHS) has changed at what seems like breakneck pace during the 1980s and 1990s, throwing up dilemmas of major proportions in the process. Chapter 7 considers the economic context in which the NHS operates, including a review of the new profit motives embodied in health-care commissioning and the growing interface with the private health-care sector; the provision of 'care in the community' and conceptualizations of informal carers; and the significance of the 'new consumerism' in health care. Chapter 8 builds on these concerns to review contemporary theoretical debates in the sociology of the professions. It is suggested that these debates have taken an overly simplistic view of the corporate structure of health care, assuming that one doctor, nurse or other health-care provider is much the same as any other as far as professional powers are concerned. In reality there are significant internal divisions within medicine and nursing which appear to be intensifying in response to health service reforms throughout the developed world. The chapter explores these changes and reflects, in particular, on their implications for a revision of professional autonomy and dominance. The final chapter in the book, chapter 9, draws some of these threads together to consider the experience of illness and health care. In particular it addresses the tension between reflexivity and the imperative of choice in illness which, it is argued, can be seen as a trope for the contemporary social condition. Thus it is suggested that now more than ever individuals, be they people with chronic illnesses, people trying to keep themselves healthy, or providers of health care, are expected to seek information and make 'informed choices'. Yet 'choices' are not easily made, surrounded as they are by the highly politicized milieu of health care. The chapter explores these issues through a number of selected themes, including the orchestration of death and dying, the imperative of health-care screening, the elevated status of high-technology medicine, and the vociferous contemporary debate on health-care rationing.

This preface has briefly highlighted the book's contents, but it is important also for me to make clear, and to regret, what is left out. As with any text of this kind, there is only so much space, and hard choices need to be made of what to include and what has to be left to one side. One choice has been to focus very much on contemporary issues, and hence any reference to health and medicine in days gone by is minimal. While I appreciate that history is itself open to contemporary reinterpretations, readers will find many excellent texts which detail important issues, such as the history of the NHS or the nature of healing in the past. A second limitation is the overwhelming focus on Western societies and, within this, the concentration upon Britain and, to a lesser extent, the United States. In substantive terms many of the concerns that currently engage sociologists of health and illness are considered, although some are given much more space than others, and readers are sure to have their own ideas about what else should have been covered, and what deserved more sustained attention! Throughout, I have tried to marry attention to theoretical debates with attention to empirical research; in this respect I am fortunate indeed to have been able to draw upon the excellent work of the many sociologists working on issues of health, illness and health care today and in the recent past.

Acknowledgements

I am very grateful indeed to Phil Brown, Kate Hunt and Richard Lampard for their comments on one or more chapters, and to Gareth Williams for reading and commenting on the whole manuscript. Discussions over many years with Judith Clark have helped to inform my thinking on feminist theories. I am also indebted to many colleagues both in the Department of Sociology at Warwick University and elsewhere for their generous support and encouragement during the writing of this book, especially Judith Clark, Sarah Cunningham-Burley, Kate Hunt, Richard Lampard, the doctoral students with whom I have had the privilege to work, and the many students who have graduated from the MA in Sociological Research in Health Care at Warwick University during the 1990s. Of course, responsibility for any errors in this work is mine alone.

Part I

Social Theory and the Sociology of Health and Illness

1

The Theoretical Origins and Development of the Sociology of Health and Illness

The sociology of health and illness has had a vexed relationship with social theory almost since its inception. A glance at any review of the field will usually make clear that its research is undertheorized and that its scholarship is marginalized from the 'mainstream' and, consequently, of little relevance to social theorists. Yet, curiously, there seems to be a change in the air as the insights of the field find their way ever more frequently into broader sociological debates, largely because of the shifting terrain of social theory itself.

As we will see in the course of the first three chapters, mainstream sociological theories grew out of the Enlightenment, an eighteenth-century movement based on notions of progress through the application of reason and rationality. While concerns with health and the body are nascent in classical social theory, the Enlightenment legacy has meant that the actions of individuals have been seen as synonymous with conscious, rational activity. The die was cast for the sociology of health and illness in significant ways. Most importantly, issues of health, illness and the body were not part of the explicit remit of early sociology which, in the work of Emile Durkheim in the late nineteenth and early twentieth centuries, for example, was founded upon a distinction from the natural sciences. As Shilling (1993: 25) writes, 'this view had an enduring effect upon sociology and meant that the natural and the biological were frequently ruled outside of, and unimportant to, the sociologist's legitimate sphere of investigation' which was based firmly upon social factors. Ironically, the sub-field of the sociology of health and illness was cast adrift, clinging to the net of the social itself, turning away from the physical body, sometimes concentrating upon the meaning of illness at the expense of bodily experience. The tide, however, seems to be turning. As wider social theory takes ever more notice of the embodied nature of experience in, for example, concerns about individual reflexivity and risk in contemporary society, the sociology of health and illness seems ever more relevant to the wider sociological endeavour.

This chapter begins by charting the intellectual terrains which gave birth to the contemporary sociology of health and illness. The focus of attention then turns to the orthodoxy that emerged around the political economy and symbolic interactionist perspectives (described below) in the 1970s and 1980s, and the insightful body of research that they have generated. Although, as we will see later in chapters 2 and 3, these perspectives are increasingly contested by, and revised in response to, a range of theoretical perspectives which have risen to prominence during the 1980s and 1990s, they continue to exert considerable influence over research in the field. Equally, however, it is apparent that as their theoretical currency has been accepted and increasingly circulated through research agendas during the 1980s and 1990s it has been worn away by use, losing its definition in the process. For these reasons it is very important to develop a clear understanding of the premises of both political economy and symbolic interactionism.

Early developments

It is commonly acknowledged that the origins of medical sociology can be found in the post-war period. Much of the theoretical impetus came from the United States through the conceptualization of illness as social deviance (discussed below), and concerns about the health consequences of social change in the wake of rapid urbanization and industrialization. British medical sociology had its roots in the emerging social medicine of the inter-war years and its concern with social patterns of health and disease (Figlio, 1987).

These twin developments have been a concern for sociologists from the early 1970s to the present day because, it is argued, they ultimately led sociology into the arms of medicine. In the early days of the discipline, sociologists tended to adopt their ideas of what was problematic from medicine, inheriting its particular value judgements (for example, that barriers to good health lie in inappropriate behaviour on the part of patients, for example their lack of compliance with medication). Murcott (1977: 157), among others, referred to medical sociology's 'medicocentrism' whereby the topics chosen for investigation were always defined against an implicit medical template – 'fringe medicine, lay definitions of illness, marginal professions, self medicine' and so on. Horobin's (1985: 95) reference to medical sociologists inhabiting the 'interstices between the citadel of medicine and the suburb of sociology' pinpoints a persistent theme of the 1970s, 1980s and arguably also the contemporary period: that medical sociology should divorce itself from medicine and develop an alternative social approach, a view which is crystallized in recurrent debates over whether the sub-field should be called medical sociology or whether titles such as the sociology of health and illness, or health and medicine are more appropriate (Brown, 1989). Through these debates an agenda was set: to supplant the problematic medical perspective with a social model of health and health care. In order to consider the way in which this took place, the first part of the chapter will take up sociology's debate with biomedicine.

The debate with biomedicine and structural functionalism

The presentation of medical science and practice as a progressive march forward in the conquest of illness to the benefit of humankind fails to recognize that medical knowledge is never disinterested. Rather, science, which includes medicine, reflects and reproduces the dominant ideas of the society of its time. Jewson (1976) charts this process through the emergence of three distinctive medical cosmologies, or frameworks within which practitioners make sense of the signs and symptoms of illness and formulate treatment plans, over the formative period between 1770 and 1870. He reveals that medical cosmologies are modes of social interaction embedded in *social* relations of the production of medical knowledge. In the early period, characterized as 'bedside medicine', medical practitioners worked within a person-oriented cosmology where judgements were made in terms of the personal attributes of the individual sick person. In order to survive in what was a competitive environment, at a time when medical practice was controlled by a small coterie of rich fee-paying patients who had access to a wealth of practitioners of various kinds (Pelling and Webster, 1979), the physician 'sought to discover the particularistic requirements of his patient in order to satisfy them to the exclusion of his ubiquitous rivals' (Jewson, 1976: 233). The personal rapport that was necessary in order to secure business depended on the physician recognizing the patient as an integrated psychosomatic totality in which physical and emotional disturbances were indivisible.

The eclipse of this person-oriented cosmology and the rise of an object-oriented cosmology began with the development of 'hospital medicine', initially in France in the early nineteenth century. With the rise of the hospital, the medical elites were no longer dependent upon patronage; instead they had a ready mass of indigent patients at their disposal. The control of medical knowledge passed from the patient, who was now expected to 'endure and wait', to the clinician and a new disease cosmology emerged, in the course of which any 'interest in the unique qualities of the whole person evaporated to be replaced by studies of specific organic lesions and malfunctions' (Jewson, 1976: 235). This cosmology was consolidated in the mid-nineteenth century with the development of what Jewson calls 'laboratory medicine'. During this period the patient as a sentient being moved out of the frame altogether to become a material thing to be analysed, and disease became 'a physio-chemical process to be explained according to the blind inexorable laws of natural science' (Jewson 1976: 238). Changes in the conceptualization of the body and medical practice are, then, as Jewson demonstrates, bound up with the changing relationship between 'medical men' and sick persons. This demonstrates that, rather than being the simple, rational progress of science, medical knowledge is produced out of particular social relationships.

As the discussion of Jewson's work suggests, modern medicine was born during the nineteenth century during the period of significant social change associated with industrialization, the movement of the population from the countryside to the cities, and the rise of capitalism (see also the discussion of Foucault in chapter 2). Although commentators have typified modern biomedicine in a variety of ways, three characteristics are usually central. First of all, in adopting what is termed a *reductivist* approach, biomedicine assumes that health and disease are natural phenomena which exist in the individual body, rather than in the interaction of the individual and the social world. This grows out of the Enlightenment view of the world referred to earlier, which sees nature as 'given' and independent of the knower. From this perspective the clinical signs that are presented to the physician are seen as objective and independent of the symptomatic experience of the patient (e.g. the sensation of pain) (Gordon, 1988). In the eighteenth century the sick person was conceived as a 'whole person'; today the body is typically viewed as a complex machine apart from the mind, a conceptualization which has its origins in the seventeenth century and the work of the philosopher Descartes, who conceived of the mind and the body as distinct entities.

The second characteristic of biomedicine, the *doctrine of specific aetiology*, is a corollary of the reductivist approach. Dubos (1960: 87) used this term to depict the change at the end of the nineteenth century away from a view of disease as lack of harmony between the sick person and the environment towards a new vision where 'disease could be produced at will by the mere artifice of introducing a single specific factor – a virulent micro-organism – into a healthy animal'. This doctrine, Dubos argued, soon spread to other areas of medicine such as deficiency diseases where there is no intrusive micro-organism but a lack of a necessary hormone or vitamin (Freund and McGuire, 1995). But, as Dubos and others have pointed out, in actuality there are few cases in which the doctrine of specific aetiology can provide a complete account of disease causation and, consequently, it has been subject to a series of criticisms. For example, it has been pointed out that infectious agents are ubiquitous; almost all people are exposed to them, yet not all people get sick. The doctrine of specific aetiology also fails to account successfully for the multifactorial effects of the broader social environment on susceptibility to disease through factors such as stress and nutritional deficiency. Further, it fails to appreciate that the simple cause–effect model inadequately represents the diagnostic process. Clinical signs, such as elevated blood pressure, do not simply present themselves to the medical practitioner, but are filtered through the individual interpretations of symptoms and experiences by both the physician and the patient (and in many cases others who are close to the patient). The physician's task, then, is not simply to grasp unequivocal signs and symptoms, but to negotiate diagnoses in interaction with patients (Mishler, 1989).

The third characteristic of the biomedical model is the claim to *scientific neutrality*, i.e. that medicine can be rational, objective and value-free, treating each individual according to their need and irrespective of any sense of moral worth. While medicine may aim to be independent of bias, numerous studies have revealed that practice is often framed normatively. For example, Jeffrey (1979) found that hospital casualty staff characterized patients who were defined as non-urgent cases, who had inflicted injury upon themselves or had disagreeable personal characteristics as 'rubbish', which often negatively affected the quality of the treatment that they received. (These issues are discussed further in chapter 9.)

Having outlined the features of biomedicine and critical responses to them, it may be useful at this point to provide a brief illustration of how, far from being objective and value-free, medicine relies in its operation upon general cultural ideas in society. Through the example of AIDS, Waldby (1996: 32) argues that 'biomedical knowledge is always a discourse about social order, worked out in bodily terms'. Her interest is in the ways in which medicine deploys sexual identity as an 'explanation' for HIV transmission by drawing upon conceptions of the female and the feminized body (e.g. that of the gay man) as pathological points of contrast to the normative heterosexual male body. Specifically, within medical texts the heterosexual male body is presented as self-enclosed and impermeable, as being able to maintain the necessary rigid boundary between the inside of the body and the outside world to avoid the transmission of the HIV virus. In contrast, the female body and that of the gay man is seen as permeable (for example, in pregnancy and birth for women, in anal sex for gay men), and therefore as unstable and vulnerable to, as well as responsible for, viral transmission. The male body, which 'penetrates but which is never penetrated, is protected from this association' as heterosexual men secure an image as stable, self-enclosed, and untroubled, while women and gay men are seen as 'fluid' and unstable (Waldby, 1996: 77). This has particular significance for the discipline of epidemiology (the study of patterns of disease) and the implementation of preventive public health measures which involve the identification of risk groups, largely in order to protect the 'general population'. Waldby argues that, in this context, the 'general population' is virtually synonymous with heterosexual males. A threat to heterosexual men, then, is perceived as a threat to all and efforts are directed at the identification of risks associated with deviant others such as (some) women and gay men. It is apparent, for example, that when attention is directed towards sex workers, interest is typically upon the risk of female sex workers to their clients and not vice versa. Similarly, considering women as a whole, there has been little concern until very recently about the infection *of* women themselves, but much about their infecting others.

Waldby (1996) demonstrates the playing out of cultural assumptions about risk within medicine through the example of the HIV antibody test. She points out that the partial and somewhat idiosyncratic nature of the antibody response to viral presence means that there has been a degree of uncertainty and ambiguity in test results, particularly in the early days of the epidemic. The possibility of error has often been dealt with through the categorization of individuals into risk categories defined against the male heterosexual 'low-risk' norm. Thus she demonstrates that when a positive result for HIV antibodies (i.e. HIV infection) is found and the individual is deemed to be from a 'low-risk' group that person will be liable to being considered a false positive (i.e. the result is an error), while for someone assigned to a 'high-risk' group, it is likely to stand. That is, scientific results alone are insufficient to determine a person's HIV status with total accuracy, and social categorization (where heterosexual men are typically taken as being at the lowest risk for infection) must be drawn upon in interpretation.

Waldby's (1996) criticism of biomedicine through the example of AIDS is, of course, a present-day illustration of the way in which medicine reflects and reproduces the dominant ideas of the society of its time. Intrinsic to this evaluation is the claim that medicine cannot be understood in its *own* terms as an objective science, since it also incorporates social values into its practice. Consequently, it must be considered from a social perspective. This argument was also of central concern to critics of medical sociology's alleged medico-centric bias during its early years for, as we saw earlier, its early research was criticized for adopting the perspective of biomedicine as its own. It was in response to these concerns that those working in the field sought to turn theory and research away from *biological* towards *social* processes. Within early medical sociology this position was consolidated in Eliot Freidson's influential text *Profession of Medicine*, first published in 1970. Freidson (1988 [1970]: 211) declared that medicine and sociology had different remits: medical sociologists, he wrote, should not be interested in the doctor's job, which is 'to test and refine medical concepts of illness and its treatment'; rather, their interest should be in the social reality of human life which 'while never wholly independent of other levels of reality, can be treated usefully as a reality in itself'. The work of Talcott Parsons, the progenitor of the structural functionalist orthodoxy within sociology in the USA until the 1970s, undoubtedly helped to establish this distinctly sociological approach to issues of health and illness.

The work of Parsons

Talcott Parsons' work has been read in a number of ways. As Frank (1991a: 205) has remarked, extremes of thought run through his writing on health where 'bourgeois apologies for professional authority alternate with a conception of the body that can be read as postmodern in its implication, whatever its intent'. Not surprisingly, conflicting interpretations abound. Of particular interest to us here is Parsons' insistence that illness should be seen as a social phenomenon rather than as a physical entity or property of individuals. In Parsons' work ill health was to be understood in terms of the functioning of society as a whole. As he wrote in *The Social System* (Parsons, 1951: 430), 'too low a general level of health, too high an incidence of illness, is dysfunctional: this is in the first instance because illness incapacitates the effective performance of social roles'. In his later work, in particular, Parsons was to take the concept of health far away from a condition of the isolated body, referring in the late 1970s to health as 'a symbolic circulating media regulating human action and other life processes' (quoted in Frank, 1991a: 206). Above all, Parsons viewed health as a valued social commodity, an essential resource for individual achievement and the smooth running of society. Although ill health was not *always* unequivocally social in origin, he was at pains to point out (Parsons, 1975) that there is likely to be a 'psychic' dimension or a 'motivatedness' to illness present to a degree in all forms of illness. It was this recognition that led him to conceptualize illness as deviance. Even apparently non-motivated illnesses such as accidents or degenerative and infectious diseases embody a motivational aspect in so far as an individual might consciously or unconsciously expose themselves to risk (Gerhardt, 1989). Clearly, Parsons' perspective on the social nature of illness is complex. He was concerned with ill health as the inability to fulfil valued social roles (such as breadwinner or parent), but alongside this, the individual's actual failure to work or look after his or her children was to be understood in psychological terms. In fact, he gave relatively little consideration to why any one individual (or social group) might be motivated (consciously or unconsciously) to withdraw from their social roles, except in so far as this lay in a generalized inability to cope with everyday stresses and strains. His concern was more resolutely with the therapeutic process. The term 'sick role' was coined to refer to the niche that is provided for the individual to recuperate from illness free from the stresses of everyday life.

The sick role, which should be viewed as a pure type rather than a literal empirical description, has four defining features, two of which can be described as 'rights' and two as 'obligations'. The two rights consist of exemption from normal social roles and from blame for ill health, and the two obligations are to get well (i.e. to relinquish the rights of the sick role as expeditiously as possible), and to seek competent professional help and co-operate with the physician (or other health-care provider). These rights and obligations are mirrored in the 'physician role' (which is less well defined by Parsons). This involves winning the patient's trust and access to their body, and the obligation to apply the highest levels of competence in caring for the patient, and to be guided by the patient's best interest (rather than by personal gain).

A range of critical comments has been levied against Parsons' work, notably in regard to the sick role. The most frequently made include the following: (1) that entry to the sick role is not as straightforward as Parsons implied; seriousness, the legitimacy of the illness and the varying cultural expectations (by class, 'race', gender, age) of how one should behave when ill all play a crucial role; (2) ill health is not morally neutral in the way that Parsons implied. Far from the patient being exempted, responsibility is uppermost. Furthermore, many health conditions are stigmatized; (3) the sick role pertains to acute conditions and cannot relate to chronic illness; (4) Parsons assumed that the patient would willingly comply with the physician, when in effect patients are not passive and the doctor–patient relationship is imbued with conflict. Discussion of these points can be found in Freidson (1988), Gallagher (1976) and Hart (1985). Parsons replied to some of these criticisms in the mid-1970s, offering a rebuttal in response to some and, to others, restating his original position. He claimed that chronic illness could be accounted for, since what he referred to was not necessarily full recovery but return to relative functioning whenever possible. He appreciated that patients are not always passive, indeed they often take an active part in their treatment. But he insisted that in the last instance, 'there must be a built-in institutionalised superiority of the professional roles, grounded in responsibility, competence, and occupational concern' (Parsons, 1975: 271).

We will not enter into detailed debate over the worth of the concept of the sick role here since our interest is more general and concerns the place of Parsons' distinctly sociological account of health, illness and health care alongside the biomedical model that caused such consternation in the early years of medical sociology. Clearly, Parsons' perspective did vivify the nascent social model. But, at the same time, it also solidified medicine's power base and arguably, along with this, its ability to set research agendas. Commentators such as Frankenberg (1974) and others expressed their concern that sociologists should be *questioning* the activities of physicians rather than taking them at face value. The theoretical perspectives which came to the fore in the 1970s (political economy and interactionism) provided the opportunity to put a critical evaluation of medical practice and the power of doctors at the heart of the discipline.

Critical challenges: political economy and interactionism

The political economy perspective

By the 1970s a clear agenda had been set for medical sociology: to liberate contemporary understandings of health and medicine from the political straitjacket of the biomedical model. The roots of the political economy approach lie in Engels' *The Condition of the Working Class in England* (1993 [1845]). Engels analysed the aetiology and distribution of typhoid, tuberculosis, scrofula and rickets in the population and concluded that, since they had a direct association with the relations of production under capitalism, medical intervention alone was insufficient for the eradication of disease. Out of these beginnings, the political economy approach has built a profound criticism of the social production of ill health under capitalism. The central tenet is that there is a contradiction between the pursuit of health and the pursuit of profit (Doyal, 1979). Medicine is enmeshed in the constant search for profit by finance and industrial capitalists, itself both contributing to and bolstered by the capitalist system and girded by the activities of the state. Crucially, this tripartite relationship operates in the interests of capitalism, (largely) in the interests of medicine, but definitely not in the interests of the health of the population.

It should be apparent that from this perspective there is little to be gained by attempting to understand health and health care by reference to the activities of individuals or to the institution of medicine; they must be placed within a broader political and economic framework. McKinlay sets this framework up nicely through the analogy of the game. He argues that

> *one can conceive of medical care-related activities as the game among a group of highly trained players, carefully selected for the affinity of their interests with the requirements of capitalist institutions, which is watched by a vast number of spectators (involving all of the people some of the time and, increasingly, some of the people all the time). And surrounding this game itself, with its interested public, is the capitalistic state (setting the rules by which the game ought to be played before the public), the presence of which ensures the legitimacy of the game and guarantees, through resources derived from spectators, that the prerogatives and interests of the park (finance and industrial capital) are always protected and advanced. (1977: 464–5)*

Capital invades all areas of life (home, work, leisure time) creating health-related problems such as unemployment, pollution and stress in the unmitigated search for profits. Social services grow to meet this demand and medicine takes on the impossible task of solving problems that are outside its control (Navarro, 1986).

So, although the profession of medicine is a target of criticism from the political economy perspective, since historically it can be seen to have actively sought a position of dominance, it is not the ultimate culprit since its power is delegated by capital. Capital operates in the field of health in the same way that it does in all other areas of society: 'invading, exploiting, and ultimately despoiling any field of endeavour – with no necessary humane commitment to it – in order to seize and carry away an acceptable level of profit' (McKinlay, 1977: 461). McKinlay (1984) refers to a logic of capital accumulation in health care which operates in cycles as follows: (1) competition forces capitalists to expand their output and sales (irrespective of the use-values of the commodities that are produced); (2) this generates profit, which (3) needs to be reinvested (in new ventures and in research); (4) profit must be realized on these new ventures; (5) there is a search for new buyers and new markets, often using deceptive advertising and the creation of a commodity-fetishist culture; (6) foreign markets are also captured; (7) profits are reinvested, returning us to the beginning of the cycle. These forces underpin the operation of formal and informal health care, and also circumscribe our definitions of health and illness.

Political economists have explored the range of ways in which capital operates in the search for profit in the field of health and health care, supported by the state and mediated by medicine. Here we will look at just two broad areas for illustration. First of all, we will consider the commodification of the body, taking the manufacture of silicone breast implants as our example. The second illustration will be the way in which the lifestyle politics of 'late capitalism' foster an ideology of health which stresses individual responsibility.

Capital and the commodification of the body

The process of industrialization, from the early development of manufacturing capital through to the high-technology industries of the late twentieth century, carries risks to health of various kinds from exposure to chemical toxins, to the E. coli outbreak and BSE crisis, to dangers in the construction trade, and the stresses and strains experienced by chief executive and shop-floor worker alike. For some commentators (e.g. Hart, 1982) it is this wider process of industrialization, rather than its capitalist variant, which is at fault. Yet political economists insist that there is an inevitable contradiction between safety and the pursuit of profit. Women's current struggle for compensation for the side-effects of silicone breast implants provides a good illustration of this. In 1963 Dow Corning (a subsidiary of Dow Chemical Company) began manufacturing a breast implant consisting of a semi-permeable envelope of silicone elastomer filled with silicone gel. The silicone gel was deemed to be inert, so if a rupture occurred the gel would not migrate or be harmful to body tissue. However, since the 1970s a minority of surgeons became concerned with the transgression of silicone across the envelope of the implant (often called gel-bleed) and began to press manufacturers and the US Federal Drugs Agency (FDA) for a moratorium on production. According to Jenny (1994) and others, this pressure went unheeded for far too long as plastic surgeons and manufacturers convinced the FDA that silicone implants were safe.

Approximately one million women had implants for cosmetic reasons and for reconstruction after surgery for breast cancer and other conditions during the 1980s and early 1990s. Levy (1994) estimates that this includes between 30,000 and 50,000 women in the United Kingdom (about 60 per cent of these implants were done after surgery for breast cancer). By 1994, 36,000 women had reported injuries (such as implant ruptures) and were seeking damages (Tran, 1995). Two major risks to health have now been identified. First of all, silicone gel bleeds into the body from the envelope and has been linked to serious diseases such as systemic sclerosis, lupus and other auto-immune and neurological conditions (many of these conditions may have a latency period of thirty years). The second problem is encapsulation, which occurs as the body reacts to the presence of silicone by developing a hard encircling capsule of fibrous tissue around the implant. In addition to these two problems, since silicone gel is radio-opaque, radiographers can have difficulty visualizing breast tissue behind the implant, which hampers the early detection of breast cancers. Several women have died as a result of the side-effects of silicone implants and a great many more live with chronic illnesses which seriously impair their lives. In August 1997 a state jury in Louisiana found that the Dow Chemical Company had knowingly deceived women by hiding information about silicone and health risks. In 1992 the FDA had banned all but their limited use in the US (in the UK the Department of Health has taken the stance that more evidence is needed before it can be concluded that they are unsafe, although at the time of writing in the summer of 1997 a new review looks imminent). Dow Corning and other manufacturers have stopped manufacturing implants, but still insist that they are safe.

During the 1980s Dow Corning (the major manufacturer) settled a number of US lawsuits out of court with confidentiality clauses attached and court protection of all findings and medical records. In 1988 Mariann Hopkins filed a lawsuit and resolved not to settle despite an offer of $1.8 million to do so. The jury ruled in her favour to the tune of $7.3 million and Dow Corning was found guilty of fraud and malice. The case opened up the floodgates to litigation, prompting Dow Corning to settle $4.225 billion in 1993 on a class action suit. In such a suit the claims and rights of many people (currently estimated at approximately 400,000 women world-wide) are decided in a single court proceeding on a 'no win no fee' basis. There are a number of benefits of opting into a class action suit, not the least being that there is no need to prove that current illness postdates the claimant's first implant. On the down side, it is rumoured that the very large number of women in the class action means that payouts may be considerably smaller than those that could be achieved in a successful individual lawsuit. Moreover, while in the class action Dow Corning and other manufacturers can continue to deny liability (it is a 'business decision' to settle cases), in separate lawsuits they can be held accountable. However, in an individual case in the US a woman would need to prove cause, and such suits have had a chequered success rate to date. Tran (1995) reports that 1,500 women have opted out of the class settlement to date to pursue separate actions. According to a spokesperson for Dow Corning 'we have consistently said that we cannot both fund the global settlement [class action] and afford large numbers of law suits outside the settlement' (quoted in Tran, 1995: 3). In May 1995 Dow Corning filed for bankruptcy protection.

Particular technologies are, then, implicated in health risks, but these risks are exacerbated by the search for profit, with medicine operating as a lucrative site for capital. In brief, capitalism despoils both health and health care.

The political economy perspective has been subject to strong criticism on a number of counts. For example, several commentators (Hart, 1982, 1985; Reidy, 1984) argue that it fails to recognize health gains – such as the increases in living standards and in longevity – that have accompanied capitalist development. In response political economists – Navarro (1985a, 1985b) in particular – have pointed to the contradictions of capitalism and the possibility for (short-term) working-class gains. In addition, many sociologists within this tradition are themselves actively engaged in activities to effect reform from *within* the capitalist system. (For example, Navarro (1994) was centrally involved in defining health policy for Jesse Jackson's Rainbow Coalition in the late 1980s and was a member of Hillary Clinton's National Health Care Reform Task Force.) To argue that improvements in mortality undermine the political economy position in particular seems to miss the mark since the concern is with *relative* differentials in morbidity and mortality between social classes (an issue discussed in more detail in chapter 4). Concerns about the ability of individuals and social groups to effect social change within the Marxist political economy perspective, however, carry more weight. While Navarro has consistently emphasized the role of working-class praxis in the struggle for health and health care under capitalism, this has often been framed at a fairly high level of generality drawing upon limited examples, leaving the complex relationship between structure and agency largely unarticulated. Gerhardt (1989: 331) raises the question of whether 'individuals are seen as anything but docile members of a pervasive social order'. Even Waitzkin's (1991) work on the micro-politics of health care, which explores the ways in which apparently humanistic and unproblematic encounters between doctors and patients mask assumptions which encourage conformity with the dominant expectations of capitalism (such as the work ethic), leaving the structural problems which foster ill health unchallenged, seems to overstate the influence of medical ideology on patients, or at least fails to explore the possibility that patients do not accept the doctors' view of their problem uncritically.

Disorganized capitalism: a new political economy of health?

Although the criticisms that have been raised deserve ongoing consideration, their immediacy as *particular* issues for debate is tempered by the weightier general question of the current status of Marxist social theory itself. Bluntly put, if Marxism is dead, what implications does this have for the political economy of health? For many, events of the early 1990s in the former Soviet Union and eastern Europe signal not only the end of communism, but also a death blow to Marxism, which is seen to have come to an 'end' itself (Makdisi et al., 1996: ix). For example, Lash and Urry (1994: 1) begin their exploration of the nature of late capitalism in a deliberately provocative tone, by asking: is 'any writer more dated, more of a "dinosaur", than Marx?' Certainly, the industrial capitalism that Marx described no longer exists, as the extraction of surplus for profit has shifted from the production of commodities with a relatively stable use-value to satisfy fairly easily defined needs, to a phase of what Lash and Urry call 'disorganized capitalism' where use-values are destabilized as capitalism becomes at once increasingly fragmented, flexible and international in form. In concrete terms, we have seen a radical shift from an economy in which people transform raw material into mass-market goods, to a flexible economy based on the production of knowledge and information. The old order where the 'capitalist core was characterised by a set of producer networks clustered around a heavy-industrial hub of the motor, chemicals, electrical and steel industries' and where 'finance, services and distribution functions were either subordinate to, or driven by, industrial production' has given way to a new cluster of information, communication and other industries (Lash and Urry, 1994: 17).

While – as has been the case for Marxism ever since the nineteenth century – conflicting interpretations abound, for many commentators what we are witnessing rather than the *end* of capitalism, is its *revitalization* as new arenas of exploitation open up quite unlike any that have gone before. As Landry and MacLean (1993: xii) put it, now 'the market is "in" everything and nothing is incapable of being commodified'. Modernity, therefore, has not been superseded, but, in the words of Lash and Urry, radically exaggerated. Individuals live in a world that has a runaway character, subject to a veritable barrage of information and new goods, many of which are more important for the status that they confer than for their use-value – status symbols, such as designer labels, for example, having more importance than the basic use of the product. Lash and Urry (1994: 3) argue that the flows and accumulations of images and symbols of disorganized capitalism do not 'just lead to increasing meaninglessness', rather, they encourage the development of a new *critical reflexivity*, or sense of freedom to act, on the part of individuals, which is itself a *precondition* of capital accumulation through consumption. For a large part of society – the professional–managerial classes and the skilled working class – this means a new empowerment, as traditional structures like social class and the family recede to be replaced by a new ability to make consumer choices; for others there is spiralling downward mobility into the de-industrialized spaces of the impacted ghetto (in the shift of manufacturing from the cities to the suburban and ex-urban locations).

Capitalism, then, is still with us and the issue that we must wrestle with is not its demise, but its revitalization in new forms. For some, Marx's social theory is still relevant to this task, while for others it has lost its usefulness and new conceptualizations are needed. For example, Giddens (1994: 87) contends that Marxist politics provide no solution to new risks associated with 'the driving expansionism of capitalistic enterprise'. To date, with just a few exceptions, sociologists of health and medicine have remained relatively quiet on these issues. However, it is possible for us to follow their implications through to a number of key areas of interest such as inequalities in health, the restructuring of health-care provision, and the experience of illness, as will be discussed in later chapters. Here we will briefly take up recent theoretical work on reflexivity, risk and health in late modernity.[1]

Reflexivity and risk, and health in late modernity

Modern society, it has been argued, is a 'risk society' which puts the phenomenon of health centre-stage. Concern now is no longer simply that economic hazards undermine health, but that environmental risks to health threaten the very existence of society as 'everywhere and eternally' they 'penetrate the economic and political system' (Beck, 1992: 83). In this new social environment, risk is increasingly opened to the public gaze and new political forms emerge. Power is decentralized from the state into the specialized division of labour which Beck refers to as 'techno-economic subpolitics'. Modes of living in risk society are very much tied to the sub-politics of medicine, that is, the broad arena of medical industries and health institutions. Medicine, defined in this way, employs a market strategy which profits from risk. Beck claims that

> *in more and more fields of action a **reality** defined and thoroughly structured by medicine is becoming the prerequisite of thought and action . . . not only is the spiral of medical formation and decision-making twisted deeper and deeper into the . . . reality of the risk society, but an **insatiable appetite for medicine** is produced, a permanently expanding market for the services of the medical profession whose ramifications echo into the distant depths. (1992: 211)*

This means that risks to health *themselves* become an economic factor as new markets are generated for products such as filters for pollutants and vitamin complexes to enhance nutrition in an age of chemically infused fast foods. Science itself turns towards the definition and management of the very risks which it itself produces. The boom industry of cosmetic surgery, on which $300 million and rising are spent every year in the USA (Davis, 1995), epitomizes Beck's medical sub-politics. As we have seen in the discussion of silicone breast implants, the health risks that it generates can be enormous, yet the decision to undergo cosmetic surgery is itself part and parcel of the emergence of the self as a 'reflexive project'. Giddens in particular stresses that under conditions of high modernity, the body is 'reflectively mobilised' becoming a 'phenomenon of choices and options' (1991: 8). As the 'visible aspect of the self', the body is not passive but needs to be monitored by individuals as they balance opportunities and risks, virtually forced to design their own bodies, and to do so under conditions of considerable uncertainty. Anorexia, Giddens claims, is symptomatic of the negative effects of what he calls manufactured uncertainty on everyday life: 'deciding what to eat', he writes, 'is also deciding "how to be" in respect to the body – and for individuals subject to specific social tension, particularly young women, the iron self-discipline of anorexia results' (1994: 82). In wider terms, of course, the billion-dollar diet industry also epitomizes the new forms of capitalist enterprise that have emerged over recent decades.

In the opinion of both Giddens and Beck, the global conditions of late modernity invite us to reconsider the nature of individual experience which, it is argued, is no longer bound by class, gender and 'race', but exposed to new social parameters of risk and uncertainty which cross-cut traditional social divisions. To be sure, these divisions still have *relevance* for people, but they are no longer, in a straightforward way, the units from which experience derives. Risks to health of various kinds, ranging from nuclear catastrophe to mysterious viral infections, contaminated foods, and stresses from unemployment and unhappy marriages, must be dealt with reflexively as the individual increasingly stands alone, looking for security in the face of uncertainty and an implosion of knowledge-systems. While arguably reflexivity might increase 'health awareness' – indeed this is a plank of contemporary health promotion – being forced to make choices by accessing an array of expert information, under conditions of uncertainty, can create considerable anxiety. How does the individual cope? The complex factors that surround the decisions that individuals make about health and illness will be discussed in detail elsewhere in the book (chapter 9), but at this point it may be useful to take one illustration, that of prenatal diagnosis. Katz Rothman's (1988) study of prenatal diagnosis vividly demonstrates the stresses that women experience in a social climate of risk that values knowledge and making informed choices. Women's reasons for refusing amniocentesis (taking amniotic fluid from the uterus to test for genetic abnormalities), which may centre around a commitment to the foetus/baby, feelings of safety (will the baby be 'normal'?), a sense of fate, or the unacceptability of abortion, are difficult to justify in a world which values the information and 'choice' that an amniocentesis result ostensibly provides. Katz Rothman shows that, far from providing choice and control, amniocentesis creates a 'tentative pregnancy'; fearful of a 'bad result', women cannot embrace their pregnancy, maintaining an emotional distance from the baby/foetus and denying or not letting themselves really feel foetal movements until the test result is available.

As Crawford (1984) has discussed very well, capitalist ideology is refracted through health beliefs, be this through the promotion and consumption of new medical technologies such as amniocentesis or silicone breast implants, or through diet stuffs and exercise programmes. In many ways foreshadowing the work of Giddens, Beck and others, he points out that 'when macro-conditions that affect health appear out of control, self-control over the considerable range of personal behaviours that also affect health is an only remaining option' (1984: 74). The burden of responsibility is placed squarely upon the individual, breaking the connection between good health and the demand for public services in the process. Yet an economy built on 'responsibility' and *self-control* alone – profitable though it may be (the diet industry, health clubs) – is ruinous to late capitalism. Consequently it exists alongside the economic mandate to *consume* market-offered goods, as immediate gratification is portrayed as a source of stress reduction and emotional and physical well-being.

This introductory discussion of the political economy perspective has highlighted its status as a theory in transition. Buffeted by the significant challenges to its Marxist foundations and by the restructuring of capitalism (and, as we will see in chapter 4, challenges to the existence of a social class structure), within the field of the sociology of health and medicine it has yet to re-establish a truly firm theoretical foundation in an era of significant social change. The continuing insights that it generally affords the discipline will be explored in the chapters that follow; at this point we turn from the present back to the 1970s and the theoretical origins of the sociology of health and illness.

As we have seen, the political economy perspective's early critical acuity was an essential plank of medical sociology's claim to authenticity as it sought to found a disciplinary project which established health, illness and health care as fundamentally social in form. The contested nature of the 'social' itself was thrown into particular relief in the 1970s when the 'macro' approach of political economy and 'micro' perspective of symbolic interactionism began an inveterate struggle for position within the sub-discipline. Although there are notable exceptions, political economists have had little truck with the bedrock principle of interactionism – that health, illness and health care must be understood by reference to the activities of individuals. The purpose of the next section is briefly to present the unfolding of the interactionist perspective from its early origins, to its enormous success as an established position within the sociology of health and medicine, and finally to what Fine (1993), referring to the discipline of sociology as a whole, has characterized as its ironic dissipation as it has become accepted into the mainstream, a victim of its own success.

Interactionism

Origins and early work

Interactionist sociology rose to prominence in the 1960s and 1970s, quickened by the loss of credibility of Parsonsian structural functionalism and by the search for 'a more humanistic sociology related to the emerging political scene of the 1960s' (Gerhardt, 1989: 75). But its origins go further back, most notably to the teachings of George Herbert Mead (published posthumously in 1934) and his student Herbert Blumer (1969).

Many interactionists have resisted the designation of their work as a 'theory', preferring instead to think in terms of a 'loosely structured cluster of fundamental ideas' (Lindesmith and Strauss, 1969: 1). At the core of this 'cluster of ideas' is the proposition that, even though there is a biological base which underlies experience, selves are essentially social products which develop out of interaction with others (Mead, 1972 [1934]). We are able cognitively to step outside ourselves and to see ourselves as others see us through the 'looking-glass self' (Cooley, 1981). The self develops through role-taking, its legitimacy dependent upon the attitude of others. Language is crucial in this process since it provides a vehicle for self-reflection, no other gesture or symbol being so successful in affecting the individual in the same way that it affects others.

Since the self is a product of social experience, it is not fixed, but emergent or socially constructed. Axiomatic to the interactionist position is the dialectic between the individual actor and the social environment. With the capacity for self-reflection individuals are self-directive with the ability to select, interpret and bestow meaning upon their interactions with others. But, by virtue of the very fact that this takes place in the presence of others (either actual or envisaged, individuals or groups), self-direction is always limited. Constraints come into play – others may not view us in the way that we view ourselves; they may not act towards us in the way that we expect, and the prior actions of others (which we may not be aware of, or may be aware of but are powerless to modify) may set up barriers to our actions. As a result of this we are called upon to be 'artful' in our everyday lives by becoming engaged in a process of 'negotiation, impression management, and meaning creation' (Fine, 1993: 64). These processes – the ways in which individuals give meaning to social events (such as childbirth, surgery, death); the ways in which they manage changed identities in ill health;

and the 'negotiation' that takes place in formal and informal health-care settings – are the subject-matter of interactionism.

It is apparent that interaction contexts must be conceived as both the seedbed of human agency and the obstacle to its growth. Tucked away all too neatly in this statement is an unresolved struggle which extends over almost three decades to understand the exact ways in which the individual both modifies and is modified by the social environments which surround health, illness and health care. This question is by no means the sole province of interactionism – some see it as significant for all sociologists – but it has been a particular preoccupation. Underpinning almost all research and commentary in this tradition is a moral alliance with the 'patient's perspective'; a concern that the patient's sense of self should be validated (rather than despoiled) by others, and that the patient should have a greater say in treatment decisions. This in itself signals a concern with undue constraints of various kinds upon individual agency, such as the failure to be heard, or to be allowed to make choices. Indeed, much of the ethnographic work of interactionists has revealed that, in the last instance, there is precious little space for patients (and to a lesser extent doctors) to establish their own individual definitions of the situation, and this is largely because of their relative lack of power and resources. Some, such as Gerhardt (1989), have taken this as a failure of the interactionist position, arguing that it fails to validate its own theoretical premise of human agency. But this is to miss the mark of interactionism's significant contributions: the rich insights that it provides into the intricacies of medical work, the delicate manoeuvring that takes place in patient–carer interactions, and the diverse individual experience of health, illness and health care.

The interactionist domain: illness, the self and the experience of health care

Although it is not possible to do justice to the depth and breadth of interactionism's scholarship here, by drawing upon some of the 'classic' and more recent work in the tradition we can sketch and illustrate key concerns: the social context of health care and the experience of health and illness. As we outline this research our focus will be on the interactionist conceptualization of agency.

Despite differences among interactionists, all react against the positivistic conceptualization of organizations with its stress on the formal structure of the organization – particularly technology and rationally defined goals – as a determinant of individual behaviour. The notion of social structure takes on a completely different hue for interactionists. Mead has explained that, like individual selves, social institutions

> *are developments within, or particular and formalised manifestations of, the social life-process at its human evolutionary level. As such they are not necessarily subversive of individuality in the individual members; and they do not necessarily represent or uphold narrow definitions of certain fixed and specific patterns of acting which in any given circumstances should characterise the behaviour of . . . individuals . . . as members of the given community or social group. On the contrary, they need to define the social, or socially responsible, patterns of individual conduct in only a very broad and general sense, affording plenty of scope for originality, flexibility, and a variety of such conduct; and as the main formalised functional aspects or phases of the whole organised structure of the social life-process at its human level they properly partake of the dynamic and progressive character of that process. (1972: 262–3)*

Here Mead simultaneously presents social organizations (hospitals, clinics, homes) as flexible and dynamic containers for human agency, and as reified actors (institutions act in order to define certain patterns of action and to uphold these definitions). Given this dual conception it is not surprising that, while sharing a view of human agency as socially emergent and a concern with individual meaning-making, interactionists have conceived of the relationship between social organization and individual social action in different ways.

Even though Goffman personally resisted classification into one or other 'school of thought', it has been customary to consider his work as falling within the interactionist tradition. As Gouldner (1970: 379) remarks, 'Goffman's is a sociology of "co-presence", of what happens when people are in one another's presence. It is a social theory that dwells upon the episodic and sees life only as it is lived in a narrow interpersonal circumference', as coming alive 'only in the fluid, transient "encounter"'. Yet it was not individuals *per se* that interested Goffman. Rather, they engaged his attention because

> *it is only in individual behaviour that it is possible to observe the nature and working of the social institutions and structures that we have – or have had – fabricated for ourselves. But he observed, and analysed, the conduct of individuals as an attribute of social order, of society, not as an attribute of individual persons. (Burns, 1992: 25)*

Although he viewed the social order as 'fragile, impermanent, full of unexpected holes, and in constant need of repair' (Burns, 1992: 26), his attraction was to the strength of the social order and an exploration of the social rules which govern interaction (Goffman, 1967). Goffman's concern with the surface structure of interaction such as rituals and ceremonies was applied to the health field in the 1970s by Strong (1979) in his observational study of paediatric clinics. In his monograph the explicit concern is not with the feelings, opinions or perceptions of parents and doctors, but with the ceremonies that they take part in, the rituals that they enact in the consultation.

Each medical encounter is framed by a series of expectations, typically embodied in what Strong calls the 'bureaucratic role format'. This ceremonial form is a collaborative effort, constructed by doctor and parent by avoiding all matters 'not fitting' with the model of an ideal parent and doctor who display themselves as mutually committed to achieving the best for the child under the medical ethos of individual commitment and gentility. Under this form the doctors in Strong's study actively worked to idealize and sanctify mothers. For example, if a mother was felt to have behaved inappropriately this was repaired by justifying her actions (offering acceptable excuses for missed appointments, highlighting future good behaviour rather than past misdemeanours). Parents complemented this by idealizing medical competence, assuming the doctor's expertise without question and avoiding reference to errors in judgement and practice. The result of this joint endeavour was the construction of an overt ceremonial order which permitted interaction to proceed in as smooth a manner as possible. Strong points out that, for Goffman, 'people are mere creatures of frames, and what we normally conceive of as a person is reduced to a set of devices for the re-creation and careful maintenance of pre-existing and super-ordinate frames' (1979: 186). Yet at the same time he

> provides us with a quite separate model; one that emphasises the margins of freedom that allow the individual some space for his or her own needs, identity and purposes. Rather than being mere puppets, individuals, in this other version, are shown to manipulate frames to their own advantage ... to make elaborate copies and parodies of more serious frames even while acting within them. (1979: 186)

In this regard, despite the ritual avoidance of moral indignation in Strong's study, doctors still used strategies to manipulate patients (e.g. to 'correct' their opinions and to guide them towards certain behaviours). Patients could also disrupt the ceremonial order, by insistent questioning for example, but this was not very successful given the medical authority invested in the bureaucratic frame. Apparently, the ceremonial order quite effectively ring-fenced the interaction of parent and doctor.

In the work of Strauss et al. (see Glaser and Strauss, 1965; Strauss et al., 1985) the social order is far less tightly circumscribed. In their own words, while Goffman 'analysed interaction as the embodiment of social order', they are 'cognisant of rules but are principally interested in . . . [the institution's] open-ended and problematic character' (Strauss et al., 1963: 14–15). The rules, rituals and ceremonies that surround health and health care are inherently precarious because they are built on the shaky foundation of a negotiated consensus. The formal institution is no more than a geographical locale, 'a site where persons drawn from different professions come together to carry out their respective purposes' (Strauss et al., 1963: 150). It does not operate according to rules, indeed 'hardly anyone knows all the extant rules, much less exactly what they apply to, for whom, and with what sanctions'. Nothing is binding or shared for all time. It is such considerations that lead Strauss et al. (1963: 148) to 'emphasise the importance of negotiation – the processes of give-and-take, of diplomacy, of bargaining – which characterises organisational life'. Negotiation connotes meaning which develops in the course of interaction; it is through meaning-making that individuals know the world and are able to act effectively in it. Consequently, action in the health-care context involves a process of definition, i.e. defining the context in which one is involved, taking account of the definitions of others, and, thereby, negotiating a consensus (which may be fleeting enough to allow one to 'get by' in a particular task, or sufficiently long-term to anticipate a changed self or new work policy). In this way, 'individuals are seen to produce rather than react to the rules and roles governing their situational conduct' (Gerhardt, 1989: 126).

The corpus of Strauss's work with his colleagues was built around observational and in-depth interview-based studies of the interaction that takes place around chronic illness and death. In their early work on dying Glaser and Strauss fashioned the term 'awareness contexts' to conceptualize 'what each interacting person knows of the patient's defined status [as a dying person], along with his recognition of the others' awareness of his own definition' (1965: 10). A range of forms – closed awareness, suspected awareness, mutual pretence awareness, and open awareness – derived from the authors' fieldwork depict the contexts in which the dying and those that surround them interact.

These forms are not fixed, but fluid, guiding the interplay between those involved and open to reconstruction as patient, doctor, or nurse engineer change. Bargaining is central to organizational life, 'every patient . . . wants to get certain things or to have certain events occur; he [or she] coaxes, wheedles, bargains, persuades, hints, and uses other forms of negotiation' to this end (Glaser and Strauss, 1965: 94). Staff, for their part, strike bargains with patients (for example over nursing regimens or how to deal with relatives) in an effort to achieve a 'job well done' (a humane and acceptable death, for example).

Negotiation is also at the heart of Roth's (1963) classic study of the timetables that are constructed in the illness career of tuberculosis (TB) patients. Timetables are an important monitoring device for TB, which at the time of his study was surrounded by diagnostic and prognostic uncertainty, providing both patients and doctors with a conception of how long a patient with given disease characteristics should need to spend in hospital. Although both patients and doctors grouped patients into categories in an effort to determine when a particular benchmark event in the career (such as taking a gastric culture) should occur, the system of grouping could differ. Roth found that patients used very broad categories, with an individual patient believing that 'anything that happens to any of the patients in that group . . . can legitimately be used as a reference point for determining what should happen to him' (1963: 36). The physician, in contrast, used more highly differentiated categories, referring to the finer points of clinical tests. Consequently,

> *the anticipation of and allowances for the reactions of the other party on both sides of a continuing bargaining system form a dialectic of constant influences operating over a period of time . . . Patients constantly press for advancing the timetable; physicians try to resist such pressures . . . The result of these opposing pressures is a continual bargaining between patients and physicians over the question of when given points on the timetable have been reached. (1963: 57, 61)*

Evidently, interactionist work on the organizational context of formal health care has endorsed Mead's contention that selves are social constructs which develop out of interaction with others. Central to the process of identity-formation is the reaction of others to the self. This principle led to a marked shift in the way that researchers sought to understand 'health behaviour', as during the 1970s a series of commentators argued that the traditional approach, which tended to adopt a medical point of view on appropriate behaviour (e.g. in help-seeking) and to conceptualize individual action as a response to structural position (e.g. social class and culture), was inappropriate (see Dingwall, 1976). In its place was a new concern with social actors who, in health and in illness, 'actively sustain their social world in every moment of their interactions with other people' (Cornwell, 1984: 19). The large and rich body of research on health beliefs and the experience of illness will be considered in chapter 9; here we touch briefly upon just two studies which exemplify interactionist work in this area.

Cornwell's (1984) in-depth interview study of working-class people in east London is about the relationship between 'way of life' and common-sense ideas about health and illness. In their 'public accounts' (that is, what is seen as acceptable to others) people revealed illness to be 'morally problematic conditions'. When speaking about health and illness,

> the person always made sure that they were seen to be in the 'right', i.e. the morally correct position in relation to them. The 'right' relationship to these terms was that of being basically healthy; if illnesses were mentioned, people made sure that they were understood to be 'real' and therefore legitimate. (1984: 124)

The quest to be seen as 'healthy' bore no necessary relation to an individual's medical history. Indeed, Cornwell recounts instances where her respondents described a series of quite serious health problems but still defined themselves as 'healthy'. The reason for this was that health was intimately bound up with moral worth; 'illness can incapacitate and prevent people from working. In doing so it can threaten not only the practical basis of their lives but also their moral reputation', a key facet of self-identity (1984: 127). Legitimacy and self-identity are, then, centrally fashioned around the response of others to the self. This has been demonstrated in a series of in-depth interview studies of the experience of chronic illness. Kelly (1992a, and 1992b), for example, portrays the tension between the private self (inner and private) and public identity (the 'public knowable aspect of the person') (1992a: 393) in his research on individuals who have undergone an ileostomy (surgical removal of the bowel). Post-surgery, individuals often experience a changed sense of self and body which impinges persistently on activities of everyday life. There may be a dual sense of a negative change in the body (the surgical stoma) and a positive sense of a self that has survived debilitating illness. But the public perception of ileostomy which 'carries a freight of more or less socially stigmatised symbols associated with dirt, pollution, loss of control and transgression of body margins' (1992a: 391), may mean that the individual wants or feels obliged to present an ordinary 'non-ileostomist version of self' to others (1992a: 403). The individual's relative success in this regard depends on being able to manage the body (which may be liable to 'let one down') and anticipate the responses of others. For Kelly these interactive processes underlie the Meadian emphasis on 'the ways in which proffered versions of self require legitimation in the process of identity construction, in order to be sustained' (1992a: 410).

Dissipation?

Fine contends that, in its shift from a marginal oppositional perspective to an accepted position, interactionism has lost its core identity. Now 'intellectually promiscuous', it blends with other positions, risking a 'diversity which may vitiate its centre' (1993: 65).

How far is this true in the area of health, illness and health care? Undoubtedly interactionism has been the dominant perspective in the field in Britain, as is demonstrated by the large numbers of published articles within the tradition. To be sure, there have always been challengers. Political economy has sustained a critique, as has the positivist tradition with the emphasis on quantitative survey research. Furthermore, there have always been dissenters from within the ranks. Ethnomethodologists, for example, inaugurated a tradition which parted company with interactionism (Garfinkel, 1967). With the intent to describe rather than to explain, the ethnomethodologist seeks to document the codes/taken-for-granted meanings that individuals use to accomplish interaction in bounded settings such as the doctor–patient encounter (see Atkinson and Heath, 1981). Conversation analysis – revealing the 'rules' that guide turn-taking and interruption, for example – has been central. The interest here is in the formal properties of language and interaction and the analysis of the organization of a commonplace activity. But, in fact, there has been little 'pure' ethnomethodological work of this kind in medical sociology, whose practitioners, with their concern to link the structure of talk to issues of power and control associated with class and gender (see Fisher and Dundas Todd, 1986), have moved into the realms of interpretation and explanation and out of the bounds of ethnomethodology.

But challenge and dissent notwithstanding, inclusion and acceptance as described by Fine have indeed been the 'fate' of interactionism. First in this regard, its key concepts (the self, negotiation, etc.) appear in abundance in published works in the sociology of health, illness and health care yet often seem devoid of their original theoretical content. Second, contemporary developments in sociology such as feminism, Foucauldian social constructionism and postmodernism to a degree rest upon but, nonetheless, subvert interactionism's original theoretical grounding. These recent developments will be reviewed in detail in chapters 2 and 3. Here, we draw our discussion to a close with a consideration of two principal criticisms that have been levied against interactionism: (1) its neglect of what Day and Day (1977: 134) dub the 'hard realities of power and politics', and (2) its cognitivist bias. I will briefly refer to attempts to reconcile the first difficulty through a resolution of the micro–macro split, and the second through the development of a relatively new sub-field; the sociology of emotions and health.

One of the central criticisms of the interactionist approach has been its conceptualization of power. The stance towards power as situational and contingent aligns with the view of individuals as conscious agents shaping the social order in the interactive process. There is minimal attention to 'how the larger structural features of . . . society influence and perhaps predetermine the limits of the negotiation under investigation' (Day and Day, 1977: 134). The conceptualization of these 'larger structural features' is, of course, the very stuff of the early political economy perspective as we outlined it earlier (remember McKinlay's (1977) analogy of the game). But interactionists have not really ignored structural features such as social class, 'race' and gender as much as they have resisted giving them a determinate role. Consequently, the interactionist contribution lies less in endorsing their influence, and more in demonstrating exactly how power is achieved and maintained.

There are clearly significant differences between the interactionist and political economy perspectives, but it is important not to overdraw the dichotomy. While there is undoubtedly a gulf between the work of, say, Navarro and McKinlay on the one hand and Strauss and Goffman on the other, there are also bridges across the divide. The work of Waitzkin (1991) on the micro-politics of health care, rooted in political economy, and the work of interactionists such as Fisher and Dundas Todd (1986) on the politics of gender in interaction have a lot in common, as do the work of the political economist Crawford (1984) and interactionist Pierret (1995) on lifestyle politics and health (see above and also chapter 9). From different positions these researchers share a concern to enjoin macro and micro levels of reality; that is, to attempt to articulate a 'seamless sociology which recognises that "separate" levels are actually intertwined and indivisible, with micro analyses implicated in macro ones, and vice versa' (Fine, 1993: 69).

The sociology of emotions

The attempt to ground interactionism in a broader politics of health care is one way in which the perspective has evolved recently in response to criticism. Other developments include the effort to resolve interactionism's cognitive bias through the emerging field of the sociology of emotions. On first glance it may seem strange to argue that interactionism neglects the emotions, but, as Faberman relates,

> *for several generations, interactionists have studied the nature of ambiguous situations, the definition of the situation, self-indication, object formation, and identity formation appropriate to situations. Throughout there has been the image of a cognitively oriented self-reflexive actor with emotions as an untheorized, empirical after-thought. (1989: 272)*

Mead and Blumer are deemed to have obscured the importance of feelings in their concern with 'deeds and thought' (Hochschild, 1979). Goffman comes under particular attack from Hochschild (1979: 551) for his concern with rule-governed behaviours to the detriment of emotions, which are seen as 'unbiddable and uncontrollable'. His concern is with emotional display rather than individuals' felt experience, with the act rather than inner feelings. She states, 'from no other author do we get such an appreciation of the imperialism of rules and such a hazy glimpse of an internally developed self' (Hochschild, 1983: 217).

Despite this questioning, most sociologists of emotions still make interactionist principles the core of their work. It is, then, much more a question of revision than abandonment. The sociology of emotions as a sub-field in sociology began to develop in the mid-1970s in the USA, stimulated by a reaction against sociology's long-standing neglect of the feelings and suspicion of all things physical (Olesen, 1990). Prior to this time, the emotions had been the undisputed province of psychology, where they were viewed as biologically given uncontrollable instincts or impulses. In Faberman's (1989) view, interactionism began to make the emotions part of its domain after the work of the psychologists Schacter and Singer (1962). They conducted an experiment which involved the injection of adrenaline (to induce a state of arousal) into subjects who were given social–emotional clues as to how they should define their feelings by briefed individuals. This suggested that people in a state of emotional arousal do not automatically know how to feel, but need to define their state by a cognitive process which takes account of the situation that they are in (Faberman, 1989). Hence, while emotion involves physiological arousal, it also involves a process of cognitive labelling which implicates social factors or, in Shott's terms, 'the actor's construction of affect'. 'Internal states and cues, necessary as they are for affective experience, do not in themselves establish feeling, for it is the actor's definition and interpretations that give physiological states their emotional significance and nonsignificance' (Shott, 1979: 1321, 1323).

Here we see the Meadian position that physiology mediates but does not determine action. Even though there is agreement that social factors are intimately tied up with emotion, there is a growing debate over the exact relationship of body, mind and emotion. Taking an approach which emphasizes the socially constructed nature of the emotions, McCarthy (1989) is critical of those who, in her opinion, layer the emotions on top of a given physiological and psychological base. She argues that sociologists must see emotions as irreducibly social, as emerging within social acts and sustained by group processes. Others are critical of this view. For example, Craib (1995) worries that it is in danger of giving priority to cognition and thereby reducing emotions to ideas. He argues instead that there is a range of emotions common to all humans, rooted in our biological make-up, but open to different cultural investment and expression. Similarly, Hochschild (1979, 1983) argues that we need to appreciate that emotion involves managing the body (since emotion is our physiological body readying itself for action), but also to be aware that feelings are socially malleable, not given. This means that emotions can be manipulated and worked at. It is in these terms that Hochschild explored the commodification of flight attendants' emotions. The concept of emotional labour is also readily applicable to health work. Defining emotional labour as 'the labour involved in dealing with other people's feelings', James (1989: 21; 1992) has explored the hard work involved in nursing the dying. Along with others (e.g. Stacey, 1981) she alerts us, in particular, to the gendered nature of emotion work as it takes place in the home and the hospital.

Taking Hochschild's attempt to reconcile organismic and interactionist approaches to the emotions more directly into the area of health and illness, sociologists have argued that the sociology of emotions can reconcile the mind–body split and other dualisms such as the micro–macro divide, that have characterized theory and research. Thus, Freund (1990) points out that social interaction with others can be expressed through the body. For example, the body may express emotions through neuro-hormonal or musculo-skeletal changes which may affect blood pressure or cholesterol levels. But, alongside this, we must recognize that these responses are not universal or automatic; most important is the social context in which the individual experiences and appraises their emotions.

Conclusion

In its development the sociology of health, illness and health care has been embroiled with biomedicine. Concerned with medicine's undue influence, early work in the field sought to supplant the biomedical with a new and distinctly *social* model of health and health care. This new approach was established during the 1970s under the theoretical frameworks of political economy and interactionism. Work that is derivative of these approaches continues to exert a significant influence over the field today. However, it does not go unchallenged. The call to incorporate a concern for the emotions is one response to what many see as the unduly social approach and its accompanying neglect of biology and the physical body. In wider terms, a critical response has been stimulated by the work of Foucault, postmodernism and feminism. It is to these more recent traditions that we now turn in chapters 2 and 3.

2

Shattering the Orthodoxy? Foucault, Postmodernism and the Sociology of the Body

Debate between conflicting approaches is a persistent and productive feature of sociological theorizing. Yet, perhaps because they repudiate virtually all that went before them, recent theoretical approaches seem to shatter the orthodoxy in an unprecedented way. Mouzelis (1993: 691) writes of 'an anarchical cacophony', 'a total lack of communication between warring theoretical schools'. Yet all contemporary theories have in common an attempt to rethink sociological theory in response to the rapidly changing world around us. Some, such as the theorists of late modernity considered in chapter 1, call for a major overhaul, but believe that, rather than having entered a new historical period called postmodernism, we have now reached a new/higher stage of modernism. For postmodernists, however, the problem goes far deeper than a need for new, more sophisticated, conceptual tools to analyse what has become a more heterogeneous and complex social world. Sociology was born out of, and grew up as part of, the particular period of Western history which followed the Middle Ages and matured with the Enlightenment. The Enlightenment world-view, as we saw in the previous chapter, championed reason as the source of progress, valuing a modern world built around secular, rational-scientific thought. Sociology's traditional task has been to explain why the world is ordered as it is by making reference to general laws. Through various propositions, such as the claim that two opposing social classes are formed out of their particular relationship to the means of production, or that women as a group are disadvantaged because of patriarchal oppression, sociology aims to show that there are clear and identifiable reasons why the world is as it is (even though these reasons are contested by different theorists). In other words, there are social patterns with identifiable causes which we can uncover through sociological analysis.

For postmodernists, the problem is that previous sociology has not so much *uncovered* the reasons for inequalities and other social phenomena, but *created* them. Sociology, then, does not *uncover* 'reality' (for there is no such thing), but its own *fabrications* of it. These fabrications are rooted in the legacy that sociology inherits from the Enlightenment way of viewing the world in terms of binary oppositions such as man/woman, reason/emotion, working class/middle class. In the case of gender, for example, we divide the world into men and women (or male and female gender) and start from the premise that men have more in common with each other than they have with women; that there is an inherent opposition of some kind between the two. From the perspective of postmodernism, this 'creates a false appearance of unity by reducing the flux and heterogeneity of experience into supposedly natural or essentialist [i.e fixed] oppositions' (Flax, 1990a: 36). For postmodernists this is not the way the world is, it is *the way that sociology views it*. There are, in fact, no intrinsic meanings, no fixed oppositions. Reality is shifting, socially constructed out of competing discourses. Consequently, in a heterogeneous postmodern social world, there is no 'truth', only multiple 'truths'.

Although it is inappropriate to label Foucault's work postmodern, it has been an important influence upon postmodernists. Moreover, in its own right it has had a notable impact upon the sociology of health and medicine, and for this reason deserves critical attention. Therefore we begin this chapter with a quite detailed review of Foucault's work, before turning to consider the significance of postmodern theories, and finally the new approaches gathered under the rubric of the sociology of the body.

The work of Foucault

As we saw in chapter 1, the early project of the sociology of health and illness was to distance itself from 'biomedicine' by stressing the socially constructed nature of illness and medical practice. Eliot Freidson (1988 [1970]: 223), for example, argues that 'while illness as a biophysical state exists independently of human knowledge and evaluation, illness as a social state is *created and shaped by* human knowledge and evaluation'. Disease (the biophysical state) and illness (the social state), therefore, were constructed as distinct entities, and illness became the province of sociology. This ultimately left a 'biological base' beyond the realm of the discipline as attention was directed towards ways in which the biological is *overlaid* by the social (Armstrong, 1987a; White, 1991). A Foucauldian perspective drives social constructionism much further on, right to the heart of the 'natural' or 'biological', arguing that what we know as diseases are themselves fabrications of powerful discourses, rather than discoveries of 'truths' about the body and its interaction with the social world (Bury, 1986). Nettleton explains that this approach is very 'different to the sociology of medical or scientific knowledge which aims to expose the social, technical or ideological interests which distort or contribute to the creation of certain types of knowledge'. Such an approach, which characterizes political economy, symbolic interactionist and other criticisms of the biomedical model discussed in chapter 1, assumes that 'whilst knowledge is socially created there exists an underlying truth, a real external world which remains more or less disguised or more or less understood' (Nettleton, 1992: 149, 136).

An innovatory treatment of power and of the individual subject lies at the heart of Foucault's work. In his own words, his objective 'has been to create a history of the different modes by which, in our culture, human beings are *made subjects*' (Foucault, 1982: 777, my emphasis). That is, contrary to the humanist view of individuals as actively constituting their own history seen in symbolic interactionism and orthodox Marxism, we have a perspective in which the subject is 'stripped of its creative role and analysed as a complex and variable function of discourse' (Foucault, 1977: 138).

The corpus of Foucault's major work from the 1960s to the 1980s is an attempt to write a new history of the subject as constituted through historically located disciplinary powers. Unlike Jewson (1976) who, as we saw in chapter 1, argued that knowledge, or particular medical cosmologies, developed out of social relations of power between particular social groups (with power shifting from the patient as patron in the late eighteenth century to the power of medical scientists a hundred years later), Foucault's starting-point is the configuration of knowledge or *episteme* which constitutes particular subjects during specific historical periods. In *The Birth of the Clinic* (1989 [1963]) he charts the emergence of a new 'clinical gaze', or way of seeing the patient's body, which paved the way for a new form of medical practice. The change in vision, from the speculatively based medicine of the eighteenth century, to the scientifically based medicine of the nineteenth, is not the result of reasoned development towards more authentic knowledge. Relatedly, disease entities and lesions are not natural phenomena now revealed more accurately by modern science. Rather, eighteenth- and nineteenth-century medicine are incommensurable visions of the body, different 'anatomical atlases' (i.e. maps of the body's structure) which can be revealed through what Armstrong (1987b) calls a 'political anatomy' of the body. Key to the changes which took place in the late eighteenth century was the new-found ability to pinpoint pathology 'in the interior of the body' and to use 'the ever more detailed methods of the [physical] examination to diagnose it' (Armstrong, 1983: 2). This was accompanied by a change in the nature of the 'reality' of disease, which moved away from the Galenic humoral model (in which disease was seen as a disturbance in the body's balance) towards the status of a 'thing', separated from the self and from how the individual feels.

This shift in the medical gaze occurred during a period of significant societal change in Europe, notably, the development of capitalism, growth in population and the concentration of large numbers of people in urban spaces. Old forms of control fell away under these conditions, to be superseded by new regimes of power built around monitoring of the body, or 'biopolitics'. People were now to be counted, monitored and surveyed, and new forms of expert knowledge – sanitary science, the study of crime and its punishment, medicine – emerged, all of which aimed to predict and control the population. Foucault's book *Discipline and Punish* (1979) begins with a description of a regicide's torture and public execution in 1757, and proceeds to chart the vast changes that took place over the next eighty-year period. In feudal times it was practicable to punish only a few wrongdoers who were used as examples to discourage the misdemeanours of others. Over the course of the eighteenth century, and the rise of a larger and more mobile population, this was no longer a cost-effective deterrent. In its place a new form of power emerged: the *surveillance of self* (i.e. self-monitoring). This was epitomized by Bentham's Panopticon, a circular building constructed around a central tower. In this architectural form individual prison inmates cannot know whether they are being observed from the central tower or not and, consequently, begin to police their own behaviour. The diffusion of this panoptic mode of power throughout society is evidenced in the growth of psychiatry and its urge to confess; in the growth of preventive medicine which relies on the internalization of powerful discourses of healthy diets and fitness regimes; and in self-help techniques (such as weight-control groups). Far from being benign in form, these humanist discourses exert a new and unprecedented kind of power over modern individuals, a form of power ultimately more repressive than any that has gone before. Now there is

no need for arms, physical violence, material constraints. Just a gaze.
An inspecting gaze, a gaze which each individual under its weight will
end by interiorising to the point that he [sic] is his own overseer, each
individual thus exercising this surveillance over, and against, himself.
A superb formula: power exercised continuously and for what turns
out to be a minimal cost. (Foucault, 1980: 155)

Sawicki (1991: 20–1) highlights three points of contrast between the traditional model of power held by Marxist and liberal theorists alike and the perspective of Foucault. First of all, in the former model power is *possessed* by individuals or groups, while for Foucault it is *exercised* by them. Second, traditional models conceptualize power as primarily *repressive*, while for Foucault it is primarily *productive*. Finally, in Marxist and liberal theories, power emanates from a *central source* from top to bottom (e.g. from the state to the population), while for Foucault it is *diffuse*, operating from the bottom up. Foucault summarizes this as follows: power is bent on 'generating forces, making them grow, and ordering them', rather than 'dedicated to impeding them, making them submit, or destroying them'. It is 'a multiple and mobile field of force relations where far-reaching, but never completely stable effects of domination are produced' (Foucault, 1980: 136, 102). Power is not embodied in individuals, social groups or institutions, even though it is clearly played out in institutional contexts such as the doctor's surgery, but operates through norms and technologies which shape the body and the mind. The control of sexuality, for example, comes not from repression but from apparently humanist discourses which rely upon the confessional form – medicine, psychiatry, sociology. In the confession, individuals are encouraged to elaborate intimate details of their lives, making it 'one of the major procedures of modern punitive powers by which the individual is tied to processes of normalisation' (Grosz, 1990a: 84).

Foucauldian social constructionism therefore repudiates sociologists' attempts to 'free' the individual who is repressed by medical powers by privileging social over scientific claims to knowledge. A number of researchers have attempted to substantiate this view through case-studies of medical practice. Arney and Bergen (1984), for example, invert the usual approach to the power-play between doctors and patients. They argue that, rather than attending to the ways in which a social model of health and health care can challenge medical dominance, sociologists should seek to understand how the power of medicine itself incites the patient to speak with the physician in a partnership which emphasizes the social nature of disease. In a historical analysis which focuses on the medical orchestration of birth and death, they argue that, far from fashioning their own liberation by *reclaiming* birth and death as social rather than medical-technical processes, the experiencing person is *put back* into medical discourse as a result of changes in the form of medical knowledge. Thus, 'it is less the patient who is forcing medicine to take him [*sic*] seriously than it is profound changes in medical logic that governs truth-speaking' (Arney and Bergen, 1984: 46).

We can consider several examples of how this occurs. First, as we have discussed, before the end of the nineteenth century the patient was not viewed as a 'person', but as a catalogue of anatomical and biophysical terms, 'a myriad of sets of mechanically juxtaposed structures each of which fulfilled specific functions' (Arney and Bergen, 1983: 3). The body was an object separate from the socio-emotional experience of the patient. Arney and Bergen give several illustrations of this, referring to such diverse phenomena as the treatment of pain, chronic illness and disability, teenage pregnancy, death and alcoholism. Alcoholism, for example, was seen as a poison that affected the structures and functions of the body. Its occurrence was a 'genetic accident' and 'medicine spoke no truth about the alcoholic's "lived body", but only about the body as an object within which the processes of disease could be mapped' (Arney and Bergen, 1983: 5). By the 1950s, a new medical logic, revolutionary in form, made socio-emotional concerns the centre of medical discourse. This can be seen in medical texts which begin to talk of the patient as having the power of perception by the senses and to refer to an enlarged doctor–patient relationship. Disease is no longer understood in terms of an event isolated in the body, but in terms of the patient's relations in the social world. For example, birth is no longer a discrete event to be controlled (often brutally), but an experience; an ideal which medicine can help women achieve. As it maps life experience and incorporates a concern for the individual 'as a person', medicine becomes omnipresent; no longer a 'closeted expert that sallies forth to meet life and death', it monitors and surveys the life-world, normalizing individual experience (Arney and Bergen, 1984: 104).

A further illustration of this process is given in Nettleton's study of dentistry. 'Dentistry's object', she argues, 'is not a pre-existent entity, a diseased mouth, waiting to be understood so it can be effectively treated', but 'variable concepts which are produced by dental perception' (1992: 7). In the nineteenth century, debate centred around whether dental health was the result of internal bodily function or whether it was vulnerable to influences beyond the body in the interaction of the individual with the external world (the effects of chemico-parasitics which enter the mouth). This latter view held sway until the twentieth century, at which point the emphasis began to shift to the problematic 'spaces between bodies and contagion'. The mouth became a vulnerable part of the body which needed to be protected as a 'boundary' between the internal body and external sources of pollution' (Nettleton 1992: 26). For example, saliva was seen as a threat, and people were cautioned not to share utensils like cups with other people. However, by the early twentieth century, with the concern to monitor the social space between bodies, dentists had moved from an assault on disease in the mouth, to acting as 'guardians of the mouth'.

A new form of surveillance grew up which empowered the dental regime, with education and training at its core. Early education (in the early twentieth century) targeted the sanitation of the *physical body*. By the inter-war period this had extended to include training the *mind*, since it was felt that a belief in the value of dental health had to be instilled in the population. Moving on, *participation* became the focus of the dental gaze in the post-war period; since it was no longer felt to be sufficient to train bodies and to impart knowledge, the patient's perspective was now sought and individuals were enrolled in a partnership with the dentist in evaluating their own mouths. Mothers, in particular, were adopted as moral guardians of dental health. Over time, then, the object of dentistry changes from what Nettleton calls the mouth/teeth, to the mind/mouth complex, to the subjective, experiencing, person. The effect of this change is a shifting dental gaze embodied in different dental techniques as dentists move from visual inspection, to listening and speaking to the patient, and finally to supporting and negotiating in partnership with the patient. Thus, for Nettleton, the 'mouth with teeth' has 'no stability, while the words body and mouth may remain the same, the objects to which these words refer change. There are no absolutes. The mouth is the effect of the specific practices that surround it and pervade it' (1992: 126).

At the heart of the Foucauldian perspective then is the view that medicine no longer controls through processes of *exclusion or repression*, but by *inclusion and normalization*. Since power is embedded in all social relations and practices, this seems to mean that it is virtually impossible to dislodge. Critics have argued that this view of power reduces the individual to a docile body with no effective means of resistance. McNay (1992: 59), for example, points to a discrepancy between Foucault's theoretical understanding of power as 'a diffuse and productive phenomenon and his concrete studies which tended to show power as a monolithic, dominating force'. In his earlier work he had attempted to resolve this discrepancy by arguing that, as soon as there is a relation of power, there is a possibility of resistance. Indeed, his view was not only that power inevitably throws up resistance, but that it actually depends on 'a multiplicity of points of resistance' to 'play the role of adversary, target, support or handle in power relations' (Foucault, 1980: 95).

Even though Foucault gave little idea himself of how this occurs, a useful illustration is provided by Sawicki (1991), who argues that women's experiences of new reproductive technologies (NRTs) are better appreciated through a Foucauldian approach to power as productive than a radical feminist perspective where power is conceptualized as an oppressive force in the hands of men. Taking Corea's (1985) work as an exemplar of radical feminism (see chapter 3), she argues that it is inappropriate to conceive of NRTs as men's last-ditch attempt to control women's procreative powers by reducing the body to a manipulable object. For Sawicki, this is only one possible facet of the problem. It is more appropriate, she claims, to see the knowledge/power invested in NRTs as controlling women's bodies not by repression but by *creating* new subjectivities – infertile women, surrogates, deficient bodies. Thus NRTs control women by making their bodies 'more useful' by *enabling* motherhood. From this perspective we can better appreciate why women submit to a practice which in the view of many radical feminists is violent and not in their interest: these technologies 'incite desire' which many women experience as enabling. Further, Sawicki claims that Foucault's disciplinary model of power permits us to view the field of reproduction as a 'site of struggle' in which women and men occupy diverse positions in relation to various 'technologies'. Thus, taking Sawicki's line of argument a little further, we may view surrogacy alternatively as men's control over women's bodies (Rowland, 1992); middle-class women's control over the bodies of working-class women, as in the case of surrogacy arrangements (Chesler, 1990); or as a practice which 'contravenes very basic patriarchal attitudes about the ownership of women's bodies (wombs) and the idealised notion of motherhood' (Smart, 1989: 109).

In his later works, the final two volumes of the *History of Sexuality* (1985, 1986), Foucault turned to explore more adequately the ways in which the individual can *resist* the effects of power, as his emphasis shifted from a focus on the body imprinted by powerful discourses towards a concern with the way in which individuals actively fashion their own existence. That is, latterly he was as much concerned with the ways in which individuals come to understand themselves, as with the ways in which they are constituted as an object of knowledge by powerful discourses such as medicine. He defines 'techniques of the self' as practices which, 'permit individuals to effect by their own means or with the help of others a certain number of operations on their own bodies and souls, thoughts, conduct and way of being, so as to transform themselves in order to attain a certain state of happiness . . .' (Foucault, 1988: 18).

The emphasis is on self-stylization, a process which is seen to carry an emancipatory impulse in so far as it embodies an attitude of self-critique on the part of the individual (McNay, 1992). Through styliza-tion (new self-images, body shapes, displays of masculinity and femininity, ethnic identities etc.), individuals explore the boundaries of their self-identity, engaging in an endless task of self-transformation. But for many critics there are problems in Foucault's conceptualization of the techniques of self. McNay (1992: 6), for instance, argues that 'by reducing all practices of the self to the level of self-stylisation Foucault does not elaborate sufficiently on the socio-cultural determinants which may impose some practices, more than others, upon the individual'. Hence, the self becomes an isolated work of art abstracted from wider political and economic structures. This, she elaborates, is far from where Foucault wanted to end up. He was highly critical of the 'cult of the self', yet in an attempt to 'block the institutional regulation of individu-ality' (or 'techniques of domination') he slides into a position which stresses the self-absorbed behaviour of individuals, unable to explain how the individual may be called out of 'a politics of introversion' (McNay, 1992: 178, 191).

Foucauldian social constructionism: a critique

With these issues in mind, we can now turn to a more detailed discus-sion of the limitations of Foucauldian social constructionism. Four issues are central to this evaluation. First, the *lack of an ethics* and the reluctance to evaluate the nature of the effects of power upon the body (i.e. are the effects positive or negative for health and the experience of the individual?). Second, the issue of *relativism*: if all forms of knowl-edge are equal and there is no 'truth', how can we evaluate the viability of Foucauldian analyses themselves? Third, the focus on the effects of power to the neglect of any consideration of the *origins* of changes in discourses of power over the course of history. Fourth, is it appropriate *to view power as a diffuse phenomenon* that operates in local contexts? If not, must we in some way also take account of powerful normalizing discourses as the province of particular privileged groups?

First of all, a series of problems flows from the lack of an ethics in social constructionist work on health and medicine. The non-evaluative stance of much research often means that we know very little about what the qualitative effects of power are for individuals concerned. To be sure, Foucault tells us that the forms of surveillance that we have discussed are the dark side of modern society (which in itself professes an ethical position). But there is a question still to be asked: does it really *matter* much to individuals that they are now the objects of this form of power? These questions are often left begging in health-related research. Raising them here is not to imply that there is an authentic patient experience that is being 'missed', but rather to ask about outcomes of various kinds, about the *benefits* that may accrue to some people and not to others (Bury, 1986).

Nettleton stresses that the social constructionist claim that disease categories and health practices are historically variable does not deny the suffering that people experience as the result of ill health. Rather, it is saying that 'self-empowerment, freedom and liberalism can be double-edged: it might be oppressive or it might be enhancing. The point is that we cannot take these values for granted. We need to question, rather than preserve, what we take to be the most caring, sympathetic and most supportive approaches to health care' (1992: 149). Yet in her analysis we never really get a feel for the particular ways in which current discourses on what she calls the 'mouth with teeth' *are* actually, in her own words 'oppressing or enhancing'. Modern individuals are constrained to police their own dental health – but what does this mean for dental health itself? For example, at the most mundane (but important) level: is the effect of modern disciplinary powers that people have more or less decaying teeth, more or less experience of pain? Of course, from the Foucauldian point of view, these questions are themselves discursively founded. This means that notions of 'patients' needs', 'more or less decay', 'more or less pain', a 'better patient experience' are all relative terms; we cannot effectively address the issue of whether people now experience less pain than they did in the past since today's 'pain' (constituted out of one kind of discourse) is incommensurable with the 'pain' of the past. This means that questions about the quality of patient experience are effectively neutralized (they become non-questions) from within the social constructionist framework. Without a normative stance, we can easily slip into *relativism* (McNay,1992), which is the second criticism to be levied against the Foucauldian perspective.

If all knowledges are equal and there is no 'truth', what is the status of our accounts of the social phenomena that we investigate? As Hammersley (1992: 49) asks, 'if what ethnographers [or, we might add, those using other research methods] produce is simply one version of the world, true (at best) only in its own terms, what value can it have?' More pointedly, how do we know that Foucauldian analyses of health and health care are themselves plausible? In the last instance, these accounts must be self-refuting (Bury, 1986). But, of course, here again, social constructionism evacuates the possibility of criticism (Jarvie, 1983). For Foucault individuals are fabrications of the same discourses that constitute a disease or a technique of health care in a particular way. Hence, there is arguably no vantage-point from which to criticize the charge of relativism (Armstrong, 1985).

The third criticism to address is the concentration on the effects of power to the neglect of any consideration of the origins of changes in discourses of power over the course of history. Studies of changes in medical knowledge often present, in meticulous detail, the various forms that medical knowledge has taken in different historical periods, but we are given no account of why knowledge changed. Critical junctures in history such as the shift towards a view of the patient as 'disembodied' in the late nineteenth century (Foucault, 1989) and the emergence of a 'new medical logic' which emphasizes the fundamentally social location of disease in the post-war period (Arney and Bergen, 1984; Nettleton, 1992), are demonstrated but not accounted for. Nettleton (1992) defends the Foucauldian position by arguing that, since power is not held by particular groups and there is no *necessity* for things to happen, it is pointless to search for explanations for events. Instead, the aim should be to look at the myriad complex factors that permitted an event to occur.

As we saw in chapter 1, political economists' accounts of changes in medical knowledge have traditionally pointed to specific structures of power which change to meet the *interests* of particular social groups (e.g. capitalists, men). For example, the emergence of the use of electrical foetal monitors during childbirth might be seen to generate profit for manufacturers and hospitals who purchase health care from insurance companies and primary care commissioning groups, as well as enhancing the dominance that obstetricians have over their clients. Irrespective of the veracity of this argument in itself, it permits us to talk of the *causes* of particular changes in the form of medical practice. Of course, for Foucault, we cannot explain historical shifts in this way since the power which produces change is not the province of a particular group (or groups) of people such as, in our example, capitalists or obstetricians.

This leads us to a final criticism. Is it adequate to view power as a diffuse disembodied phenomenon that operates in local contexts? Or, must we find a way to also take account of points of power which reside in dominant institutions and the powerful normalizing discourses embodied in particular privileged groups? For many commentators this is the locus of Foucault's problems. For example, Best and Kellner (1991:

70) contend that the Foucauldian approach 'occludes the extent to which power is still controlled and administered by specific and identifiable agents in positions of economic and political power, such as members of corporate executive bodies, bankers, the mass media, political lobbyists, land developers'. It is notable that most work in the area of health and medicine draws upon Foucault's earlier work emphasizing the dangers of normalization. There have been few attempts to engage with his later work, which argues that individuals must promote new forms of subjectivity by reflexive transformation of the self. However, Susan Bordo (1993a: 195) and others alert us to the problems of such an approach. In her own words, 'how helpful is . . . an emphasis on creative agency in describing the relationship of women and their bodies to the image industry of post-industrial capitalism, a context in which eating disorders and exercise compulsions are flourishing?' The body, she remarks, is not a plastic entity that can be remade at will. There is, then, in Bordo's view, a need for a better alignment of Foucault's emphasis on the *normalizing* politics of biopower, especially as it is racially, ethnically and heterosexually inflected – people do not tend to make themselves over to look more 'Jewish' or 'African' – with the possibility of resistance. The co-presence of normalizing discourses and discourses of resistance on the part of individuals is refracted through the media. Her analysis of the portrayal of women's 'healthy bodies' in advertisements makes this point quite well and is worth quoting at length. She refers to a magazine advertisement

> *which pictures a lean, highly toned, extremely attractive young woman, leaning against a wall, post-workout; 'I believe', the copy reads, 'that if you look at yourself and see what is right instead of what is wrong, that is the true mark of a healthy individual'. Now, those convinced that 'resistance is everywhere', might see this advertisement as offering a transgressive, subversive model of femininity: a woman who is strong, fit and (unlike most women) not insecure about her body. What this really neglects is that we have a visual message here as well: her body itself – probably the most potent 'representation' in the advertisement – is precisely the sort of perfected icon which women compare themselves to and of course see 'what is wrong'. (Bordo, 1993a: 198)*

For Bordo and others, resistance and the ability to be 'different' must be viewed as hard-won, forged against normalizing discourses (of ageism, sexism, racism and heterosexism).

Our discussion of Foucault suggests that his work is likely to continue to be a fruitful theoretical resource for sociologists of health and medicine as well as a continued source of controversy. As mentioned earlier, it is one source for the postmodern challenge to modernist theory, and it is to this perspective that we now turn.

Postmodernism

We have yet to see a sustained application of postmodernist ideas to the sociology of health and medicine, although there is certainly an interest among many to explore their relevance for the field. Since their impact is beginning to be felt, it is important to explore postmodernism's guiding ideas and potential. In doing so, we will draw upon Bauman's (1988) useful analytic distinction between a *postmodern sociology* and a *sociology of postmodernity*. The former refers to theorists who attempt to develop a new epistemology or way of knowing the world, emphasizing its fundamentally socially constructed nature, while the latter refers to sociologists whose aim is to explore the empirical nature of the postmodern world. We begin by looking at postmodern sociology which involves a deconstruction (or undoing) of past understandings of health and health care, including those put forward by sociologists, focusing upon competing discourses (or ways of seeing) and how they achieve their claims to knowledge, and power, in the field of health.

Postmodern sociology

In common with most of the theoretical frameworks considered so far, postmodernism is not a unitary body of thought. In fact, in many ways it is even more difficult to define and summarize than other perspectives, for even speaking of *a* postmodernism can be seen to run the risk of 'violating some of its central values – heterogeneity, multiplicity, and difference' (Flax, 1990a: 188). Moreover, there are quite significant differences between authors whose work is generally subsumed under the label 'postmodern'. Nevertheless, it is still possible to draw out common threads in a general way. Flax (1990b) sees postmodernism as throwing the following modernist views into doubt:

1 the existence of a stable, coherent self
2 the notion that science and reason can provide an objective foundation for knowledge
3 the idea that this knowledge will be 'truth'
4 the notion of a transcendental reason (independent of individuals), and
5 the view that language accurately reflects 'reality'.

For postmodernists, there are no 'real things', no objective realities 'out there' in the world that language (including the language of sociology) tells us about. Language does not reflect 'reality', it *creates* it. A crucial tenet of postmodernism, therefore, is that the 'truths' that seem to exist for us in the world (for example, that there are men and women, able-bodied and disabled people) have themselves been created by the way that we use language. That is, the subject positions that we refer to (old or young, sick or healthy) are discursively created. The use of *binary logic* has been central to modernist ways of viewing the world. Indeed, we are so imbued with this logic that it is extremely difficult to see beyond it (Smart, 1990). Yet this is precisely what postmodernism asks us to do. The aim is: (1) to show how 'knowing the world through opposition' creates a false appearance of unity; and (2) to reveal that the 'dualisms which continue to dominate Western thought are inadequate for understanding a world of multiple causes and effects' (Lather, 1991: 21). Postmodernism achieves this through a process of *deconstruction*, a methodology which takes its impetus from the works of Derrida (see e.g. 1982). A process of deconstruction involves:

1 looking at an imputed opposition (able-bodied/disabled, for example)
2 showing that the dominant privileged position (able-bodied) is created out of a contrast with the oppressed position (disabled), i.e. we can only conceive of able-bodiedness by conceiving of what it is not – disability. Similarly, being 'white' only has meaning against being 'black', and
3 thereby, revealing that what appear to be dualisms are not really opposites, but are interdependent (they derive their meaning from an established contrast).

The important point then is that postmodernist sociology aims to deconstruct the dualities of modernist thought and to reveal them as artefacts of a particular way of knowing the world. In their place we are exhorted to put plurality and heterogeneity.

Now, the sociology of health and medicine, which is said to be caught up in the traditional modernist world-view of sociology, is implicated in the construction of a social world built around duality. Specifically, it has fabricated its own privileged perspective in binary opposition to what is positioned as the 'biomedical model'. It pits its own social model against the biomedical and, through this process, enhances and places value upon its own position. It can be seen to 'pull out' biomedicine's references to the social and to see them as tainted by its, variously defined, mechanistic and individualistic ethos. Waitzkin's (1991) political economy approach to doctor–patient interaction, for example, undermines medicine's use of the social as a mechanism of social control in the direct service of capitalism, and privileges its *own* 'social' model, which stresses the need for patients to have more power, in its place. Although not endorsing a postmodern view, Kelly and Field suspect that 'the real issue behind medical sociology's attempt to assert the superiority of the social model is ideological, and has its origins in the view that its version of reality is a superior one to that of the medical scientist' (1994: 36). For Fox (1993a), who advocates a postmodern position, championing a social model is a claim to authority that is itself a discursive product; in effect, it is just another power. Through a deconstructive reading it is, then, possible to understand why the disciplines of sociology and medicine are often viewed as standing in opposition.

Few sociologists have directly applied the method of deconstruction to the field of health and medicine. However, in a series of publications Fox reveals the ways in which the surgical enterprise is fragile and open to contestation. Specifically, the surgeon's perspective (on the patient or the success of surgery, for example) is not a given product of his or her technical work, but is actively constructed in contest with other views of the same phenomena; the anaesthetist's view, for example. In contrast to modernist theories which 'look for structure' and assume that organizations like hospitals employ rational means to achieve rational ends, Fox's postmodern approach views 'all organisations [as] mythologies constituted discursively to serve particular interests of power, and contested by other interests of power' (1993: 49). Power is not given to particular groups (by virtue of their technical skills, status and so on), but is constantly recreated and vulnerable to challenge. An example of this from his ethnography of surgery is the contested powers of anaesthetist and surgeon in the operating theatre. The anaesthetist is interested in the overall *fitness* of the patient (i.e. the patient's ability to withstand surgery), while the surgeon is more focused on the resection (removal) of the *disease*. The problem for the anaesthetist is that surgery can itself compromise fitness. The anaesthetist's ability to establish power through a discourse of fitness is generally limited because the organizational context privileges the surgeon's view. The point, however, is that the dominant position of the surgeon is itself formed in a struggle with the alternative discourse of the anaesthetist. But, Fox (1994: 15) argues, there is inherent '*undecidability* in organisation, the potential for the meaning of events to be re-constructed in a way which no longer favours the (currently) powerful'. Often such challenges arise from contingency. For example, he found that when a patient sustained a bleed after the removal of a brain tumour, authority shifted from the consultant neuro-surgeon (who had previously sustained a discourse of the patient as diseased, i.e. she was too ill to give rise to significant concern for residual fitness) to the anaesthetist. The surgeon had compromised fitness and had also failed to improve the patient's condition. When this happened an emergency operation was conducted under the control of the anaesthetist (but conducted by a senior registrar) 'with the simple objective of restoring fitness compromised by an earlier unsuccessful piece of surgery' (Fox, 1992: 74).

In this, and other examples from the same research, Fox conveys a principle of deconstruction – that the meaning of the two discourses (here of fitness and of eliminating disease) which are seemingly conflicting are, in fact, interdependent and can only be articulated through a contrast ('fitness', for example, only emerges as a discourse when it is open to challenge by the surgeon's focus on 'disease elimination'). This follows Derrida's (1982) principle discussed above: that oppositional positions, in effect, depend on each other for their own authenticity.

What Fox's approach does not do is explicitly to reveal the heterogeneity that is suppressed in binary oppositions. Yet for some this is the core of a postmodern politics. For example, writing from a feminist perspective, Eisenstein (1988: 7) claims that we need a 'radical epistemology – one that denies duality and its hierarchical, oppositional conceptualisation of differences – which *begins* to shift political discourses, which begins to shift relations of power'. Deconstruction can begin to disrupt and erode the power of the normalizing discourses that are highlighted in the Foucauldian understanding of individual experience of health and health care. At this point it might be useful to give an illustration of how, in theory at least, this might occur. As discussed earlier, the status 'disabled' depends for its existence upon the supposedly opposite position of being 'able-bodied'. From this perspective two contrasting 'liberatory positions' present themselves: one arguably modernist and one postmodernist in form. Modernist politics might call for the recognition of difference perhaps through its celebration of, and/or through the call for the appreciation of, particular needs on the part of the disabled in order to achieve equality. The postmodern position, in contrast, would be to argue that this is still politically problematic, since it continues to establish difference. In its place, the categories of disabled/able-bodied need to be eroded (since their use in language only serves to establish a related subservience/dominance). The line of argument might continue that only when we cease to think (and therefore act) in these binaristic terms can we begin to appreciate that notions of disability/ability are constructed out of a continuum of characteristics. Only when we are able to think in terms of a range of abilities and experiences (e.g. mobility, pain, dexterity) will we overcome the tendency to normalize (and stigmatize) people who are pushed into the particular group labelled 'disabled'.

The sociology of postmodernity, medicine and the body

So far we have been sketching the ways in which a postmodern epistemology (or way of knowing the world) might approach issues of health and medicine. By adopting the method of deconstruction, we have also used this epistemology to consider the status of sociology's own perspective. That is, we have been considering aspects of a *postmodern sociology*. Explicit in this perspective is the belief that experience can no longer be contained within the narratives of modernist thought, which are ill equipped to understand a social world which has become increasingly heterogeneous and complex. The objective of *sociologists of postmodernity* is to understand the nature of contemporary postmodern society.

Marxist social thought has often been the target of postmodern critiques of modernist social theory. As discussed in chapter 1, theorists such as Lash and Urry (1994) have seriously questioned the ability of orthodox Marxism to explain the nature of contemporary capitalism. Capitalism, however, still persists, albeit in a radically altered form, as its 'logic' extends way beyond the economic forms of capital described by Marx into the aesthetic or cultural domain. For Jameson postmodernism is itself the cultural logic of late capitalism as commodification penetrates all spheres of social life. Capitalism, he argues, has 'finally succeeded in transcending the capacities of the individual human body to locate itself, to organise its immediate surroundings perceptually, and cognitively map its position in a mappable external world' (1984: 83). The individual is debilitated, forced to live a schizophrenic existence. Thus, as distinct from Lash, Giddens and others who refer to the increased ability of most individuals to make choices and fashion their own existence in 'late modern' society, postmodernists are often pessimistic about the ability of individuals to locate themselves within 'post-capitalism'.

Orr (1990) contends that panic disorder is the response to postmodern contemporary existence. Her discussion begins with the juxtaposition of extracts from Marx's *Capital* (vol. 1) and a contract between Jose Borain (a fashion model who appeared in television commercials for Calvin Klein's Obsession perfume) and Calvin Klein Industries. The commodification of Borain's body is evident in the contract, which states that, where applicable, a consultant shall 'cause Borain to main-tain Borain's body weight, hair style and color and all other features of Borain's physiognomy as they are now or in such other form as Calvin Klein may from time to time reasonably request' (Orr, 1990: 461). Under conditions of postmodern capitalism, women's bodies (and, we could also argue, men's bodies) are 'worked over' to create use-value and become objects of circulating capital. No longer a solid form to be used for the production of physical capital, the body becomes a liquid commodity. 'This compulsion toward liquidity, flow, and an accelerated circulation of what is physical, sexual or pertaining to the body is the replica of the force which rules market value: capital must circulate; gravity and any fixed point must disappear . . . value must radiate endlessly and in every direction' (Baudrillard, quoted in Orr, 1990: 475). Mental illness (panic disorder) Orr writes (1990: 475), is the high price that individuals pay for their 'hook-ups in the postmodern market's shifting central (nervous) system'.

Self-evidently, the narratives of *orthodox* Marxism have no place in interpreting our contemporary existence from this perspective. Its theo-retical construction of 'the world' through 'systemic, essentialising, totalising, and hierarchical conceptual categories' is said to have im-posed a kind of 'realist tyranny', reducing all our understandings to the primacy of social class (Callari et al., 1995: 3, 4), with the collective working class the vanguard of a new social order. The notion of collec-tive social action – be this on the part of 'capitalists' or the 'working class' – is, of course, anathema to many postmodernists who proclaim the 'death of the subject', that is, of the ability of individuals to effect change. The work of Baudrillard expresses this position in arguably its most extreme form.

Baudrillard, dubbed by Best and Kellner (1991: 111) the 'high priest of the new epoch', argues that, in the move from a period of modernity dominated by industrial production to a high-technology postmodern world, we enter an era of 'hyper-reality'. In this new world individuals are no longer controlled by the needs of capitalists, but by new forms of technology: models, codes and cybernetics. The boundary between 'real-ity' and simulation implodes and models and codes become the basis of experience. For example, actors who play doctors on television are viewed as more credible than our local general practitioners. It is not just that the boundary between image and reality is dissolved, but that the simulated real becomes more real than the 'real'. Simulations come to constitute 'reality'. There is an extreme reversal of the subject/object dichotomy as objects elude control and themselves dominate the individual subject. 'We are living in the period of the objects', Baudrillard writes, *that is, we live by their rhythm, according to their incessant cycles. Today, it is we who are observing their birth, fulfilment, and death; whereas in all previous civilisations, it was the object, instrument, and perennial monument that survived the generations of men [sic]. (Baudrillard, in Poster, 1988)*

Individuals are no longer citizens, but consumers. Under such conditions there are no stable structures (class, 'race', gender); power is totally dispersed, too dispersed to struggle against. In these terms Baudrillard (1987) offers a critique of Foucault, whose argument that power is mobilized through localized discourses fails to appreciate that power is, in effect, 'dead', totally dispersed in the implosion of boundaries between the real and the illusory. Meaning too is lost in the same process as 'information dissolves meaning and the social into a sort of nebulous state leading not at all to a surfeit of innovation but to the very contrary, to total entropy' (Baudrillard, 1983: 100).

The hyper-real, then, is a condition in which any tension that we may feel between reality and illusion disappears. When this happens 'reality is no longer checked, called to justify itself' (Sarup, 1993: 166). For example, we no longer even appreciate the 'reality' of ill health and starvation in war-torn nations. It passes us by; we 'know' about it from the television news, but, living under conditions in which we are bombarded with information, we are unable to take it in. We come to accept starvation, which we see as 'just an image', our ability to do this fostered by the way in which the media promote form (image) over content (Kellner, 1989).

What can we say of health in the Baudrillardian depiction of the postmodern age in which the organizing principle of society is no longer the production of goods but models/simulation codes? Under conditions in which it is no longer possible to distinguish the 'real' and the 'image', the body becomes ripe for reconstruction. Kroker and Kroker (1988) assert that in the postmodern condition the natural body becomes obsolete, no longer needed in the technologically advanced capitalist age. Reproduction, for example, is no longer exclusively inside the natural female body as it becomes possible to develop an artificial placenta, lactation in males, and, potentially, to implant an embryo in any abdomen, be it male, female or animal. Under such conditions the body is a site for rhetorical investment. Public crisis is projected on to the body as it becomes an inscribed surface for 'a whole contagion of panic mythologies (AIDS, anorexia, bulimia, herpes) about disease, panic viruses, and panic addictions (from drugs to alcohol) for a declining culture where the body is . . . the inscribed text for all the stresses and crisis-symptoms of the death of the social' (Kroker and Kroker, 1988: 27).

As for Orr (1990), postmodernity is a panic condition; a scene of loss, cancellation, and extermination. When this happens, Kroker and Kroker claim, it is not surprising that power is the product of biological discourse, since what is at stake is the life and death of the species itself. Panic without is projected on to the body, which absorbs 'all the grisly symptoms of culture burnout' (1988: 22). The physical, sentient body disappears as it is deflated 'to the quality of its internal fluids' (1988: 11). The postmodern age is an age of 'panic sex' likened to the dark days of plague-ridden Athens of the fifth century, where

> *the invasion of the body by invisible antigens, the origins of which are unknown, the circulation of which is unpredictable as it is haphazard, and the pathology of which is disfiguring as it is seemingly fatal, has generated a pervasive mood of living once again, at the end of the world. (Kroker and Kroker, 1988: 14)*

Since it is very difficult to visualize the immune system, to see it as 'there inside us', scientific and popular literature makes it earthy and real by constructing military images of cells as invaders (an imagery that has clearly been evident in literature on AIDS):

> *in the supposedly earthy space of our own interiors, we see non-humanoid strangers who are supposed to be the means by which our bodies sustain our integrity and individuality, indeed our humanity, in the face of a world of others. We seem invaded not just by the threatening 'non-selves' that the immune system guards against, but more fundamentally by our own strange parts. No wonder autoimmune disease carries such awful significance. (Haraway, 1989: 27)*

Under immune-system imagery it is no longer clear that the body is an integral bounded unit where ill health is an invasion from outside. Stress, viewed as a form of communications breakdown, becomes the privileged pathology.

The postmodern body is, then, vulnerable and semi-permeable. New diagnostic techniques and therapies such as 'imaging' and 'visualization' emerge as central to postmodern medical practice. Frank (1992) contends that modernist medical sociology, which is premised upon the existence of a corporeal body as the raw material of medical practice, is ill equipped to appreciate the significance of these changes. Following Baudrillard, he contends that medicine now deals not with sensual bodies, but simulacra or images of bodies. In the place of the body at the centre of medical practice, we now have images and codes. The video screen, not the sentient patient in the bed, is now emblematic of the hospital. Four types of screen predominate: screens which exteriorize images of the bodily interior, such as ultrasonic scanners; screens which display on-line digital images of body processes such as electrocardiographs (ECGs); screens which display symbolic images such as patient information; and, finally, the television screens which, in US hospitals, appear in almost every patient's room. In such a context the traditional doctor's round of modern medicine takes on a new hue.

> *It is less for [the physician] to see the patient, than for both patient and physician to assure themselves that the other is still there, each a nostalgic token of the other's productive desire. Real diagnosis takes place away from the patient; bedside is secondary to screen. For diagnosis and even treatment purposes, the image on the screen becomes the 'true' patient, of which the bedridden body is an imperfect replicant, less worthy of attention. (Frank, 1992: 83)*

Hence, images of the body displayed on screens are the hyper-real, more real than the patient's actual body which is displaced by videotapes of angiograms and ultrasounds, files of CAT (computerized axial tomography) scan images, graphs of blood cell counts and serum levels. When as a patient I am asked how I feel, Frank writes, 'it is to these that I refer and which refer to me. In the medical simulacrum, I lose myself in my image . . . Hospitalised, I respond to those who ask me how I feel: I do not know how I feel; the tests are not yet back' (1992: 87, 86). Under the sway of medical simulacra, the subjectivity of the doctor disappears alongside that of the patient; no longer productive but transductive, the doctor is merely part of a network of images (see also the discussion in chapter 9).

Outside as well as inside the hospital, 'the person experiences his or her own body within the context of a media environment of repeating images' (Glassner, 1989: 183–4). The body is reinvented *under the direction of objects* – such as exercise videos. Glassner analyses the current 'fitness craze' in these terms. The video, he explains, is constructed of simulacra far removed from original experience. The Jane Fonda exercise-class videos, for example, are not real classes: 'according to the director . . . the video required three days to shoot in order to get all the angles right; it was shot without music, the sound-track was dubbed in later; and the "class" was recorded separately, without Fonda present' (1989: 184). Consequently, 'rather than the image [the video] being a copy of the real, in the exercise video, the real [body] strives to become a copy of the image. The viewer mimics the images on the tape and strives to alter her or his appearance to resemble them.' (1989: 184).

Postmodernism and human agency

As we have discussed postmodern considerations of health and medicine, we should not be surprised that the 'body', rather than the individual 'subject', has been the focus of our attention. There have been no thorough considerations of phenomena that are crucial to the so-called 'modernist' approach; that is, to the social patterning of health and illness or to the individual's experience of health and illness (issues which are taken up in detail in chapters 4 and 9). Such considerations seem to be 'ruled out of court' as postmodernists 'decentre the subject', directing their attention to different discourses and new social formations that construct the individual in particular ways; however, some have argued that while the author – i.e. the sociologist who lifts the veil on the 'true' experience – is indeed dead, as are the collective actors (such as 'the working class') which the sociologist creates, the *individual* subject lives on, engaged in a process of meaning-making in an effort to cope with the barrage of information that is symptomatic of postmodernity. Lyotard (1986), for example, decries what he calls the 'totalising narratives' of Marxism, championing in their place plurality and heterogeneity as a basis for postmodern politics. As it is no longer possible for individuals to grasp what is happening in society overall, 'truth' and legitimation for action are dispersed, now residing not in grand narratives (i.e. theories which suggest a working out of particular ends, such as a proletarian revolution), but in localized contexts. With postmodernism,

> what has 'died' is the unified, monolithic, reified, essentialised subject capable of fully conscious, fully rational activity, a subject assumed in the most liberal and emancipatory discourse. Such a subject is replaced by a provisional, contingent, strategic, constituted subject which, while not essentialised, must be engaged in processes of meaning-making given the bombardment by conflicting messages. (Lather, 1991: 120)

Glassner provides an illustration of this in his study of fitness activities. 'By means of vital, rationalised, and self-directed action', he writes, 'the practitioner of fitness strives to construct an integral biography during a time when roles and collective morality are inconsistent and rapidly changing' (1989: 183). Under such conditions there is a blurring of the polarity of self and body at the level of individual experience. Echoing our earlier discussion of Derrida, health-related practices are seen to have a deconstructive role. Glassner argues that 'fitness activities afford [people] the opportunity to disenthrall their selves from the perceived shortcomings of everyday life in modern culture – in particular, from constraining dualities such as expert versus amateur, self versus body, male versus female, and work versus leisure' (1989: 182). The polarity of inner and outer body is also undermined, since inner-body mainte-nance is claimed to enhance outer appearance, and work on the outer body aids inner health (i.e. mental well-being). In modern contexts work and leisure are seen as separate modes, but in postmodernity, *leisure* becomes work (the work-out); people must keep themselves fit and healthy to actually keep their jobs and, in some industries, fitness time is built into work time.

Glassner's work suggests, then, that health-related practices may themselves serve to deconstruct contemporary dualisms. This idea is pursued more critically by Bordo (1993b), who portrays the anorexic woman as responding to the dual demands (for 'female domesticity' and 'male mastery') that are placed upon contemporary women. The anorexic pursues slenderness through the conventional feminine prac-tice of attending to appearance and, once engaged in this practice, 'discovers' male values of self-mastery and control (over the body); at the point of anorectic excess 'the conventionally feminine deconstructs, we might say, into its opposite and opens onto those values our culture has coded as male' (1993b: 179). No wonder, Bordo continues, anorexia is experienced as liberating. But, of course, this 'power' is illusory; in effect anorexia is not a protest or liberation but hopelessly counter-productive, an unconscious collusion with patriarchy.

Quite clearly, there are contrasting views of the body and subjectivity in the variously termed world of high modernity, postmodernity, or late capitalism (as discussed here and in chapter 1). For some, the body is a passive site of repression, for others a site of self-directed transfor-mation which has subversive potential. We turn now to consider this point further as we look at recent work which has emerged under the rubric of the 'sociology of the body'.

The sociology of the body

It is not merely that sociologists are becoming aware that the body is 'in fashion', they are increasingly aware that the social actors that

populate their theories have bodies that are integral to human exist-
ence and thus a central consideration in any theory. (Freund, 1988:
840)

'Bringing the body back into sociology' is the clarion call of the sociology of the body. Fearful of biological determinism and striving to
establish its own perspective built around the social, sociology, it is
argued, has taken flight from the physicality of the body. This is said to
have had the most damaging of effects upon our attempts to understand social action: we have stressed the conscious action of individuals, failing to recognize that this action is inevitably *embodied*, failing to
appreciate that our bodies are intimately bound up with our actions
both shaped by, and themselves shaping, social relations (Shilling,
1993; Turner, 1992).

The sociology of the body crystallizes a number of recent developments in social theory already discussed in this chapter: a critique of
sociology's replication of the mind/body dualism of post-Enlighten-
ment thought; the influence of the Foucauldian reconceptualization of
power; and changes in the social conditions of life in late capitalism/
postmodernity which permit us to control the body in ways that were
never possible in the past, yet which throw us into doubt about what
the body actually is, 'about where one body finishes and another starts'
(Shilling, 1993: 38). (We can transplant organs, but who will qualify for
them? We can artificially support the body, but how shall we decide
when to end life?) The sociology of the body also draws significantly
upon the feminist insistence that we attend to the body as a key site of
oppression (discussed below in chapter 3).

As we have already discussed, Western social thought has construed
the body and the mind in opposition. The Greek philosopher Plato
described the body in the following way:

> *a source of countless distractions by reason of the mere requirement of*
> *food . . . liable also to diseases which overtake and impede us in the*
> *pursuit of truth; it fills us full of loves, and lusts, and fears, and fancies*
> *of all kinds, and endless foolery, and in the very truth, as men say,*
> *takes away from us the power of thinking at all. (Plato, quoted in*
> *Bordo, 1993b: 145)*

Still today, the body is construed as 'something apart from the true self
(whether conceived as soul, mind, spirit, will, creativity, freedom . . .),
and as undermining the best efforts of that self. That which is not-body
is the highest, the best, the noblest, the closest to God; that which is

body is the albatross, the heavy drag on self-realisation' (Bordo, 1993b: 5). If this perspective has had a negative impact upon the parent discipline of sociology, its effects are argued to be especially pernicious for the sociology of health and medicine.

In response, sociologists of the body are concerned to demonstrate the dialectical (or two-way) relationship between the physical body and human subjectivity, often expressed through the concept of the 'lived body'. This conception is, in fact, part of a theoretical legacy that predates thinking that now goes under the banner of the sociology of the body. As already noted, feminist work has been an important, although often underacknowledged, resource in this regard, as has phenomenology, particularly through the work of Merleau-Ponty, which stresses the irreducible fusion of mind and body. 'The vision of soul and body is not', Merleau-Ponty writes, 'an amalgamation between two mutually external terms, subject and object, brought about by arbitrary decree. It is enacted at every instant in the movement of existence' (1962: 88–9). Thus our experience, our being-in-the-world, is lived through our body's habitual relation to the world.

Clearly then the sociology of the body intends to do more than just call our attention to the physiological. The aim is to recognize that 'in addition to understanding the social construction of bodies, it is very important to appreciate the ways in which social structured physiology affects social behaviour' (Freund, 1988: 857), for example, through physiological responses to stresses in the environment. In simplified terms, there is a 'feedback' in operation, in which social environments construct bodies, which impacts back on social behaviour, which can then further modify the body. An illustration of this process – or dialectic between the physical body and social environment – is given in Connell's (1987) discussion of how gender identities 'contradict' physiology. Ten-year-old girls are generally defined as weak and fragile when, in fact, their bodies are usually larger than those of boys. These gender identities themselves become incorporated into girls' bodies; their bodies may actually *become* weaker because of the social practices that are inscribed on the body. For example, passive rather than active pursuits are sanctioned, which are less likely to develop the body.

Turner argues that, once we realize this dialectic, we can appreciate that

> *the sociology of the body represents a major counter-position to the medical model and to reductionism in socio-biology because, in the concept of embodiment, we can break out of the dualism of the Cartesian legacy, phenomenologically appreciating the intimate and*

necessary relationship between my sense of myself, my awareness of the integrity of my body and experience of illness as not simply an attack on my instrumental body . . . but as a radical intrusion into my embodied selfhood. (1992: 167)

In an attempt to establish a new approach which attends to the dialectic between the 'physiological body' and the 'minded self', through the exploration of the experience of the 'lived body', the sociology of the body has so far operated at a fairly abstract level. As a result, the early literature was largely devoid of practical experiences of embodiment (Frank, 1996; Watson et al., 1995), although this is now beginning to change. A further concern relates to the relative lack of attention to the political 'here and now' in which the body is experienced in health and illness. The lived body that has been attended to – as wide-ranging as the man or woman undergoing cosmetic surgery, the adolescent anorectic, or the male body-builder – is often curiously decontextualized. In this regard, Eagleton (quoted in Marshall, 1996: 256) rails against both the focus on the 'exotic' and the neglect of the oppressed, when he remarks on a lack of any moral immediacy in the sociology of the body where there are 'mutilated bodies galore' (e.g. body-piercing, surgical transformations), but 'few malnourished ones', belonging as they do, he writes, 'to bits of the globe beyond the purview' of Western universities.

Conditions and practices which are emblematic of troubled times, such as eating disorders, have been the focus of attention. We know little as yet, for example, about the lived experience of the 'aged body' or the relatively untroubled body (for example, healthy middle-aged men). In short, there is a need to look at 'ordinary' experiences of the body in health and illness. Drawing together data from three studies – of women and men in the 'middle years' (aged 45–59), men aged 30–40, and disabled men and women of all ages, Watson et al. (1995) argue that 'a theory of embodiment grounded in *lay accounts* recasts the problem of theoretical dualities such as biology : culture, individual : society . . . in experiential terms'. Central here is the recognition that embodiment – or the subjective experience of the body – is 'predicated upon flux and indeterminancy . . . rather than the assumption of key dichotomies so prevalent in western society' (1995: 28, 29). Their respondents' accounts, for example, revealed the way in which perceptions of their own bodies, as well as the bodies of those known to them and those of generic 'types' displayed in the media, are variable and derived from everyday experience. In similar terms, Marshall (1996: 255) draws upon the metaphor of the mobius strip – the 'rubber band formed into a figure eight in which inside and outside endlessly merge' – to conceptualize the 'ordinary experience' of pregnancy and birth. Originating conceptually in the work of Lacan and deployed by Grosz (1994: xii), 'the mobius strip has the advantage of showing the inflection of mind into body and body into mind, the ways in which, through a kind of twisting or inversion, one side becomes the other'. Marshall draws upon her own personal account of pregnancy to reveal 'a multiplicity of bodies' which populated her own experience, 'shimmering like images in a kaleidoscope according to the focus applied to them' (1996: 262). At various points in time she could both experience her body as pregnant/not pregnant; hugely pregnant/tidily pregnant; in control/out of control (depending, for example, on whether she focused on biological parameters, personal feeling states, or the perceptions of others).

Earlier in the discussion of health and illness under conditions of late modernity/postmodernity, we noted that for some theorists the body is a passive site of repression, for others a site of transformation which has subversive potential. Efforts to understand anorexia display these *contrary perspectives* on the sociology of the body. On the one hand, anorexia makes the contemporary mind/body dualism explicit; it is a battle of the mind over the body, an attempt to control the body's rebellious desires and appetites, in effect to overcome them, to cease to experience hunger and desire. A female student's diary exemplifies this experience: 'When I fail to exercise as often as I prefer, I become guilty that I have let my body "win" another day from my mind. I can't wait until this semester is over . . . my body is going to pay the price for the lack of will it is currently getting. I can't wait' (respondent quoted in Bordo, 1993b: 147).

Yet at the same time that anorectics objectify their bodies (which are conceived of as alien to the self), anorexia is part of a process of creating and bestowing meaning on the body: 'it is an attempt to embody certain values, to create a body that will speak for the self in a meaningful way' (Bordo, 1993b: 67). However, referring back to our earlier discussion of Foucauldian perspectives, we are still left with the thorny question of whether what appear in narrative accounts as moral choices are in effect merely a ruse of disciplinary powers making individuals agents of their own subjection (Frank, 1996). Frank argues that, although disciplinary powers undoubtedly do exert control, there remains a space within which we can construct our personal ethics and our lives. Illness narratives (discussed in detail in chapter 9 below), he claims, are not simply confessional techniques, but entail 'practising a technique of the self', providing the opportunity to speak from the 'centre of the lived body' (1996: 63). Attention to the 'lived' body, therefore may provide the opportunity to rupture the dualistic thought that postmodernists, sociologists of the body and others argue has long animated thinking within the sociology of health and medicine.

Concluding comments

The sociology of health and medicine has travelled a long way in a relatively short period of time. In the space of less than three decades its practitioners have sought authenticity by contesting the biomedical model and founding a distinctly *social* perspective in its place. As we have seen, the nature of the social is itself highly contested. In one sense we seem to have come back full circle: the turn away from a physical in favour of a social model has now turned back on itself, but in a reconstituted form as sociologists of health and illness seek to 'reclaim the body' and develop a more sophisticated theoretical framework which takes account of the dialectical relationship between biological and social processes, the individual and society.

These developments notwithstanding, attempts to theorize the social context that surrounds health and medicine in the contemporary period appear to be at a crossroads: the established positions of interactionism and political economy certainly still hold sway but are increasingly subject to revision as new perspectives such as theories of late modernity, Foucauldian social constructionism and postmodernism force themselves into view. Although poorly articulated to date in relation to health and medicine, these newer approaches may cause consternation for some, while being greeted with enthusiasm by others. The struggle to establish a feminist agenda within sociology occurred at broadly the same time as medical sociology's development as a major subdiscipline. This, along with feminists' significant attention to issues of women's health, has meant that feminist theory has been entwined with the debates that we have been exploring in this chapter for over three decades or more. It is to feminist perspectives that we turn in the next chapter.

3

The Feminist Challenge

A review of trends in the study of gender in sociology begins by
remarking that 'it is difficult now . . . to recall the time when gender
relations were not regarded as a legitimate focus for sociological study'
(Maynard, 1990: 269). However, behind this growing acceptance lies a
hard-fought battle for recognition.

Early challenges to male dominance in the discipline emphasized
women's *invisibility*. For example, back in 1974, Oakley wrote that
discrimination against women in society was mirrored by concealment
in academia. In much sociology, she proclaimed, 'women as a social
group are invisible or inadequately represented; they take the insub-
stantial form of ghosts, shadows or stereotyped characters' (Oakley,
1974: 1). Areas of social life which, *because* of sexism, particularly concern women, such as the domestic sphere, were excluded from the
sociological agenda as male sociologists from the early days of the so-
called founding fathers onwards gave their attention to work, industry
and the state (all constructed as male, and therefore as the most important, domains of social life) (Stacey, 1981). Alongside this process of
exclusion, Oakley pointed to the way in which sociological theory gave
a distorted picture of women as it tried to fit them into 'pre-defined
male-oriented sociological categories' (Oakley 1974: 4). She gives several examples of this, drawing on the sub-fields of deviance, social
stratification, power, the family and work and industry. Ironically,
Oakley failed to include the domain of health and illness in her review –
in these early days when feminists tended to argue for an awareness of
women *within existing* areas of male interest, it seems that women's
health could not be put on the agenda precisely because it was not yet of
interest to men. As feminist research gained momentum during the

1970s, it was increasingly recognized that women's experience could not easily be accommodated within existing theoretical paradigms. Subsequently, some feminists have sought to extend and revise existing theories developed by men, while others, less happy with revisionism, have argued for a more radical overhaul.

Although there are exceptions, feminist theory has often been used tacitly in research on gender and health. This means that, more often than not, interpretative frameworks are implicit rather than explicit. For example, in *Women, Health and Medicine* (1991) Miles gives a thought-provoking introduction to social science research on women's health and health care, drawing attention to a number of important debates around the medical control of women's lives. The problematic nature of women's experience is highlighted and related to factors such as doctors' attitudes and gender-related influences on women's experiences (socialization, differences in terms of work and lifestyle and so on), but there are no explicit references to patriarchy, power or social class, nor to the ways in which, when linked in a theoretical framework, these concepts can help us to *explain* women's circumstances and their relationship to their health. While it is somewhat invidious to critique one book, it illustrates a problem that underpins a lot of gender-related research, which is that women and also, where they are included, men often appear as a bundle of statuses – domestic worker, paid worker, mother, father, working-class, middle-class etc. From a woman's point of view these statuses are appropriately interpreted as problematic for health because of 'patriarchy', 'gender-related exploitation' and the 'control of women', yet these concepts often lack clear definition and articulation within a broader feminist theory. This neglect can partly be explained by feminists' insistence that women's *subjective* experience should always be put at the centre of research in order to highlight the very real suffering that they have experienced in attempting to care for their own health and the health of others. However, while recourse to subjective experience is crucial, by itself it is an insufficient challenge to patriarchy. Rather, through the use of theory we can 'address women's experience by showing where it comes from and how it relates to material social practices and the power relations that structure them' (Weedon, 1987: 8). As Stacey (1993) argues, theory has a central role in overcoming subordination. In the first place it has a *critical* purpose, that is, to expose and challenge, rather than to legitimate, oppression. Second, feminists can use analytic categories to move beyond the descriptive and the anecdotal, that is, to generalize beyond the individual case (an individual person, health clinic, health-care system).

Feminist differences

Only at a very general level can we talk of a common feminist vision. Broadly, all feminisms share an understanding that patriarchy privileges men by taking the male body as the 'standard' and fashioning upon it a plethora of valued characteristics (health, mastery, rationality, reason, and so on) and, through a comparison, constructing the female body as deficient, associated with illness, with lack of control and with intuitive rather than reasoned action. In associating these 'deficiencies' with women's reproductive capacity, patriarchy conflates biological sex and social gender. A major task of feminism has been to question this elision between sex and gender by showing that gender is socially constructed; the social processes that construct the female body as inferior and that discriminate against women (and favour men) can then be identified and acted upon to improve the conditions of women's lives, including their health.

The sociology of health and illness made a major contribution to the development of second-wave feminism (from around the late 1960s), yet recently it seems to have drifted away from core debates in feminist theory. Although there is a growing recognition of the fragmentation of feminism among some writers in the field (see Doyal, 1995; Lupton, 1994), many still seem to work from the assumption that feminist theory is an internally coherent body of thought. This means that the implications of the growing differences within feminism for the way in which we conceptualize the influence of patriarchy upon women's bodies and their health have not yet been fully appreciated (Annandale and Clark, 1996). Even though in some circumstances it may be strategic to draw on what various feminist approaches hold in common at a broad level (such as the analysis of patriarchy and the will to abolish the oppression of women), at the current time it is far more appropriate to talk of *feminist theories and feminisms* in the plural than of *feminist theory and feminism* in the singular.

Having recognized this, we are left with the thorny problem of how to talk and write about different feminist ideas. It is possible to argue that there are groups of thinkers who hold more in common with each other than with other groups of thinkers, but at the same time to recognize that they are not identical. In this respect it has become usual to refer to the following different 'types' of feminism: liberal feminism, radical feminism, materialist feminism and postmodern feminism (although there are other valid classifications). Some object to categorization, arguing that it obscures more than it reveals and can lead to the stereotyping of particular views. Undoubtedly there is something artificial about grouping the works of various feminists together in this way. However, categorizing is, if nothing else, an effective way to begin to understand a complex issue. As we explore feminist approaches and the understanding of issues of health, illness and health care that they suggest, it is important to bear in mind that while the various 'types' do have some internal coherence, they may conceal differences between individual writers. It is also important to appreciate that, although there are significant debates between 'types' of feminist theory and between individual theorists, some feminists now talk of a greater tolerance of different approaches. Jaggar and Rothenberg (1993), for example, make a virtue of divisions using the metaphor of several lenses through which we can look at the same time.

The next section considers in turn liberal, radical, postmodern and materialist feminist critiques of: (1) the elision of gender and the body under patriarchy; and (2) the ways in which patriarchal social structures damage women's health. We will emphasize the quite different conclusions that each perspective affords on how to improve the conditions of women's lives and their health.

Liberal feminism

Liberal feminism has its roots in political liberalism. In liberal thought the uniqueness of human beings lies in their capacity for rationality. A good and just society is one that allows the individual the potential for autonomy and self-realization, ideas that originated in seventeenth-century England and took root there in the eighteenth century. During this period John Locke espoused a political liberalism at variance with the sixteenth- and seventeenth-century view which saw the political order in familial terms, as natural or ordained by God, and built around the 'rule of the father'. For Locke, this was antithetical to the individualism inherent in bourgeois liberal society. But this view of the liberal individual did not extend to women. Indeed, Locke felt that the hierarchical division of the sexes was necessary for the operation of the market. However, Mary Wollstonecraft (1757–97), often proclaimed the first major feminist, developed an impassioned attack upon the sexism of late eighteenth-century society in her feminist declaration of independence, *A Vindication of the Rights of Woman* (1792). As Brody (1992: 1) writes, 'Wollstonecraft dared to take the liberal doctrine of inalienable human rights, a doctrine which was inflaming patriots on both sides of the Atlantic, and assume these rights for her own sex.' She argued for women's parity with men, making a great virtue of women's involvement in the sphere of paid work, alongside their responsibility for childrearing.

Even though Wollstonecraft and others of her time only argued, in effect, for the equality of middle-class women on men's terms, they nonetheless recognized the need for institutional change – notably in the areas of education and the law. In this way, their work called for a degree of structural reform. As we turn to second-wave feminism of the post-Second World War period, something of this is lost. For example in *The Feminine Mystique* (1963) Betty Friedan wrote through the language of individual will, emphasizing the ability of the individual to make rational choices and to act upon them. Her focus was, as Tong (1992: 24) explains, the 'dissatisfaction of the suburban, white, middle class, heterosexual housewife in the United States', making work outside the home the goal of the women's liberation movement. Crucially, the aim was not to take power from men, but to be *included in men's power* (Eisenstein, 1993).

The stress upon rational action and the ability to achieve equality with men through concerted action within the existing structures of society also remains central to contemporary feminist work such as Naomi Wolf's (1991) *The Beauty Myth*. Wolf's identification of the body as a site of oppression (revealed, for example, in the increase in eating disorders such as bulimia and anorexia) is not in question. Rather, what concerns us is her premise that the way out of the devastating effects of 'bodyism' for women is via a collective act of will, a denial of the beauty industry and male control through a third wave of activism from young women – in her own terms, the view that women can create a 'new perspective themselves' (Wolf, 1991: 288). These arguments are developed further in *Fire with Fire* (Wolf, 1994: 187, 83), where women are urged to view feminism as a humanist movement in which men are not enemies but partners in the fight for social equality, and where activism is a 'journey to a social contract that includes men and women fairly'. She responds to feminist poet Audre Lorde's (1984) dictum that 'the master's tools will never dismantle the master's house', with 'it is *only* the master's tools that can dismantle the master's house; he hardly bothers to notice anyone else's'. Women are called upon to 'walk into the "palace of power", and unapologetically use its mighty resources for change' (Wolf, 1994: 59, 74). For critics this betrays a fundamental problem: liberal feminists fail to see that male bias is *intrinsic* to the institutions that they wish to gain access to (Gatens, 1992). Consequently, women could never gain full access on men's terms even if they wanted to: they have not simply been excluded from the rational (male) world of reason; rationality itself has been defined against 'the feminine' and traditional female roles. There is, therefore, an inherent contradiction within liberal feminism: a fundamental belief in individual autonomy, but a failure to recognize that these liberal ideas are patriarchal in form (Eisenstein, 1993). Put another way, liberalism itself has patriarchal roots.

Although liberal feminism takes the male body as the implicit norm or standard of the 'liberated individual', the body itself is mute, reflecting the privileging of mindful, rational action – action which Jaggar (1983), among others, identifies as 'male'. This deprecation of bodily functions and activities no doubt grows out of a wish to negate the patriarchal elision of sex and gender – i.e. to substantiate that gender does not follow from sex/biology, but is socially constructed and, therefore, that there is no intrinsic reason why the female sex cannot have access to male-gendered social experiences. Here the connection between femininity and the morphology (i.e. form) of the female body (and masculinity and the male body) is arbitrary; the body is passive and merely mediates the inscription of social 'lessons' (through gendered socialization) on to the mind. As a result, we have what Moira Gatens (1983: 144) believes to be a 'simplistic solution to female oppression: a programme of re-education, the unlearning of patriarchy's arbitrary and oppressive codes and the re-learning of politically correct and equitable behaviours'.

But in Gatens' (1983, 1992) view, there *is* no neutral body; it is always sexed. This becomes evident, she argues, when we appreciate that behaviours (be they stereotypically 'masculine' or 'feminine' in form) have different social significance when acted out by a male or a female body. In the context of health care, for example, significant others (family, doctors, nurses) respond not 'just' to symptoms, but to symptoms that are attached to a particular (gendered) body (see Wallen et al., 1979). Hence, the body is not passive or mute but calls forth particular responses based on its own physicality. This is not to argue that the physical body is in any way essentially given or fixed around sex-typed features (such as genitalia), but that biological features themselves are open to cultural investment, i.e. that biology itself is a social construct, and that social gender, in fact, has its *genesis* in our views of the body (Gatens, 1983).

Contrary to the radical feminist view (considered below) that attention to the specificity of the female body is crucial in understanding women's enslavement to and liberation from men, liberal feminists emphasize mindful action over embodied experience. This perspective had a very influential impact upon the large and very productive body of research which began to emerge in the 1970s which stressed the relationship between social roles and health status (see Nathanson, 1980). Quite clearly, the underlying aim of this research was to demonstrate that health is not a straightforward product of women's biology, but is socially constructed out of gender-related roles and experiences. As we have seen, liberal feminism emphasizes freeing women from the oppressive gender roles used to justify their exclusion from the valued public sphere. It is not surprising, therefore, that research on gender roles and health focused from the outset on the world of paid work outside the home. This is seen in the considerable attention given to the roles of paid worker and 'housewife' (and their combination in women's lives), notably in the debate over whether women in paid work are in better health than those who work full-time in the home. In early work of this type in particular there was a tacit use of male lives as a reference point. For example, conditions of paid work were often considered through the lens of traditionally male occupations, on the assumption that they affect women's health in the same way (Hall, 1989). Although, as we will see in the detailed discussion in chapter 5, research on gender and health status is now far more sophisticated than it was in the 1970s and early 1980s, its liberal feminist legacy is still felt in the tendency to put the 'social' aspects of gender to the fore, as attention is directed towards 'mindful action' rather than 'embodied experience'.

Scott and Morgan (1993) relate the privileging of mind over body to the centrality given to knowledge as power over the body in liberalism, something which has been central to the women's health movement, which views access to information and the right to decision-making in health matters as vital. The women's health movement embodies diverse perspectives. Ruzek (1980), for example, identifies three alternatives to the traditional male authoritarian model of health care: the *traditional egalitarian* (professionals assume responsibility but patients are expected to be informed and involved); the *traditional feminist* (the balance of medical authority is altered but not undermined – e.g. by the use of female para-professionals such as nurse practitioners); and the *radical feminist* (women assume major responsibility, physicians have only technical status performing tasks prohibited to others under law, such as writing prescriptions). The traditional egalitarian and traditional feminist models relate most closely to the liberal feminist position: there is an attempt to include women in a system which still ultimately operates as a male-defined preserve, and to assume that the sex-typing of health occupations and the related problem of sexism in medicine can be dealt with by feminization of the medical profession (see discussion in Fee, 1975). Even where activists recognize that quite radical change is needed, there is an underlying sense that this can be achieved through informed individual or collective political action (e.g. seeking the information that you need to make decisions about your health) with little discussion of structural impediments to such action (e.g. financial barriers) or of the need for concomitant change in women's lives outside of the health-care system.

Radical feminism

One of the limitations of liberal feminism identified by its critics is its willingness to work *within* the patriarchal system. Radical feminism breaks completely with this, arguing that patriarchy is the *root* of women's oppression – there can be no equality on men's terms; patriarchy must be eliminated. Ramazanoglu (1989) identifies radical feminism as the feminism most difficult to define because of its diversity. Like all feminisms, the category does not refer to writers who hold identical ideas, but to those who share certain basic premises. Central to radical feminism has been the idea that what women have in common is greater than the factors which might divide them (social class, 'race' and sexual orientation, for example). What they share is the common experience of oppression built around male control of women's bodies. This means that liberating the body is fundamental to transforming women's political consciousness. Through consciousness-raising, and positing the 'personal as political', radical feminism made sexuality, rape, and other forms of male violence (including the practices of obstetrics and gynaecology) into public issues (Ramazanoglu, 1989). In distinction to other feminist perspectives, radical feminism was effectively built around control of the body and thus women's health. To map the development of radical feminism, therefore, is simultaneously to chart radical feminist views on health, illness and health care, notably as they relate to reproduction and childbirth.

One of the early statements that helped to define the radical feminist position was Kate Millett's *Sexual Politics* (1991 [1970]). Millett identified patriarchy as the basis of all power relations, existing prior to and superseding economic and political forms of oppression. This, and other works, establish reproduction as central to women's oppression, although radical feminists have, in fact, proposed quite different solutions to women's oppression through biology. Shulamith Firestone (1970) identifies women as a sex-class (i.e. a class unto themselves), arguing that we can understand their position through the forces of reproduction rather than production. The historical struggles between biological sexes – over the form of marriage, control of reproduction and child care – are identified as the moving forces of history. She concludes that women need to be liberated from their biology through technology; they need to seize the means of reproduction – in the 1970s this was limited to contraception, abortion and sterilization – in order to liberate themselves from childbearing, which she identifies as 'barbaric'. Other radical feminists retain the emphasis on women's difference from men built around the specificity of the sexed body, but dissent from Firestone's view that the solution to male control lies in repudiating women's capacity to reproduce. There is nothing problematic about reproduction; rather, the problem lies in patriarchy's response to it. From this perspective, technologies such as contraception, abortion and *in vitro* fertilization (IVF) need to be viewed with extreme caution, as they are male attempts to wrest control from women. For Gena Corea (1985) reproductive technologies are means for men to control the female body, to satisfy their unconscious desire to procreate and, ultimately, to do away with the need for women altogether. A woman's body is a source of power undermined by men. The Feminist International Network of Resistance to Reproductive and Genetic Engineering (FINRRAGE) called for a halt to the development of *in vitro* techniques and urged that we put in its place a self-conscious move away from male/misogynist scientific control of reproduction and birth towards feminist self-help and home birth (Sawicki, 1991).

The call for feminized control over reproduction is a general position which characterizes radical feminism as a whole, but, nonetheless, conceals a range of views. The 'strong' end of radical feminism is often identified with the work of the American writer Mary Daly, who aims to show how, despite different historical, political and cultural formations in the societies in which women live, they share the common experience of patriarchal oppression. Daly's work is difficult to summarize, since her ideas have changed over the course of her writing. In her early book *Beyond God the Father* (1973) she was concerned with God as the paradigm for patriarchs, arguing that this constructs woman as 'other', as an object, against the male subject who emerges in God's likeness. She proposes a form of androgyny (a mix of masculine and feminine virtues), which would retain the feminine traits of love and compassion which are distorted into excesses of self-sacrifice under patriarchy. On this view, when a woman refuses to be an 'other', she is no longer a slave; with no slaves man has no one to control; patriarchy then loses the conditions for its existence. In *Gyn/ecology* (1990 [1978]), Daly rejects the concept of androgyny, now recognizing that the constructs of femininity (nurturing, compassion etc.) that she referred to in her previous work should be appreciated for what they are: namely, man-made constructs that have nothing to do with 'true femaleness'. The book has been very influential, notably for its criticism of gynaecology. She writes that

> *there is every reason to see the mutilation and destruction of women by doctors specialising in unnecessary radical mastectomies and hysterectomies, carcinogenic hormone therapy, psychosurgery, spirit killing psychiatry and other forms of psychotherapy as directly related to the rise of radical feminism in the twentieth century. (1990: 228)*

Medicine condenses woman's being into particular parts or organs of the body, making her, in Daly's words, shrunken/frozen, manipulable/manageable. By this process, gynaecologists 'vampirise their feelings of effectiveness/potency from women' (1990: 236).

In this work Daly positions woman's difference from man. As Tong relates, Daly calls for a recapturing of women's true biology as a subversive strategy against patriarchy: 'to become a whole person, to make contact with her true, natural self, a woman need only strip away the false identity – femininity – that patriarchy has constructed for her' (Tong, 1992: 107). There is, then, a sense of an original self beyond that which has been imposed by patriarchy. What patriarchy has created as good for woman is bad for her; what it sees as bad for her must be good. Thus the inversion of male values is a political strength, as seen in Daly's discussion of the 'hag':

> *Hag is . . . defined as 'an ugly or evil-looking old woman' [in Old English]. But this considering the source, may be considered a compliment. For the beauty of strong, creative women is 'ugly' by misogynist standards of 'beauty'. The look of female-identified woman is 'evil' to those who fear us. As for 'old', ageism is a feature of phallic [i.e. male-defined] society. For women who have transvaluated this, a Crone is one who should be an example of strength, courage and wisdom. (1990: 14–15)*

In her later work, Daly views woman as close to nature (see *Pure Lust*, 1984) where true femaleness is seen as wild and untamed. In accord with this 'strong' version of radical feminism, others celebrate women's bodies. Lipshitz, for example, sees women as 'witchlike in being able to give birth to live beings', as 'possessors of an invisible internal substance that provokes fear because it links them to another world than that of male culture' (1978: 39).

In her critique, Di Stefano identifies this position as anti-rationalist:

[It] celebrates the designated and feminised irrational, invoking a strong notion of difference against the gender-neutral pretensions of a rationalist culture that opposes itself to nature, the body, natural contingency, and intuition. This project sees itself as a disloyal opposition and envisions a social order that would better accommodate women in their feminised difference rather than as imperfect copies of the Everyman. (1990: 67)

This 'strong' position, then, seems to put forward the female body as superior to the male body. Since this is the case for *all* women, it has been seen as universalizing women's experience. Jaggar (1983) dubs it a 'woman culture movement' which fails to address issues of class and 'race'. Lorde (1984: 67) echoes this view, referring to black women's experience. She remarks that to argue that women all suffer the same oppression 'simply because we are women is to lose sight of the many and varied tools of patriarchy'.

Radical feminism undoubtedly vivified both popular and academic work on women's health in the 1970s, and its influence continues to be felt today. A large body of research has explored women's experience of health, illness and health care, detailing the ways in which patriarchy, viewed as an intrinsic part of the formal health-care system, undermines women's health. A very clear agenda is set: to explore the ways in which patriarchy, manifest most clearly in male control of women's bodies, undermines women's health.

Dreifus dedicates *Seizing Our Bodies: The Politics of Women's Health* (1978) to the memory of her mother: 'an early health feminist who knew that a woman's right to her body was a woman's right to her life'. This dedication, and the title of the book, point to the heart of the radical feminist struggle for women's health against men. A number of very influential studies have revealed how, throughout history, men have controlled women through their bodies. For example, Ehrenreich and English document how middle-class femininity was seen as synonymous with sickness from the mid-nineteenth century to the turn of the century, when the myth of female frailty was used to justify women's exclusion from higher education (notably medicine) and from voting. The authors remark that 'medical arguments seemed to take the malice out of sexual oppression: when you prevented a woman from doing anything active or interesting, you were only doing this for her own good' (Ehrenreich and English, 1978: 128). This was premised on the view that the sexual organs, in particular, competed with other organs in the body for a limited supply of vital energy. Since, according to nineteenth-century physicians, 'reproduction was women's grand purpose in life, doctors agreed that women ought to concentrate their physical energy internally, toward the womb' (1978: 131). Ehrenreich and English write that doctors 'found uterine and ovarian "disorders" behind almost every female complaint, from headaches to sore throats and indigestion' (1978: 132). Writers have also revealed that the view of 'female anatomy as destiny' is still rife in much of contemporary Western medical practice, contributing, for example, to the view that changes in women's bodies, such as the menopause, are problems to be dealt with by medicine (see the discussions in Foster, 1995 and Martin, 1987).

Given their intention to reveal the way in which patriarchy seeks to control reproduction, it is not surprising that radical feminists have given significant attention to childbirth. Along with others, they have sought through historical analysis to demonstrate that, by scapegoating midwives for high maternal death rates and offering heroic interventions (such as the use of forceps), male obstetricians wrested control of birth from female midwives in the late eighteenth century. Before this 'male take-over', they argue, birth was a natural and normal event. Among a great many others, Rich (1992) and Oakley (1984) write that still today obstetricians use the concept of 'risk' to turn an essentially natural experience into one that is replete with dangers, thereby justifying technologically assisted hospital birth and denying women a fulfilling birth experience. Arms (1975: 83), writing in the 1970s about an experience that is still relevant today, likened women giving birth in US hospitals to prisoners, arguing that birth was 'slow and agonising, full of risk, expensive, lonely, demoralising if not demeaning, and heading in the direction that may someday eradicate the need for the woman's body (except her uterus) altogether'.

From the 1970s onwards there has been an outpouring of research which draws upon the radical feminist premise that men's and women's bodies and, by extension, their experience, are engendered. The radical feminist emphasis upon women's experience in interaction with male physicians has been central. For example, in an influential article, Graham and Oakley (1986 [1981]) argued that doctors and mothers have a qualitatively different way of looking at the nature, content and management of reproduction. Dundas Todd looked at how the 'disease model' draws physicians' attention away from the social context (work, home, family) which informs women's experience of gynaecological health and illness. Echoing the conclusions of other research, she shows how, when physicians do delve into the context of women's lives, they use this information to exert more control; to reinforce stereotypical sex roles and ignore women's health needs (1989: 97). The call for female-controlled alternatives to mainstream gynaecology and obstetrics resonates throughout the women's health movement. In the United States self-help has been promoted through feminist health collectives, the best known being the Boston Women's Health Collective, who publish the book *Our Bodies, Ourselves* (Boston Women's Health Book Collective, 1973). In Britain, there have been few alternatives outside the NHS (Doyal, 1995), but groups like the Association of Radical Midwives, pressure groups such as the Association for the Improvement of Maternity Services and the National Childbirth Trust, and the work of individuals like Sheila Kitzinger have organized to effect change (Stacey, 1988). The alternatives that have developed, of course, span the range identified by Ruzek (1980), with only those in which women assume major responsibility, and where physicians are allowed only a technical status, fitting the radical feminist ideal.

Having briefly detailed the issues that were taken up in response to this perspective, it is important to reflect back upon the treatment of the sex/gender distinction in radical feminism. The important and difficult questions that we must ask are: to what extent does research on women's health essentialize and valorize the female body? To what extent does it universalize women's experience? And, in reality, *can* radical feminism deliver women from patriarchal control when it is founded on a politics of difference from men?

As we have seen for all feminisms, patriarchy oppresses women by eliding sex and gender, attributing negatively valued characteristics to the female body and, therefore, to female gender. Liberal feminists attempt to counter this by severing the association between sex and gender, thereby rendering the body mute and privileging rational, minded behaviour. The strategy of radical feminism is very different: it in effect endorses a strong *connection* between sex and gender, but reverses the privileges of patriarchy, valorizing the physicality of the female, rather than the male, body. The body is no longer mute; instead we have an animate, lived body (Gatens, 1983). This position came under considerable attack from other feminists in the 1980s and 1990s for its implied essentialism, i.e. the view that there is an essential femininity untainted by patriarchy. This suggests that the 'natural' female body is unproblematic and that women's health problems arise because biomedicine 'disrupts women's natural needs and rhythms' (Scott and Morgan, 1993: 9). Since authentic experience is built on the sexed body, which is seen to a large degree as biologically 'fixed', this means that men and women are conceptualized in opposition to each other, developing what we can call an 'engendered perspective' where, in Eisenstein's (1988: 3) words, 'differences among women are silenced and differences between men and women privileged; the sameness among women is presumed and the similarity between men and women is denied'. Critics of radical feminism have argued that its essentialism means that it denies differences between women (e.g. differences of social class) and that it pits women against men by holding up a female 'counter-culture' premised on women's biological superiority.

As has already been noted, the question of whether radical feminism presumes a fundamental biological (i.e. essential) difference between men and women is highly contentious. Calls for alternative models of childbirth appear to endorse the view that, free from male control, women's experience of birth would be essentially different. For example Calloway writes, 'no longer a passive, suffering instrument . . . [woman] retains the power of self-direction, of self-control, of choice, of voluntary decisions and active cooperation with doctor and nurse' (1993 [1978]: 23). The problem with this view, and others like it, is that there is an appeal to a return to childbirth 'as it really is'; there is an assumption that there is an authentic natural birth which can be rediscovered outside of patriarchy. Yet what *is* natural birth? It is typically only ever evoked in very general (and positive) terms in radical feminist literature, appearing as an antithesis to obstetrics and built around assumptions of the sisterhood among women (Annandale and Clark, 1997). Several writers have characterized the radical feminist assumption that all women need a woman-centred alternative to male-controlled health care, as a middle-class 'white' view. bell hooks (1984), for example, argues that the notion of sisterhood is inappropriately based on the idea of 'common oppression', a view that all women's bodies and, therefore, their experiences are the same.

These criticisms culminate in the view of many feminists in the 1990s that, by arguing for fundamental differences between men and women, radical feminism ironically buys into the male-defined world-view that it attempts to undermine. Grosz writes that feminism becomes

> necessarily complicit in reproducing patriarchal values: in claiming that women's current social roles and position are the effects of their essence, nature, biology, or universal social position, these theories are guilty of rendering such roles and positions unalterable, necessary, and thus of providing them with a powerful political justification. (1990b: 335)

Thus, counter-intuitive though it may seem, the radical feminist position may be implicated in patriarchy. This can occur in the following way: in much radical feminist work, it is argued that women can escape the profoundly negative influence of patriarchy by emphasizing their positively valued difference from men. This difference centres on re-production. The problem is that, just like the male biomedicine that it criticizes, radical feminism can thus find itself making reproduction the centre of women's lives. It has been argued that women then accept, rather than challenge and displace, the social relations of patriarchy that were defined as the problem in the first place.

However, other writers view the argument that radical feminism is essentialist as fundamentally misplaced. Diane Bell and Renate Klein (1996: p. xxiv), for example, remark that radical feminism is 'the femi-nism that everyone loves to hate', as witnessed in continual taunts of essentialism and in the charge that it universalizes women and there-fore masks differences between them. Andrea Dworkin, whose own work has been criticized in these terms, writes of the negative response that she received when she spoke out in the 1970s against what she calls the 'ideological rot, articulated of late with increasing frequency in feminist circles: women and men are distinct species or races . . .; men are biologically inferior to women; male violence is a biological inevit-ability; to eliminate it, one must eliminate the species/race itself' (1988: 42). For Dworkin, this is a biologically determinist logic virtually equiv-alent to Nazism. Few radical feminists would, of course, adopt the 'strong' position that Dworkin rails against. Yet few feel able to ques-tion, or even want to let go of, the view that there is a 'raw material' that women hold in common which provides at least the *starting-point* for the social construction of differences between men and women (Fuss, 1989), perhaps because to do so would appear to undercut the notion of engenderment altogether. For example, Rowland and Klein see the criticism of biological determinism as a ploy to undermine the effective-ness of radical feminism, and stress that differences between men and women 'may have been generated out of the different worlds that we inhabit as social groups'. But they still remark that

> it is possible that differences between women and men arise out of a biological base but in a different way to that proposed by a reductivist determinism. The fact that women belong to the social group which has the capacity for procreation and mothering, and the fact that men belong to the group that has the capacity to carry out, and does, acts of rape and violence against women, must intrude into the conscious-ness of being male and female. (1990: 297–8)

The discussion so far in this chapter has shown that liberal and radical feminists share the premise that patriarchy oppresses women by conflating sex and gender, attributing negatively valued characteristics to the female body and, therefore, to female gender. As we have seen, the liberal feminist response has been to argue that, since gender is socially constructed, there is no intrinsic relationship between sex/ biology and gender. Traditionally, emphasis has been placed on women's access to positively valued 'male roles' and male experiences which are associated with good health. As a consequence of focusing on rational minded behaviour, the body is mute and passive. Radical feminism appears to take a contrasting approach, in effect endorsing a strong connection between sex and gender. It often attempts to undermine patriarchal privilege by positively valuing what is distinctive about the female, rather than the male, body. Women's reproductive capacity has been a central concern. Far from being mute and passive, the body is central to and, although this is disputable, seems for some radical feminists effectively to determine, women's experience. There are, then, important differences in the way in which liberal and radical feminists have sought to understand women's health. Yet, from the vantage-point of postmodern feminism, these differences pale into insignificance. Although, as was discussed at the beginning of the chapter, it is important to approach both radical and liberal feminism as umbrella terms for a range of ideas, in their ideal typical form at least, they have been criticized for constructing male and female health in oppositional and often universal terms, whether this be on *social* (liberal feminism) or *biological* (radical feminism) grounds (Annandale, 1998). As we will now go on to discuss, for postmodern feminists there are inherent dangers in this position.

Postmodern feminism

Feminist theory is widely recognized to have experienced a major transformation during the late 1980s and early 1990s. As Michele Barrett writes, 'contemporary Western feminism, confident for several years about its "sex-gender" distinction, analyses of "patriarchy", or postulation of "the male gaze" has found all these various categories radically undermined by the new "deconstructive" emphasis on fluidity and contingency' (1992: 202).

The crux of the postmodern challenge to prior feminisms is an insistence that both their theory and their politics are premised on the assumption of a fundamental difference between men and women that is artificial and the result of a modernist view of the world. Although it is not always made explicit, radical feminism is often the critical target. Its assumption of difference built around biology, as we have seen, is said to universalize experience and to take it as 'given' that women have more in common with each other than they have with men. The concept of sisterhood has particularly been subject to attack, and here the work of black feminists, who have highlighted modernist feminism's promotion of the notion of a generic white, middle-class woman, has been very important. Bryan et al. vividly display the white bias in feminist activism in the context of health care (the issue of 'race' and health in a wider context is discussed in detail in chapter 6). For example, when the Women's Liberation Movement took up the issue of 'abortion on demand' in the 1970s,

> black women had to point out that we have always been given abortions more readily than white women and are indeed often encouraged to have terminations we did not ask for. It's for this reason, too, that when the women's movement demanded 'free, safe and available contraception for all women', we had to remind them that for Black women this often means being used as guinea-pigs in mass birth control programmes . . . And when the same women talked about 'a woman's right to choose', we responded that for Black women, this must also mean having the right to choose to have our children, planned or not planned. For us, the politics of women's health have always had that added racist dimension – a dimension which has been overlooked far too often by the white, middle-class women who constitute the majority of the women's health movement. (Bryan et al., 1985: 105)

Many black feminists argue that we must be aware of 'interlocking systems of oppression': that there are 'few pure victims or oppressors' in a matrix of domination. Rather, 'each individual derives varying amounts of penalty and privilege from the multiple systems of oppression which frame everyone's lives' (Collins, 1990: 222, 229). This helps us to appreciate women's oppression of each other. As hooks (1984) writes, black women often work under white women, so why should they join with women who exploit them to help liberate them? It is evident from this brief discussion that there is an empathy between many black feminist writers and postmodern feminists (which, of course, includes black women) who claim that we should be *as* concerned about differences among women, and similarities between women and men, by 'race', class and sexual orientation as we should about what women hold in common, although of course it is important to appreciate that a concern to explore the complexity of experience does not necessarily call for a thoroughly postmodern perspective.

Although it is fairly prolific, the debate between postmodernist and other feminist positions still operates at a fairly abstract level. There have been no sustained attempts by sociologists to apply postmodern feminist ideas to the field of health and health care to date, but it is possible tentatively to draw out a number of implications. Stated most broadly, from a postmodern feminist perspective other feminist research on women's health gets into difficulties because it begins with an *assumption of difference* by sex or by gender. The response to the question of why it is so important to contest this view pivots on the argument that to take women's difference from men as basic effectively plays into patriarchy's hands. As Grosz expresses it, binary oppositions are inherently patriarchal, since their 'very structure is privileged by the male/ *non-male* (i.e. female) distinction' (1990a: 101, my emphasis). Therefore, if we accept the modernist view that men and women are opposites (irrespective of whether we conceive of sex/gender as biologically or socially based), then all women are doing is colluding in their oppression, since under patriarchy, women's 'opposite position' will always be defined in a negative way. As a fundamental opposition, gendered difference underwrites (i.e. supports) other oppositions which attach to it – for example, men are rational, women are irrational; women are caring, men are uncaring, and so on. It is by this process that the positively valued 'health' attaches to men, while the negatively valued 'illness' becomes the province of women. Two things follow: first, it makes it difficult for women to be viewed as well; and second, it makes it difficult for men to be viewed as ill. This is because when we think in binaristic terms, each term depends on a *contrast* with the other for its authenticity.

There are a number of ways in which binaristic conceptions of gender and health tend to privilege male bodies as healthy through the pathologization of women's bodies, of which we will take just two examples. First of all, research on body shape and size. In his theoretical study on the sociology of the body, Shilling (1993) looks at what he terms 'naturalistic views of the body' (by which he means analyses which take the body as a pre-social, biological entity). He focuses overwhelmingly on women's bodies, arguing against the premise that they have natural shapes and sizes which are distorted by patriarchy. Irrespective of the merits of this criticism in and of itself, his foregrounding of it to the neglect of any possible equivalent concerns among men only serves to promote body shape and size as 'women's difficulty' and to demote any problems experienced by men. And, consequent upon this, body size and shape as an issue that might cross-cut gender is removed from discussion altogether. A second example of the way in which men's health problems are rendered invisible is in the area of assisted reproduction. Although feminists working on this topic have questioned why men have not been the focus of *medicine's* attention, they have gone little way towards an understanding of male infertility themselves. In an interview-based study, Mason found that men remain 'shadowy figures when it comes to matters of fertility' (1993: 3). As one man reported,

> *they [clinic staff] tried to make out my wife had a problem instead of acknowledging that my infertility is the cause of our problems ... I need people to recognise that the problem is mine, that I do exist and that I am important in the investigations, but my experience has made me feel that I'm useless, just a spare part in the wings. (1993: 67)*

As Pfeffer (1985: 31) remarks, 'implicit in the medical definitions and unchallenged by feminists, is the assumption that the male reproductive system is structurally efficient, and that its functions proceed smoothly'. Ironically, then, at the same time as they criticize biomedicine's pathologization of women, feminists tend to replicate a focus on the 'abnormalities of women's reproduction'.

Further, it might be argued that if we start from the position that women are different from men and see this difference as rooted in reproduction, we collude with biomedicine's viewpoint (which, as we have already seen, tends to take woman's reproductive capacity as her defining feature). The debate with biomedicine is played out on biomedicine's own (binaristic) terms: feminists clearly point to the iatrogenic consequences of medical practices for women (important issues such as problematic childbirth experiences and unnecessary gynaecological surgery, for example) but, through this, attend only to women's negative experiences. As we focus on ill health, we learn little about what promotes good health or what constitutes good health care. This is because women's well-being is largely only understood as the antithesis of what makes them ill, rather than as something which exists in its own right. In early radical feminism in particular women's good health or good health care (the antithesis) tends to have no substance of its own since it is typically produced in negative terms as an opposition to biomedicine, or to male practices and experiences. In this way, we end up knowing more about what is wrong with women's health and health care than what is right. The irony is that, if women's problems are continually emphasized in the academic and popular press, women may buy into the view that they are inevitably going to be unhealthy. Indeed, it does seem quite difficult to see women as well nowadays (witness the large number of books on women's *ill* health in the bookstores). By this process women's health is pathologized.

From a postmodern perspective, a different political position is formed through the deconstruction of the binary positions of male/female, man/woman, sex/gender to reveal that they are artefacts of a modernist world-view, rather than apt descriptors of men's and women's experience of health and illness. The aim in deconstructing gender is to show that real-life experience does not work in terms of clear-cut structures and oppositions; attributes and experiences like acting rationally, being caring, or being healthy cross-cut gender and are not the province of *either* men *or* women as a group. Central to postmodern feminism's political agenda is the claim that *if oppositions are dislodged, then men can no longer easily be associated with all that is valued in society and women with all that is devalued*. We are urged to conclude that our modernist world-view has blinded us to the heterogeneity and plurality that now characterizes the postmodern world. The challenges that this poses for empirical research on gender and health status are discussed in detail in chapter 5.

Given the highly contentious nature of contemporary feminist theory, it is not surprising to find that postmodern feminism has been subject to considerable critical debate. Two concerns are uppermost. First, if postmodern feminists argue that the neglect of male health undermines our ability to understand women's health, and that differences within men and within women and similarities across the two are as important as what women hold in common, they put male health and male bodies on the agenda in the same conceptual terms as women's. From this perspective it is no longer possible to see men as powerful oppressors and women as victims or survivors in a straightforward way, since there must be a recognition of powerful discourses that traverse gender. For example, to present a perfect body, not only women, but also men are opting for cosmetic surgery in increasing numbers. An article in the *Sunday Times* remarked that, for men the message is clear: 'change your body, change your life. In short, men are acting and feeling like women' (Helmore, 1994: 14). We are led to ask not only whether men are increasingly exposed to the same pressures that women feel, but to begin from the premise that gender, traditionally conceived, may not *matter* at all. This is self-evidently a contentious area for feminists. Men as well as women may become the victims of patriarchy – a discourse which no longer 'belongs' to men. If this happens, 'the exploration of men's pain is then an area which needs very careful critical attention if men are not to emerge as both the dominant gender and as the "real" victims of masculinity' (Ramazanoglu, 1992: 346). The second, and

related, criticism of postmodern feminism concerns the political implications of the turn away from 'gender as difference'. If gender is
deconstructed and patriarchy has no 'owner', it is made invisible and
cannot exist as a target for political resistance. As Bordo (1993b) puts it,
the protean standpoint of multiple axes of identity can end up as a
'view from nowhere'. It is for these reasons that many leading feminists
have savoured the use of the postmodern deconstruction of gender as
'an instrument of critique and subversion' (Barrett, 1991: 165), but have
pulled away from fully embracing a 'strong' position such as that
aligned with the work of Baudrillard, in which, as we saw in chapter 2,
there are no stable structures of class, 'race', gender – and, we might
add, patriarchal medicine – and power is too dispersed to struggle
against. The repudiation of structure would seem to bring postmodern
feminism into direct contrast with materialist feminism, which has its
genesis in Marxism.

Materialist feminism

The term materialist feminism connotes the uneasy partnership of feminism with Marxism. Historically, drawing upon radical feminism *and*
Marxism has meant questioning both (Ramazanoglu, 1989), generating
heated debates which began in earnest in the 1970s over whether the
two are equal partners and, if not, which has greater analytic purchase
in the attempt to develop a more complete understanding of women's
oppression. As if these debates were not contentious enough, contemporary challenges to Marxism and prophecies of the 'end of capitalism'
(as discussed in chapter 1) pose additional challenges for materialist
feminists.

Feminists began to question their engagement with Marxism in the
1960s and 1970s. On the positive side, Marxism raised doubts about the
radical feminist idea that women constitute a sex class (as discussed
earlier in this chapter), showing that class interests could cut across
gender in significant ways. But, on the negative side, Marxism was sex
blind as women's relationship to men was subsumed under workers'
relation to capital. Many Marxists argued that feminism was 'at best
less important than class conflict and at worst divisive of the working
class' (Hartmann, 1981: 2). Materialist feminists raised a number of
profound criticisms of this position, arguing that the Marxist 'woman
question' is not the feminist question because it fails to recognize the
differences between men's and women's experience of capitalism which
derive from men's vested interest in women's subordination. (For ex-

ample, if patriarchy places women in the home as supporters of men, then men are better able to occupy valued positions in the market.) The message of feminists in response to the classic Marxist view of women is, then, that 'women's oppression is *more than* class oppression', 'since capital and private property do not cause the oppression of women as *women*, their end alone will not result in the end of women's oppression' (Hartmann, 1981: 5). The crucial question became how to put patriarchy on the agenda as a legitimate issue in the larger struggle against capital, with feminism's answer hinging upon being able to specify the exact nature of the relationship between capitalism and patriarchy.

The crux of the internal debate within 'Marxist feminism' during the 1970s and early 1980s was whether patriarchy and capitalism could be seen as distinct but coexisting systems mutually reinforcing women's oppression (so-called *dual systems theory*), or whether patriarchy should be viewed as the core, or backbone, of capitalism (*unified systems theory*).

The *dual systems* approach is exemplified in Heidi Hartmann's (1981) work of this period. In her work both capitalism and patriarchy are identified as having a material base; for capitalism this lies in the relationship to the means of production, for patriarchy in men's broader control over women's labour power. This latter control is achieved by restricting women's sexuality and their access to resources. Hartmann argues that only by taking account of the *separate but intersecting* operation of capitalism *and* patriarchy can we fully understand why it is that women fill certain places in the capitalist hierarchy and men others. Of course, she goes on, there is a 'healthy and strong partnership ... between patriarchy and capital' (1981: 19), but it is not an inevitable one since men and capitalists can have different interests in the use of women's labour power. For example, most men may want women at home to service them, while a smaller number (who are capitalists) want them in the labour market. Hartmann attempts to identify the separate operation of patriarchy through historical analysis. During the nineteenth century for example, women and children were good for capital since their labour was used to keep male wages down. Men resisted women's entry into the labour force both on this basis and through the argument that it disrupted family life. Thus, men did not fight for *equal* wages but rather for high wages for *men* (the 'family wage'). Hartmann (1981: 21) proposes that 'in the absence of patriarchy a unified working class might have confronted capitalism, but patriarchal social relations divided the working class, allowing one part (men) to be bought off at the expense of the other (women).'

When exploring issues of women's health, from the perspective of dual systems theory we would presumably want to look at the ways in which patriarchy might exert more of an influence upon health and health care in *some* (capitalist) contexts than others. Patriarchy might even operate in ways that do not benefit capital (for example, maintaining women as health carers in the home means they are not available as cheap waged labour). While it may be appropriate to think along these lines in theory, as Hartmann herself remarks, though not referring to issues of health and health care, 'the same features, such as the division of labour, often reinforce both patriarchy and capitalism, and in a thoroughly patriarchal society, it is hard to isolate the mechanisms of patriarchy' (1981: 29). This probably explains why, in research on women's health and health care, patriarchy is generally seen as working in the service of capital, but the possible independent (but interrelated) effects of patriarchy and capitalism are difficult to identify. In most research the underlying premise is that, while capitalism undermines the health of men and women, women experience the *added effect* of patriarchy. Writing about health care, Zalewski (1990: 238) proposes that 'the realities of patriarchy and capitalism mesh together to create a society in which men as well as women suffer oppression, but women suffer the double oppression of both patriarchy *and* capitalism'. For example, leaving aside the not insignificant problems of conceptualizing social class and material circumstances in Marxist terms and of finding comparable measures of class/material circumstances that are sensitive to gender, the body of research which explores women's health status through a focus on the material conditions of their lives (discussed in chapter 5) reveals significant gender differences in morbidity within class groups (see Popay et al., 1993). This suggests that capitalism undermines the health of those in the least favourable material circumstances (manual workers, the unemployed), but that patriarchy works *alongside* this to further disadvantage women.

Iris Young (1981) established this framework by arguing that women's situation is not conditioned by two distinct systems – capitalism and patriarchy – but should be understood as *one unified system* which has women's oppression as its core attribute. This speaks for a gendered Marxism; 'instead of marrying Marxism and feminism', she wrote, 'feminism must take over Marxism and transform it' (1981: 50). Like Hartmann she sought to establish her theory historically. Women's marginalization is, she argued, an essential characteristic of capitalism since it does not need all able-bodied people to work. Women are marginalized because, under patriarchy, sex is available as a natural criterion of exclusion (women are 'needed' to care for small children). Women have been marginalized by capital as strike-breakers (e.g. in the 1930s) and, in the nineteenth century, through the cult of domesticity which was used to keep their wages low. For Young, these and other factors illustrate that, far from having a separate trajectory, capitalism is inherently structured by a gendered division of labour; capitalism does not *draw upon* gender hierarchy, it is *founded on* it. Thus, the front line of women's struggle lies not with patriarchy, but with its embeddedness within capitalism.

In the context of health and health care, the unified approach would appear to render any need to sort out the *relative* influence of capitalism and patriarchy upon women's health unnecessary: *their effect is as one.* The health-care system under capitalism is *founded on* patriarchy and, therefore, is inherently sexist: obstetrics must profit from the patriarchal oppression of women; capitalism is premised upon the exploitation of women's health. Research on women as carers and recipients of health care from what can be identified as a materialist feminist perspective often views the operation of patriarchy through ideologies which support capital. Medicine supports capitalism by viewing health as the ability to work, and patriarchy by defining women's health as the ability to reproduce the family through domestic work in the home and to biologically reproduce the species (Doyal, 1979). Taken together these factors significantly undermine women's health. In the context of health care 'medical language transforms important social problems facing women – family roles, occupational aspirations, sexuality, childrearing, and so forth – into objectified disorders of the sexual and reproductive organs' (Waitzkin, 1991: 113). A functional fit is found between the objectification of women's bodies around reproduction and the corporate interests of medicine and patriarchy. Defined in this way, women's bodies become ripe for intervention through the use of high-technology, high-profit procedures such as electrical foetal monitoring in childbirth, caesarean sections, cosmetic surgery and so on.

As was noted at the beginning of this section, recent changes in the operation of capitalism pose significant challenges to materialist feminism. Has capitalism, as some postmodern feminists might suggest, changed to such an extent that gender inequality is no longer a feature of contemporary experience? Or could it be that, rather than being superseded, *new* forms of gender inequality are emerging which, while not premised upon a clear-cut division between the privilege of men and the oppression of women, might be just as injurious to health? In rethinking the relationship between feminism and Marxism, contemporary discussion within materialist feminism recognizes that gender identities have become more fluid under late capitalism, loosened by patterns of consumption which increasingly seem to traverse traditional gender distinctions. Indeed, as Ebert (1996) remarks, new sites of exploitation emerge which actually *rely* upon a deconstruction of gender as a duality. For example, as consumption patterns which were traditionally gendered, such as smoking (male) and dieting (female), are increasingly 'opened up' to men *and* women (at least in some social strata – see chapters 4 and 5), and traditional gender roles – such as male breadwinner and female homemaker – are undermined by shifts from an industrial to a service economy, then arguably gender is more productive for capital *if* it is more flexible. To talk of a post-feminist age is to assume, as Landry and MacLean (1993) put it, that women have already won whatever struggles once made feminism necessary. In an era in which capitalism is intensifying across the globe this is way off the mark. From a materialist feminist perspective which continues to emphasize the importance of women's relationship to the means of production, the stress that some postmodern feminists place upon revealing the fluidity and contingent nature of gender identities may *itself* contribute to the revitalization of capitalism in ways that are injurious to women's health, such as increases in cigarette-smoking and of eating disorders associated with the targeting of 'health' and the body as key sites for the operation of capital.

Conclusion

The discussion in this chapter has highlighted that, even though all feminists share a common objective of identifying the ways in which patriarchy undermines women's health, there are nonetheless significant and highly politicized differences between them. We have explored these by thinking in terms of different 'types' of feminism, namely, liberal, radical, postmodern, and materialist feminism. But, as noted at the beginning of the chapter, these are umbrella terms at best. At worst they distort what is in effect a shifting terrain. As Jaggar and Rothenberg, cited earlier, explain, 'few feminists any longer insist on unswerving loyalty to a single theoretical framework' (1993: xvii). Rather, particular perspectives shift and accommodate to challenges which come equally from changes in the social world around us and other, initially competing, theoretical frameworks.

This point of course holds true for social theory generally. We are clearly at an eventful juncture in the history of social theory as 'modernist' and 'postmodernist' thinkers stand head to head in debate. It may be some time before there is a resolution – if there is to be one. But one thing that does seem clear is the window of opportunity for sociologists of health and medicine to contribute to theoretical debate as issues of health and illness assume centre stage as we approach the turn of the century. As we turn in the following chapters to particular issues that engage sociologists of health and medicine, it will be possible to explore the relevance of many of the theoretical issues that have been raised in this first section of this book to concerns such as health inequalities, the provision of health care and the experience of illness.

Part II

Contemporary Health Inequalities

4

Class Structure, Inequalities and Health

There is considerable evidence to suggest that the hardening of inequalities between people in recent years has been accompanied by a widening of inequalities in health. Yet in sociology, many theorists are assiduously pursuing the theme that 'class is dead'; that it is no longer a useful marker for people's life chances. Has class been eclipsed by other axes of inequality? Does it no longer have relevance in identity formation? If so, what are the implications for research on inequalities in health? These are the issues that will be addressed in this chapter. We begin with a descriptive account of trends in economic inequality over the last decade and their association with inequalities in health. We then turn to the significance of economic restructuring and 'the demise of class' for sociological research on health inequality. The chapter concludes with a consideration of the recent turn away from class identity towards consumption and 'lifestyle' as a basis for understanding health inequality.

Economic inequality and health

Townsend (1993: 92) writes that during the 1980s and on into the 1990s 'social layers in Britain have been partly reconstituted, more deeply etched and more widely spaced'. This process of social polarization is partly hidden by misleading 'average' improvements in standards of living which conceal wide variations, and the fact that while the conditions of the well off have got even better, those of the poor have changed very little, and may even have deteriorated by some indicators. Figure 4.1 shows that disposable incomes have risen since 1971, but at a much faster rate at the top than the bottom. Adjusting for

Fig. 4.1

Real household disposable income, UK 1971–92 (£ per week)

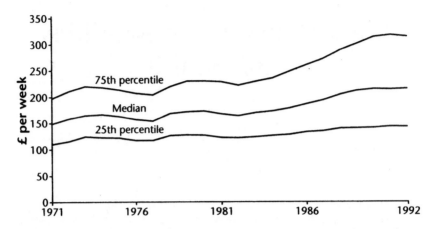

Note: Before housing costs, at January 1994 prices deflated by the retail prices index.
Source: CSO (1995a), *Social Trends 1995 Edition* (London: HMSO), fig. 5.1.

household size and composition (in order to take account of differing demands on resources), the incomes of households in the bottom and top 25 per cent of the population have gradually diverged from the median over time: between 1971 and 1992 income at the 25th percentile point increased by 28 per cent, the median by 46 per cent, and at the 75th percentile point by 60 per cent.

There is a now a considerable body of evidence that the growing wedge between rich and poor has particular significance for households with below-average income who rely on welfare benefits. In 1979 only 8 per cent of the population had less than half the average income; the corresponding figure for 1992/3 was 20 per cent (DSS, 1995). Families with children are over-represented at the lower ends of the income distribution, making up 4.5 million of the poorest group of people whose income is less than 40 per cent of the UK average. Membership of low-income groups for households with dependent children is clearly associated with unemployment, lone parenthood, and low wages combined with high outgoings such as mortgage costs (Benzeval and Webb, 1995).

These rather stark aggregate data come to life when they are related to the circumstances of people's lives, particularly their health. Recent

Fig. 4.2

Percentage change in standardized mortality rates between 1980–2 and 1990–2 by age-group and sex

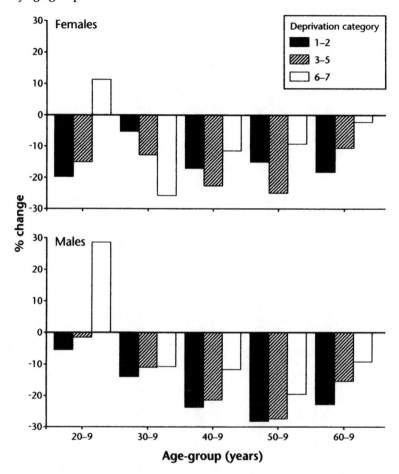

Source: P. McLoone and A. Boddy (1994), Deprivation and mortality in Scotland, 1981 and 1991, *British Medical Journal,* 309, fig. 3 (p. 1467). Reproduced by permission of the BMJ Publishing Group.

research shows clearly that, in common with trends for economic inequality, overall mortality has declined over recent decades, but at a faster rate among more affluent groups. Contemporary evidence for widening inequalities in health by various economic measures is beginning to look incontrovertible. This is most clearly demonstrated through

Table 4.1 Trends in age-specific mortality in most deprived and least deprived fifths of electoral wards in Northern region of England. Values are SMRs[a] (numbers of people)

Year	Age-group of most deprived fifth of wards					Age-group of least deprived fifth of wards				
	0–14	15–44	45–54	55–64	65–74	0–14	15–44	45–54	55–64	65–74
1981–3	116 (620)	117 (1,116)	130 (2,041)	145 (6,304)	123 (9,562)	80 (195)	86 (428)	79 (574)	92 (1,549)	94 (3,178)
1983–5	117 (580)	119 (1,085)	135 (1,892)	149 (6,206)	122 (9,256)	77 (170)	84 (406)	81 (560)	96 (1,626)	90 (3,042)
1985–7	119 (588)	120 (1,072)	145 (1,778)	151 (5,789)	127 (9,441)	70 (145)	87 (427)	79 (546)	88 (1,531)	87 (2,962)
1987–9	114 (551)	128 (1,141)	152 (1,624)	153 (5,302)	130 (9,474)	71 (135)	79 (400)	78 (535)	85 (1,460)	87 (2,995)
1989–91	130 (566)	128 (1,144)	162 (1,575)	151 (4,745)	133 (9,397)	79 (131)	77 (390)	83 (549)	87 (1,433)	88 (2,981)

[a] Standardized to national (England and Wales) mortality of 100 in each three-year period. Deprivation defined on basis of 1981 census.

Source: P. Phillimore et al. (1994), Widening inequality of health in northern England, 1981–1991. *British Medical Journal*, 308, 1125–8, table IV (p. 1127). Reproduced by permission of the BMJ Publishing Group.

recent trends in mortality. McLoone and Boddy (1994) compared over a thousand postcode sectors in Scotland ranked according to a deprivation score in 1981 and 1991 (consisting of the proportion of the population in households without a car, with the head of household in occupational class IV or V, in overcrowded households, and in households with unemployed men). They found that, although the age- and sex-standardized mortality for ages 0–64 declined from 400 to 311 per 100,000 population, or by 22 per cent, the reduction in the deprived categories was only about half that of the affluent groups. Moreover, for the most deprived category there was a deterioration as the standardized mortality ratio[1] rose from 144 to 165 (a finding which also held for men and women taken separately). This is highlighted in the more detailed breakdown (by age-group and gender) given in figure 4.2 (where category 1 is the least and category 7 the most deprived). The worsened mortality rate for those aged 20–29 (which rose by 29 per cent for men, and 11 per cent for women) in deprivation categories 6 and 7 is largely attributed by the authors to a disproportionate increase in suicides and undetermined deaths combined with a smaller than average decline in the rate for accidents. The trend of an overall decline in mortality, coupled with an increased differential between the least and most deprived in most age groups, is mirrored for cause-specific mortality. For example, the death rate for ischaemic heart disease in categories 6 and 7 was 74 per cent greater than in categories 1 and 2 in 1980/2, but 130 per cent greater in 1990/2. For cancer of the lung and bronchus, the figures for the equivalent time periods are 120 per cent and 170 per cent.

In a similar analysis, but using a slightly different measure of deprivation, Phillimore et al. (1994) have ranked electoral wards in the north of England. Table 4.1 compares trends in age-specific mortality in the most and the least deprived fifths of wards (as measured by deprivation in 1981). In all age-groups the gap between the least and the most deprived appears to have widened. Interestingly, this was not invariably because standardized mortality ratios improved in the most affluent areas of the north (substantial improvement is only evident in the 15–44 age-group), but because of rising (worsening) ratios in the poorest areas for all age-groups, but particularly noticeable in those aged 45–54. The findings summarized here overall highlight Wilkinson's (1986: 2) conclusion that health is a 'barometer of the social and economic conditions in which people live', something which is confirmed by the recent rise in the incidence of tuberculosis – a recognized disease of poverty – which has been restricted to the poorest communities in Britain (Bhatti et al., 1995).

Absolute and relative deprivation

Recently, commentators have drawn our attention to an important distinction between *absolute* and *relative* deprivation. Wilkinson (1996), for example, proposes that for developed countries there is a threshold beyond which the *absolute* standard of living of the population loses its association with improvements in life expectancy. This threshold is signalled by the epidemiological transition, a term which refers to the shift away from infectious towards degenerative diseases as the major cause of death within a society. He argues that 'apparently regardless of the fact that health differences within societies remain so closely related to socioeconomic status, once a country has passed through the epidemiological transition, its whole population can be more than twice as rich as any other country without being any healthier' (Wilkinson, 1996: 3). This suggests that there is a clear limit on the health returns, at least as measured by life expectancy, of more and more material wealth (i.e. GNP per capita) at the level of the total population. However, *within* a society differences in income between people are crucial: here it is not the *absolute* standard of living that matters, but where individuals stand in relation to others, i.e. *relative* deprivation. This proposition is supported by Ben-Shlomo et al.'s (1996) research which finds an association between degree of variation in deprivation within an area (here small area census data for England) and all-cause mortality between 1981 and 1985. Specifically, there is evidence that the more heterogeneity there is in the socio-economic status of an area (measured by an area deprivation index), the higher the mortality rate, an effect which seems to hold when the absolute level of deprivation within the area is controlled for.

This leaves us with the important question of *why* relative differences in wealth are so important. Wilkinson argues that the major effect is psychosocial. As income differences widened in Britain during the 1980s, psychosocial stress increased and we saw a slow-down in the improvement in mortality rates. Britain, he remarks, has become a 'cash and keys' society, where 'cash equips us to take part in transactions in the market' and keys to our homes (presuming we have one) 'protect our private gains from each other's envy and greed' (1996: 226). As individualism and the ethos of the market increasingly hold sway and civic morality declines, our health is compromised. Feelings of hopelessness, anxiety, insecurity and anger among those living in relative deprivation leave their mark on health, both directly, through weakened immunity, and indirectly, through unemployment and negative health-related behaviours such as the consumption of alcohol, and high-fat and high-sugar 'comfort foods'.

Since health in Britain, the USA and other rich countries is now almost unrelated to measures of economic growth, Wilkinson argues that relative poverty will not be solved by us all getting richer together. Within the developed world, it is not the richest countries which have the best health, but the most egalitarian. He gives a number of illustrations of this, including wartime Britain, which saw a rise in life expectancy among civilians alongside a narrowing of income differentials and an increase in social cohesion, despite the fact that absolute material circumstances declined for many people. A second example relates Britain and Japan. In 1970 the two countries were quite similar in terms of life expectancy and income distribution. Subsequently, the income distribution for Japan has narrowed considerably while life expectancy has increased quite dramatically to reach the highest recorded for any country reporting to the World Bank. By comparison, in Britain income differentials widened substantially over the 1980s and its place on the life-expectancy league table has fallen. Wilkinson estimates that, if Britain had the political will, 'a difference of only about 7 per cent in the share of income going to the bottom 50 per cent of the population' would yield a two-year increase in life expectancy (1996: 107).

The discussion so far has pointed to an enduring association between economic inequality and mortality. Westergaard's (1995: 113–14) protestation that class cannot be declared dead or dying in social significance 'at a time now when its economic configuration has become even sharper' would seem more than appropriate in the field of health. Yet while many sociologists of health and illness continue to draw upon income and indicators of material deprivation at the individual and population levels, as well as occupation (discussed below), as markers of class, commentators on social stratification point increasingly to the declining relevance of class analysis in sociology. Put like this, there would seem to be a contradiction between claims that social class no longer has significance and the data we have considered. Part of the confusion in sorting out the relationship between class and health lies in the multiple meanings or metaphorical quality of the concept of 'class' itself (Crompton, 1993; Holton and Turner, 1989). *Crucially, it may be that, while inequalities in health between people exist, these can no longer be viewed in class terms.* Before we can begin to address this possibility, we need to give some attention to the meaning of class in contemporary sociology.

The demise of class?

Given that much of the discipline of sociology was effectively built around the concept of social class (Esping-Anderson, 1993), it is not surprising that the herald of its demise has thrown up a debate of considerable proportions. Should we, along with Holton and Turner (1989: 173), question whether we now even want to 'organise our understanding of the social structure in class categories' given that modern society is now predominantly 'characterised by individualism'? Or should we concur with Navarro (1994) that class divisions are as entrenched as they ever were and that the possibility of class action still exists? Despite the hotly contested nature of the debate around class, one issue is central to everyone's concern – is class compatible with recent economic and social changes such as the internationalization of capital, the decline in manual work, the shift to a service economy, the higher employment of women, and the reconceptualization of the citizen as a consumer rather than producer? The major factor that lies behind the various theoretical articulations of these changes is the collapse of the manufacturing industry. Manufacturing's share of employment was reduced from 32 per cent in 1973 to 25 per cent in 1983, to reach just 19 per cent in 1993, representing a decline from 7.8 to 4.6 million people working in manufacturing over the twenty-year period (OPCS, 1995a). The number of miners, often popularly stereotyped as the archetypal working class, declined from 600,000 in the 1940s, to 200,000 in the 1980s, and to just 30,000 by the early 1990s (Savage and Miles, 1994). In comparison to manufacturing, the service sector has increased substantially growing from 55 per cent to 71 per cent between 1973 and 1993. Predictions for the year 2000 indicate that, while manufacturing's share of employment will continue to fall to 17 per cent (4.4 million people), the service sector's will rise to 74 per cent (17 million people) (OPCS, 1995a). These shifts in employment are not at issue, rather, debate centres around their significance for class formation.

Significant implications follow from the decline of the 'traditional working class', the old cornerstone of class theory. Perspectives on the working class have shifted considerably during the second half of the twentieth century. From 1945 to 1960 class seemed to be the fundamental divide in British society during a time when manual workers were 70 per cent of the workforce and the Labour Party and the trade union movement enjoyed unprecedented popularity (Savage and Miles, 1994). A shift began to occur in the 1960s and 1970s as revolutionary politics and any 'natural alliance' between Labour and the working class were questioned, and studies such as the Affluent Worker series (Goldthorpe et al., 1969) began to point to the so-called fragmentation of the working class and the irreducibility of beliefs, attitudes and behaviours to class location. By the 1980s, commentators were moving to the view that 'the idea of class did not seem to appreciate that people actually had choices as to how they identified themselves and lived their lives, and that class might be only one, relatively unimportant, form of self-expression which people chose to adopt' (Savage and Miles, 1994: 13). On top of this, the post-structuralist turn to textual analysis claimed that, rather than being literal accounts of working-class life, studies such as *Coal is Our Life* (Norman et al. 1969) are constructions of a particular image, possibly influenced by romantic academic visions of 'working-class community'. Fundamentally, then, commentators have begun to draw away from conceptions of class that have a concern with class-based identity, collective action or consciousness, or the potential for this, at their heart.

Holton and Turner make a distinction between stronger, Gemeinschaft-based (community formation) class idioms and weaker, Gesellschaft-based (the distribution of individuals within roles) ones. In the former approach, a theory of class is coterminous with a theory of society where 'class idiom operates both as a structural account of relations of power, inequality, and exploitation, and simultaneously an account of consciousness, group formation, and social movements as emancipatory social change' (Holton and Turner, 1989: 161). In the weaker idiom, class is one of several patterns of power and inequality. For these authors, we have now reached a point where we should treat with scepticism any attempt to hold on to the strong *gemeinschaftlich* approach to class; bluntly put: class is a redundant issue, meaningful only 'in the weak sense as a means of delineating forms of economic power relations which generate and reproduce inequalities' (1989: 194). From this point of view, class as community and collective identity can no longer be called upon as an explanatory variable in the search for an explanation for inequalities in health. In its place we are exhorted to put an emphasis on non-class-based social movements and consumption cleavages that are not reducible to the production and reproduction of economic life. This implies that macro-narratives which seek to determine a class system by reference to various structuring principles, such as Marx's labour theory of value and class conflict, are equally futile.

Others, however, wish to retain the primacy of class as a structuring principle. Fundamentally, they point out that the decline of the traditional working class should not be taken to signify the decline of all classes. As Westergaard (1995) argues, the new 'forget-about-class' wisdom has paid little or no attention to dominance and privilege at the top.

For Navarro (1994), in particular, it is more than ironic that recent social theory refers to lack of class solidarity and class action at a time when the class interests of capital are more than evident in the US policy arena (for example, in mobilizing against a National Health Program). Indeed, it could be argued that most of the changes in the economy that we have been discussing are driven by capitalists, either as individuals or as agents of large capitalist enterprises. Therefore, it is by no means contradictory to recognize that workplace feelings of class and collective identity – the traditional locus of class – are being eroded, while structural class relations of ownership, production and the market persist, since the very nature of employment and workplace relations (for example, new managerial styles, devolved responsibility, economic insecurity) may increasingly mask, rather than reveal, their operation (Crompton, 1996).

Undoubtedly, an enormously privileged group of people occupies positions of considerable economic power in Britain, and there are indications that the number of relatively high incomes is increasing. Townsend (1993: 109) refers to the emergence of an 'overclass' (the counterpart to the 'underclass', discussed below); a 'pedestal elite' consisting of 'socially remote rich people' with quite immense power and wealth. The capitalist business class which comprises about 0.1 per cent (approximately 43,500 people) of the population was estimated to hold 7 per cent of all wealth in 1986, each of these individuals having at least £740,000 in bank deposits, shares, land and other forms of property. Scott (1991) approximates that in 1990 there were more than 200 families with more than £50 million each in Britain (with aggregate wealth of just under 10 per cent of GDP). The question remains, however, of whether this elite should be conceived as a nominal category of office-holders, or an active social group. Clearly, with changes in the legal and financial structure of business enterprises, the separation of ownership and control, and the new managerialism, the orthodox Marxist capitalist class no longer exists in its pure form. But in Scott's view we still do have a capitalist class, even though it differs considerably from its historical counterparts. As capital interests become fragmented, they tend to be less immediately visible as an interlocking system of privilege. Thus the old 'enterprise capitalists' (who own their own business) still exist, but take their place alongside new 'rentier capitalists', who have a stake in a number of businesses; 'executive capitalists', who are directors of firms, and 'finance capitalists', who sit on the executives of a number of companies. Viewed in this way, there is both a statistical top and a 'privileged class rooted in a position of economic dominance in a capitalist system of production' (Scott, 1991: 63). An 'overclass' and 'underclass' exist in relation to each other as distinct social conditions defined by 'catastrophic' boundaries in the distribution of resources. Or, as Navarro (1994) puts it, the working class is weak precisely because the capitalist class is strong.

For many sociologists, then, there is still considerable merit in trying to rank distinct social groups in relation to each other in an ordered way. Despite the variety of class maps that have developed in recent years, they 'all view that structure as hierarchical, with proportionately more of the population in the lower reaches than the higher; but whereas some conceive the structure as a pyramid with a very small apex ... others suggest the possibilities of the development of a more onion-shaped distribution' (Crompton, 1993: 191). In light of the economic changes that have been outlined, all of these maps refer to the need to shift attention away from a manual/non-manual divide; all identify some form of middle class or, more accurately, middle classes (discussed below); all include a reconstituted working class; and, for some, there is also a new 'underclass'.

The 'underclass'

Amidst the theoretical controversy over class, no issue has generated as much heat as the so-called underclass debate. It has begun seriously to challenge the historical tendency to see class position as primarily based on occupation; it has resurrected concerns of citizenship and social inclusion; and it has polarized the political left and right.

At first sight 'under-class talk has an understandable appeal when used only as ready rhetoric to sum up the downside impact of ... trends to polarisation, or to give snapshot descriptions of life today in localities of concentrated deprivation' (Westergaard, 1995: 14). But, despite its common usage, there is no shared view on what the concept of underclass implies, although theories do tend to stress three characteristic features: this group suffers from 'prolonged labour market marginality'; experiences deprivation that is greater than that of the manual working class; and has its own distinctive subculture (Gallie, 1994: 737). Opinions diverge quite radically, however, on the reasons for the formation of an underclass (which, it must be said, stretches back to the early period of industrialization). First of all we have a position, epitomized in the work of Murray (1990: 4), which marks out a sub-section of people living a life not 'just' of poverty, but a life deliberately apart from the rest. This is a group whose lifestyle is characterized by unemployment, illegitimacy and crime; a 'growing population of working-aged, healthy people who live in a different world from other Britons, who are raising their children to live in it, and whose values are now contaminating the life of entire neighbourhoods . . .'. In many commentaries the rise of an underclass is linked to the development of the welfare state, with questions raised about whether it has 'gone too far', creating a culture of dependency with too many rights and too few obligations. The second position on the underclass stresses structural factors rather than personal or behavioural characteristics. Here the underclass are victims of extrusion from labour markets consequent upon economic restructuring, their worsening circumstances and social segregation 'exacerbated by Government policies towards public welfare services, such as health and education, which have been cut back while the private sector has been subsidised; a policy designed to produce private affluence and public squalor' (Walker, 1990: 56).

Whatever position we take on the 'causes' of the underclass, it is apparent that, in both the more conservative and the more radical view, we have set before us an emerging group which is cut adrift from the majority. This poses a significant challenge to class schema which rely upon occupational rankings. When this is accompanied by the further challenge of accommodating 'the changing nature of employment and the phenomenon of what is often termed underemployment: chronic insecurity and non-standard patterns of work' (Morris, 1994: 5), it is perhaps easy to see why social scientists might be tempted to contain these 'troublesome' features in a residual underclass category. The wisdom of this notwithstanding, we are still left with the question of whether it is really viable to lump together as a *class* people in such potentially disparate circumstances as being unemployed, homeless, a recipient of welfare, a single parent, prosecuted criminal, or an ex-mental patient. Even within a category such as the unemployed (which it must be said is likely itself to be marked by considerable diversity), there is little evidence for the formation of the distinctive culture heralded by the conservative and radical perspectives alike (Gallie, 1994).

Class or inequality?

Whether we predict class restructuring or, more radically, the demise of class depends in good part on what we actually mean by 'class'. The diagram in figure 4.3 depicts a trajectory between four ideal typical positions which result from the intersection of two analytic distinctions. The first of these relates to whether we conceive of class in its strong Gemeinschaft-based or its weaker Gesellschaft-based form. The second differentiates between those who believe that class still exists but no longer resembles its traditional form (i.e. it has been restructured), and those who claim that it has been superseded by other forms of inequal-

Fig. 4.3
Class transformation

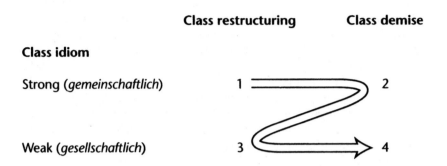

ity (i.e. class demise). The arrow on the diagram indicates a fluid move away from a strong sense of class as collective identity (position 1) towards the more extreme position in which class has very little meaning at all (position 4).

In the first position, the strong class idiom, classes still exist, but they have been restructured through capitalist class action. For Navarro in particular, class is far from dead; attempts by capital to fragment the working class and weaken the support for organized labour attest to this. Of Republican Party health policy in the USA he writes, 'in the unrestrained pursuit of its interests, it has exhibited the most aggressive class behaviour shown by a capitalist class since the beginning of this century' (1994: 20). Moreover, the potential for working-class solidarity is still strong. The second position is not viable analytically, since if you contend that the strong class idiom still has relevance, you are unlikely to simultaneously argue that 'class is dead'.

It is the third position which claims so many advocates at the present time. Theorists argue, as we have seen, that the strong class idiom is no longer applicable in a modern world in which the links between market position and life chances are uncoupling due to economic change. Here 'class' is best conceived in its weaker form, referring not to collective identity, but to a range of inequalities which distinguish a set of relatively autonomous individuals along a number of axes which are unlikely to align to form a strong collective economic or social identity. Interestingly, the same process of economic restructuring, which in the first position is said to lead to the hardening of class differences, is linked in the third position to the retrocession of strong class structure. This is the view of Lash and Urry (1994: 299), who refer to the metamorphosis of capital (the shift from manufacturing, the emergence of global markets, the rise of new markets for information and communication) and the emergence of a phase of 'disorganized capitalism' in which we are likely to see 'the loosening or destruction of group and grid'. Thus as capital mutates in form with increasing velocity we see 'an ongoing process of de-traditionalisation in which social agents are increasingly "set free" from the heteronomous control or monitoring of social structures [such as class] in order to be self-monitoring or self-reflexive' (1994: 3–4). This position is neither incompatible with inequality nor with the emergence of geographical 'dead zones' of literal disorganization and severe deprivation. Interestingly, Lash and Urry make direct reference to class in this regard, writing of an 'impacted underclass' generated by the process of capital accumulation at the top. However, this is 'class' as a collection of individuals – disorganized capitalism is accompanied by the loss of shared meaning, as 'selves' are converted to 'Is' through a process of 'individuation, normalisation and atomisation' (1994: 314).

The recent work of Pakulski and Waters (1996) moves somewhat closer to, but still does not fully embrace, the fourth position. Although they have some empathy with the work of Holton and Turner, in their view it stretches class too far, so far in fact that it becomes meaningless, standing for both everything and nothing. In arguing instead that class has been replaced by stratification based on cultural distinction, they abut the fourth position identified in figure 4.3, where even the weaker class idiom preferred by Holton and Turner and others is repudiated. Pakulski and Waters argue that our attention should be directed to status distinctions (pursued through consumption) which consist of a 'virtually infinite overlap of associations and ideologies that are shifting and unstable' (1996: 155). It is crucial, however, to appreciate that they are 'not arguing for a decline in inequality and conflict but for a decline in *class* inequality and conflict' (1996: 157). The work of Baudrillard (1987) takes us even further towards the demise of class, into a postmodern world where (as we saw in chapter 2) the boundary between image and reality dissolves, power is totally dispersed, and the subject ceases to exist. In such a world stable 'structures' such as class have no meaning at all.

Research on health inequalities tends to fall most clearly (though not exclusively) into the third position, where class has been restructured and is best viewed through the weaker class idiom. In many cases this has less to do with a theoretical revision of class than with a rather unreflective use of a range of 'class indicators'. To explore this we turn now to review, in more detail than has been possible so far, the body of current empirical research on health inequalities, paying particular attention as we do to the models of 'class' and the operational measures that are used.

Researching class, inequality and health

As Crompton and Mann point out, while the discipline of sociology as a whole has turned away from class as an explanatory variable, it is still included in most quantitative research. It would appear then that 'the need for class measurement endures, even when class theory becomes unfashionable' (1994: xi). The problem, however, is that, until very recently at least, many researchers have been less than clear on what theoretical position they actually want to take on class. This may explain the tendency for theoretical debates to turn into debates on methodology. In the sociology of health and medicine, as elsewhere, for those who wish to retain some reference to 'class divisions' (even in their weaker *gesellschaftlich* form), research is beset with disputes about 'the relative significance of this facet of inequality versus that, and about boundary lines in the hierarchy or hierarchies of inequality' (Westergaard, 1995: 148). We begin, then, with a discussion of measurement issues.

Measuring the relationship between class and health

At the operational as well as the theoretical level, to enter into a discussion of class is to enter into an area of conceptual confusion and muddied waters. This is clearly seen in the use of the Registrar General's (RG) occupational measure of social class in Britain (OPCS, 1991). This classification is self-consciously no more than 'an undefined proxy for

Table 4.2 Mean number of symptoms reported as being experienced within the last month

Age	Social class							
	Males				Females			
	I–II	IIINM	IIIM	IV–V	I–II	IIINM	IIIM	IV–V
18–29	1.5	1.5	1.6	1.6	1.9	2.1	2.3	2.4
30–44	1.8	1.9	1.8	1.9	1.9	2.4	2.3	2.6
45–59	1.5	1.6	2.1	2.4	2.5	2.7	2.9	3.4
60–69	1.7	2.3	2.5	2.6	2.6	2.3	3.0	2.9
70+	2.2	2.5	2.7	2.8	2.8	3.0	3.4	3.7

Source: M. Blaxter (1987), Health and social class: evidence on inequality and health from a national survey. *Lancet*, 4 July, 30–3. © The Lancet Ltd. 1987. Reproduced by permission.

Fig. 4.4
Percentage of people in Britain declaring high rates of psychosocial malaise

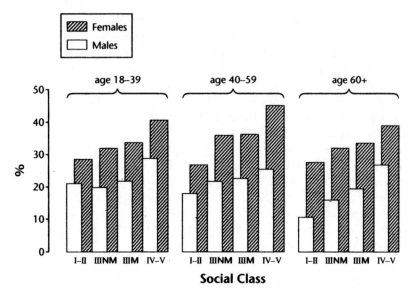

Source: M. Blaxter (1987), Health and social class: evidence on inequality in health from a national survey, *Lancet*, 4 July, 30–3. © The Lancet Ltd. 1987. Reproduced by permission.

the effects of unknown socio-economic differences' (Wilkinson, 1986: 18). As Bartley et al. (1996: 459) discuss, the fact that it is seen to 'measure' a wide range of aspects of class is problematic because it leaves class gradients in health open to a wide range of alternative explanations referring, among other things, to 'prestige, education, social support, material living standards, and lifestyle in various combinations'. The research literature is replete with provisos that employment aggregate measures are inadequate to capture the 'reality' of social class, but that, for the sake of comparison with other studies (particularly when looking at trends over time), or because of the need to make use of limited secondary data sets, they will have to suffice. Perhaps the factor above all that induces researchers to use the RG occupational measure is its predictive value. That is, putting the not inconsiderable problem of not knowing exactly what we are measuring aside, occupational social class does seem to yield consistent gradients in morbidity and mortality. For example, table 4.2 shows a range of self-reported symptoms of ill health from the British Health and Lifestyle

Survey. We see a 'steep and regular trend towards more frequent illness in manual social classes', particularly after age 30 for women and age 45 for men (Blaxter, 1987: 31).

The same study also found clear class differences in psychosocial well-being using a 'malaise' score (a simple additive score of symptoms of self-reported depression, worry, sleep disturbance, feelings of strain and other factors), with the percentage of those with a high malaise score rising consistently with RG class (see figure 4.4).

Similar class gradients have been reported for mortality. For example, in a recent follow-up study, Harding (1995) has assessed the relationship between RG class in 1971 and the risk of dying (measured by SMR) over specified intervals up to 1989 for men aged between 15 and 64 (see table 4.3). The far right-hand column shows that mortality rose progressively from class I to class V over the duration of follow-up. Men in class I show a deficit in mortality of 34 per cent (i.e. over and above all men), while those in classes IV and V show excesses of 11 and 34 per cent respectively.

RG social class is an ordinal (ranked) measure which is basically defined according to skill levels, drawing (in a poorly defined manner) upon occupational title and employment status (self-employed, supervisor, foreman, employee). Through a detailed coding procedure, it is possible to collate the range of occupations into five groups: class I (broadly professionals), class II (managerial and technical occupations), class IIINM (skilled non-manual), Class IIIM (skilled manual), class IV (partly skilled), and class V (unskilled). Socio-economic group (SEG) is a somewhat different, but still occupationally based, measure, which combines information about employment status, authority and establishment size with the occupational data outlined above. At a broad level ('condensed SEG'), it generates seven nominal categories. Currently, researchers seem to be making considerably more use of SEG as a measure of social class than they have in the past. For example, table 4.4 presents data from the 1991 Census which, for the first time since 1911, included a health-related question, referring on this occasion to any long-term illness, health problem or handicap (including problems which are due to age) and a further sub-question asking whether this illness limited work or daily activities. The total number of persons (resident in households) who reported a limiting illness of this kind was 6.67 million, or around 12 per cent of the population. The breakdown by SEG shows that those with a limiting long-term illness are more likely to live in households headed by a 'manual' or 'personal service worker' (67 per cent compared to 50 per cent for residents in other households). Conversely, they are much less likely to live in households headed by

Table 4.3 Mortality of men aged 15–64 at death by social class in 1971 and period of death

Social class in 1971	Period of death											
	1976–81			1982–5			1986–9			1976–89		
	Deaths	SMR	95% CI[a]	Deaths	SMR	95% CI[a]	Deaths	SMR	95% CI[a]	Deaths	SMR	95% CI[a]
I	159	69	(59–81)[b]	87	61	(49–75)[b]	93	67	(54–83)[b]	339	66	(59–74)[b]
II	749	78	(73–84)[b]	424	78	(71–86)[b]	362	80	(72–89)[b]	1,535	79	(75–83)[b]
IIINM	524	103	(95–113)	280	98	(86–110)	214	85	(74–97)[b]	1,018	97	(91–104)
IIIM	1,698	95	(91–100)	1,052	101	(95–107)	931	102	(96–109)	3,681	99	(96–102)
IV	913	109	(102–116)[b]	507	113	(103–123)[b]	414	112	(102–123)[b]	1,834	111	(106–116)[b]
V	425	124	(113–137)[b]	240	136	(119–155)[b]	222	153	(134–175)[b]	887	134	(125–143)[b]
Armed forces	25	102	(66–151)	18	98	(58–154)	19	88	(53–137)	62	96	(74–123)
Inadequately described	92	173	(139–212)[b]	40	144	(103–196)[b]	37	145	(102–200)[b]	169	159	(136–185)[b]
Unoccupied	272	212	(187–239)[b]	99	165	(134–201)[b]	83	137	(109–170)[b]	454	182	(166–200)[b]
All men aged 15–64	4,857	100		2,747	100		2,375	100		9,979	100	

[a] 95% confidence interval for SMR.

[b] 95% confidence interval for SMR excludes 100.

Source: S. Harding (1995), Social class differences in mortality of men: recent evidence from the OPCS Longitudinal Study. *Population Trends*, Office for National Statistics, Crown copyright 1997. 80, 31–7: table 2 (p. 32).

Table 4.4 Economically active household residents aged 16–59[a]: socio-economic group of household head and limiting long-term illness (LLTI), Great Britain

SEG of economically active household head	Adults resident in households			
	No LLTI		With LLTI	
	Number (000s)	%	Number (000s)	%
Professional	246.9	6.9	7.1	5.0
Employers and managers	774.8	21.8	9.3	6.6
Intermediate non-manual	400.2	11.2	14.4	10.2
Junior non-manual	360.4	10.1	15.4	11.0
Skilled manual (inc. self-employed)	1,096.0	30.8 ⎫	48.7	34.7 ⎫
Semi-skilled manual and personal service	471.1	13.2 ⎬ 50%	26.4	18.8 ⎬ 67%
Unskilled manual	143.6	4.0	10.0	7.1
Other	65.9	1.9 ⎭	9.1	6.5 ⎭
Total	3,558.9	100.0	140.4	100.0

[a] Data taken from census 10 per cent tables.

Source: J. Charlton et al. (1994), Long-term illness: results from the 1991 Census. *Population Trends*, Office for National Statistics, Crown copyright 1997. 75, 18–25: table 5 (p. 23).

an 'employer or manager', and slightly less likely to live in a household whose head is a 'professional' or 'intermediate non-manual' worker (Charlton et al., 1994).

Research has tended to concentrate on people of working age, leading to a reliance on so-called premature death and a neglect of health in older people. In part this can be explained by the disincentives posed by the difficulty of class measurement for people no longer in paid work, but alongside this it seems likely, as Victor (1991) explains, that ageist stereotypes lead researchers to treat older people as a homogeneous group, all inevitably sick and in need of health care (in ever-increasing amounts). In reality, while there is an increase in acute and chronic conditions with age, it is mistaken to view ill health as a universal feature of later life. For example, 42 per cent of men and 45 per cent of women aged 65 and over reported a limiting long-standing illness in 1993, which represents a rise from 28 per cent and 29 per cent for men and women in the 45–64 age group. But when we concentrate solely on rising percentages we can overlook the fact that the majority of those past retirement age did not report a condition that limited their activities. However, as with younger groups, there is clear evidence of class patterning (by SEG of 'head of household'): for those aged 65 and over only 32 per cent of men and 33 per cent of women in the 'professional group' reported a limiting illness, compared to 51 and 52 per cent respectively in the 'unskilled manual' group (OPCS, 1993a). As Victor (1989: 87) suggests, data such as these are very likely to reflect 'the culmination of a lifetime of disadvantage and inequality'.

Reporting on a recent review by the Economic and Social Research Council (ESRC), Rose (1995: 3) points out that, for many analysts, the fact that RG social class and SEG appear able to summarize complex data and reveal social variations that are relevant to policy and resource issues (i.e. the measure's reliability) is far more important than any quest for a clear theoretical and conceptual basis or knowing what they are supposed to measure, and whether they do this successfully (i.e. ensuring validity). However, it was the firm recommendation of the review group chaired by Rose that an explicit and coherent theoretical base should be sought, with the result that research is being commissioned to this end. The remit of the ESRC review, in fact, went much wider than a concern with class theory: concerns were raised about the issue of the limited population coverage of RG and SEG, as well as the fact that the underlying schema relies on a male-defined classification of the labour market (the issue of gender and class measurement is discussed in more detail in chapter 5, and the issue of 'race' in chapter 6). Rose (1995: 7) points out that, in many circumstances, current occupation-based class measures cover just half of the population, and it is often the most 'disadvantaged and precariously placed individuals' such as the long-term unemployed, never employed (potentially those lumped into an 'underclass'), and people in the growing temporary and 'flexible' job market who are left uncovered and among whom morbidity and mortality are likely to be high. While there are 'solutions' within the schema, such as coding people by their last occupation or the occupation of the 'head of household', they are far from unproblematic. In addition, the RG classification lumps together a range of disparate occupations into one or other class, potentially hiding more finely graded variations in morbidity and mortality. This possibility is suggested in research by Marmot (see Marmot, 1986, 1996) which looked at various employment grades of Whitehall civil servants (who all work in one location and in a sedentary occupation) over time and revealed strong and consistent correlations between grade and various causes of death and of illness, which are generally stronger than those found using RG classes.

But, even bearing these various problems in mind, the overall conclusion of the ESRC review group (Rose, 1995: vi, 8) was that an occupationally based classification should be retained both for pragmatic reasons (occupation data are widely and relatively easily collected) and because 'it remains the case that a person's employment status is a key determinant of life chances, ... access to other types of social good and subjective quality of life'. This view is shared by class theorists. Westergaard (1995: 15), for example, believes that it is essential to retain an approach to class that marks its boundaries primarily by reference to what people actually do. But, because we cannot easily locate the 'economically inactive', we need also to look at what people get. In his own words, class arises from inequalities in command over scarce resources, gains force as a set of inequalities of 'people's conditions and prospects in life' and then finds a wide range of social and cultural expression, for example, in 'lifestyles' and health-related behaviours.

A number of researchers, including the ESRC review group, have pointed out that command over key resources may be a more satisfactory and discriminating way to look at socio-economic circumstances than occupation. At the present time there is a fairly limited amount of national health-related survey data which contain non-occupational measures. The Longitudinal Study (LS) (Goldblatt, 1990a), which covers approximately 1 per cent of the population of England and Wales (half a million people at any one time), starting with a sample drawn from the 1971 Census, contains information on two frequently used measures: housing tenure and access to a car. Table 4.5 shows more marked mortality differences for these measures than for own RG social class for both men and women. Access to a car would seem to be particularly important, perhaps, as Davey Smith et al. (1990) suggest, reflecting income levels. Also drawing on the LS data, Fox and Benzeval (1995: 14) report that, between 1976 and 1981, 'women and men in owner-occupied accommodation with access to a car had an SMR of 78 against that of 138 for women and 129 for men in local authority rented accommodation without a car'. Finally, recent research on general practice (OPCS, 1995b) suggests that, while occupational social class is a significant predictor of consulting behaviour, its effect is significantly reduced when other socio-economic measures are taken into account. For example, if we look at men aged 16–44, the likelihood of consulting for a serious illness is 50 per cent higher in classes IV and V than in classes I and II. When other variables (notably housing tenure and employment status) are taken into account, this is reduced to just 20 per cent.

Table 4.5 Mortality of men and women, 1976–1981, by occupational social class, housing tenure and access to a car

Social classification	Men aged 15–64 (SMR)	Women aged 15–59 (SMR)
Own RG class		
Non-manual (I, II, IIINM)	84	78
Manual (IIIM, IV, V)	103	96
Other	189	106
Husband's RG class		
Non-manual	—	73
Manual	—	108
Tenure (private households)		
Owner-occupied	85	82
Rented	114	110
Car access		
One or more cars	87	84
None	122	122

Source: Derived from P. Goldblatt (1990b), Mortality and alternative social classification. In P. Goldblatt (ed.), *Longitudinal Study: Mortality and Social Organisation 1971–1981* (London: HMSO), 163–9. Office for National Statistics, Crown copyright 1997.

The muddied waters which surround the measurement of social class get murkier still when we also bring in health. A number of health measures (SMR, long-standing illness, self-reported symptoms, malaise), from an even wider range in the health inequalities literature, have been used rather unproblematically in the preceding discussion. Yet putting aside SMRs, since death (though not necessarily its cause) is generally incontestable, how do we know what respondents have in mind when they use the terms health and illness? It is impossible to deny that the measures which we have considered are any more than compressions of the 'complex, subtle, and sophisticated' nature of lay concepts of health (Blaxter, 1990: 14). Two particular concerns follow on from this. First, as operationalized in interview-based surveys, indicators of self-reported health status are explicitly designed to yield statistically comparable data so that we can look at differences between groups of people, yet the very way that individuals perceive and report health is likely to be patterned by these same socio-economic variables.

There is a body of more qualitative data which attests to different thresholds on what counts as 'illness', particularly as this varies by social class and age. But, given the inverse association between socio-economic status and morbidity, the important question is whether lower socio-economic groups 'over-report' ill health. This is a difficult question to answer, although recent research by Elstad (1996) using Norwegian survey data on long-standing illness implies that it may in fact be middle-class respondents who report less serious and inconsequential illnesses, suggesting that current data may actually *underesti-mate* class differentials in health. Much more research, however, is needed on this issue. The second concern relates to the potentially misleading statistics that can result from allowing just one or two measures to stand for overall health status. Ford et al. (1994: 1038) have found that 'for all studies which include a range of health outcomes there are some dimensions of health which show no significant or consistent patterning by class, have flattish class gradients, or show more complex patterns of interaction by, for example, sex and age.' Finally, it is evident that, despite the claim to be measuring 'health', most indicators really tap 'disease', or negative rather than positive health.

Explaining inequalities in health

In the discussion so far we have simply looked at associations between class and health rather than attempting to explain them. We have worked with the implicit assumption that somehow class or socio-economic status are causally implicated in the construction of health differentials. Yet there would appear to be a number of reasons for contesting this assumption. One of these is, as we have already seen, theoretical: sociologists have questioned the contemporary relevance of 'class' as a causal mechanism, especially in its strongest *gemeinschaftlich* form. Sociologists of health and illness have, however, tended to raise methodological rather than theoretical question marks over any causal relationship between class and health. We have already looked at many of these concerns in our discussion of health and class measurement, but others come to the fore when we consider the methodological biases that might be artificially distorting the imputed relationship between class and health.

Is the relationship between class and health artefactual?

Although the question of whether the relationship between class and health is artefactual rather than real is frequently raised in the health inequalities literature it is, in fact, a poorly researched area. Nonetheless, two issues tend to be singled out for attention, both related to mortality. First of all, with the shift away from manufacturing over time, RG class V is likely to shrink in size and any rises in mortality could be based on a small and extreme group. Specifically, the argument is that newer, younger workers are likely to be recruited into skilled and white-collar work (classes IV, IIIM and IIINM), while those left in class V will be older and likely to be less healthy by virtue of their years. While undoubtedly there is a need to bear in mind that, with shifts in the occupational structure, we are not comparing like with like, there is much to suggest that the RG class differentials that we have observed are the result of more than a pull from an extreme group of individuals. Age effects can be taken account of by age-standardizing data, and, when we combine classes IV and V, or IIIM, IV and V, we still see a pattern of widening differentials (Blane, 1985). The second way in which artefacts may enter into the class–health relationship is via the coding of death. One of the major shortcomings in the way mortality rates are collected is what is known as numerator-denominator bias. The numerator is the occupation taken from the death certificate, the denominator is the RG class taken from the census. Death rates may be distorted if the biases in the recording of occupation at death are greater than or different from those biases arising from occupational recording at census. Problems are most likely to occur with the recording of occupation at death: relatives may 'promote' the deceased by recording a higher-ranked occupation than they actually had, or may have quite limited information on the individual's actual job. In addition, the deceased's last occupation may be very different to their lifetime's work. Although these errors no doubt occur, they only really become problematic if they contain systematic biases which inflate working-class and/or deflate middle-class mortality. Evidence from the Longitudinal Study suggests that this does not happen. As was discussed above, the LS began with a 1 per cent sample of the population drawn from the 1971 Census (where occupation is recorded by the individual concerned) and, unlike most mortality rates, which rely on aggregate or group data, has been able to link census data prospectively with vital events, such as death, for the particular individual concerned. These data show that the class differentials reported elsewhere are unlikely to be grossly distorted by numerator-denominator bias (see Fox et al., 1990; Goldblatt, 1990b).

A further aspect of artefact related to coding of death concerns cause-specific rates. Specifically, the given cause of death may be influenced by the diagnostician's knowledge of the social class of the individual. Again, if errors in recording cause of death are random, then the observed class differentials are unlikely to be distorted since false positives and false negatives will balance each other out. However, there is evidence (albeit limited) to suggest that there may be some bias towards systematic under- or over-recording of particular causes of death by class. Bloor et al. (1987) give an interesting account of this process. In the 1930s it appeared that the male death rate for coronary heart disease was higher among members of the middle classes, but by the 1960s there seemed to be a reversal of fortune, with the working class experiencing higher rates. We could speculate on a range of explanations for this shift, including changes in the health behaviours of the better off and/or worsening social conditions of the less well off groups. However, the authors point to the role of changing diagnostic fashion: it seems probable that in the earlier period working-class men were more likely to be diagnosed into the residual category 'other myocardial degeneration' (OMD), which is generally taken to be an imprecise term for arterioscle-rotic (ischaemic) heart disease, while the middle classes were given the more accurate and specific diagnosis. In other words, working-class men may have been suffering from ischaemic heart disease at equal or even higher rates than their middle-class counterparts, but it was just not recorded as such and, in more recent times, the reverse trend might be an artefact of a decline in the use of the OMD category.

Clearly, as Bloor et al. (1987: 511) note, 'the measurement process may be construed as both producing and concealing health inequalities'. An example of possible concealment is the tendency to code the immediate cause of death rather than its underlying cause, possibly leading to the under-reporting of deaths due to degenerative occupationally related diseases such as pneumoconiosis (a lung disease caused by the continued inhalation of dust). On the present evidence, which it must be admitted is scant, we must conclude with Bloor et al. that any assessment of artefact explanations for inequalities in health 'must be both partial and tentative' (1987: 251). Fortunately, by way of contrast, there is a growing body of literature on the other major explanations of health inequality: health selection and social causation.

Inequalities: health selection or social causation?

If there is a causal relationship between class and health, in what direction does it flow – is it more likely that class influences health (social causation), or that health influences class (health selection)? Surprisingly, this question has generated a 'highly charged' (West, 1991) debate in recent years. The controversy is in good part explicable by the form that the discussion took in the Black Report on Inequalities in Health (Townsend and Davidson, 1982: 105). The Black Report imbued health selection with a distinctly social Darwinist hue, referring to a process by which 'those men and women who by virtue of innate physical characteristics are destined to live the shortest lives also reap the most meagre rewards' as they are sorted into lower social-class groups (conversely, the innately more healthy would be sorted upwards). However, to frame health selection in this way is to strip it of its fundamentally social dimension; to fail to recognize that social sorting is as likely, if not more likely, to occur through a process of negative social discrimination on the basis of (ill) health than by the physical properties of sickness and disability in and of themselves (West, 1991). Recently, there has been greater acceptance that illness can indeed act as a mechanism of social selection, but debate still abounds with questions about the manner by which processes of selection operate, and the size of the contribution that selection is likely to make to class gradients in health.

In trying to address these questions it is important to bear in mind the distinction between direct health selection, that is, direct discrimination on the basis of health, and more indirect processes of selection whereby social mobility is not driven by social responses to health *per se*, but by factors linked to health and to class, such as educational achievement. Thus, people with disabilities or poor health may 'underachieve' educationally (not only because they miss some of their schooling, but because social labelling by teachers, careers officers and others means they are given fewer opportunities), and this then has a negative impact on their achieved adult social class. Perhaps because of the legacy of the Black Report, there has until recently been a tendency to focus on intra-generational social mobility, or a drift down the occupational class structure because of more direct processes of health selection (i.e. people are not able to maintain their adult occupational class for health reasons). In this regard there are a number factors which work against the argument that health selection can account for the large class differentials in health that we have observed. For example, if RG class or SEG is our measure of socio-economic status, it is simply not likely that people with significant illnesses will appear in the data (since those who have not been in work for some time or who have never worked are excluded). Moreover, as Fox et al. (1990) note, the large class differentials in health that we observe in the post-retirement age-group, whose RG class is assigned according to their main job before retirement, are unlikely to be explicable by reference to health selection, since those who died at age 75 or over retired ten or more years previously. This means that they cannot have drifted down the occupational class structure for health reasons prior to death. Rather, the differentials that we observe are most likely to be related to longer-term or immediate socio-economic circumstances or lifestyle.

If direct health selection seems unlikely to be a major contributor to class gradients in health, recent commentaries suggest that indirect selection may have more of an impact, although, again, it is difficult to pin down the magnitude of its effect. West (1991) suggests that indirect selection is likely to be revealed most clearly in inter-generational mobility (i.e. in the movement between class of origin to achieved class position). Here the argument is that social mobility favours the healthy, something that was suggested some time ago by Illsley (1955: 1521), who discovered that Aberdonian women who married 'upwards' 'tended to be taller, with better physique and health [as assessed by their obstetricians], than those who remained in the same class at marriage or who fell in social status'. Interestingly, in the context of childbearing, these women tended to have lower prematurity and obstetric death rates than those whose social class was stable or fell.

Most of the more recent research on inter-generational mobility by health has focused on the youth–adult transition. For example, considering a cohort of people born in 1946 and followed up thereafter, Wadsworth (1986: 65) found that boys who had been seriously ill in childhood (measured somewhat problematically as those who had been hospitalized for twenty-eight consecutive days or who had a school/ work absence of three or more consecutive weeks) 'were more likely than others to experience a fall in their fortunes', whatever their class of origin (Wadsworth was unable to make a similar estimate for women since a large number were not in work at the time of follow-up). Cross-sectional research undertaken in Glasgow (Macintyre and West, 1991; West et al., 1990;) suggests that the period of relative class equalization of health in youth (marking a move from marked differentials in childhood) is lost by age 35 when clear class gradients begin to (re)emerge. The fact that a change seems to take place around the period of occupation (i.e. class) sorting is consistent with processes of direct and indirect health selection, though the extent to which this actually happens can only be explored by following the same individuals over time.

Of course, at the end of the day, the health status of any group of individuals is likely to be the product of a very complex interplay between processes of social causation (social circumstances impacting on health) and health selection, that is, they are not mutually exclusive explanations for class differentials in health. This is demonstrated by Shaar et al. (1994) in their research on physical disability in West Beirut. They ask the question, to what extent is discrimination (in terms of achieved social class) attributable to social class of origin (social causation), and to what extent is it due to social selection and drift down the class structure because of negative labelling, stigmatization and discrimination? This is explored by comparing the fortunes of individuals who contracted poliomyelitis in childhood with a matched control group of siblings, and a general sample drawn from the Beirut population. Even though an individual's disability was in itself insufficient to block fluid movement in the job market, the people with poliomyelitis tended to end up in lower class positions than the general population. In part this may be because their parents were in lower occupational class groups. However, since those who came from non-manual backgrounds tended not to hold on to their parental social class or to match the class of their siblings, this can only be a partial explanation. Interestingly, those from skilled and semi-skilled manual backgrounds tended to hold their class position. So, irrespective of class of origin, people with poliomyelitis tended to cluster in skilled occupations, something which is explicable, according to Shaar et al., by the tendency to steer disabled people in Beirut towards skilled vocational work. Thus we see both causation and selection at play: individuals with poliomyelitis tend to come from relatively disadvantaged backgrounds, explicable by the fact that the condition itself is linked to social disadvantage, but there is a clear process of occupational sorting by health operating alongside this.

Macintyre (1997) has pointed out that the publication of the Black Report on inequalities in health within a highly politicized arena made it expedient for its authors to raise and then reject *stronger* versions of the artefact, health selection and cultural/behavioural explanations. This was done in order to pre-empt attempts by others to explain away the significance of theories which stress socio-economic inequalities as the cause of health differences *through* these other explanations, and to argue on the back of this that social inequalities in health are not a problem requiring political attention. However, it is rather unfortunate that the relative outpouring of research post-Black has tended to confuse the stronger or 'hard' version – i.e. that socio-economic differences in health do not present problems of measurement and that health selection and individual health-related behaviours do not play a role in causing them – with the 'softer' version discernible in the report, which allows a role for each of these factors, albeit in a way that is secondary to the prevailing structural–materialist explanation. Understandable though the continued re-buttal of the 'hard' version is in political terms, the attention that it has received has, in Macintyre's view, diverted research energy from explor-ing the precise mechanisms or pathways through which health inequali-ties are generated and maintained. The 'selection versus causation' and 'artefact versus real differences' distinctions can, she writes, 'thus be seen to be politically and conceptually important, but as becoming false anti-theses if treated as being mutually exclusive' (1997: 740). It seems likely, therefore, that the sense of stand-off between explanations for inequalities in health is likely to cede in the future as attention turns to the more fruitful task of exploring the difficult issue of the interplay of selection and causation in the production of health differentials for various class groups at different stages of the life-cycle by reference to a range of measures beyond those of RG class, mortality, and the limited measures of morbidity that have been used to date.

Class and health: the relationship reconsidered

Having explored the range of methodological issues that run through research on health inequalities, we can return more directly to the question of whether the differentials in health that we have observed can be interpreted in class terms. In particular, can they be understood through the theoretical lens of the strong class idiom, with its emphasis on structured class relations and class action (as the data considered in this chapter would lead us to believe), or must we shift our attention to the weaker theoretical perspective, where 'class' refers to a range of inequalities between people which are unlikely to align to form a strong collective experience of health and ill health? Or does it no longer make any sense even to think in class terms? As Esping-Anderson (1993) asks, are the links between ownership, market position and life chances uncoupling altogether? It might be claimed that all we have before us is an edifice created by modernist reasoning! To talk of a postmodernist approach to class inequalities in health is, of course, something of a contradiction in terms. As we saw in chapter 2, postmodernists reject attempts to search for the underlying causes of experience such as class membership. Rather, attention is directed towards the deconstruction of binary oppositions – such as the working class and the middle class, the healthy and the unhealthy – and to reveal that they are artefacts of a particular way of knowing the world. From such a perspective (embod-ied in the fourth position in figure 4.3), pushing people into constructed class groups or health status groups creates divisions and hides the heterogeneity of social life. Quite obviously, the authors whose work we have considered in this chapter are unlikely to find much of merit in this position (although it is conceivable that it will capture more empirical attention in the near future). However, it does at least have the virtue of drawing our attention to the fact that there may be as much variance in health within class groups (however they are defined) as there is across them.

Some, however, would go further, raising questions about the very process of grouping people as a route to explanation. By this process, as Kelly and Charlton (1995: 83) remark, we can end up reifying the social system, promoting the view that 'the system is found to be working in a way that disadvantages particular groups'. When this happens, they continue, 'the individual is relegated to being nothing more than a system outcome, not a thinking and acting human'. But, as these authors recognize all too well, what is the alternative? As they say, we can easily fall into the position that class has little relevance at all. At the extreme we can end up with a view epitomized in some forms of health promotion where 'health is idealised as self-governed lifestyle choice' (Bunton and Burrows, 1995: 210). This comes close to the perspective of the Department of Health's *Health of the Nation* documents which set out targets for reducing the level of ill health and death caused by particular diseases. From the first document in 1992 to the follow-up published in 1995, there was no mention of inequality, but, rather, brief reference to variations between groups associated with a 'range of often inter-linking factors: geography, socio-economic status, gender, environment, ethnicity, culture and lifestyle' (DoH, 1995a: 27). When the risk factors associated with conditions like coronary heart disease and stroke were reviewed, attention was squarely on the so-called voluntary behaviours of smoking, diet, alcohol and physical activity, with no reference to the environmental factors alluded to earlier in the document. Yet there is a growing body of research which suggests that individual risk factors account for relatively small amounts of the variance in health. For example, the Whitehall study of civil servants revealed that only a quarter of the mortality gradient in coronary heart disease could be explained by factors such as cigarette-smoking, cholesterol level, blood pressure, body mass index and physical inactivity (Marmot, 1996).

The question of whether health status can best be explained by the behaviour of individuals, the material circumstances in which they find themselves, or the interplay between the two has been a topic of highly charged political debate for many years. Commentators alert us to a lack of political will to explore materialist explanations during consecutive Conservative administrations, as well as a strong resistance to instituting redistributive economic policies (Davey Smith, 1996; Wilkinson, 1996). There is a strong indication that, with the appointment of a minister for public health (an unprecedented appointment in central government), the current government may shift the focus of the *Health of the Nation* by giving more attention to the health consequences of poverty and inequality (here it is instructive that the term health *inequalities* is being used rather than health *variations*). A green paper, *Our Healthier Nation* will be published in 1998 and an updated Black Report has been commissioned. However, in broader terms, Macintyre (1986: 410–11) alerts us to two major shifts of focus over the last century: first, away from material conditions of life (poverty, polluted water, occupational hazards) towards 'psychosocial aspects of living' (stress, social support, living environments); second, away from a view of the factors that intervene between social position and health as largely outwith the control of the individual, to seeing them as within the individual's control. In academic terms, these trends have undoubtedly been given impetus by recent developments in social theory which shift our attention from class to the individual. Central in this regard has been the argument that the major cleavage in con-temporary society is not class but consumption. In the final part of this chapter we consider the implications of this debate for inequalities in health.

Health, consumption and lifestyle

As we saw in chapters 1 and 2, it has been argued by theorists of late modernity and postmodernity alike that in the contemporary developed world the self has become a reflexive project. Cast adrift from the erstwhile constraints of class, individuals are recurrently engaged in a process of constructing 'lifestyle identities'. For Bauman (1987: 189), in today's world self-identity is inextricably bound up with the 'need to possess, and consume, market-offered goods'. From this perspective, since consumption patterns float free from economic production, we should no longer seek to sort individuals into social or economic groups with particular world-views based on their occupation or (some measure of) social standing, but turn our attention instead to alternative lines of social division located in various household, workplace and leisure consumption activities.

The emergence of consumption as a new axis of inequality has been linked to changes in the occupational structure, notably to the development of a new (swelling) middle class associated with the growing service sector. As attention has shifted away from production as the locus of class, and with this any concern with a manual/non-manual divide, it has turned upon the new middle class. The defining character-istics of the new middle class have been very elusive, with many theorists concluding that above all it is a 'class' marked by diversity and fragmentation, its members perhaps having nothing more in common with each other than 'the fact that they are not manual workers' (Crompton, 1993: 175). Those who might be included comprise 'low-level' service workers (e.g. the hospitality industry), teachers, techni-cians, those in advertising and the media, and the new service professionals (like social workers and counsellors).

However, occupation is no longer the determining factor; if we can-not 'read lifestyle off class', we cannot assume that occupational posi-tion necessarily influences lifestyle; it may be the other way round. For Bourdieu (1984), for example, occupational class itself is likely to be achieved by individuals engaged in a search for social distinction. From this perspective, class is ever shifting like 'a flame whose edges are in constant movement, oscillating around a line or surface' (Bourdieu, quoted in Crompton, 1993: 174). As the world of middle-class work changes (people no longer have a 'job for life'; in many organizations there is a loss of rigid hierarchies, and innovation and flexibility become the order of the day), 'a "healthy lifestyle" is in effect becoming instrumentally converted into health for increased earning capacity and the accumulation of economic assets' (Savage et al., 1992: 114–15). It is through this process that different segments of the middle class with different cultural assets emerge. Savage et al. (1992) identify three such groups: the very high earners who are tagged, with tongue in cheek, as 'postmodern' in lifestyle, living a life of extravagance and excess (in terms of diet and alcohol consumption, for example) alongside cultivat-ing a 'culture of the body'; a second 'ascetic' group, pursuing a lifestyle based on health and exercise (a group typically high in cultural, but low in economic, capital – teachers or social workers – dubbed by Savage et al. as 'intellectuals'); and finally, an 'undistinguished' or conventional group, a legacy of the 'organizational man' whose life is tied up with the firm and cannot be said to have a distinctive lifestyle. This work (which draws on Market Research Bureau data) is useful in so far as it illus-trates the turn towards lines of social division that no longer rely on a traditionally class-based understanding. However, its handle on issues of health and illness as they have been discussed in this chapter is weak. There are many questions still to be addressed, notably the association between lifestyles, consumption and actual health status. Moreover, how far can we actually go in applying these nascent theoretical ideas outside the confines of the 'new middle classes'?

Lash and Urry contend that economic restructuring is giving rise to a new service class, but also to 'what is becoming the bottom and excluded part of the "two thirds society"':

> *A new lower class [now] takes its place at the bottom of a restructured stratification ladder in which the hierarchy of capital and labour is replaced by a three-tiered ordering – a mass class of professional-managerials (alongside this a very small capitalist class), a smaller and comparatively under-resourced working class, and this new lower class. (1994: 145–6)*

Increasingly visible though the lifestyles and health practices of the new service class may be, it is hard to see how they are practically accessible to those at the bottom of the ladder. Homelessness is notoriously difficult to put a figure to, but on the basis of a head count and knowledge of the number of hostel places, a Salvation Army study estimates that there were 75,000 homeless single people living in London in 1989 (Everton, 1993). For these people, maintaining health and gaining access to health care is an intractable problem. Local area studies especially have brought the related effects of the restructuring of the workforce and unemployment into sharp relief. David Widgery (a GP in the East End of London for over twenty years up to his death in 1992) viewed the effects of the deregulation of finance and decline in manufacturing upon life in Hackney, Tower Hamlets and Bethnal Green as a microcosm of what had happened nationwide in Britain since the 1980s. Portraying the pathos of daily life and ill health in an area with over 30 per cent unemployment, 30 per cent 'out-of-wedlock' birth rates, and 25 per cent technical overcrowding, he referred to the 'classless society' as 'an incoherent edifice without logic or enquiry, a crazy house whose apparent doors are mysteriously barred, whose entry points are impenetrable and whose views are without perspective or horizon' (1991: 110).

Conclusion

Class has become a concept that 'we cannot do without when discussing socio-economic groups, political action, and cultural behaviour', and yet in research on health inequalities as much as in the broader context discussed by Holton and Turner, 'the ambiguities in its meaning and intellectual function seem to be proliferating in an ever more confusing way than before' (1989: 172). There has been a tendency to turn theoretical debates on class into concerns of methodology, such that we are not really sure exactly what the inequalities in health that we observe through our research actually mean in class terms. If we reflect back briefly on the four ideal typical positions outlined in figure 4.3, clearly, for some researchers class in its strongest form (position 1 – class as collectivity formed out of relations to other classes) still impacts profoundly on health. But, more commonly it would seem, sociologists of health and illness use the concept of class more loosely, referring to inequalities, but not necessarily locating them in class terms (position 3). We may increasingly begin to see a turn towards other axes of inequality such as consumption and lifestyle which, it has been argued, do not align with class as it has traditionally been conceived in sociology, in the bid to understand why some groups of people are healthy and others not. Finally, in perhaps the most radical position of all (position 4), even the attempt to search for underlying causes of health status by reference to class would be rejected.

5

Gender Inequalities and Health Status

The refrain 'women get sick and men die', which has been at the heart of research findings in the area of gender inequalities in health, still rings true but increasingly belies the complexity of the relationship between gender and health status. In this chapter we will explore the rich insights that have emerged from the large body of research on gender differentials in health, but also consider some of the assumptions on which they are based. In particular, we will reflect critically on the somewhat over-generalized nature of the established sociological wisdom of men's higher mortality and women's higher morbidity, and question the search for male/female difference that underpins much of the research in this area.

The chapter begins by considering gender differences in mortality. Here we will explore explanations for the emergence of a female advantage at the end of the nineteenth century and the suggestion that this advantage may be reducing as we approach the turn of the present century. Since explanations for men's higher death rates typically refer to the penalties of masculinity, we will weigh the potential of current theoretical debates in this area to inform our understanding. We will then consider how useful the predominant gender role framework is as a conceptual basis for the exploration of gender differences in morbidity.

Men, women and mortality

We are thoroughly accustomed to thinking of longevity as a female advantage in contemporary Western societies. But this has not always been the case. Indeed, there is evidence of a substantial male advantage

Fig. 5.1
Sex mortality differentials in cohorts born between 1871 and 1921, England
and Wales

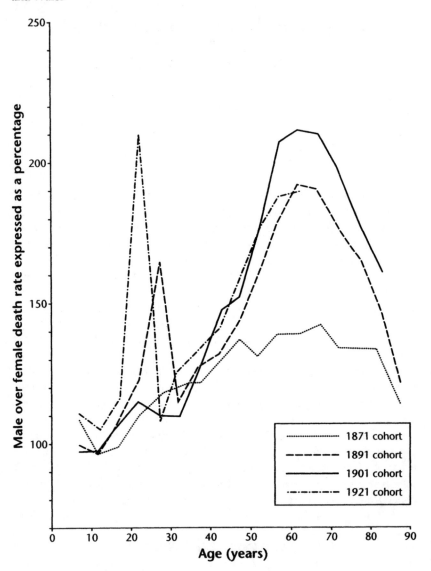

Source: N. Hart (1989), Sex, gender and survival: inequalities of life chances
between European men and women. In J. Fox (ed.), *Health Inequalities in
European Countries* (Avebury), 109–41: fig. 6.4 (p. 118).

in longevity from studies of sixteenth- and seventeenth-century European villages (Shorter, 1982). In the first half of the nineteenth century, male and female life expectancies were more or less equal, but by the early 1960s women could expect to live, on average, for 5.8 more years than men (CSO, 1996). How can we begin to explain the gradual birth of the female advantage and its persistence well into the late twentieth century in developed countries? Hart contends that 'whatever underlies the widening gap in survival between European men and women, it seems to have begun among those who started their lives in the late nineteenth century' (1989: 117). She goes on to ask, 'what events or processes at the turn of the century could have the capacity to alter the balance of advantage between the sexes so spectacularly?' One possibility is that the Great War of 1914–18 led to a 'burnt out' generation of men 'depleted by battlefield death and disablement' (Hart, 1989: 122). This would seem to be supported by figure 5.1 which shows a peaking of the male excess mortality during this time. We see a rise when the cohort born in 1871 reach their mid-forties and a marked excess when those born in 1891 reach their mid-twenties, during the First World War. (The significant male excess for the cohort born in 1921 represents deaths in the second World War.)

Since it was likely to have been the fittest men who entered the armed forces, the excess male deaths for this period could be a form of health-related selection, whereby the unhealthy survivors and the unfit to fight were left to appear in the mortality figures. For example, physically weakened, many died in the flu epidemic of 1918–19. But Hart believes that, while selection may play a role, it is unlikely to be the whole of the explanation since, as we can see in figure 5.1, after a drop to pre-war levels, the male excess continued upwards among those born in the 1920s. Indeed, the excess in male mortality reaches its highest level for those born in 1901, who were too young to fight in the war.

A second explanation for the emergence of a female advantage is the decline in mortality during women's reproductive years, where later childbearing, reduced family size and improved child-spacing may have contributed to women's improved health. The average family size for those who got married in 1865 was over six children; this had fallen to two for those who married during the Depression. Figure 5.2 shows the marked divergence at age 20, when after 1931 the female death rate declined far more rapidly than the male (Kane, 1994). Similar trends can be observed for women in their later reproductive years.

A third explanation for the shifting balance of advantage between the sexes can be summarized under the umbrella of patriarchy and the adverse social circumstances that prevail for women and girls under

Fig. 5.2
Index of age-specific mortality rates, Great Britain 1911–1981 (age 20)

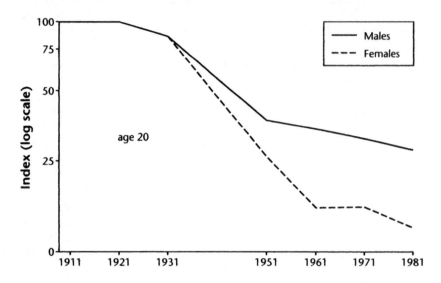

Source: P. Kane (1994), *Women's Health: From Womb to Tomb* (2nd edition; Macmillan), fig. 1.7 (p. 18). Reproduced by permission of Macmillan Ltd.

conditions of economic scarcity. Over the last 150 years in England and Wales, the death rate for baby boys has always been at least 20 per cent higher than for girls (even though mortality rates for both male and female infants have been drastically reduced). Mortality during *childhood*, however, presents a somewhat different picture. From the mid-1880s and for most of the period up to the turn of the century, the difference between the death rates of boys and girls was 3 per cent or less, and even showed a reverse pattern (i.e. a female disadvantage) in the late 1800s. The reverse pattern is even more marked for children aged between 10 and 14 where, aside from just a few years when rates were equal, boys had a 3–8 per cent advantage right up to the mid-1930s (OPCS, 1992). For adolescents (ages 15–19) a female excess continued into the late nineteenth century. Even for women aged 25–34, this pattern continued until 1860.

As is well known, this female excess mortality is mirrored in the experience of many children in the Third World today, most notably in South Asia (India, Pakistan and Bangladesh) and in parts of the Middle East. Female infanticide is still practised in societies with strong patriar-

chal ideologies. For example, Zhang (quoted in Vallin, 1993: 196) estimates that infanticide, which accounts for 60 per cent of all infant
deaths in Anhui province in China, is responsible for the 12 per cent
excess mortality that is experienced by girls. Among forty-five developing countries, there are only two where the death rates of girls
aged between 1 and 4 are not higher than for boys of the same age
(MacCormack, 1988). Koenig and D'Souza's (1986) analysis of data for
rural Matlab Thana in Bangladesh, for a cohort born during 1973–1974,
shows the typical male disadvantage in the first year of life, but a female
disadvantage of 59 per cent between ages 1 and 4. The important point,
then, is that the contemporary experience of girls in the Third World
mimics that of their historical counterparts in developed countries
during the late nineteenth and early twentieth centuries.

The interaction of economic scarcity and patriarchy has especially
been noted for women's health in the mid-nineteenth century. For example, the fact that women were more susceptible to tuberculosis (then the
number one killer during the childbearing years) in the mid-nineteenth
century, has been associated with their greater exposure to malnutrition
(Shorter, 1982). Interestingly, unable to admit to this, the Registrar General of the day blamed much of women's illness on the fashion for
wearing tight corseting which, it was said, constricted the chest and
made breathing difficult. As Johansson writes, 'making a culprit of the
corset made it seem as if women themselves were responsible for dying
so often from consumption; it also implied that they could change this
sorry state of affairs as easily as their frocks' (1977: 171). Discussing the
higher mortality of girls and younger women in mid-Victorian England
more generally, she explores the ways in which government policies
might have 'influenced the construction of gender during the process of
development, in a way that made it temporarily hazardous to be a young
female during a period of accelerated social and economic change'
(Johansson, 1996: 35). Female mortality was particularly high in the
countryside where female excess mortality spanned ages 5 to 64. The
economic marginalization of women was particularly marked in rural
areas, as paid employment in the agrarian sector declined alongside the
enclosure movement and technological change, and jobs got increasingly
scarce for women. Johansson hypothesizes that, as women's economic
value declined, families from the poorest to the most wealthy may have
found it more prudent to invest in the health of males. As urbanization
proceeded apace, and women were able to obtain work in the cities,
excess female mortality disappeared.

Overall then we have seen that the pattern of female mortality advantage to which we have become accustomed is a contemporary phenom-

enon. In the past men tended to fare better than women. This may in part be explained by the risks of childbirth, but the most likely reason is that women's mortality advantage emerged alongside a remarkable improvement in their social status and economic circumstances, a situation which some, such as Vallin (1993), have argued pertains right up to the current day. But, how likely is this to continue?

The gap closes?

Commentators are beginning to suggest that we may soon see a trend away from the marked female mortality advantage that has prevailed

Fig. 5.3
Death rates 1841–1995, all ages, per 1,000 population England and Wales

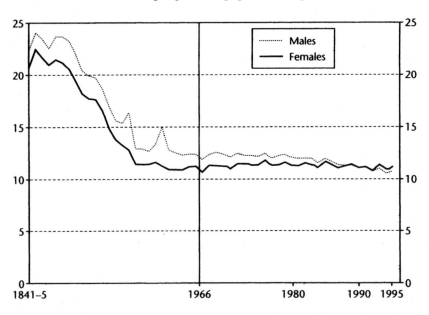

Note: Rates to the left of 1966 are given for five-year periods; after 1966 annual rates are given. This means that decreases to the left of 1966 are steeper than they would appear if annual rates were given.
Source: Author's analysis, based on the following sources: OPCS (1992), *Mortality Statistics, Serial Tables: England and Wales* (London: HMSO), Series DH1, No. 25; OPCS (1993b), *1991 Mortality Statistics, General: England and Wales* (London: HMSO), Series DH1, No. 26; OPCS (1994b), *Mortality Statistics: Serial Tables* (London: HMSO), Series DH1, No. 27; ONS (1996), *Population and Health Monitors* (London: HMSO), DH2 96/1 & 2.

Table 5.1 All age sex mortality ratios for selected years between 1841–5 and 1995 for England and Wales

Year	Ratio (M/F)
1841–5	1.073
1861–5	1.102
1896–1900	1.133
1916–20	1.289
1931–5	1.114
1941–5	1.360
1951–5	1.147
1961–5	1.107
1971	1.100
1981	1.062
1989	1.000
1990	1.009
1992	0.989
1993	0.974
1994	0.972
1995	0.973

Source: OPCS (1992), Mortality Statistics, Serial Tables: England and Wales (London: HMSO), Series DH1, No. 25; OPCS (1993b), 1991 Mortality Statistics, General: England and Wales (London: HMSO), Series DH1, No. 26; OPCS (1994b), Mortality Statistics: Serial Tables (London: HMSO), Series DH1, No. 27; ONS (1996), Population and Health Monitors (London: HMSO), DH2 96/1 & 2. Office for National Statistics, Crown copyright 1997.

for most of the twentieth century (Hillier, 1991a; Kane, 1994). A new trend began to emerge in the United States during the late 1970s where the ratio of male to female deaths (called the sex mortality ratio) for all causes decreased from 1.8 to 1.72 between 1979 and 1989 (Waldron, 1995). Waldron reports that the female advantage in life expectancy decreased from a peak of 7.8 to 6.8 years over the same period. Data for England and Wales point towards a similar conclusion although, historically, the gender gap in life expectancy has never been as wide as in the United States, or as in some other European countries. Figure 5.3, which depicts death rates for men and women separately between 1841–5 and 1995, shows the now familiar decreases in the death rate: for women, we see a decline from a peak of 22.6 per 1,000 population in 1846–50 to 11.1 in 1995; and, for men, from 24.1 to 10.8 over the same period.

As we would expect from these data, there is evidence of a quite marked shift in the sex mortality ratio. In Table 5.1 the familiar female advantage emerges quite clearly over the course of the second half of the nineteenth century (from just over a 7 per cent advantage to women in 1841–5 to around 13 per cent by the closing decade of the century) and persists well into the second half of the twentieth century (note once again the peaks during the two world wars and their aftermath). But a different pattern begins to emerge from the 1960s onwards: despite some fluctuations, we see a gradual decline in the female advantage until male and female mortality rates reach virtual parity by the early 1990s. Data from 1992 onwards even hint at a reversed trend of female disadvantage. It would be rash to draw any firm conclusions from this – particularly given that changes in the age structure (not accounted for in these figures) can induce changes in the male/female differential. But looking at age-standardized rates to account for this, Tickle (1996) finds little difference between the overall improvement in mortality for women at 17 per cent and for men at 18 per cent over the period 1982 to 1992 in the UK. It will be interesting to watch closely to see how these trends develop in coming years.

Trends in the sex mortality ratio are very tentatively supported by life-expectancy data. Men born in 1901 could expect on average to live 3.5 years less than women, while for those born in 1961 the gap had risen to approximately 5.8. Although life expectancies have continued to rise for both men and women (it is expected to level off gradually after 1996), the difference between them may be reducing. Thus there is a projected differential (itself taking account of recent gender-related changes) of 5.5 years between men and women born in 1991, of 5.2 for those born in 2001, and of just 5 years for those born in the year 2021 (CSO, 1996).

There are three possible explanations for a move towards convergence (Kane, 1994): it could be due to improvements for men (i.e. men may be 'catching up' with women); there could be a deterioration or plateauing of women's death rates; or both trends could be taking place simultaneously. Changes in death rates provide a clue as to what might be happening. If we look at male rates, especially from the 1960s onwards, we see a very gradual but continuing decline (that is, an improvement) from 12.4 per 1,000 population in 1966 to under 11 into the early 1990s. For women, there is much less change over the same period: the death rate was 11.2 per 1,000 population in 1966 and, despite some fluctuations upwards, was around 11 in the early 1990s. The picture that begins very tentatively to emerge, then, is that convergence is not occurring because women's health is getting worse, but, rather, because men's health is improving. However, while this forms a useful working hypothesis, we must be wary of generalizing too far from these data, since there are likely to be different risks of death for men and women at different ages. More specifically, particular age cohorts of men and women may face gender-specific health risks associated with the social and cultural circumstances they are born into and experience during their lives.

Tables 5.2 and 5.3 reveal different trends in sex mortality ratios for different age-groups. If we look first of all at the data in table 5.2: for all of the age-groups depicted, the death rates show an increasing gender differential from around the beginning of the twentieth century in the direction of a growing female advantage. The very low rates for both men and women, which are rounded to one decimal place, make the calculation of sex mortality ratios crude (and hence they are not in-

Table 5.2 Death rates per 1,000 population and sex mortality ratios for age-groups between 15 and 44, 1841–1944, England and Wales

Year	Age-group 15–19		Age-group 20–4		Age-group 25–34		Age-group 35–44	
	M	F	M	F	M	F	M	F
1841–5	6.8	7.7	9.0	8.6	9.4	9.9	12.2	12.1
1861–5	6.4	6.9	8.7	8.2	9.8	9.8	13.2	12.1
1896–1900	3.6	3.4	4.9	4.1	6.5	5.6	11.1	9.1
1916–20	3.9	3.7	6.6	4.5	8.6	5.5	9.1	6.4
1931–45	2.5	2.2	3.2	2.8	3.3	3.1	5.4	4.3
1951–5	0.9	0.5	1.2	0.7	1.4	1.1	2.7	2.1
1961–5	1.0	0.4	1.1	0.5	1.1	0.7	2.8	1.8
1971	0.9	0.4	0.9	0.4	1.0	0.6	2.3	1.6
1981	0.8	0.3	0.8	0.4	0.9	0.5	1.8	1.3
1989	0.7	0.3	0.9	0.3	0.9	0.5	1.7	1.1
1990	0.7	0.3	0.9	0.3	1.0	0.4	1.7	1.1
1992	0.6	0.3	0.8	0.3	0.9	0.4	1.7	1.1
1993	0.6	0.3	0.8	0.3	0.9	0.4	1.7	1.1
1994	0.5	0.2	0.8	0.3	1.0	0.4	1.7	1.1
1995	0.6	0.3	0.8	0.3	1.0	0.4	1.7	1.1

Source: Author's analysis based on the following: OPCS (1992), *Mortality Statistics, Serial Tables: England and Wales* (London: HMSO), Series DH1, No. 25; OPCS (1993b), *1991 Mortality Statistics, General: England and Wales* (London: HMSO), Series DH1, No. 26; OPCS (1994b), *Mortality Statistics: Serial Tables* (London: HMSO), Series DH1, No. 27; ONS (1996), *Population and Health Monitors* (London: HMSO), DH2 96/1 & 2. Office for National Statistics, Crown copyright 1997.

Table 5.3 Death rates per 1,000 population and sex mortality ratios for age-groups between 45 and 84, 1841–1995 in England and Wales

Year	Age-group 45–54 Death Rate		Ratio	Age-group 55–64 Death Rate		Ratio	Age-group 65–74 Death Rate		Ratio	Age-group 75–84 Death Rate		Ratio
	M	F	(M/F)	M	F	(M/F)	M	F	(M/F)	M	F	(M/F)
1841–5	17.2	15.1	1.14	30.3	27.2	1.11	65.5	59.1	1.11	143.7	131.8	1.09
1861–5	18.9	15.5	1.22	32.8	27.9	1.18	66.4	59.1	1.12	145.9	133.8	1.09
1896–1900	18.4	14.3	1.29	34.1	27.4	1.24	68.3	58.5	1.17	143.1	127.0	1.13
1916–20	14.0	10.4	1.35	27.9	20.4	1.37	63.0	47.7	1.32	139.4	115.1	1.21
1931–45	11.2	8.0	1.40	23.6	17.0	1.39	56.7	42.8	1.32	135.2	108.9	1.24
1951–5	7.9	4.9	1.61	22.5	11.8	1.91	54.6	33.1	1.65	126.7	92.4	1.37
1961–5	7.4	4.4	1.68	21.7	10.6	2.05	54.0	29.8	1.81	121.3	83.6	1.45
1971	7.1	4.3	1.65	20.1	10.0	2.01	50.5	26.1	1.94	113.0	73.6	1.54
1981	6.1	3.8	1.61	17.7	9.5	1.86	45.6	24.1	1.89	105.2	66.2	1.59
1989	4.7	3.0	1.57	14.8	8.8	1.68	39.5	22.6	1.75	95.7	60.3	1.59
1990	4.6	2.9	1.59	14.4	8.6	1.67	38.7	21.9	1.77	93.3	58.1	1.61
1992	4.4	2.8	1.57	13.5	7.9	1.71	38.1	21.7	1.76	95.1	58.8	1.62
1993	4.4	2.9	1.52	13.4	7.9	1.70	38.6	22.1	1.75	97.7	61.0	1.60
1994	4.2	2.8	1.50	12.6	7.4	1.70	36.7	21.2	1.73	93.2	58.0	1.61
1995	4.3	2.9	1.48	12.4	7.3	1.70	35.8	20.7	1.73	96.6	59.3	1.63

Source: Author's analysis based on the following: OPCS (1992), *Mortality Statistics, Serial Tables: England and Wales* (London: HMSO), Series DH1, No. 25; OPCS (1993b), *1991 Mortality Statistics, General: England and Wales* (London: HMSO), Series DH1, No. 26; OPCS (1994b), *Mortality Statistics: Serial Tables* (London: HMSO), Series DH1, No. 27; ONS (1996), *Population and Health Monitors* (London: HMSO), DH2 96/1 & 2. Office for National Statistics, Crown copyright 1997.

cluded here). A gender difference, however, does persist even though for those under age 35 this corresponds to a death rate of less than 1 per 1,000 people for both men and women. Table 5.3 begins to hint at a different story. Since in most cases the death rates are higher, sex mortality ratios are less liable to misinterpretation as a result of rounding. Sex mortality ratios for men and women aged 45–54 show a gradually widening gap to women's advantage up to around the mid-1960s, and then suggest a reduction. This trend is a little more marked for those aged 55–64, where the ratio has steadily decreased from 2.05 in the mid-1960s to around 1.7 during the early 1990s. For both of these age-groups the change seems to be related to a slower pace of decline in the death rate for women compared to men, which began in the late 1950s.

In summary, the data in tables 5.2 and 5.3 suggest that the narrowed gap seen in figure 5.3 may in part be explained by very low death rates among younger adults (even though there are still significant gender differences within this), and by a declining advantage among women in middle and late middle age. While this should not obscure the fact that, on average, most women still have greater life expectancies than men at all ages today, it does suggest that something may be happening to improve men's mortality to a greater extent than women's.

Social circumstances, gender and mortality

At this point it is useful to return to some of the issues that were raised when we looked at the excess female mortality for certain ages in the mid-nineteenth century and the emergence of a male excess by the turn of the century, that is, the relationship between gender differences in mortality and social circumstances. If improved social circumstances can be invoked to explain the decline in the female mortality disadvantage in the past, might they also explain the incipient improvement in male mortality today? The factor that immediately comes to mind in this regard is the reduction in cigarette-smoking among particular cohorts of men, alongside its continuation among women.

Referring to male excess mortality Hart (1989: 133) remarks that 'the epidemiological search looks complete. Men die before women because of alcohol and cigarettes. If their consumption could be reduced, sex inequalities in life chances might be eliminated or at least cut to a lower level.' There is some indication that this is exactly what is beginning to happen. Smoking, which was considered improper for women until the early twentieth century, became more acceptable with the suffrage movement. By 1935 in the United States, 18.1 per cent of women and

Fig. 5.4

Prevalence of cigarette-smoking among men and women aged 16 and over, 1948–1990, Britain

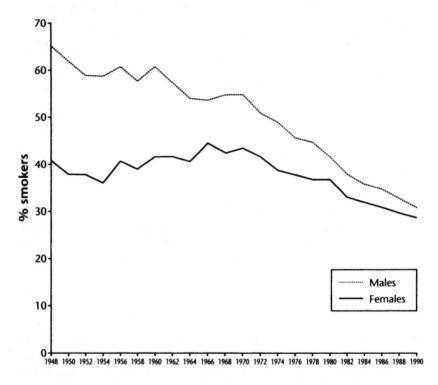

Source: H. Graham (1994), Surviving by smoking. In S. Wilkinson and C. Kitzinger (eds), *Women and Health* (London: Taylor & Francis), fig. 7.2 (p. 109). Reproduced by permission of Taylor & Francis.

25.5 per cent of men smoked; by the 1950s, when the link with lung cancer was being made, the respective figures were 38 and 62 per cent (Chollat-Traquet, 1992). Trends for Britain are clearly documented in figure 5.4, which highlights the more rapid rate of decline in smoking among men than women and the move to a situation where 'today, an almost equal proportion of women (28 per cent) and men (29 per cent) report that they smoke cigarettes' (Graham, 1995: 513).

Given the association between smoking and morbidity and mortality, it is not surprising to find that in the United States there was a substantial increase in mortality for lung cancer and chronic obstructive airways disease among women, but not among men in the 1980s: while men had a lung cancer death rate of 59.3 per 100,000 in both 1979 and 1989, women's rates for the equivalent years were 17.3 and 25.4. So, while male rates remain higher, the sex mortality ratio (i.e. women's advantage) for the disease has declined from 3.43 to 2.33 (Waldron, 1995). Data for selected regions in the United Kingdom and for Denmark reveal differences in lung cancer incidence for males and females aged 30–74 (see figure 5.5). The figures for Scotland, in particular, are striking: while for men aged 30–74 there has been an overall rate of decline of 2.4 per cent every five years since the mid-1980s, for women there has been a rate of increase of 26.2 per cent (OPCS, 1994a). For England and Wales, male deaths from lung cancer nearly halved between 1971 and 1992, while female rates increased by a sixth over the same period (CSO, 1995a). In the words of Jacobson (quoted in Graham, 1987: 49), 'in smoking-related mortality women are achieving an equality in death that most never achieved in life'.

This discussion suggests that the decline in smoking and smoking-related deaths among men might well be a contributory factor in the recent decline in male death rates, and thereby to the reduction in the sex mortality ratio for both the United States and Britain. Other factors may also play a role. Men (especially younger ones) have traditionally experienced a higher death rate from motor vehicle accidents. Stricter controls on drinking and driving in recent years and the introduction of compulsory seat-belts may, again, be leading to a decline in male deaths. For example, in the United States the male death rate per 100,000 population for motor vehicle accidents (for all ages) was 35.8 in 1979; by 1989 this had dropped significantly to 26.8. For the equivalent years, women began with a lower rate of 12.1, which reduced to only 11.2. This smaller decline may be related to the substantial increase in female driving overall during the 1980s. Consequently, over the period 1979–1989 the sex mortality ratio for motor vehicle accidents in the United States changed, in men's favour, from 2.96 to 2.39 (Waldron, 1995). The decline in male employment in energy, manufacturing and construction, sectors traditionally associated with fatal injuries, may also be contributing to the reduction in male death rates, although given the long and variable delay in the period between first exposure and the onset of terminal illness (for example, pneumoconiosis in mining), this may not show up in significant terms for some time yet. (Work in the female-dominated service sector may be just as unhealthy, but is probably more likely to generate chronic ill health than terminal illness.) Of course, there are areas of mortality in which men have traditionally predominated and continue to do so, for example suicide and self-inflicted injury, where there are twice as many male deaths as female

Fig. 5.5

Cumulative risk per 1,000 (30–74 years) for successive birth cohorts 1900–1940: lung cancer incidence, UK and Denmark

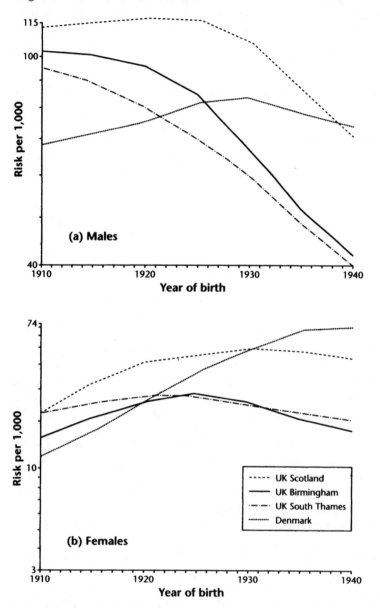

Source: OPCS (1994a), *Cancer Statistics: Registrations* (London: HMSO), Series MB1, No. 22: fig. 2 (p. 11).

ones, a trend that seems to be on the increase (OPCS, 1993b). This point notwithstanding, the data lend some support to the trend depicted in table 5.3: that any possible drift towards a reduced mortality gap is not because women's situation is worsening, but because men's is improving. Yet this seems counter-intuitive in light of compelling evidence that women's social circumstances have worsened in a number of areas in recent years.

As Payne reveals, women's 'secondary position in the labour market and their first position in the home' signals their economic dependence on men and, relatedly, their greater vulnerability to poverty and deprivation (1991: 3). There has been a well-documented trend towards greater female participation in the labour force over recent years. The proportion of economically active women rose from 44 per cent in 1971 to 53 per cent in 1994, and is set to rise to 57 per cent by the year 2001 (CSO, 1995a). Women's greater involvement in paid work might be expected to enhance their life chances. However, as Graham contends, 'the increase in women's employment is closely meshed into the growth of flexible working and service-sector employment' (1993a: 110). Thus, by the mid-1990s, nearly twice as many men as women worked full-time, while more than five times as many women as men worked part-time in Britain (CSO, 1995b). In addition, women are twice as likely to be in temporary work (with poor terms and conditions), and twice as likely to be in it because they cannot find a permanent job. Moreover, at all ages their wages are, on average, lower than those of men. As we saw in chapter 4, the earnings gap between the better and the less well paid has increased over the last twenty years. Since women work in less well paid jobs, the number in the low-pay range has also increased. In 1994, a third of women earned £190 per week or less, compared to 13 per cent of men. Conversely, three-quarters of men earned over £230 per week, compared to only half of women. Taking all independent income (i.e. money from wages, state benefits, and pensions and investment) into account, women have roughly half as much money as men (CSO, 1995b).

Some of the links between socio-economic circumstances and the reduced mortality gap between men and women at certain ages may already be beginning to emerge. As we saw in chapter 4, there has been a significant widening of the mortality gap between rich and poor in recent years. For example, the research by McLoone and Boddy (1994), which grouped residential postcode sectors in Scotland using a measure of deprivation, found that although standardized mortality ratios (SMRs) (all causes of death combined) had improved between 1981 and 1991, this trend was far more marked in the more affluent areas. It is particularly interesting to note, in light of our discussion in this chapter, that the reduction in death rates for women between the ages of 40 and 69 in the most deprived areas was only about a third of the reduction seen in other areas. For men this trend was somewhat less marked. Since, as we have seen, it is precisely within this age-range that the sex mortality ratio seems to be narrowing, these data lend some support to the possibility that men's relative material advantage/women's disadvantage may be an important contributor to any possible reduction in the sex mortality ratio.

The associations between material circumstances and health that were documented in chapter 4 would suggest that if overall women's circumstances are worsening then, as noted above, we would expect their death rates to be gradually rising rather than staying more or less the same. However, it may be far too early to see this effect for many causes of death. Referring to changes in women's lives in terms of increased work outside the home (alongside considerable responsibilities in the home), stress, and the consumption of cigarettes and alcohol, Kane remarks that:

> most of these changes in women's behaviour are comparatively recent. Deaths from ailments like ischaemic heart disease, or lung cancer, tend to come only after a long exposure to their contributory factors, and hence at older ages: there is little immediate impact. Any increases in death rates of women who have been exposed to these behavioural changes for the past thirty years or so will only begin to show up in the mortality statistics towards the end of this century. (1994: 51)

Clearly, the evidence that has been presented on the closing gap between male and female mortality rates at the current time is tentative and highly speculative. It is important to bear three things in mind. First, we need to watch closely to see if men's rates continue to decline at specific ages, and to see if women's begin to rise as the present century draws to a close and a new one begins. Second, if there is evidence of a swifter pace of decline in male death rates, much more research will be needed to identify the social mechanisms underpinning the change, which at the current time are very vaguely specified. However, the third, and perhaps most important, point to emphasize is that all we have been referring to is a *trend* towards a reduced gap (i.e. where women's mortality advantage may be declining) not to an *endpoint* where men have gained the advantage in longevity. Therefore, we are still left with the question of why, at least at the present time, most men still die at an earlier age than women.

Masculinity, risk and early death

The social context of men's risk of early death is vividly portrayed by Stillion. In the male world, she writes, the cultural message is 'kill or be killed, and the statistics show that this violent moral is being heard, internalised, and to some extent, grafted onto men's gender identities' (1995: 54). After years of relative invisibility, male health has achieved a new prominence on both academic and public health agendas during the 1990s as well as in the popular media. For example, the annual report of the Regional Director of Public Health of one (then) Regional Health Authority in England stated that 'the most important new conclusion that we have reached is that something should be done about the health of men' (WMRHA, 1994: 118). The report continues,

> *What can be done? It is time that men started to think about their health in a serious way. This may require more thought than just keeping fit and eating fruit. A significant number of the male deaths are associated with risk taking behaviour that leads to accidents and injury, but there are also too many suicides. It may be that men are poor at seeking or obtaining help when things are not going too well. It is necessary not only to keep fit and avoid smoking but also to play and drive safely and be prepared to admit weakness or difficulty in life, seeking help when depressed. For the stereotypical male such a list is full of contradictions. The fit healthy male who avoids a heart attack is also likely to be the person who plays dangerous sports and drives too fast and who would probably find his macho image somewhat dented by seeking counselling or support if things were not going too well. (WMRHA, 1994: 19)*

This lengthy quotation quite neatly captures the theme of the wider literature: that 'masculinity is dangerous to your health' and is in urgent need of redefinition. The claim that patriarchy represents privilege for men, which has been central to feminist theories (see chapter 3), is therefore under direct challenge, particularly from the 'sociology of masculinity'.

The sociology of masculinity

Privilege, it might be argued, is largely invisible to those who have it (Kimmel, 1990). Patriarchy has carried with it an ironic twist: by creating history as an ungendered and universal process, it has not only concealed female oppression, but also sidelined men's experience as men. This has meant that it has been difficult for men to appreciate the gendered character of their experience. Attempts to understand male experience in these terms began as part of 1970s counter-culture, culminating today in the view that masculinity is not simply privilege, but wounded and in need of healing (Connell, 1995).

Not surprisingly, the sociology of masculinity has a tense relationship with contemporary feminism; it has recognized its indebtedness, but feels the need to distance itself from it. Seidler (1994) has discussed this at length, arguing that too close an identification with the feminist agenda can lead individual men to internalize patriarchy's guilt with serious negative consequences for the male self. For this reason he argues that men need to take on feminism's challenge, but not reject masculinity as inherently negative. Feminists, not surprisingly, have questioned the political project of the sociology of masculinity. As Hanmer (1990) relates, if the concern is with liberating men, this neglects a critique of men as part of the problem.

One response has been to emphasize the *plural* character of masculinity. Sabo and Gordon, for example, refer to a 'system of intermale dominance in which a minority of men dominates the masses of men'. The fact is, they continue, 'that all men are not alike, nor do all male groups share the same stakes in the gender order. At any given historical moment, there are competing masculinities – some hegemonic, some marginalised, and some stigmatised – each with their respective structural, psychological, and cultural moorings' (Sabo and Gordon, 1995: 10). (Clearly there are parallels here with feminism's recent stress on patterns of super- and subordination within women – see chapter 3.) This permits theorists to refer to two hierarchies – male dominance of women, and inter-male dominance – which reflect and feed on one another. Considerable emphasis has been placed on the concept of hegemonic masculinity (sometimes also called hyper-masculinity), as the form of masculinity which, at any one specific point in time, is 'culturally exalted' (Connell, 1995: 77). This form of masculinity would seem to mesh well with the features of masculinity that are seen as negative for health. In the context of a discussion about masculinity and risk-taking, Kimmel and Levine write that:

> *until daring has been eliminated from the rhetoric of masculinity, men will die as a result of their risk taking. In war. In sex. In driving fast and drunk. In shooting drugs and sharing needles. Men with AIDS are real men, and when one dies, a bit of all men dies as well. Until we change what it means to be a real man, every man will die a little every day. (Kimmel and Levine, 1992: 327)*

Since the sociology of masculinity suggests that male experience can be as much about privation as about privilege, it might be a fruitful basis for the study of men's higher average mortality. Conceptualizing masculinity in plural terms provides a theoretical context to explore health inequalities within men as a group, attending not just to differences, but also to actual relations of dominance and subordination. However, there is a marked tendency for the sociology of masculinity to view ill health as an assault on a man's sense of self and to neglect the association between masculinity and health through patterns of power and domination, including, it is important to appreciate, the effects of power/masculinity on *women's* health. There is an affinity between this attention to the male self and the wider social changes of late modernity as they have been conceptualized by sociologists. In chapter 1 we discussed Giddens' contention that social life has become a highly reflexive project in an environment of chance and risk. Men's position, in the public domain, he argues, 'has been achieved at the expense of their exclusion from the transformation of intimacy' (Giddens, 1992: 67). However, it seems important that sociologists looking at men's health attend not only to personal experiences, but also to wider structures of power to counter the tendency of the sociology of masculinity to 'turn inward' to individual experience and men's inability to 'fulfil their emotional needs' (Hearn, 1996). When attention is fixed exclusively upon men's personal pain, 'the reality of male power tends to be washed away with the tears shed for men's underlying vulnerability' (Segal, 1992: 68).

A more structural approach would also seem to be called for to explore the changing gender patterns of general and cause-specific mortality referred to earlier in this chapter. It has been suggested that women's life expectancy may begin to decline if their lifestyles 'become more like those of men' (Hart, 1989; Kane, 1994). In this regard it is important not to lose sight of the fact that the 'lifestyles' and health-related risks that people experience, and the 'roles' that they occupy, are not just reflexively chosen, but are structured by the economic imperatives of late modernity, where health and the body are new and important sites of personal and social capital (see chapters 1 and 2). But research has tended to subsume changes in cigarette-smoking, diet, exercise, and paid work under the rubric of health-related behaviour or the convergence of gender roles. A social role framework has also been the starting-point for research on gender differences in morbidity. It is to this issue that we now turn.

Gender and morbidity: whose advantage?

The social role framework has been a very rich source for research on gender and morbidity. As was noted in chapter 3, by linking various combinations of social roles to health status, its chief objective has been to determine that the observed pattern of women's higher morbidity can be explained by the social roles that they occupy, rather than by their 'biology'. Although, as we will see, it is possible to draw some broad conclusions, this body of research is extremely complex, sometimes contradictory and very difficult to synthesize. The problem is partly methodological: since the role concept is very diffuse it can mean quite different things to different researchers. Concepts such as role accumulation and role conflict are defined and operationalized in different ways in different research projects (often because researchers have to rely on secondary data). When this is combined with the wide range of ways in which morbidity is measured, it is difficult not to agree with the sentiments of Kandrack et al. (1991) that research seems to have reached a conceptual impasse. Kane (1994) concludes that, on the question of why men's and women's health is different, nobody really knows!

Are women sicker than men?

But even though we may not quite know why, it is commonly accepted that women are in worse health than men. For example, although the differences are small, figure 5.6 shows that a consistently higher proportion of women reported a limiting long-standing illness, and re-

Table 5.4   Self-reported general health by age and sex (per cent)

Health category	Males Age			Females Age		
	25-34	35-44	45-54	25-34	35-44	45-54
Very good	46	40	38	41	39	35
Good	42	43	43	47	44	42
Fair	11	14	14	11	14	19
Bad	1	3	5	2	2	4
Very bad	0	1	1	0	1	1

Source: Health Survey for England, 1994 Vol. 1 (1996a). London: HMSO.

Fig. 5.6

Percentage of males and females reporting (a) long-standing illness; (b) limiting long-standing illness; (c) restricted activity in the fourteen days before interview (Great Britain, 1972–1994*)

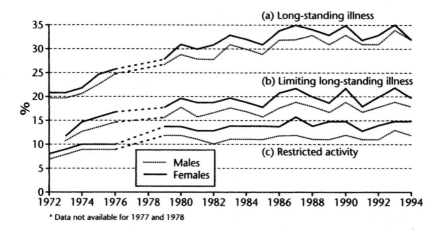

* Data not available for 1977 and 1978

Source: OPCS (1995c), *Living in Britain: Results from the 1994 General Household Survey* (London: HMSO), fig. 3a (p. 44).

stricted activity due to ill health, in the fourteen days before interview, between 1972 and 1994. However, recent national surveys of global self-ratings of health seem to reveal quite small gender differences. For example, the *Health Survey of England* (DoH, 1996a), which was conducted in 1994 (table 5.4), shows that gender differences tend to be in the direction of men being somewhat more likely to report 'very good' health than women, and women being a little more likely to report 'good' health than men (a pattern which also tends to hold for age-groups not shown in table 5.4).

Hospital admission, general practitioner contact, and community surveys tend to reveal higher rates of psychosocial ill health among women. With regard to mental illness, Pilgrim and Rogers (1993) show that, for all diagnoses combined, women's rate of admission to hospitals in England and Wales was 29 per cent above the rate for men in 1986. The female excess in admission rates for affective psychoses was 98 per cent and for neurotic disorders 91 per cent, although rates for schizophrenia, and for alcohol psychoses and alcoholism were 12 and 55 per cent less than for men. Figure 5.7 shows that, from around age 10 to the mid-sixties, women seem much more likely to consult their general practitioners

Fig. 5.7

All diseases and conditions (ICD, chapters I–XVII): Patient consulting rates per 10,000 person years at risk.

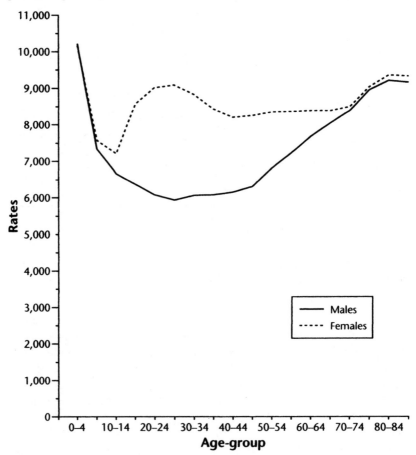

Source: OPCS (1995b), *Morbidity Statistics from General Practice: Fourth National Study 1991–2* (London: HMSO), fig. 2.1 (p. 25).

(GPs) than men. When we look into episodes of ill health diagnosed by their GPs (table 5.5), it is apparent that women suffer far more frequently from mental disorders, specifically from anxiety states and depression, osteoarthritis, migraine, obesity, and iron deficiency anaemia. For a range of other conditions, notably heart attacks and angina pectoris, male rates are somewhat higher than female.

Table 5.5 Gender differences in episodes of ill health seen by GPs: England and Wales 1991–2, prevalence rates per 10,000 at risk (all ages)

Condition	Male	Female
Serious neoplasms (cancers)	77	95
Diabetes	119	102
Obesity	38	124
Iron deficiency anaemia	19	87
Mental disorders	503	944
Anxiety states	135	290
Neurotic depression and depressive disorder	91	246
Migraine	58	169
Acute myocardial infarction (heart attack)	38	20
Angina pectoris	130	98
Asthma	429	422
Chronic bronchitis	54	37
Osteoarthritis	228	398
Rheumatoid arthritis	28	54
Back pain	259	339

Source: OPCS (1995b), *Morbidity Statistics from General Practice: Fourth National Study 1991–2* (London: HMSO). Office for National Statistics, Crown copyright 1997.

While these data do suggest a picture of overall higher female morbidity, we should be cautious about taking this conclusion too far. In a recent consideration of a range of data, Macintyre et al. remark that they were 'struck not by the consistency of a female excess in reported ill-health, but by the lack of the predicted female excess, and by the complexity and subtlety of the pattern of gender differences across different measures of health and across the life course' (1996: 617). The data that we have looked at so far have already highlighted this. For example, reports of the simple presence or absence of a long-standing illness (shown in figure 5.6) were exactly the same for men and women in 1994, while (as noted above) female rates were higher for the related measures of limitations on activities. Macintyre et al. (1996) take this point further in their consideration of a sample of individuals aged 18, 39 and 58 from the West of Scotland Twenty-07 Study alongside a sample aged 18–22, 36–40 and 56–60 from the British Health and Lifestyle Survey on a range of comparable health measures. In both studies, although proportions reporting their health as 'fair' or 'poor' were higher among women, this was only statistically significant for one age-group, that is, those aged 18 in the Twenty-07 Study. For no ages were there significant differences in long-standing illness in either study (reflecting data in figure 5.6). Symptoms of 'malaise' (e.g. nerves, worrying, always feeling tired) were higher for women at all ages in both studies; however, 'physical' symptoms (e.g. colds/flu, stiff/painful joints, trouble with eyes) showed a female excess only at age 39 in one study and at age 56-60 in the other. Looking at younger age-groups, Sweeting (1995) reveals that, prior to entry into adolescence the familiar female excess morbidity is very small or even reversed. Macintyre et al.'s (1996: 621) conclusion that 'female excess is only consistently found across the life span for more psychological manifestations of distress, and is far less apparent, or reversed, for a number of physical symptoms and conditions' certainly suggests that we need to avoid drawing any sweeping conclusions that women are sicker than men.

One point that does seem to emerge from this and other research, however, is a persistent pattern of higher rates for mental, or psychosocial, ill health among women, as well as a higher incidence of reporting of milder physical conditions. If men and women experience different kinds of health problems, then this could help to resolve the paradox of why men tend to die younger, while women seem to be sicker throughout their lives. As Verbrugge contends, 'women's days and years are filled with discomfort and illness restrictions, but contain less threat of life ending from illness'. Therefore, she continues, one sex – women – is indeed sicker in the short run, and the other – men – in the long and ultimate run (1988: 139). The argument, then, is that men's health problems are more serious than those of women. It has also been suggested that, since milder forms of illness allow greater discretion in terms of perceptions of symptoms and health actions (such as visiting the doctor), differential rates by gender may reflect a greater propensity among women to admit to illness and men to deny it (Verbrugge, 1985) as well as a greater inclination for others, such as doctors, to define women as ill. This would suggest that data reporting milder forms of ill health in particular may not reflect 'real' differences in health status, but artefacts of gender-related attitudes and behaviours. Male stoicism, it might be suggested, is complemented by the cultural acceptance of vulnerability and sensitivity to symptoms (linked to the caring role) within women.

At the end of the day, the question of 'whether women's higher morbidity is real' may be unanswerable. As Popay (1992: 101–2) explains, the point that women over-report and men under-report illness assumes 'that there are objectively identifiable categories of illness or symptoms to be expressed and acted upon which are in some sense more real than people's subjective accounts of them'. Who can act as the 'objective' arbiter of experience? Two studies have tried to address this by looking at independent assessments. Both reach the conclusion that women are not over-reporting illness. Davis (1981) looks at chronic joint symptoms associated with osteoarthritis, an area which one would expect to be open to significant influence by socio-cultural factors. The three symptoms that are considered – chronic pain, chronic morning stiffness, and chronic joint swelling – reveal that men and women are more similar than different in their own reporting (although women tend to report more of each, this is not statistically significant). Radiographic evidence, graded independently by two rheumatologists using standard diagnostic criteria, was used to assess whether osteoarthritis was present or not in a way that is blind to gender and independent of the patients' symptom reports. Davis explains that if women are more willing to report symptoms, when we control for disease and treatment category we would expect to see them consistently reporting symptoms at a higher rate. Yet this does not seem to be the case. Within those men and women diagnosed (by radiographic evidence) with osteoarthritis who were under medical treatment, 83.95 per cent of men reported pain compared to 69.64 per cent of women. For those with the disease but not undergoing treatment, the equivalent figures were 21.02 and 15.22 per cent. When she conducted a multivariate analysis, Davis found that, when other variables were held constant, most of the probability of reporting pain was explained by the diagnosis of the presence of osteoarthritis and use of treatment, and that gender was non-significant. She concludes that not only is there no evidence for women's over-reporting, but there is little support for men's under-reporting. Indeed, men may actually be more willing to report since, although women's disease was rated as more severe than men's, at all levels of severity men reported a higher level of pain.

This finds support in Macintyre's study of the common cold which, again, is a good model for those 'minor, acute, episodic conditions which women are hypothesised to be more likely to perceive and report than men' (1993: 16). A total of 1,700 male and female volunteers who were resident in the British Medical Research Council's Common Cold Unit rated the presence/absence of a cold and its severity, as did clinical observers who visited them daily. Macintyre found that, while men and women were both likely to 'over-rate' the severity of their cold compared to the observer, this was true for significantly more men (20 per cent) than women (14 per cent). When a range of other factors, such as age and occupational social class, were controlled for, men were 1.6 times more likely to 'over-rate' than women. Macintyre asks whether what we are seeing here is the possibility that at a given level of symptoms men are more likely to complain than women ('the whingeing male' explanation), or the possibility that doctors are more likely to observe and diagnose symptoms in women (the 'chauvinist interpreter' explanation). Whatever is going on, the one thing that does seem clear is that 'at given levels of clinical signs of a condition, men and women are either equally likely to report related symptoms, or men are likely to report more severe symptoms' (Macintyre, 1993: 19).

Gender, health and social roles

The consensus then is that where women's morbidity is higher than men's (and vice versa) this is a product of the social roles that they occupy. In other words, gender differences in morbidity are 'real' rather than artefactual. The underlying premise is that, if men and women were in the same role positions, there would be little or no difference in their health status. However, this has been a difficult hypothesis to explore since most research has been directed towards identifying differences in health status among women rather than between men and women. Moreover, the explicit or implicit intention has been to establish that, since health variations are closely associated with roles and circumstances, their origins are social rather than biological. The organizing principle of this research has been the concept of multiple roles, chiefly the combination of being a paid worker outside, and an unpaid worker inside, the home. At first glance, the general conclusion of this research – that the more roles that women, and presumably men, have the better their health tends to be – might seem surprising. Researchers' early concerns that combining a paid job with work in the home would generate stress and poor health were soon countered by the argument that multiple roles might enhance health. For example, work outside the home may offer not only financial rewards, but also opportunities for social support and improved self-esteem (Sorensen and Verbrugge, 1987). If this is true, then it is no wonder that women who are full-time 'housewives' tend to be in the worst health of all (Kane, 1994).

Other socio-demographic factors such as age and the number of children in the home have been shown to mediate the relationship between work and health for women. For example, Arber et al. (1985) have found that paid work is most beneficial for women of all ages without children, and for women over 40 with children. In contrast, there is evidence of role strain and poorer health for women under 40 years old with children. Clearly, 'the key question is not whether paid work in general is good for all women, but rather what the conditions are under which specific types of work will be harmful or beneficial for particular women in particular circumstances' (Doyal, 1994a: 67). The unwritten assumption that the benefits of paid work outweigh the costs, flies in the face of considerable evidence that work in 'women's employment ghettos' (such as nursing, office and shop work, and the electronics industry) can be arduous and unhealthy (Baker and Woodrow, 1984; Coleman and Dickinson, 1984). Evidently, the material circumstances of people's lives are very important.

Women's health and socio-economic circumstances

A woman who works a 'double shift' in a paid job and in the home, who has a satisfying career, a good income, her own home, the support of a partner, and time to relax and unwind is in qualitatively different circumstances to a woman caring for children on her own in rented accommodation, in a poorly paid job, and far away from the support of family and friends. Although sociologically intuitive, the association between socio-economic circumstances and health for women has been the source of considerable debate, much of which pivots on the question of how women's socio-economic status can be measured. Social class based on a woman's own occupation, assuming that she currently has one, is problematic for a number of reasons. First and foremost, since the Registrar General's classification is based on a male occupational structure (see chapter 4) it fails to differentiate adequately between the jobs that women do. Pugh and Moser point out that

> *the lesser importance given to women's jobs as compared to men's, the assumption that breadwinners are male, that women are depend- ent on men, and that women's role is primarily that of homemaker, all contribute to the many problems associated with using own occupa- tion to classify women. (1990: 94)*

In fact about two-thirds of women in paid work end up coded as social class III non-manual (e.g. secretaries, shop assistants, clerical workers) and to a lesser extent as class II (e.g. teachers, nurses). Because of this concentration it is hardly surprising that we find steeper class gradients in health for men than for women. These conceptual problems have surely contributed to the paucity of research on women's health and social class. But, as Pugh and Moser (1990: 94) state, 'hard though it may be to consider women's mortality in relation to their social class, if the difficulties had pertained to men's mortality researchers would by now undoubtedly have found a way!' This point is taken up by Payne, who likens research in this area to a detective job which, she says, 'speaks volumes for the predominantly male focus of research on inequalities in health' (1991: 118).

One solution has been to turn from women's 'own class' to that of the male 'head of household' (where there is one). This so-called 'conventional approach' has been strongly advocated by Goldthorpe (1983) and contested by many feminists for the reasons that it defines women in terms of men; ignores women's contribution to the home and their experiences outside the home; and, in more practical terms, because it makes it difficult to compare different groups of women (e.g. those who are married and those who are not) since you are not comparing like with like. Despite these considerable difficulties, the conventional approach is adopted quite widely, often because it seems to have a greater ability to discriminate among women. Aware of the problems of using women's occupation as a measure of class and unhappy with the reliance on male occupation, some researchers prefer to use household asset-based measures of socio-economic status, such as access to amenities, often in conjunction with occupational class. For example, Pugh and Moser (1990) find significant differences when they cross-classify a range of variables for groups of women with particularly low and high SMRs. As we can see in table 5.6, the standardized mortality ratio (SMR) for women in non-manual occupations, whose husbands are also in a non-manual occupation, who own their own homes, and have a car is 70. This compares to a SMR of 113 for women and their husbands who are both in manual jobs, rent their home and have no car. However, we do need to be wary of relying on asset-based measures alone. In actuality women may have little access to assets like cars and videos, and the lack of amenities, which appears at first glance to be communal, may have a different significance for men and women. For example, lack of hot water means something different to the man who uses it to wash and shave in the morning, and the woman who is responsible throughout the day for childcare, the washing of clothes and cleaning the house (Payne, 1991).

This all serves to remind us that knowing that a person *occupies* a particular role or social position tells us very little about their *experience* of it. Social roles are often taken to 'stand in' for experience, which means that we lose the sense in which gender is made and constructed in interaction (Connell, 1995). Researchers in the area of health are beginning to stress the need to take account of (1) the variable *quality* of a role (for example, the terms and conditions of work), and (2) the differential *meanings* that a role might have for men and women. Simon (1995), for example, hypothesizes that work and family roles will have

Table 5.6 Measuring mortality differences

	Low mortality	High mortality	% of expected deaths covered by these two groups
Single women			
Characteristics	Non-manual Car(s)	Manual No car	44
SMR (95 CI[a])	69 (47–98)	178 (131–236)	
Observed (expected) deaths	30 (43.5)	48 (26.9)	
Married women *(a) With an occupation*			
Characteristics	Non-manual Husband non-manual Owner-occupier Car(s)	Manual Husband manual Rented housing No car	31
SMR (95% CI[a])	70 (56–86)	113 (91–138)	
Observed (expected) deaths	90 (129.3)	93 (82.0)	
(b) Housewives			
Characteristics	Husband non-manual Owner-occupier Car(s)	Husband manual Rented housing No car	44
SMR (95% CI[a])	65 (53–79)	161 (135–188)	
Observed (expected) deaths	104 (159.1)	147 (91.5)	

[a] 95% confidence interval for SMR.

Source: H. Pugh and K. Moser (1990), Measuring women's mortality differences. In H. Roberts (ed.), *Women's Health Counts* (London: Routledge), 93–112. Original source: HMSO. Office for National Statistics, Crown copyright 1997.

different meanings for men and women and that this will help to explain gender differences in psychosocial distress. Using a combination of large-scale survey data and in-depth interviews, she looked at the meaning that being a good wife/mother or husband/father held for women and men, and their respective views on whether home and work roles fitted together well or were in conflict with each other. Men tended to express a feeling of interdependence between work and family roles, while for women there was a sense of independent or competing obligations. Interestingly, there were differences between those men and women who *both* spoke of conflicting roles: for women conflict was non-specific and pervasive, while for men it was rather specific and delimited (e.g. not being able to attend their children's after-school activities). Popay et al. (1993) also highlight the fact that it is not 'just' the social positions that men and women occupy that explain their health status. Looking at a range of health measures from the British Health and Lifestyle Survey, they found that the relationship between variables such as employment status, income, marital status and health is very complex, but broadly similar for men and women. Where women's health is worse this is generally because they are situated in worse social circumstances. However, the authors state that since women report higher rates of illness even *within* the positions that *both* men and women occupy, 'it would appear that the experience of a particular social position must be different for men and women in ways which are not captured by the crude measures of class, household incomes, marital status and work status' that were used in their study (Popay et al., 1993: 31).

The problem is that most data sets lack the type of information that would permit researchers to explore the meanings that men and women attach to social roles and statuses. Moreover, many make a priori assumptions about which roles and which statuses are relevant to men and which to women. Rarely, for example, is it possible to look at the significance of paid work (attending to terms, conditions and the experience of work) for the health of both men and women within one analysis, let alone to explore the importance of domestic work in the home and family life (Bartley et al., 1992; Hunt and Annandale, 1993). To date, gendered assumptions have been effectively built into the heart of research on social roles and health, so much so that there is a quest for gender difference to the neglect of any similarities across gender.

Conceptualizing women, men and gender

The conceptualization of gender through social roles can lead us away from the social relations of gender towards the scripts of a male/female dichotomy built on biological difference. Ultimately, research on gender and health, or any other area of experience for that matter, gets trapped within the ideological context of what it is trying to analyse as gender difference is sought from the outset (Carrigan et al., 1987).

The positivistic methodology that attaches to work in the area of gender inequalities tends to reinforce this. The reporting of similarities (or null results) is prohibited by the scientific community. As Kandrack et al. report:

> *negative (read: not statistically significant) findings tend not to be reported, or if they are, they are not able to counter all of the pre-existing research which shows differences between women and men. Sex differences are magnified, the duality of these 'differences' is reinforced, and our attention is turned away from the common humanity which men and women share. (1991: 588)*

This point is exemplified in a comment made by Macintyre et al. who report that, when they presented their paper highlighting the fact that female excess morbidity is not universal at the 1994 European Society for Medical Sociology conference in Vienna, 'several listeners afterwards told us that they had not found the "expected" gender differences in self-reported health in their surveys, but had never drawn attention to this because they assumed it was due to a peculiarity in their sample or social setting, or to some other "anomalous" circumstance' (1996: 623).

Using *data categories* such as male/female, married/not married, in work/out of work is economical and practical, but imposes 'boundaries that do not reflect unclear distinctions' (Fuchs Epstein, 1988: 337). Since any methodology has its theoretical corollary, the problem is more than one of research technique. As we discussed in chapters 2 and 3, we are now thoroughly accustomed to thinking in categorical terms. Postmodern theorists have argued that this is the legacy of Enlightenment thinking, which views the world as structured around binary oppositions such as male/female and blinds us to the heterogeneity and plurality of experience that characterizes contemporary social life. As we saw in the discussion of postmodern feminism, in a modernist world view, men and women are viewed in opposition. This opposition attracts another – that of health and disease. Under patriarchal privilege, women are viewed as unhealthy and men as healthy. Even though we know that there are a great many unhealthy men and healthy women, when we work from a position of opposition we are led away from this towards an explanation of sickness that attaches itself irrevocably to gender as a dichotomy. As we have seen here, there may indeed be a lot in women's experience that makes them sick, and in men's that makes them well, but in a search for the causes of illness in gendered positions we neglect the similarities in health (and disease) between men and women and the differences within men as a group and within women as a group. There would, then, seem to be a need to recognize at once that certain social positions do still carry significant privilege, but also to be more open than research has been to date to experiences that cut across gender. This should not necessitate a wholesale rejection of existing approaches to research in the field, but rather a willingness to think of gender as more than a social or biological dichotomy (Clarke, 1983).

Masculinity, femininity and health

Adding a more in-depth qualitative dimension to existing survey approaches (in the manner advocated by Simon (1995)) is one fruitful way to deconstruct gender aggregates. Another is to use alternative ways of conceptualizing gender. Annandale and Hunt (1990) have used a measure which does not assume that sex and gender are coincidental to explore the possibility that observed male/female differences in health status might mask an association of a 'feminine' gender role orientation with relatively poor health and a 'masculine' gender role orientation with relatively good health, in *both men and women*. The Bem Sex Role Inventory (BSRI) (Bem, 1974) is a psychological measure which asks individuals to endorse a series of adjectives or characteristics which have been judged to be stereotypical of either men (masculine) or women (feminine), in terms of how far they feel they describe them personally. From these endorsements, it is possible to derive two separate 'masculinity' and 'femininity' scores for each individual. A multivariate analysis sought to consider the relative importance of 'sex' (male/female) and high/low 'masculinity' and high/low 'femininity' for the health of a sample of individuals aged 35 living in the west of Scotland. The results are interesting in so far as they show that, for self-reported measures of health, when the measures of 'masculinity' and 'femininity' were included in the analysis, the significance of 'sex' (male/female) disappeared. Moreover, high 'masculinity' scores were associated with better health than low scores for both men and women. Conversely, high 'femininity' scores were associated with poorer health than low scores, again for both men and women. The association of high 'masculinity' (defined *inter alia* as being independent, assertive, self-sufficient and ambitious) with better health for men and women is interpreted by the researchers as reflecting the high social value and related health benefits that accrue from a more 'masculine' gender-role orientation. Of course, this does not suggest that men and women who have a more 'masculine' gender-role orientation are necessarily more healthy by some objective standard, but rather that they define themselves as such. It could, of course, be the case that the more socially valued 'masculine' self-concept of these individuals itself incorporates a more positive sense of self-esteem which in turn prompts a more positive self-evaluation of health. This may be particularly important for the reporting of mental health and milder symptomatology.

The finding that *better* health is associated with 'masculinity' for both men and women deserves some discussion in light of the association that has been made between masculinity and health risk-taking. The BSRI intentionally aims to capture 'positively valued' dimensions of masculinity. So it includes 'assertive' rather than 'aggressive', 'ambitious' rather than 'arrogant'. As we have seen, masculinity as it is conceived by sociologists of masculinity has a plural character and it is *hegemonic* or *traditional* masculinity that has been most closely linked with poor health. The BSRI clearly does not permit us to explore this. However, Helgeson (1990, 1995) is able to do so by using a conceptually similar approach, the Extended Personal Attributes Questionnaire, which contains scales of 'positive masculinity' (e.g. self-confident, stands up under pressure) and 'negative masculinity' (e.g. hostile, looks out for self). In her study of coronary heart disease in the USA, Helgeson (1990: 758) finds that negative, or 'traditional masculinity' seems a prescription for 'the most dangerous components of coronary-prone behaviour'. For example, higher scores on 'negative masculinity' were associated with a longer period between the awareness of symptoms and the onset of the heart attack. Moreover, high 'negative masculinity' was also the best predictor, for men *and* women, of heart-attack severity.

Measures of gender-role orientation are useful because they permit us to look at the relationship between gender and health without relying on a male/female dichotomy. However, other problems persist. First, the scripted quality of the wider role framework is still evident. As with male and female so too with 'masculinity' and 'femininity' we are left with the question of the meaning that gender roles have for individuals, how they are enacted and how they influence health on a routine basis. Second, in common with the wider literature on gender inequalities in health, research within this framework seems to draw a fairly hard line between the 'social' and the 'biological'.

The social and the biological

The conceptualization of biology as fixed and social roles as malleable was fundamental to feminism in the 1970s (which was precisely the time when research on gender inequalities in health began to emerge), and remains very influential to this day. For example, prefacing her discussion of premature death among males, Stillion (1995) makes a distinction between sex and gender, where sex refers to genetically determined and biologically maintained physical differences between the sexes and gender is a cultural artefact. Helgeson writes in similar terms about gender-role orientation in her analysis of variables, such as Type A behaviour and social support, that might mediate the relationship between masculinity and heart attack. In her analysis she says, 'it was important to control for subject's sex in order to show that gender role characteristics were related to mediating variables after considering the effects of biological sex' (1990: 764).

The feminist theories that we looked at in chapter 3 tend to reinforce this division between the 'biological' and the 'social'. As we saw, liberal feminism challenges the patriarchal assumption that women's health problems stem from a biological weakness (usually linked to reproduction), by showing that health status is really bound up with particular social roles and social circumstances. By way of contrast, the radical feminist legacy induces us to strip away the social to reveal women's natural superiority (and, relatedly, men's natural inferiority) in biological terms, that is, to show that under social conditions of equal privilege women's natural health advantage would shine through. The legacies of these traditions sit somewhat uneasily side by side in research on gender inequalities in health today (see discussion in Annandale, 1998). The dominant position, that gender differences in morbidity and mortality are social, not biological, in form has already been presented in some detail. We end this chapter by looking at the more limited body of research which seeks to consider whether, in the last instance, women really do enjoy a biological advantage.

First of all, support for a female biological advantage has been found in the stable pattern of excess male mortality during infancy referred to earlier in this chapter. Male vulnerability in infancy has been linked to the fact that, although boys are typically of greater birth weight, they tend to be less mature (i.e. they are born at lower gestational ages). Moreover, even at equal gestational ages their lungs tend to be less developed, which may predispose them to respiratory distress (Waldron, 1983). Second, support has also been found in the historical relationship between the emergence of women's mortality advantage and changes in socio-economic conditions and social relations of gender (also discussed earlier). Could it be that 'the improvement in the status of women may have enabled them to benefit from their innate advantage, which had previously been nullified by the social disadvantages from which they suffered' and from the actions of men. (Vallin, 1993: 191) Similarly, Hart (1989: 121) questions whether women's greater longevity 'expresses a natural superiority revealed only in conditions of adequate female nutrition'. This is a point which Payne (1991) takes up in her discussion of social class and health. She suggests that if relatively poor social conditions depress women's natural physiological superiority and relatively good social conditions allow it to emerge, then we would expect sex ratios in illness to be wider in lower social class groups compared to higher ones. That is, she suggests that even though (at least by some measures) women's health is poorer than men's, it is less poor among those at the top end of the class structure than at the bottom. The fact that women's health improves more than that of men as we go up the class structure, then, could be because their health benefits more when resources are more plentiful. However, in broader terms, Hart (1989) cautions against too quick an acceptance of the argument that improved living conditions reveal a female biological advantage. For example, historically it has not been the case for all countries that a rise in living standards has occurred alongside a widening of the sex mortality differential to women's advantage.

Nonetheless, if conditions of relative gender equality permit women's biological health advantage to emerge, might this be complemented by a biological disadvantage for men? Verbrugge (1988) speculates that this could very well be the case. Her study of the health of men and women in Detroit reaches the now familiar conclusion that gender differences in morbidity are the product of the different social risks to which men and women are exposed. When she controls for these risks (that is, makes them statistically similar) she finds that the health differences narrow considerably. This leads her to conclude that if men and women were more alike in experiences then their health status would be much more similar than we see it today. For the current discussion, the most interesting and unexpected finding of her analysis was the emergence of what she calls a 'flip' to male excess morbidity for a number of health measures. Even though these 'flips' were statistically non-significant, they lead Verbrugge to suggest that *if* women's and men's circumstances were more similar we might see the emergence of a male disadvantage. Since a range of social factors has been accounted for in her model, by a process of elimination Verbrugge concludes that this disadvantage is biological. She writes that 'modern life masks something enduring, and unwelcome, about men's health. If women's lives were indeed more healthful ... their morbidity would decline. And we might then begin to see some comparatively higher morbidity rates among men. ... Men's fundamental health disadvantage is present, but hidden, in health survey data' (1988: 160). On the back of this finding she calls for more research on 'women's biological robustness'.

While this research is intriguing, the question of whether men or women have an advantage in morbidity or mortality cannot be answered in terms of *either* social *or* biological factors, even though feminists' endeavours to contest patriarchal definitions of the female body in terms of weakness and vulnerability can predispose us to frame debates about gender differences in health in these terms. Sociology, as we saw in chapter 2, has been criticized for taking flight from 'biology' as it sought to establish its own social model of health. But, as sociologists of the body and others remind us, there is not just the biological body on the one hand and the social on the other; they exist in a dialectical relationship. Hood-Williams relates that 'writers within the sex/gender problematic have acted as if the body possessed a peculiar ability to generate the true meaning of sex. But sex does not simply stand like a base beneath the super-structure of gender because the existence of sex itself is an object of the discourse of gender' (1996: 8). That is, the very ideas that we have about 'sexed bodies' are socially constructed. While we would not claim that biology is irrelevant to the late twentieth century, social practices – the worlds of work, leisure, personal relationships etc. – which have significance for health, construct the body but not in a way that is singular, fixed or inextricably 'sex-linked'. In these terms the question of whether either men or women have a stronger biological base for health would seem to have little meaning.

Conclusion

The aim of this chapter has been to demonstrate that research on gender inequalities in health defies the easy summaries that often appear in the literature. To be sure, on average women do still live longer than men, and, by a number of measures, their health is worse than that of men. However, this is by no means always the case. In the first place, there are instances in history, as well as in the third world today, where women's *mortality* rates are higher than those of men. For example, in the early part of the chapter we saw that before the late nineteenth century it was generally men who had the advantage. Moreover, there are suggestions that the extent of women's longevity advantage in both the USA and Great Britain may be declining as we approach the end of the current century. Second, the extent to which men fare better than women in terms of health seems to vary significantly depending on what aspect of health is being measured. The chapter has also sought to highlight the contested nature of the explanations that have been put forward to explain 'why women are sicker than men'. Although important findings continue to emerge from this body of research, it seems to have reached a conceptual impasse. In particular, there is a need to get beneath the socially scripted nature of the role framework that has dominated research in this field for so long to explore the actual experience of social roles and the meanings that they carry for men and women. Finally, there would also seem to be a need to remove the theoretical blinkers that have led us to make certain gendered assumptions about *which* social roles and *which* experiences are relevant for men's and which for women's health in advance of our empirical research, as well as to be more open to the possibility that, in some areas of health and health behaviour, there may be important similarities as well as differences between men and women.

6

'Race', Ethnicity and Health Status

The discussions in chapters 4 and 5 have highlighted the dynamic character of debates on social class and gender inequalities in health. Economic and social restructuring has induced many sociologists to reflect critically on whether social class as traditionally conceived within the discipline is eroding to be replaced by new forms of stratification. Similarly, it has been suggested that many of the customary tools of feminism, which stress the dichotomous character of gender, may now be inadequate for an understanding of the highly complex nature of contemporary health inequalities. As we have seen, the ability of sociologists of health and illness to engage with these debates in empirical terms has been restricted by the lack of sophisticated conceptual and methodological tools to match new theoretical developments in the discipline. Nowhere is this more apparent than in the field of 'race' and health, where a lack of sensitivity to the meaning of categories such as 'race', ethnicity and the concept of racism, alongside the propensity of sociologists of health and illness to keep their heads 'buried in the sand of white health concerns' (Ahmad, 1993: 23), has all but inhibited the development of an effective body of research in the field.

However, there is reason for optimism. The broader sociology of 'race' and ethnicity has, in recent years, gained new momentum following the challenges posed by the rise of new racisms and nationalisms in Europe, and the new intellectual terrains of cultural studies and postmodernism. As Rattansi and Westwood argue, a forceful question mark now hangs over the ability of existing social science narratives to adequately explicate 'events in an era characterised by culturally heterogeneous, rapidly changing social configurations, structured by new forms of globalisation and the all but complete collapse of communist blocs' (1994: 2). The current period then is arguably one of dynamism not only for gender and class but also for social science research on 'race'. Moreover, sociologists of health and illness are now beginning, albeit belatedly, to engage with these debates and to highlight the crucial importance that they have for the relationship between racism and the experience of health and illness. In this chapter we begin by exploring the racialization of the body and the ascendance of racial categories. Integral to this will be an examination of the particular definitions and classifications that are used and their implications for research in the field. With these points in mind, we then turn to consider the health-related research that has engaged with survey statistics as well as qualitative studies. Here it will be important to emphasize that, since all classifications of 'race' and ethnicity are themselves political products, research findings cannot be taken easily at face value. Indeed, any classification inevitably requires 'the invention of fixed, discrete and mutually exclusive ethnic categories' (Smaje, 1995: 24) which are bound to hide the diversity that many have argued characterizes the experience of modern society as we approach the turn of the century. As in the previous discussions of social class and gender inequalities in health, we are destined to come up against the vexed question of how to signify axes of inequality without creating falsely universal categories which distort the complex reality of individual experience.

Racial landscapes

Rattansi and Westwood contend that 'the spectre that haunts the societies "of the west" is no longer communism but, both within and outside their frontiers, a series of racisms and ethno-nationalisms' (1994: 1). With the increased mobility of 'capital, commodities and human beings across national boundaries' which accompanies the globalization of capital, the nation state is increasingly open to 'international (and industrial) intrusions of various kinds (Miles, 1994: 215). The internationalization of capital vitalizes the racist imagination and highlights a persistent contradiction in the simultaneous dissolution and reproduction of national boundaries. For example, the plan to abolish internal border controls and to implement a common European immigration policy has led some to refer to the development of a 'Fortress Europe'. In common with others, Mason explains that, 'given that in some countries of the Union there are large populations of non-citizens, it is not difficult to see how appearing to be different, and particularly having a darker skin, could be taken as prima-facie evidence of non-citizen status – or even of illegal entry' (1995: 122). In particular, concerns have been expressed that the Mediterranean Sea will become Europe's Rio Grande and 'no more than a minor obstacle for the millions of Africans' who might seek to enter the European Community illegally (discussed in Miles, 1994: 199).

As 'the world becomes more mixed and transnational, and borders are redefined, the hatreds and psychic fears become more virulent' (Eisenstein, 1994: 6). Boundaries of the physical body and the body politic have attained panic proportions as they are marked with the emergence of a new kind of colonial domination in which the 'totalising grand history of nations has given way to a transcendent account of chance intersections of germs and bodies'; of 'borders gone out of control' (Patton, 1992: 218, 224). The map of the postcolonial world has been 'redrawn as a map of epidemiological strike rates' in which a 'new Africa-with-no-borders functions as a giant agar plate, etched by the "natural history" of the AIDS epidemic' (Patton, 1992: 218). Perhaps nothing so neatly conveys the image of the West being 'overrun' by 'others' as AIDS, 'the quintessential invader from the Third World' (Sontag, 1988: 62).

Ironically, then, globalization means that national boundaries are becoming more pervious, but also susceptible to being reworked in ways that signal new racialized identities. This dual move towards openness and closure is mirrored at the level of individual identity and marks a vigorous debate within the social sciences over whether 'ethnic categorization' is increasingly being imposed on individuals, or whether such identities are ever more open to personal investment and choice. This is an issue that we will take up again later in the chapter in the section on cultural fragmentation. For the moment it is important to set the current concerns about racialization and globalization in historical context. For as serious as the events that have been referred to certainly are, what we are in fact witnessing is the contemporary legacy of a long history of the bodily imprint of racism which had its genesis in early modern society.

Bodily impresses: the birth of modern racism

Although the idea of 'race' first appeared in the English language in the early seventeenth century, it was not until the late eighteenth century that it began to be used in Europe and North America to name and explain phenotypical (or 'observable') differences between human beings. By the mid-nineteenth century the idea that there were a number of distinct 'races', each with a 'biologically determined capacity for cultural development' (Miles, 1994: 28), was firmly etched into the collective consciousness. Colonial expansion of the West and the recognition of 'difference' that this entailed, coupled with the rise of science during the same period, provided a firm foundation upon which to build a 'race science' which 'characterised human diversity as a division between fixed and separate races, rooted in biological difference' (Mason, 1995: 6–7). It was also during this period that medicine saw a spectacular shift from the speculatively-based practice of the eighteenth century to the wondrous new scientific medicine of the nineteenth century, with its ability to pinpoint pathology in the interior of the body by the use of ever more detailed methods of investigation such as the stethoscope and the thermometer. This was the period of great Western optimism during which the scientific revolution transformed human understanding of the body and how it worked

The 'impetus to biology' with its sense of fixed, natural and distinguishable bodies was as keenly felt in the field of 'race' as it was in gender. As Laqueur writes,

> the importance in the eighteenth century of new theories of knowledge generally, and with respect to the body particularly, is a commonplace. Scientific race, for example – the notion that either by demonstrating the separate creation of various races (polygenesis) or by simply documenting difference, biology could account for differential status in the face of 'natural equality' – developed at the same time and in response to the same sorts of pressures as scientific sex. (1990: 155)

Like gender, then, the new 'facts' of racial difference were premised on a particular vision of the body read through the oracles of the new science. As with the positing of 'sex differences' and sexism, racism not only draws upon imputed biological characteristics, it is also fundamental to a 'discourse of marginalisation which is integral to a process of domination' (Miles, 1994: 101). Thus, no matter the historical time or place in which it is articulated, differential exclusion is the deep structure of racism (Goldberg, 1990). However, it needs to be made clear that, despite this core element, racism in fact takes various forms, so much so that current theorists in the field of 'race' and ethnicity stress that it does not have a single logic. Indeed, it is far more appropriate to speak not of racism, but of racisms which assume different forms in different places in history. The way in which this takes place can be illustrated by looking at how *medicine* has been enmeshed with the racialization of the body.

As Eisenstein (1994: 13) writes, 'the body is a visual site which makes it crucial for marking differences; and it is a felt site: one feels one's body. This makes the body unique in its utter intimacy as a location of politics. Torture, slavery, and death camps all bespeak the body as a powerful site of struggle.' The Cartesian 'mechanical philosophy' of the seventeenth century was in effect the *precondition* of racist discourses. The new and docile body, which presented itself as the objective and observable natural basis of racial difference, lent itself readily to the classificatory impulse of the new science. Consonant with Cartesian mind–body dualism, the subjectless body was available to be 'analysed, categorised, classified, and ordered with the cold gaze of scientific distance' (Goldberg, 1990: 302). Medicine was, and continues to be, a prime vehicle for the imposition of the classificatory gaze upon the body. In light of the attention that we are giving in this part of the chapter to racism's historical roots, the US medical debate on slavery is illuminating since it throws the role of physicians in the racialization of the body into particular relief.

Medicine, science and racialization: historical contexts

Krieger's (1987) analysis takes us back to the period between the early nineteenth century and the year 1865 when Abraham Lincoln outlawed slavery for ever, to a time when the United States of America was the greatest slave-carrier of the world. Physicians, of course, were never disinterested commentators on the 'slavery debate', in the Southern states: for example, many hired their services to plantation-owners or inspected slaves for auction at the block. As the abolitionist movement gained momentum in the 1830s, physicians were compelled to enter the fray in ostensibly less partisan terms through the guise of science and the classificatory gaze referred to earlier. The ideology of innate racial difference found clear expression in medical studies of the day. Krieger discusses, for example, a text by one Dr Pendleton of Sparta, Georgia, who argued in 1849 that the fact that twice as many 'blacks' than 'whites' died of tuberculosis was because they were not suited to the cold even of Georgia's warm climate. Here he neglected to make any reference to a life of slavery in which men and women were 'forced to live in crowded, poorly heated, leaky cabins without adequate clothing or blankets and were overworked to boot' (1987: 263). Faced with the problem of why it was the 'coarse muscular Negress' rather than the 'delicate white female' who had more miscarriages, Dr Pendleton neglected the social causes of overwork, favouring the conclusion that the problem must originate from 'the unnatural tendency of the African female to destroy her offspring' (quoted in Krieger, 1987: 264). In 1850 Dr Samuel Cartwright, an ardent defender of slavery, authored an infamous article: 'Diseases and Physical Peculiarities of the Negro Race', which proclaimed the natural status of the 'Negro' as slave. As Krieger outlines, Cartwright claimed in the article to have discovered the 'ultimate physical basis of black inferiority: their inability to consume as much oxygen as whites, a consequence of certain "peculiarities" of the black nervous system' (1987: 268). This oxygen insufficiency, he went on to claim, predisposed slaves to lethargy, the only antidote to which was forced labour.

By the 1850s a new voice entered the debate to contest its reductionist stance: that of the new 'black' physicians, one of the most outspoken of whom was Dr John Rock, who countered existing medical science and its biological rationales for slavery with a social model which stressed 'the white man's desire for cheap labour' (Krieger, 1987: 271). This position was taken up by Dr James McCune Smith, who argued that traits which appeared to be innate were, in fact, a product of the social environment; hence the diseases of slaves were the effect of racism, rather than being caused by 'race'. The ongoing debate between the reductionist medical science of many 'white' physicians of the time and their nascent 'black' detractors, took a new turn in the aftermath of the Civil War as slaves were turned from property into people. But, as history testifies, racism did not die with the abolition of slavery. Indeed it has lived on in the midst of the 'discoveries' of science and medicine of the twentieth century, enlivening the popular imagination. For example, new impetus was found in social Darwinism and the belief that the 'negro problem' would resolve itself through the process of natural selection. Such views fed into the eugenics movement of the early twentieth century.

Arguably the most horrifying manifestation of 'scientific racism' in the twentieth century lies in the aiding and abetting of the racial policies of the Nazi state by the psychiatrists and anthropologists who provided the 'scientific' basis for assumptions of racial and genetic inferiority (Muller-Hill, 1988), as well as in the involvement of physicians and nurses in the classification of mental patients and those of 'inferior races' for sterilization, forced labour and death. Going back to the nineteenth century, Gilman (1991: 38) writes that 'there is no space more highly impacted with the sense of difference about the body of the Jew than the public space of "medicine"'. In an intriguing analysis he explores the way in which the pathologies that were attributed to the Jewish foot marked men out as unfit for military service and, therefore, for full citizenship. By this process 'the foot became the hallmark of difference, of the Jewish body being separate from the body politic' (1991: 44). This medical vision spread to the wider body, as the sign of the 'limping Jew' was read into a number of diagnostic categories of nineteenth-century neurology. Intermittent claudication (manifest in chronic pain and tension in the lower leg and resulting in stiffness and inability to move the leg) was seen as the cause of an inhibited gait and ultimately as a sign of the inherent constitutional weakness of Jewish people.

The examples of US slavery and Nazi genocide have highlighted the way in which the body is marked by racial discourse through the complicity of medical science. Skin colour, head shape, body size, smell, hair texture and other phenotypical features were the markers of the gaze of medical science which professed to be cold and objective (Goldberg, 1990). We know today that there is no genetic basis for racial classifications: indeed most genes occur identically in all human beings. Indeed, 85 per cent of all identified variation in human genetics can, in fact, be accounted for in terms of individual differences, while only 7 per cent is due to differences between 'races' (Bradby, 1995). As Hill (cited in Smaje, 1995: 13) explains,

> *the amount of variation within a racial group is considerably greater than the average genetic difference between races. Clearly the genes responsible for the morphological features that allow us to classify individuals into broad racial groupings are atypical and extremely unrepresentative of the true degree of interracial genetic difference.*

But even today, at a time when the scientific gaze has penetrated even further into the hidden recesses of the body, indeed at a time when some have argued that the 'natural body' is obsolete (see chapter 2), the 'lived body' is still racially inflected. Hence,

> *the striving for classificatory systems, articulated with the modern projects of constructing disciplined, managed, healthy nations continues to involve the weeding out of contaminating 'Others' who appear to disturb the social order, who fall foul either of cultural/ethnic boundaries or seem to transgress conceptions of the 'normal' as defined by . . . biology, medicine, psychology and psychiatry, sociology . . . and their associated disciplinary and regulatory institutions such as hospitals, prisons, schools and factories. (Rattansi, 1994: 25)*

'Scientific racism' has in many respects now been superseded by a new 'cultural racism' which, it should be noted, exerts no less power and is no less repressive because it has swapped the language of biology for a cultural inflection and a preoccupation with national belonging. As already noted, racism is plural in form and highly adaptive to the changing contours of modern society. Although they are fluid and unstable, racial identities are typically constructed by an attempt to naturalize the difference between 'belongingness and otherness' (Hall, 1992: 255). Gilroy contends that, although it does not draw explicitly on biological differences or 'race', in the wake of postcolonial and economic crises, as well as strident social change in Europe, Britain's populist crisis racism of the late 1980s and into the 1990s is linked to a preoccupation with drawing lines of inclusion and exclusion. By this process, he writes,

> Britons are invited to put on their tin hats and climb back down into their World War II air raid shelters. There they can be comforted by the rustic glow of the homogeneous national culture that has been steadily diluted by black settlement in the post war years. The unsullied culture can be mystically reconstructed, particularly amidst national adversity when distinctly British qualities supposedly emerge with the greatest force and clarity. (Gilroy, 1990: 266)

These concerns stick steadfastly in the collective consciousness, reflecting immigration policies and influencing the reception that migrants to Britain, and other countries, receive. It is to British immigration that we now turn.

Migration, minority ethnic status and population classifications

The contemporary British population is one forged from successive migrations stemming from earliest recorded history and resulting from impulses as diverse as conquest, refugeedom, and labour shortages (Mason, 1995). In fact, there have been people of non-European origin in the British Isles since at least the sixteenth century. Eighteenth-century estimates put the African population in England at 0.2 per cent, consisting mostly of male servants from the West Indies who entered the country as slaves. The migrant population began to decline in the early nineteenth century with the abolition of slavery and the reduction in naval recruitment after the Napoleonic Wars (Coleman and Salt, 1996). This means that, effectively, before the twentieth century Britain had a very small 'black' population, usually estimated to be just a few thousand people. While it is very important not to neglect well-

Fig. 6.1

Trend in total ethnic minority population 1966–7 to 1989–91, Great Britain

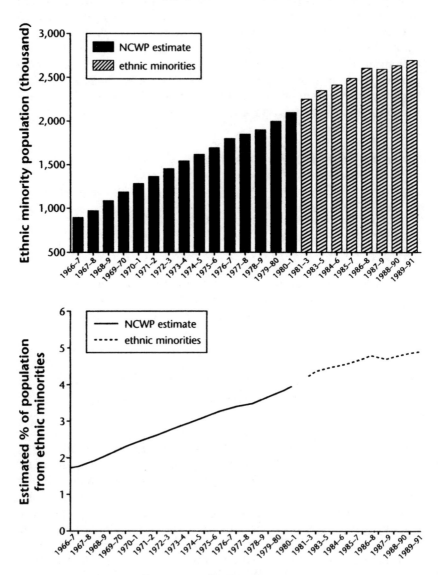

Source: D. Coleman and J. Salt (1996), The ethnic group question in the 1991 Census: a new landmark in British social statistics. In D. Coleman and J. Salt (eds), *Ethnicity in the 1991 Census*, Vol. 1 (London: HMSO), fig. 4.1 (p. 83).

established patterns of Irish migration, and the immigration to Britain of those fleeing persecution, such as many Jewish people between the two world wars, the period of large-scale British immigration is usually identified with the post-1945 labour shortage. In its early period of office after the war, the Labour government estimated that approximately one million workers were needed, principally in agriculture, coal mining and textile production.

As many have pointed out, immigration to Britain is now taken to be virtually synonymous with migrants of 'New Commonwealth' origin i.e. the British Caribbean and the Indian subcontinent (South Asia). Peak first-generation immigration from the Caribbean occurred in the early 1960s, and from India and Pakistan in the late 1960s and early 1970s, tailing off thereafter until the early 1980s when there was an increase in the number of migrants from Bangladesh, Hong Kong and Africa. The NHS, which is today the largest employer of the minority ethnic population, was a major site for the recruitment of nurses and doctors from the ex-colonies: in 1964 almost one in five nurse trainees were from the Commonwealth, and there was a flow of 1,600 doctors from India and Pakistan in the 1970s, many of whom were shunted into lower-grade posts and lower-status specialties (Johnson, 1993; Ward, 1993) (aspects of the contemporary situation are discussed in chapter 8).

In actual fact, it is notoriously difficult to begin to estimate the minority ethnic group population of Britain. As we will see below, the 1991 Census was the first ever to ask individuals to identify their own ethnic status, which means that for trend data we are often forced to rely upon country of birth. This draws attention to the tunnelled focus on migration and the sense of Britain being 'swamped by people with a different culture' that has marked British immigration policy since the late 1960s (Mason, 1995). In technical terms alone, reliance upon country of birth as an indicator of ethnic group membership presents a significant problem since it has been difficult to identify the growing number of second-, and now third-, generation descendants of early migrants. Figure 6.1 depicts the trend in the total minority ethnic population in Britain between 1966–7 and 1989–91. The data for the period between 1966–7 and 1980–1 refer to the New Commonwealth population (NCWP) and are derived from country of birth information, while those from 1981–3 onwards are drawn from the annual Labour Force Surveys[1] (see Owen, 1996: 82).

The two parts of the figures depict a trend of almost continuous growth in the minority ethnic population, expressed both in terms of numbers and as an estimated percentage of the total population of Britain. Clearly the umbrella term ethnic minority population is highly problematic, hiding considerable diversity. Table 6.1 presents data disaggregated under Labour Force Survey categories of 'ethnic status'. Plainly, those classified as 'white' constituted the largest ethnic group with little percentage change between 1981 and 1989–91. Although those who identified themselves as Indian comprised the largest minority ethnic group at both time periods, the fastest population growth was displayed by Bangladeshis and people assigned to the 'Other' category, whose numbers more than doubled. Significant increases are also evident for the smaller minority 'ethnic groups', such as people of Chinese and African origin.

If we want to make *comparisons over time*, we are at the moment more or less reliant upon the Labour Force Survey. However, although it is not without its own problems of under-enumeration, the snapshot 1991 Census is generally thought to be more reliable. For this reason, table 6.2, based on census figures, is included here to show the most up-to-date designated ethnic group composition of the population.

The language of racial categories

The racial subject positions of the 1991 Census categories (and those of other classificatory schema) are fundamentally ideological fabrications. From this perspective our choice of language is far from neutral. Indeed, it is the medium through which we actively construct 'race' or ethnicity and it is hardly surprising, therefore, that it has occasioned considerable debate within the social sciences. The 'ethnic question' in the 1991 Census, for example, was the outcome of almost twenty years of deliberation, initially on its desirability and more recently on the form that it should take (Coleman and Salt, 1996). Therefore, before we look at recent health-related research, it is important to give a little more thought to the vocabulary that shapes the research agenda.

Since it attributes negativity to those designated 'non-white' and, in any case, fails to recognize that 'white' itself is a very heterogeneous category, a 'white/non-white' classification is clearly inappropriate to any understanding of racialized difference. Similarly, the term 'black' is problematic since it collapses people from many different origins into one group. Bearing these points in mind Cole (1993) argues that the most appropriate aggregate term to use is 'Asian, Black and other minority ethnic groups'.[2] This helps us to keep in mind the fact that ethnicity is equally a characteristic of 'white' people, who can be designated a 'majority ethnic group' where this is appropriate (clearly, in some countries such as South Africa, and in some locales within countries, 'whites' are *not* the majority). In such an approach, minority and

Table 6.1 Estimated population of Great Britain by ethnic group, 1981 and 1989–1991

Ethnic group	Estimated population			
	1981 (000s)	1989–91 (000s)	Change (000s)	Change (%)
White	51,000	51,808	808	2
All ethnic minority groups	2,092	2,677	585	28
West Indian	528	455	−73	−14
African	80	150	70	88
Indian	727	792	65	9
Pakistani	284	485	201	71
Bangladeshi	52	127	75	144
Chinese	92	137	45	49
Arab	53	67	14	26
Mixed	217	309	92	42
Other	60	154	94	157
Not stated	608	495	−113	−19
All ethnic groups	53,700	54,980	1,280	2

Source: D. Coleman and J. Salt (1996), The ethnic group question in the 1991 Census: a new landmark in British social statistics. In D. Coleman and J. Salt (eds), *Ethnicity in the 1991 Census*, Vol. 1 (London: HMSO), 1–32. Office for National Statistics, Crown copyright 1997.

Table 6.2 Resident population by ethnic group, Great Britain, 1991

Ethnic group	Number (000s)	Proportion of total population (%)
White	51,874	94.5
Black – Caribbean	500	0.9
Black – African	212	0.4
Black – other	178	0.3
Indian	840	1.5
Pakistani	477	0.9
Bangladeshi	163	0.3
Chinese	157	0.3
Other – Asian	198	0.4
Other – non-Asian	290	0.5

Source: C. Smaje (1995), *Health, 'Race' and Ethnicity* (London: King's Fund Institute), table 1.1 (p. 28), based on 1991 Census Local Base Statistics. Office for National Statistics, Crown copyright 1997.

majority are used simply in numerical terms. However, as this chapter betrays, it is difficult to abide by a particular vocabulary, not the least because if we wish draw upon existing research data we are forced to employ their own lexicon.

The categories that were eventually adopted for the census (as seen in table 6.2) are clearly a mixture of racial, national and ethnic classifications. Thus, 'black and white are pseudo-racial categories, referring, rather inaccurately to perceived skin colours, but Indian, Pakistani and Bangladeshi are all legal nationalities although they may also be regarded as ethnic categories. Chinese is a nationality, but also an ethnic description as well as a linguistic group, and so on' (Skellington, 1996: 26). In effect, the seven precoded categories (designated White, Black – Caribbean, Black – African, Indian, Pakistani, Bangladeshi and Chinese) and the 'Black – other' and 'Other – other' designations, which asked respondents to write in their 'ethnic or racial group', yielded thirty-five classifications, although these are usually collapsed into the ten shown in table 6.2 for most analyses. One of the most important things to bear in mind in this regard is the omission of a separate code for 'mixed' minority ethnic origins (diverse though this may be). Instead, people who identify themselves in this way are included in one of the residual 'Other' categories, some of which are shown in table 6.2. As Owen (1996: 89) writes, 'this is problematical, because it confounds the characteristics of people of mixed parentage with those of people from less numerous ethnic groups and those of people who have a perception of their ethnicity that did not match the seven major categories'. It is important to observe that 'Other – other' (not shown in table 6.2) contained 290,000 people (or 0.5 per cent of the total population). Owen (1996) reports that fully 52.8 per cent (or 153,000 people) within this aggregate are of mixed 'black and white', 'Asian and white', or other 'mixed' parentage.

Since the admixture of the census categories is replicated in various ways in other schema, this means that there is little that we can do to avoid racialized classifications if we wish to engage with survey statistics. At the strong end objections can be raised that to fix racialized identities under labels, no matter how nuanced they may be, will inevitably do violence to the sheer complexity of the ethnic identities that are forged by individuals. However, many social epidemiologists, sociologists of health and illness, and policy-makers are prepared to live with the recognized injury to the representation of diversity that occurs in the process of classification, since they feel that a classificatory schema is the best way to signify the stark realities of oppression as revealed in the social and material inequalities that are frequently attached to minority ethnic status. This has been the view of the Commission for Racial Equality (CRE) and some health researchers (see Smaje, 1995, 1996), and it is also part of the official rationale for the 1991 Census question. However, as we read the data we must always be aware of their socially constructed nature. Sheldon and Parker (1992: 62–3) remind us, 'there is nothing so powerful as a large and available data set for encouraging the suspension of disbelief'. In the process of analysis the issue of what a variable like 'ethnic status' actually means can get lost, as ethnic categories are reified and health outcomes frozen into static entities, with little attention given to the processes of power and racism that are involved in their construction, both analytically in research, and in terms of individual experience (Stubbs, 1993).

Minority ethnic groups and aspects of health status

As well as the general problems that accompany the use of any classificatory schema, research on ethnic status and health has some additional limitations of its own: the data that exist are often rather outdated and attend to specific health conditions rather than to more general problems of morbidity. Moreover, the specific health problems that are chosen for study tend to be those which predominate in minority ethnic groups (for example, sickle cell disease and thalassaemia). When this is coupled with a focus on 'problematic' rather than 'good' health, and a failure to make comparisons with the majority 'white' population, it is easy to see why Ahmad (1993) and others accuse health researchers of racist bias.

There is a singular dearth of good-quality large-scale survey data which contain both a measure of general health status and allow us to look at minority ethnic groups alongside the majority 'white' ethnicity in Britain. For this reason, the combination of the 'ethnic question' and the measure of long-term illness in the 1991 Census is an unprecedented source of data.[3] Figure 6.2 provides information on limiting long-term illness (that is, a long-standing illness that limits daily activities or work) for the ten designated 'ethnic groups' separately by gender. Because at the present time the age profile of minority ethnic groups is typically younger than that of the majority 'white' population, data have been age-standardized to the 'European population', the reason being that, since limiting long-term illness tends to increase with age, if we do not do this we risk an underestimation of minority ethnic group ill health.

Fig. 6.2

Household residents (all ages) with limiting long-term illness: directly
standardized* rates by ethnic group and sex, 1991, Great Britain

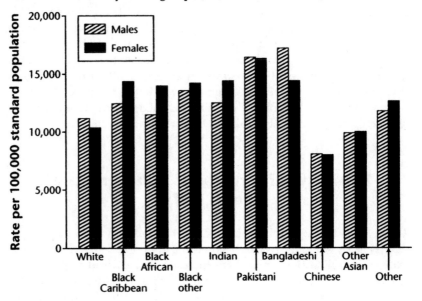

* Standard = European standard population

Source: J. Charlton et al. (1994), Long-term illness: results from the 1991
Census. *Population Trends*, 75, 18–25: fig. 5 (p. 22).

The data show that standardized rates of limiting long-term illness
are the lowest among men and women who identified themselves as
Chinese. Other Asian and white men and women, and Black African
men also fare relatively well. Rates are significantly higher for Pakistani
men and women and for Bangladeshi men. The extent of gender differentials within minority ethnic groups varies, although very broadly
speaking the data seem to point to a female disadvantage. However, an
apparent counter to this is the notably higher rate of self-defined illness
for men in the Bangladeshi group.

The new question on long-standing illness is as far as the census can
take us. However, a recent English survey of just over 3,500 men and
women aged between 16 and 74, which has been conducted under the
auspices of the Health Education Authority (HEA, 1994), covers aspects
of self-assessed health. Table 6.3 shows perceived health status for the
four designated minority ethnic groups in the study and the UK population (with the latter taken from the British Health and Lifestyle sur-

Table 6.3 Perceived health status (base: all adults)

Health status	All adults				Standardized				
	African-Caribbean %	Indian %	Pakis-tani %	Bangla-deshi %	African-Caribbean %	Indian %	Pakis-tani %	Bangla-deshi %	UK population %
Very good	43	45	37	35	39	45	38	34	47
Fairly good	43	39	43	38	44	39	43	36	45
Fairly poor	8	11	14	18	9	11	14	20	6
Very poor	6	6	6	9	8	5	6	10	2

Source: HEA (1994), *Health and Lifestyles: Black and Minority Ethnic Groups in England* (London: HEA), table 19 (p. 42). © Health Education Authority 1994. Reproduced by permission.

vey). The data are presented in two forms: first, each group in the survey sample is weighted to the 1991 Census characteristics of that group, and second the data are standardized to the age-sex profile of the UK population. Overall, the table shows that minority ethnic groups defined their health in less positive terms than the UK-wide population. If we consider those who described their health as 'fairly poor' or 'very poor', Bangladeshi people stand out as especially disadvantaged.

A recent community-based survey undertaken by Fenton et al. (1995) in Bristol also found an excess of poorer health among minority ethnic groups. Thus, as table 6.4 shows, 47.7 per cent of the combined minority ethnic population described their health as 'fair' or 'poor' which compares to only 29 per cent in the Health and Lifestyle Survey. In this Bristol sample it is self-assessments of health among the Pakistani population which stand out as revealing especially poor health. Fenton et al. alert us particularly to the wide variation *within* minority ethnic groups, notably in relation to gender. For example, at one extreme just 33.3 per cent of *Bangladeshi men* said that their health was 'fair/poor', while at the other 61.1 per cent of *Pakistani women* described their health in this way. Interestingly, while Bangladeshi men would appear to report the best general health of all (though only marginally better than Black Caribbean men), we have seen that they also have the highest rate of limiting long-standing illness as assessed by the 1991 Census (see figure 6.2). Although it is important that we do not make too much of this particular comparison given the different nature of the samples, it does serve to remind us of a point that was made in chapter 5; namely, that patterns of advantage and disadvantage are far from consistent across samples and across measures of health. Moreover, we need to be

Table 6.4   Demographic variables and self-assessed health

Group		n =	% of respondents in whom self-assessed health described as	
			Excellent/good	Fair/poor
Total survey group		512	52.3	47.7
Sex	Male	150	56.0	44.0
	Female	362	50.8	49.2
Age-group	Under 35	177	62.1	37.9
	35–64	267	44.9	55.2
	65 and over	47	55.3	44.7
Ethnic group				
'Black Caribbean'	Male	53	66.0	34.0
	Female	184	54.9	45.1
	Total	237	57.4	42.6
'Indian'	Male	27	63.0	37.0
	Female	67	56.7	43.3
	Total	94	58.5	41.5
'Pakistani'	Male	55	40.0	60.0
	Female	90	38.9	61.1
	Total	145	39.3	60.7
'Bangladeshi'	Male	15	66.7	33.3
	Female	21	47.6	52.3
	Total	36	55.6	44.4

Source: S. Fenton et al. (1995), 'Self-assessed health, economic status and ethnic origin'. *New Community*, 21, No. 1, table 2 (p. 62). Reproduced by kind permission of Carfax Publishing Ltd, PO Box 25, Abingdon, Oxon OX14 3UE.

sensitive to the fact that self-assessments of health status are strongly influenced by cultural beliefs and practices and, for this reason, to be wary of assuming that the definitions of 'poor' health that people give are equivalent. This point, which has already been stressed in the context of gender and class inequalities in health, may be especially acute when we make comparisons between minority ethnic groups, as well as when comparisons are made with the majority ethnic population.

There is a particular need to heed these cautionary points when we consider health service use. Research has tended to reach the conclusion that minority ethnic groups consult their general practitioners more frequently than the majority white population. For example, the average annual consultation rate is estimated to be 3.6 based on the British Health and Lifestyle Survey, while the Health Education Authority study gives the rate for African-Caribbeans as 4.2, for Indians 5, for Pakistanis 7.1 and for Bangladeshis 7.9 (HEA, 1994). The more detailed Fourth National Morbidity Survey of General Practice in England and Wales (OPCS, 1995b) shows that there was no difference in the proportion of each ethnic group (defined in the study as White, Black-Caribbean, Indian, Pakistani/Bangladeshi, and Other) who consulted their general practitioner in 1991–2. However, the proportion of minority ethnic respondents as a whole who consulted for 'symptoms, signs and ill-defined conditions' was found to be remarkably higher than for whites. It is difficult to know why this might be the case. The findings are as likely to reflect problems of doctor–patient interaction and racist assumptions on the part of physicians as they are to reveal 'over-consulting' for ill-defined complaints. Patterns for the more specifically defined conditions in the Morbidity Survey are complex, varying as they do by specific ethnic group and also by gender. The survey highlights in particular: that there are significantly high consultation rates for blood disorders among minority ethnic women compared to white women; that men and women from Pakistan/Bangladesh, Indian men and Afro-Caribbean women consult more than white people for endocrine and nutritional disorders; that Indian and Pakistani/Bangladeshi men consult more than white men for respiratory conditions; and that Pakistani/Bangladeshi men and women and Indian women consult more than white people for musculoskeletal problems (see OPCS, 1995b). The little research that there is on the utilization of acute services seems to conclude that, when morbidity, the availability of care, and socio-demographic factors are taken into account, there is little difference in the utilization of hospital services (Smaje, 1995). It is worth noting that more detailed evaluations will soon be possible with the collection of data on ethnic status for NHS in- and out-patients which became mandatory in April of 1995.

Although there are insufficient national data to enable us to compare the self-perceived *general health status* of ethnic groups, more attention has been given to *specific diseases*, even though much of the research is dated, reliant upon country-of-birth data, and focuses on death rather than ill health. The major source for contemporary discussions is a report edited by Britton (1990) which reviews geographic patterns of mortality in England and Wales in the mid-1980s drawing upon a range of (then) Office of Population and Census data sets. These data, in fact, place a number of limitations on analysts, most notably the classifica-

Table 6.5 Mortality at ages 20–69 from all causes by sex and country of birth, 1979–1983

Country of birth	Males (SMR)	Females (SMR)
Scotland	118	118
All Ireland	128	120
Indian subcontinent	106	105
Caribbean Commonwealth	79	105
African Commonwealth	109	114
Mediterranean Commonwealth	87	78
Australia	85	83
Canada	96	85
New Zealand	84	96
France	80	75
Germany (East and West)	87	93
Italy	65	78
Poland	99	97
Spain and Portugal	70	56
USSR	96	95
Republic of South Africa	97	94
USA	89	85
England and Wales	100	100

Source: R. Balarajan and L. Bulusu (1990), Mortality among immigrants in England and Wales. In M. Britton, *Mortality and Geography: A Review in the Mid-1980s* (London: OPCS), Series DS, No. 9: Table 4. Office for National Statistics, Crown copyright 1997.

tion of people born in Pakistan, India and Bangladesh under the rubric of the 'Indian subcontinent'. Table 6.5 gives standardized mortality ratios at ages 20–69 by country of birth for men and women separately. As can be seen, with the exception of Caribbean Commonwealth men, persons from the Indian subcontinent, the Caribbean Commonwealth (women) and the African Commonwealth all experienced excess mortality when compared to the host population of England and Wales. However, it is interesting to note that ratios are also higher for men and women who migrated to England and Wales from Scotland and Ireland. Moreover, from trend data not presented here, Britton (1989) shows a significant decline in mortality levels for African and Caribbean groups between 1970–72 and 1979–83, alongside little movement among the Scots and the Irish.

If we turn to cause-specific mortality, again by country of birth, it is

Table 6.6 Mortality (SMR) from selected diseases by place of birth, age 20+, England and Wales, 1979–1983

Place of birth	Sex	Circulatory disease	Coronary heart disease	Cerebro-vascular disease	All cancers	Respiratory disease	Diabetes
'Indian subcontinent'	M	133	136	153	59	88	297
	F	136	146	125	68	104	103
'Caribbean Commonwealth'	M	77	45	176	65	61	292
	F	141	76	210	71	101	424
'African Commonwealth'	M	127	113	163	71	105	219
	F	136	97	139	83	106	161
'England and Wales'		100	100	100	100	100	100

Source: Adapted from C. Smaje (1995), *Health, 'Race' and Ethnicity* (London: King's Fund Institute), table 3.1 (p. 52), based on R. Balarajan and L. Bulusu (1990), Mortality among immigrants in England and Wales 1979–83. In M. Britton (ed.), *Mortality and Geography: A Review in the Mid-1980s* (London: OPCS), series DS, No. 9. Office for National Statistics, Crown copyright 1997.

evident that despite some differences between groups, the major causes of death are similar to those in the indigenous population, namely, circulatory diseases, respiratory diseases and cancers (Hillier, 1991b). While this highlights the importance of not seeking out medically 'exotic' conditions to the neglect of more 'typical' causes of death, we also need to bear in mind that many immigrants often have higher death rates within these conditions. Table 6.6 reveals a complex pattern of mortality differentials, some of which can be highlighted. All three of the minority ethnic aggregates experienced a high burden of death from diabetes, and from cerebro-vascular diseases (strokes). A similar pattern is observed for circulatory disease, with the exception of a notably lower death rate among men from the 'Caribbean Commonwealth' compared to the rate for England and Wales and for other minority ethnic groups. For coronary heart disease a similar picture applied to both men *and* women from the Caribbean Commonwealth, and women from the African Commonwealth. Most notable are the significantly lower rates of death from all cancers combined for all minority ethnic groups when compared to the rate for England and Wales.

Of course, the presentation of these data, which are themselves subject to numerous qualifications, tells us nothing at all about the *reasons* for the differentials that we have observed. This is a point that has been highlighted for health inequalities in a broader context. Yet however high the political stakes might be over the relative merits of 'material' versus 'cultural' explanations in the context of class, gender and health, they are multiplied many times over when we add 'race' and ethnicity into the equation.

'Race', ethnicity, social class and health

As we saw in chapter 4, social class is in the conceptual spotlight at the current time as protagonists line up on either side of a divide which questions whether class, as traditionally conceived, any longer has relevance to late modern society. On the one hand, it has been argued that economic inequalities are more sharply drawn now than ever before and are central to class divisions, while on the other they are viewed as simply one of a number of dimensions of power and inequality that place people within the social order. Also contained within this debate is the issue of whether class can now be viewed in terms of *collective identity*, or whether it is more appropriate to think in terms of a range of inequalities which distinguish relatively *autonomous individuals* along a number of axes which are unlikely to align to form a strong collective economic or social identity. Debates within the field of 'race' and ethnicity are both paralleled and cross-cut by these concerns. In order to explore this we begin by looking at the debates which accept the continued significance of economic inequalities and racialized identities, but raise concerns about their relative primacy in structuring the experience of health and illness. Later in the chapter we consider research which focuses on ethnicity, including the implications of a more radical postmodern approach.

'Race' or class, or 'race' and class

This subheading is borrowed from the title of an article by Navarro (1989) in which he dissents from any reduction of class to 'race', working specifically from the political standpoint that to think from racial divisions effectively weakens class solidarities that traverse the 'black–white' divide. Others also contest reductionism, but from the vantage-point of not subsuming 'race' under class. For example, Ahmad (1993: 31) argues that there is a 'danger that a radical field of "race"/health research will encourage material reductionism where all phenomena are reduced to material disadvantage or class oppression'. But clearly, putting other differences between these authors aside, they agree that any form of reductionism (be it class to 'race', or 'race' to class) is unacceptable, and that ultimately we must find a way of looking at the influence of 'race' *and* class upon health status, a point of view which is shared by many other researchers (e.g. Smaje, 1996).

Before we move on to look at some of the rather limited empirical research that has actually tried to disentangle the interaction of 'race' and class in the production of health inequalities, it is important to make some reference to the meanings that are given to 'race' and social class in these particular debates. First, in this context 'race' often supplants terms like 'ethnic group' to signal the central role that racialization plays in the construction of inequalities. Thus, theoretically at least (since there is unfortunately little direct research on this), attention is directed to the ways in which racism drives individuals into social circumstances (such as poor housing, unemployment), which generate personal stressors that are inimical to good health. Second, social class is often left undefined and implicit, something which is undoubtedly assisted by the multiple meanings and the rhetorical qualities of the very concept of class at the present time. Although, of course, this is not peculiar to studies of 'race' and ethnicity, researchers often seem to slip from initial discussions of social class into references to 'material' or

Table 6.7 Infant mortality by mother's place of birth, England and Wales, 1982–1985

Mother's place of birth	Infant mortality		Perinatal mortality		Neonatal mortality		Post-neonatal mortality	
	Rate	N[a]	Rate	N[b]	Rate	N[a]	Rate	N[a]
UK	9.7	21,515	10.1	22,503	5.6	12,438	4.1	9,077
Eire	10.1	269	10.4	279	5.9	158	4.1	111
India	10.1	459	12.5	576	6.1	278	3.9	181
Bangladesh	9.3	145	14.3	225	6.5	101	2.8	44
Pakistan	16.6	892	18.8	1,022	10.2	549	6.4	343
Caribbean	12.9	274	13.4	288	8.4	179	4.5	95
East Africa	9.3	255	12.8	351	6.3	172	3.0	83
West Africa	11.0	128	12.7	149	8.0	93	3.0	35

[a] Number of deaths

[b] Number of deaths and stillbirths

Source: C. Smaje (1995), Health, 'Race' and Ethnicity (London: King's Fund Institute), table 2.2 (p. 39), based on R. Balarajan and V. Raleigh (1990), Variations in perinatal, neonatal and post-neonatal and infant mortality by mother's country of birth. In M. Britton (ed.), Mortality and Geography: A Review in the Mid-1980s (London: OPCS), series DS, No. 9. Office for National Statistics, Crown copyright 1997.

'socio-economic differences', making it difficult to know how social class is being theorized, if at all. This means that class seems ultimately to be reduced to indicators of material advantage/disadvantage. Ethnicity, which is loosely taken to refer to cultural distinctiveness, then tends to be lined up as a contrasting explanation replicating the 'material versus culture' agenda of the Black Report on inequalities in health. Consequently, although it can be argued that this well-worn debate has outlived its usefulness, it still continues to animate research in the field (Smaje, 1996).

At the heart of the debate on the relative significance of ethnicity and socio-economic factors for health inequalities is the recognition that, although ethnicity tends to be strongly associated with material disadvantage, the correlation is not perfect and consequently, more often than not, the health issues under investigation cannot be fully explained by reference to socio-economic measures alone. That is, there is an independent effect of culture/ethnicity upon health. One of the most often-cited illustrations of this comes from the study of infant mortality rates. Table 6.7 shows various measures of infant mortality by mother's place of birth (note that 'UK-born' mothers includes all ethnic groups) between 1982 and 1985. If we look first of all at infant mortality rates, which comprise deaths of children under 1 year of age per 1,000 live births, we see that a number of migrant groups had elevated rates when compared to the 'UK population', something which was most marked for Pakistani-born mothers. Clearly, however, the rates for children of mothers born in Bangladesh and East Africa were lower (Smaje, 1995: 38). This result has occasioned much discussion since, by conventional measures of socio-economic status, people of Bangladeshi origin are often seen to be among the most deprived. Furthermore, as Andrews and Jewson (1993) explore, a straightforward materialist explanation would seem to be contradicted by more finely grained data. Thus, they report that, notwithstanding the similarities in the occupational class profiles of Pakistani and Bangladeshi migrants, there were marked differences between them in terms of post-neonatal (deaths between twenty-eight days and one year) and perinatal (deaths in the first week of life) mortality rates (as seen in table 6.7).

If we wish to look at indicators other than infant mortality we come up against significant barriers given the marked lack of a literature which addresses the three-way interaction of 'race', class and health. Put in oversimplified terms: in Britain the constraints stem from the lack of national data which attend to 'race'/ethnic status, whereas in the US authors have bemoaned the lack of any regularized way of collecting social class data. Thus, from the British vantage-point, there is the risk of neglecting facets of deprivation that are not bound up with class, while from the point of view of the US there is an inherent danger of essentializing 'racial difference' in the absence of any significant attention to the part that social class plays in the construction of health differentials. Of course, an essentialist stance is not the prerogative of the US; as Sheldon and Parker (1992) have explained, 'race' is sometimes even taken as a *proxy* for deprivation, as is the case in some area measures of deprivation (such as Jarman scores, made on the basis of capitation payments to general practitioners). The research on infant mortality that we have considered here might be seen to come close to this since the connection with socio-economic status is merely *imputed* from other 'known' research, rather than demonstrated through analyses which link the actual circumstances of the women concerned to the fate of their children.

In the absence of large-scale data that are sensitive to detailed measures of socio-economic status and to ethnicity, locality-based studies (which it must be said are also scarce) provide some insights. We can return here to the Bristol study by Fenton et al. (1995) which was referred to earlier in this chapter. As we have seen, this study revealed excess morbidity (as measured by self-assessed health) among minority ethnic groups when compared to the population of the British Health and Lifestyle Survey, but alerted us also to differences *across* ethnic groupings, particularly in regard to the relatively poor health of Pakistanis. As a vital extension to this analysis the researchers wished to explore the relationship with socio-economic disadvantage. In the first instance they examined the various socio-economic variables from the sample population alongside the 1991 Census data for Bristol, concluding that, even though there was a clear pattern of disadvantage in the sample (mirroring the minority ethnic population of the city), this needed to be qualified since, although Pakistanis and Black Caribbeans showed relative disadvantage, this was not the case for Indians. In the next stage of the analysis, they considered whether the link between minority ethnic status and health would persist if the effects of socio-economic status, age and gender were statistically controlled for (using standardization). As we can see in table 6.8, since the differences between designated groups do not significantly change after standardization, those which remain are unaccounted for by the control variables. (Note that the socio-economic variables in this analysis were restricted to whether there was an 'earner' in the household, and whether respondents could afford to keep the house warm in winter.) Presumably, then, although socio-economic status plays an important role, 'ethnic differences' are also important.

Table 6.8 Self-assessed health and ethnic group

Standardized for	% respondents reporting fair/poor health				
	Black Caribbean	Indian	Pakistani	Bangladeshi	Total
Nothing	43.5	41.8	60.6	42.9	48.2
Gender	42.2	41.9	60.8	45.8	48.0
Gender and age	41.0	38.6	62.6	48.0	47.5
Gender, age and earners	41.7	28.6	61.0	51.1	45.6
Gender, age, earners and keeping warm	42.0	35.9	57.9	45.9	45.9
$n =$	207	91	142	35	475

Source: S. Fenton et al. (1995), 'Self-assessed health, economic status and ethnic origin'. *New Community*, 21, No. 1, 55–68: table 7 (p. 65). Reproduced by kind permission of Carfax Publishing Ltd, PO Box 25, Abingdon, Oxon OX14 3UE.

Although this specific research begins to resolve some of the difficulties that can arise when measures that were developed for use on the majority white male population are used, it is nonetheless worth highlighting problems that can occur more widely in research of this kind. The well-known difficulties of the Registrar General's measure of occupational social class are, of course, magnified when we consider minority ethnic groups. To take 'South Asian' people as an illustration, many who would be classified to higher occupational classes because they are self-employed live in social environments that are akin to those of lower class groups. As we saw in chapter 4, many social scientists argue that the aggregation of individuals into classes and the 'search for difference' across these groups is artificial, hiding the possibility that there may be as much variance in health *within* groups as there is *across* them. This may be compounded for the minority ethnic population given that, even within a common occupation, they tend to be found in lower grades, with less job security and lower wages and salaries (Andrews and Jewson, 1993). These points suggest that conventional measures may, in fact, obscure the extent of deprivation within minority ethnic groups. Readily available non-occupation-based measures such as housing tenure may also lack sensitivity. Thus, although the proportion of home-owners is higher in most 'South Asian' groups than among whites, there is evidence that the quality of accommodation tends to be poorer (Smaje, 1995). Of course, the wider dilemmas of using traditional occupational and other measures are redoubled for *women* from minority ethnic groups, since it is often (though certainly not always) the case that markers which rely on male occupation and household aggregate measures fail to capture women's experience, given the more marked gender inequalities among some minority ethnic communities (see chapter 5 for a wider discussion of this issue).

Clearly, research has a very long way to go before we can gain a full picture of the exact nature of inequalities in health. At the moment we are perhaps best advised to conclude with Grimsley and Bhat (1988: 201) that minority ethnic groups 'endure working-class health inequality and then some'. However, there is undoubtedly a need to be acutely aware that not all individuals from minority ethnic groups are disadvantaged in every instance of health, and that much still needs to be done to demonstrate the precise *mechanisms* that link socio-economic status and health (Smaje, 1996). Racism has been unduly neglected in this regard. In the next section we look at this issue through the lens of research on culture/ethnicity and health.

Racism, ethnicity and health inequalities

Racism is chameleon-like in its nature: sometimes overt (as in racist violence); sometimes more guileful as it is expressed through a variety of coded signifiers which 'produce a racist effect while denying that this effect is the result of racism' (Solomos and Back, 1994: 156). The current social attention to cultural or ethnic 'difference' has been deemed part of this 'new' more covert racism.

The intersection of racism and attributions of cultural difference is clearly seen in the context of mental health, where higher rates of illness among particular minority ethnic groups seem to be almost taken for granted. Mental illness is, of course, a complex phenomenon which manifests itself in various forms. However, two particular statistics have been picked out for attention in the literature. The first of these is higher rates of diagnosed schizophrenia among Afro-Caribbean males. For example, one interview-based study of referrals to mental health services in Nottingham by Harrison et al. (1988) gives an incidence that is 12 to 13 per cent higher than for the general population of the city. The second, somewhat lesser, focus of attention is high rates of suicide and parasuicide among female 'South Asian' migrants to Britain. Balarajan and Raleigh (cited in Smaje, 1995: 72), for instance, found that suicide among 'South Asian' women aged 20–49 was 21 per cent higher than for the general female population in 1979–83, while for those aged 15–24 there was a threefold difference. Debates on Afro-Caribbean men and schizophrenia have centred on the degree to which these differences can be attributed to cultural variations in the presentation of symptoms; to the material stresses of racism; and to the propensity of indigenous white people (including mental-health workers) to label them as mad without a cause (Pilgrim and Rogers, 1993). Racialization is made more apparent by the fact that Afro-Caribbeans are far more likely to reach the mental health system via the police, the courts, and prisons, and to experience more harsh and invasive forms of treatment (such as electro-convulsive therapy) than others. It is also revealed in the analytic attention to *threats* to the white community, rather than the *distress* of those who experience mental health problems. Indeed, there is a strong 'predisposition on the part of white people in Britain to interpret black people's behaviour as signs of insanity and danger'. Thus it can be argued that the debate on 'race' and madness is central to the inner workings of the new racism with its intent to banish and exclude undesirable 'Others' (Pilgrim and Rogers, 1993: 51). A feeling of unbelonging was, for example, central to the narrative accounts of schizophrenia among individuals from a range of minority ethnic backgrounds in Westwood's (1994) interview-based study. It was also apparent in Donovan's research among 'Asian' women in London who highlighted the pervasive effects of racism on their mental well-being. As one woman explained,

> *It affects your mind. If you feel depressed that you are not treated as other people are or they look down on you, you will feel mentally ill won't you? It will depress you that you are not treated well racially, it will affect your health in some way. It will cause you depression, and that depression will cause the illness. (Donovan, 1988: 205)*

In these contexts, as Westwood (1994: 262) explains, 'racism becomes the modality through which mental illness is represented, and this is something which is reinforced by psychiatric discourses and practices'. Coercive psychiatry then becomes part of a 'postcolonial, Europeanised alternative to repatriation' as minority ethnic groups with mental illnesses are excluded from the community (Pilgrim and Rogers, 1993: 61).

Clearly, then, since racism has many guises there is little merit in trying to treat it as a separate factor that can be parcelled out in analysis, whether this is done through an attention to material or to cultural determinants of health, or to both. Rather, racism should be viewed as 'integral to whatever analysis that is developed' and the question posed not *whether* it operates but when, where and how (Andrews and Jewson, 1993: 149).

Historically, attempts to explain health differences of various kinds by reference to cultural difference have been strongly disparaged as racist in form, given that minority ethnic group cultures have more often than not been negatively stereotyped in terms of difference from the 'white' norm. By this process health-related research has itself been identified as racist. Examples of this abound in the literature, one of the most notorious of which is the case of 'Asian rickets'. Rickets, which is caused by vitamin D deficiency, is known to be a disease of poverty. During the 1940s it was tackled among the 'white' population of Britain through the fortification of margarine; however, when a high prevalence was observed among 'Asian' school children in the 1970s, it was 'explained in terms of un-British eating and living habits' and its solution sought in a change towards a 'British' diet and lifestyle. Thus rickets, a disease of poverty, is racialized through a cultural inscription among 'Asians' (Ahmad, 1993: 21). There are many other illustrations of how cultural 'difference from us' is manifest in health care. We have already touched upon mental health in these terms, but one of the most striking examples comes from Bowler's (1993) ethnographic study of midwives' crude racial stereotypes of patients of 'South Asian' descent. In contrast to their attitude to their 'white' British patients, midwives approached their 'Asian' patients as a rigid homogeneous group who were 'all the same', and negatively typified their behaviours and characteristics, seeing them as non-compliant, tending to 'make a fuss about nothing', and lacking a requisite maternal instinct.

Health education, medicine and the social sciences can, therefore, be criticized for an 'intellectual apartheid' in their conceptualization of minority ethnic groups as carriers of problematic cultures and 'exotic' illnesses. Ahmad forcefully points out that when researchers employ simple, rigid and essentialist notions of culture they pursue a politics of victim blaming,

> *which constructs minority communities as dangerous to their own health. To save them, it is necessary to save them from their own cultures which shackle their minds, their beliefs and their behaviour; their problems are located in their difference; their salvation is in being more like 'us'. A view of culture as a source of nurturing and strength, as providing alternatives to oppressive state systems or mobilising family and state resources to fight racism and disadvantage ... as providing essential tools for resisting oppression, is nowhere to be seen in such constructs. (Ahmad,1996: 196)*

All too often the research that we have before us uses a concept of culture emptied of any racialized content as ethnicity is used as a 'variable' to 'explain' patterns of disease (Sheldon and Parker, 1992). Commodified, frozen in time and space and linked to health through its difference from an often undisclosed 'white' standard, the world of culture and medicine in relation to minority ethnic groups has been the world of 'lifeless, limp, cellophane-wrapped and neatly tagged cultures, rather than one of living and lived in cultures with all their vitality, complexity, complementarities and contradictions, cultures that are empowering, changing, challenging and flexible – cultures that are real' (Ahmad, 1996: 199).

An article chosen at random from the new journal *Ethnicity and Health* (first issue March 1996) by Gregory Lip et al. (1996) on heart disease prevention amongst Afro-Caribbean, 'Asian' and 'white' women betrays this approach. From their study the authors conclude that currently identified risk factors for heart disease, such as exercise, smoking and diet, are distributed in such a way that 'Asian' families are least likely to take regular exercise, less aware of cholesterol or of dietary content (fibre, sugar, salt), but the least likely to smoke cigarettes (this finding on smoking is replicated in the wider Health Education Study (HEA, 1994: 79)). The interesting point for the current discussion is the targeting of 'Asian' women for health education, alongside the lack of any similar attention to 'white' women and their relatively high levels of smoking. 'White' ethnicity, then, becomes little more than a foil. In much the same way that patriarchal privilege is not discernible to men, so too 'white' privilege is invisible to both 'white' men *and* women, as 'whiteness' is 'unmarked and unnamed' as only 'Others' are seen to be the carriers of 'culture'. Whiteness, therefore, is a 'space defined only by reference to those named cultures that it has flung to its perimeters' (Frankenberg, 1993: 231). In this context Frankenberg makes an incisive point about research on women's experience of work that pertains equally well to health; namely, that any consideration of Afro-Caribbean women will 'probably address race and culture; a study of white women . . . probably will not' (1993: 18). The pervasive tendency to homogenize 'white' ethnicity is arguably part and parcel of its invisibility. Thus, with some limited exceptions such as attempts to understand the relatively poor health of the Irish (see Kelleher and Hillier, 1996), 'white' ethnici*ties* remain largely unexplored in the context of health. In recognition of this problem, Smaje (1996) contends that silence on the construction of 'white culture' is one of the biggest omissions in health-related research.

A number of serious problems follow on from the use of 'white' culture as an unarticulated standard by which to judge minority ethnic culture and health, the most important of which has already been mentioned: the tendency to subsume people under an oppressive and deterministic cloud of cultural difference. In the context of health-related research this is most clearly manifest in the attribution of negativity and its corollary of focusing on problematic, to the exclusion of positive, health. This seems to come through even in research that self-consciously tries to avoid these pitfalls, largely, I think, as a result of the sequestration of 'white' culture. For example, in an otherwise perceptive discussion which attempts to vindicate a cultural focus, Kelleher (1996: 79) cautions us against lumping all '"non-white" people together as "black"'. Yet it would seem that by his very use of the term *non*-white he does just this, creating all those who are *not* 'white' (itself essentialized) as the 'Other'. Ironically, his own objective of demonstrating that culture is a dynamic entity is weakened by his failure to put 'white' ethnicities on the conceptual agenda both as cultural resources for living in their own right and as forces of oppression for minority ethnicities.

The shortcomings of research are brought most clearly to the fore when *only* minority ethnic cultures (beliefs, attitudes, behaviours) are considered. There is, for example, merit in Pierce and Armstrong's (1996) research on the beliefs that older Afro-Caribbeans hold about diabetes (an unexplored issue). In their study, individuals came across as unsure, perhaps even confused about what diabetes is, and the implications that it has for their long-term health. The authors, however, tend to set this against a rather authoritative medical 'truth' of the disease against which the 'lay' voice is almost bound to be 'confused' not only if it is that of predominantly older Afro-Caribbean men, but also if it comes from various majority 'white' ethnic groups. The authors themselves recognize that any attribution of the accounts of their respondents to 'ethnic beliefs' must be tentative in the absence of any empirical comparisons, but still feel able to conclude that 'a number of views were expressed that clearly did seem to reflect a specific and different ethnic culture' (Pierce and Armstrong, 1996: 99). The question that arises from this, of course, is different from *what*?

'White' essentialism clearly jeopardizes attempts to conceptualize the relationships between racialization, ethnicity and health. But the recognition that minority ethnic groups do not constitute monolithic entities and that there may be as many similarities as differences across 'ethnic groups' is really only putative at the present time given the dearth of systematic comparative studies in the health field. Moreover, recent postmodern approaches suggest that even moves in this direction which conceptualize culture as a 'flexible resource', or a 'recipe for living' in the world (Ahmad, 1996; Donovan, 1988) may not go far enough in acknowledging the fluid nature of contemporary ethnic identities.

Cultural fragmentation

Taking us back to the concerns raised at the beginning of the chapter, Rattansi and Westwood ask, 'in an age of multiple and shifting subjectivities or identifications, and new interconnections between the "local" and the "global", what meaning can be given to "identity" at all?' (1994: 4). This resonates with the work of Stuart Hall, who suggests that racism itself not only marks and fixes differences between belongingness and otherness, but also *subverts* them since it simultaneously positions minority ethnic groups as inferior and expresses desire and envy on the part of the 'white' majority. Global diaspora and the emergence of syncretic cultures (notably in the context of youth music scenes) have been put forward as evidence of the more fluid and dynamic quality of 'ethnic identification'. Hence it has been argued that racism can be rescued from Otherness and used to signal the fact that 'we all speak from a particular place, out of a particular history, out of a particular experience, a particular culture, without being contained by that position' (Hall, 1992: 258). This position has much in common with the debates on class that were discussed in chapter 4, where we considered the argument that social class as collective identity is diminishing to be replaced by more fluid self-stylizations built around the consumption of particular lifestyles, which here would be bound up with the appropriation of a range of 'ethnic' identities. Although not adopting a postmodern approach, Nagel (1994: 152) refers to a model of culture which recognizes that the 'origin, content, and form of ethnicity reflect the creative choices of individuals and groups as they define themselves and others in ethnic ways'. Ethnicity, in her view, becomes a dialectic of self-ascription and the inscription of others, which is both volitional and mandatory as individuals carry a 'portfolio of ethnic identities that are more or less salient in various situations and vis-à-vis different audiences' (Nagel, 1994: 154). One of the illustrations that she gives is of affirmative action policies in the US, for example, in the context of university admissions, where 'the multi-ethnic ancestry of many Americans combines with ethnically-designated resources to make choosing an ethnicity sometimes a financial decision' (1994: 160).

To date there has been little attempt to engage with these positions in the context of health. On the one hand, we might see the more fluid approach to identity as the ultimate 'way out' of the problems that have arisen when an individual's health status, health beliefs and health behaviours are rather uncritically 'read off' their designated 'ethnic group' status (in both quantitative and qualitative research). But, on the other hand, concern has been expressed that euphemisms of diversity can act as a smokescreen for the entrenchment of inequality (Smith, 1993). For example, in suitably evocative terms, Smaje (1996: 143) cautions that 'no amount of strategic manipulation alters the direction of the racist's fist'. While some imply that more fluid identities are a product of global social change, particularly in the European context, others warn that postmodern approaches are often profoundly Eurocentric and deeply racialized themselves as they generate a 'vision which renders the immiserated irrelevant and blacks, in particular, as ornaments without agencies or resistance' (Harris, 1993: 35). Racism by this process can be made invisible. As bell hooks reminds us, notably absent in these debates are the voices of minorities, especially those of women. Should we not, she writes, 'be suspicious of postmodern critiques of the "subject" when they surface at a historical moment when many subjugated people feel themselves coming to voice for the first time?' (1991: 28). In associated terms she cautions us that the 'politics of difference' must not be separated from the 'politics of racism'.

Concluding comments

This chapter has sought to demonstrate that social science research on 'race' and health status suffers from a number of problems. Somewhat ironically, it has uncovered the racist ideologies of medicine both in contemporary and past times, but has failed to develop the adequate conceptual tools to tackle the issue of 'race' and health inequalities itself. At the present time research is inhibited by deficiencies in the scarce data that are available. For example, the categorizations that are employed in survey research are, as we have seen, often saturated with racist assumptions. In more qualitative research, conceptualizations of minority ethnic cultures tend to be racially inflected with negative qualities and reduced to static and unchanging entities that 'determine' health beliefs and behaviours. A lack of sensitivity to social class (often reduced to crude indicators of relative material deprivation) means that, to date, research has made little progress in exploring the interaction of racism and cultural and economic factors in the production of health inequalities.

More broadly, sociologists of health and illness as a group have yet to engage in any significant way with the wider social science literature on 'race' which, at the current time, points to the seeming paradox of a concurrent hardening of racism alongside an emerging 'ethnic diversity'. The fact that fixity seems to coexist with fluidity, both empirically and in the conceptual frameworks of social scientists, raises two significant issues: first it reminds us that racism itself is packaged in a variety of ways and is highly adaptable to changing circumstance; second, it alerts us to the fact that individuals are never *wholly* slaves to ascribed 'ethnic identities'. Together these points are highly relevant to the exploration of health inequalities of various kinds since they suggest that we should try to find the theoretical tools to enable us both to recognize the impact of racisms of various kinds upon health and also to explore the ways in which the cultural and material resources of individuals from both minority and majority 'ethnic groups' facilitate and impede good health.

Part III

Accomplishing Health and Health Care

7

Health Care in the 1990s and Beyond

The British National Health Service (NHS) and its future have dominated the domestic political agenda since the beginning of the 1990s, its problems emblematic of the wider process of economic and social restructuring that has affected health-care organization internationally. In this chapter we explore the reforms that have taken place since the mid-1980s and their implications for the provision of care to patients. First we briefly outline a conceptual framework to help us interpret health care in the context of broader economic and cultural change. The chapter then sketches the evolving structure of health and community care, paying attention to changes in the nature of the internal market over the 1990s and the growing union between the public and private sectors. This will lead us into a discussion of the rhetoric and reality of the new patient consumerism.

The NHS and the new economic order

The existence of a new economic order is central to theories of late capitalism and postmodernity. Although, as we saw in chapters 1 and 2, there is considerable debate over whether this new form should be signified as a complete rupture from, or an extension of, what went before, there is broad agreement that we are witnessing a shift from an industrial economy in which people work to transform raw material into mass-market goods, to a flexible economy based on the production of knowledge and information.

With the shift from an industrial to a service economy built around a new cluster of information, communication and other services the production of 'objects' has been replaced by the production of 'signs' (Lash and Urry, 1994). Informational and aesthetic goods like videos, magazines and genres of popular music are purchased as much for their sign-value (or the status that they confer) as for their use-value. There is a heightened design component invested in all of these goods. For example, clothes carry 'designer labels', and institutions such as hotels, and even hospitals nowadays, market their product through slogans and logos which mark them out from other goods and services in an attempt to establish a niche market. This transition has been conceptualized by some as a move from a Fordist to a post-Fordist mode of economic regulation. In the first decade of the twentieth century Henry Ford (the car manufacturer) lent his name to a new form of work organization at the core of which was 'the notion that management needs to control the work force by specifying in some detail what is to be done, how it is to be done, and in what quantity it is to be done' (Harrison et al., 1992: 14–15). This Fordist mode can be contrasted to post-Fordism, which is premised on 'a belief that workers can be more productive if they are encouraged to use all their abilities in a relatively free rather than closely monitored way', and where responsibility is directed downwards to the point of contact with clients (Walby et al., 1994: 8). This 'new management' induces producers of goods and services to be keenly aware of and responsive to consumers, something which is deemed to be necessary because commodities and services are now tailored for a highly specialized (rather than mass) market in response to an increasingly diverse pattern of consumer demand. Workers are encouraged to develop close involvement with clients (so that they know what product or service is desired); are allowed autonomy and entrepreneurship (embodied in notions such as 'productivity through people'); and work within lean and non-complex management structures with maximum autonomy at the level of production or the provision of services (while still being subject to resource allocation from the centre).

There is considerable disagreement over what post-Fordism actually *means* for workers and consumers. Some emphasize the liberatory potential of flexible work conditions and the individual accountability that it signifies (Piore and Sabel, 1984), while others paint a more pessimistic picture, referring to a dark underside where 'devolved control' is really 'remote control' (Hoggett, 1994), and where a periphery of numerically flexible workers bears the brunt of fluctuations in demand for services created by a volatile consumer market. The optimistic/pessimistic visions of post-Fordism parallel debates taking place among sociologists of postmodernity who, as we saw in chapter 2, contest whether postmodern society holds out the potential for individuals increasingly to construct their own lives, or whether it portends the demise of individual agency. Indeed, discussions of the transition from modern to postmodern society, and from Fordist to post-Fordist modes of economic regulation, are interconnected. For many commentators post-Fordism is quite broadly understood as 'the economic basis for a postmodern culture' (Allen, 1992: 184). For Lash (1994), the new reflexivity which characterizes the activities of both producers and consumers is a *direct outcome* of changes in the infrastructure of society and a precondition of future economic growth. In the new information and communication structures where capital accumulation is based on the acquisition of knowledge, both the production of goods and the delivery of expert services, such as health care, call for the 'freedom' of flexible post-Fordist economic forms in order to innovate to meet the demands of an ever-changing consumer market.

Economic restructuring and the reformed NHS

Social scientists have recently begun to use Fordism and post-Fordism as sensitizing concepts which might help us to understand welfare reforms. For example, Williams reflects on the possibility that, if changes in the wider economy are being reproduced in welfare provision, we are likely to see a transition from

> mass production to flexible production; mass consumption to diverse patterns of consumption; production-led to consumer-led; from mass, universal needs met by monolithic, bureaucratic/professional provision to the diversity of individual needs met by welfare pluralism, quasi-markets, reorganised welfare work and consumer-sovereignty. (Williams, 1994: 49)

In many ways this shift might be said aptly to characterize the new NHS. The radical changes set in train by the Conservative government's NHS and Community Care Act of 1990 have gained so much momentum that in formal terms at least the structure of health care now bears little resemblance to that which existed a decade before. These changes were premised on a vision of a costly and inefficient NHS marked by stultifying bureaucracy and driven more by the needs of professionals than the provision of quality care to patients. Competition was to be injected into the system through the introduction of a quasi-market. During the early 1990s health care *providers* (such as hospitals and community health services) were put into direct competition with

each other as they sought contracts from *purchasers* (then general practitioners and health authorities) who held budgets and bought health
care on behalf of patients. Patients have been reborn as 'consumers'
who are theoretically empowered to make health-care choices (through
contracts placed on their behalf by purchasers) and to hold health-care
professionals to account through new citizens' rights embodied in the
Citizens' and Patient's Charters. We turn now to a discussion of the
backdrop to these reforms.

Crisis, what crisis?

Although 'the rhetoric of imminent disaster' is almost as old as the NHS
itself (Butler, 1994: 16), the 1970s saw the emergence of a heightened
sense of crisis that extended far beyond a concern with the NHS. The
'managed capitalism' of the Keynesian post-war welfare state had meant
that it had been possible to nurture the conditions for capital accumulation while also fulfilling a range of social welfare functions to legitimate
the system (Offe, 1984). But, as many commentators have sought to
demonstrate, 'as the 1990s dawned, the conditions essential to the
survival of the welfare state in its conventional form have been transformed' (Allen, 1992: 108). Underpinning this has been economic reces-
sion, the global economic crises of the 1970s and the intrusion of global
forces into national economies. Expensive welfare programmes proved
difficult to sustain in the context of an unregulated global economy, and
costs burgeoned, leading to the general assent that the state was in
'fiscal crisis' resulting from a structural gap between state expenditure
and revenues (O'Connor, 1973).

Health-service expenditure in Britain rose from £444 million in 1949
to £29 billion in 1990. Taking account of inflation, this represented a
fourfold increase in costs over the life of the NHS. The majority of
expenditure currently goes on hospital care (48 per cent) and, within
this, on in-patient care (DoH, 1996b). These rising costs are generally
attributed to demographic changes, notably rises in life expectancy and
an ageing population, the costs of technological advances, and public
demand. Not surprisingly, the volume of work in the NHS has risen
quite dramatically. For example, the total number of discharges and
deaths increased from approximately 3 million in 1949–50, to about
8 million in 1989–90. New out-patient cases doubled over the same
period (Appleby, 1992). Clearly more patients were being treated (although it would be wrong to assume that there were always health
gains on the back of this). That is to say, it was not *simply* a case of
money being swallowed up by an inefficient system. But inefficiency

was the perception that prevailed, and the NHS came to be seen as 'unresponsive, producer-dominated, inefficient, and providing services of a poor quality' (Walsh, 1994: 189).

Three key developments prepared the ground for the changes of the 1990s (Butler, 1994). First of all there was the growth of managerialism. Professional dominance has been effectively built into the NHS since its inception in 1948, when Minister for Health Aneurin Bevan permitted GPs to remain as independent contractors to the health service (rather than making them salaried employees) and 'stuffed consultants' mouths with gold' (with generous salaries, merit awards, and the option of combining NHS work with private practice) in a successful bid to buy off medical opposition. Once in place medical power seemed intractable and soon became associated with rising costs. Simply put, clinical autonomy meant that decisions about treatment for a particular patient were almost totally in the hands of consultants who, it was argued, had no real incentive to restrict their spending. There were several attempts to change this during the 1970s through the introduction of a new management ethos. The first of the major managerial reforms came in 1974 with the Labour government's introduction of 'consensus management' into the health service. As Strong and Robinson (1990: 18) write, 'the health service was to be managed, but its management was to be conducted not by a boss, but by a group of equals, of fellow professionals, each representing the interests of a different occupation'. While this may have improved the co-ordination of care, it did little to confront the power of medicine. The Conservative government reforms of the early 1980s took a very different tack. In 1983, the Secretary of State for Health appointed the late Sir Roy Griffiths, who was the Deputy Chairman and Managing Director of the Sainsbury's supermarket chain, to head a management inquiry into the NHS (DHSS, 1983). The mood of the report is conveyed in its observation that 'if Florence Nightingale were carrying her lamp through the corridors of the NHS today, she would almost certainly be searching for the people in charge' (quoted in Baggott, 1994: 122). Consensus management, it concluded, was simply not working and should be replaced with a system of *general management* where there would be one identifiable individual in charge at every organizational tier (then regional, district and unit levels) of the service. With the Griffiths reforms, each general manager was to be 'a real boss, in charge of the treasurers, the cleaners, the nurses, the doctors, the personnel department – the lot' (Strong and Robinson, 1990: 23). Mohan (1995: 141) retorts that 'if Florence Nightingale actually returned' today and 'searched for the person in charge as Griffiths suggested, it may not be too great a caricature to suggest that she might have found a virile, macho figure, armed with the latest computer systems and filofaxes – the antithesis of the legendary nurse!' There is evidence, nonetheless, that the new general management largely failed to tame medical power. For example, fieldwork conducted by Harrison et al. (1992) during 1987–8 revealed that general managers seemed to have little effect on physicians or other staff at ward level; in fact most managers did not even seem to *expect* doctors to change. As we will see in chapter 8, the reforms of the 1990s were to address unfinished business and tackle the management–medicine interface head on.

The introduction of general management, then, is the first of the important foundations for the new NHS; the second is the contracting out of services. Health authorities were instructed to begin competitive tendering for catering, laundry and domestic services in September 1983. A few weeks after this the Conservative government abolished the Fair Wages Resolution Act of 1946 which had required contractors to provide terms and conditions at least equivalent to those in the service. In 1987 tendering was extended to other non-clinical services like portering, and then to areas such as diagnostic and pathology services. Over this period those who do domestic, catering and laundry work (very largely women) have come to be seen as a flexible and casualized workforce on the periphery of the post-Fordist economy. This is exemplified in Pulkingham's (1992) study of two Lothian (Scotland) hospitals, where managers explicitly stated that they increased part-time work to cut costs and improve work performance. It was reported that employing one worker for forty hours a week cost £300 per year *more* than employing two workers at twenty hours each. From the management point of view, concentrating work into four- or five-hour blocks means that the worker does not tire as easily and works at a more consistent and intense pace. Hence ancillary workers now not only have a more onerous workload, but have far less time in which to complete their work. (It should be noted that at the time of writing compulsory tendering in the NHS is under review by the NHS Executive, having already been halted in the local government sector following the election of the Labour government in 1997.)

The final seed of the new NHS sown in the mid-1980s was the introduction of income-generation schemes. 'A new ethos of entrepreneurship' (Butler, 1994: 15) had entered the NHS that was resonant of the USA, where revenue-generation is the order of the day and hospitals have diversified into areas like fast-food restaurants and the health and fitness business. In Britain, hospitals could now sell space for in-hospital shops, advertising, and land for developments such as car-parks. In 1990–1 income generation schemes in England, Wales and Northern Ireland had raised £90 million (National Association of Health Authorities and Trusts, cited in Appleby, 1992: 29). In addition, the government did much to lay the groundwork for a partnership between private health care and the NHS during the 1980s by allowing NHS consultants to do more private work and halting the phasing out of NHS pay-beds. In summary, the nucleus of a new management structure, contracting out, and income-generation had begun to establish the basis for the development of the internal market of the 1990s.

By the late 1980s there was a distinct sense that the NHS was in acute crisis. During the winter of 1987 the media drew ever more attention to cancelled operations and bed closures. Political pressure began to mount. Between October 1987 and February 1988 there were fifty-two Early Day Motions in the House of Commons which drew attention to the closure of facilities and to the fiscal crisis in the health authorities, as well as five full debates on the NHS and the emergency cash injection of an additional £100 million into the service (in 1987). In December 1987 the presidents of the Royal Medical Colleges publicly said that the NHS had reached breaking point. Hitherto, the political sensitivity of the NHS had conferred on it a relative immunity from the widespread reforms that had been affecting the public sector since the mid-1970s. Quite simply, 'electoral pragmatism almost invariably tempered ideological impulses' (Klein, 1995: 136). But, somewhat ironically, the crisis that came to a head late in 1987 provided a key opportunity for the Conservative government to 'do something' about the NHS.

The reforms and their implementation

In January 1988, the then Prime Minister, Margaret Thatcher, announced on the *Panorama* television programme that a ministerial group had been set up to review the operation of the NHS. This culminated, a year later, in the White Paper *Working for Patients* (DoH, 1989 – papers for Scotland and Northern Ireland came later), and the NHS and Community Care Act of 1990, which was implemented in April 1991 (with the community care element delayed until 1993). The reforms cost around £600 million to implement (between April 1991 and April 1993) and brought about 'the biggest explosion of political anger and professional fury in the history of the NHS' (Klein, 1995: 131). In the eyes of the opposition Labour Party and the health-service unions the reforms were the prelude to privatization. In a document which it claimed to be possibly the most important that it had issued for forty years, the British

Medical Association (BMA, 1989) stated that the proposed changes would exacerbate the already serious damage to patient care caused by chronic underfunding, and went on to mount a high-profile media campaign of opposition.

As has been discussed, although in retrospect we can see that the foundations for these reforms were laid in the 1980s, at the time they took a great many people by surprise. Like a ship setting out into uncharted waters, the health service was set on a new, almost wholly untested, course. The aim was to introduce market principles into health care, turning what was perceived to be a sluggish, expensive, and provider-led system into a cost-efficient, consumer-led quality service. The power of consultant physicians was to be tempered through an internal market where health-care providers would compete for contracts from purchasers, yet even quite late on in the deliberations of the ministerial review group the structure of the market was still unclear. The identity of the purchasers, in particular, was subject to considerable debate. Several proposals had been put forward, including one that had been mooted since the mid-1980s – American Alain Enthoven's argument that health authorities should purchase on behalf of their populations. In this model the district health authorities would function like US prepaid health-care plans called Health Maintenance Organizations (HMOs) where, when a patient becomes ill, the HMO covers the cost of care, which is provided either by in-house physicians or through contracts which are placed with local hospitals and other health-care providers. Since the HMO has a fixed income, in theory there is an incentive to contain costs by avoiding expensive tests and procedures and engaging in preventive care. But the working group felt that the HMO model had a number of problems, not the least being the tendency to underprovide for the poor and chronically ill. In addition, while it has always been recognized that small HMOs are particularly vulnerable to the financial consequences of 'costly patients', the late 1980s saw the collapse of several very large HMOs including the giant Maxicare which once covered over two million people (Freund and McGuire, 1995). According to Glennerster et al. (1994: 9), by the summer of 1988, midway into the working party's deliberations, Margaret Thatcher's Policy Unit became increasingly concerned that the group was getting 'bogged down and the proposals on the table less and less radical'. The GP funding idea was revitalized and what in fact emerged was a modification of the HMO model in which *both* health authorities *and* GPs would act as purchasers. Yet, as we will see as this chapter unfolds, the identity of purchasers continued to be a source of debate during the 1990s, and is set to change again in April 1998 (DoH, 1997). However, we begin our discussion of the internal 1990s.

Purchasers

Although GP fundholding was quintessential to the reformed NHS, it was one of the least specified aspects of *Working for Patients*, which contained no detail on how budgets would be set or what aspects of care would be covered. But even in its most rudimentary form, fundholding incited considerable opposition, so much so that it looked like it might lose the Conservative government the 1992 General Election. The BMA in particular was vociferous in its dissent, writing to all general practices and asking them not to participate in the scheme in mid-1990. This climate of apparent opposition may help to explain why the regional health authorities (who took the initial lead in setting up fundholding) only expected a modest interest from practitioners (Glennerster et al., 1994). The way that fundholding took off, then, was all the more surprising because it was unexpected. By 1996 there were 3,000 fundholding practices covering over 10,000 GPs and almost 50 per cent of the population.

The fundholding initiative had a twofold political objective: to cut costs and improve the quality of care. These objectives were very much bound together under the assumption that, if competition was introduced into the system, hospitals would be more responsive to GPs and GPs more responsive to patients: GPs would now have the power to vote with their purses and patients with their feet if the service provided was unacceptable to them. With the advent of fundholding, GPs were no longer to be supplicants pleading with hospital consultants on behalf of their patients, but powerful actors who had the might of money behind them. With their own budgets, they would not only be able to influence the quality of care, but would also have an incentive to be cost-efficient themselves since they would now assume a personal financial risk for their decisions.

In 1991, the first year of the scheme, 291 practices in England (covering 7 per cent of the population) had been screened and accepted to become fundholders (Glennerster et al., 1994). Individual budgets were eventually set according to past referral activity, amounting to approximately £100 per patient for the year. This money was to be used to contract with trusts for a range of non-emergency services for patients. The full detailed list of around 110 procedures to be covered in the scheme, which did not become available until March 1993, itemized out-patient and in-patient treatments including most surgery. The budget was extended in 1996 so that many GPs could also purchase more surgical treatments and community health services (for example, district nursing, health visiting and mental health care). However, even though in 1995 fundholders commanded a budget of £2.8 billion (Petchey, 1995), this consumed a relatively small percentage of hospital and community spending. This was estimated at 15 per cent in April 1996 (Chadda, 1996).

The role of local health authorities shifted from providing services in their own hospitals (which have taken on trust status) to one of assessing health-care needs and purchasing care on the behalf of residents. At the time of writing, health authorities continue to purchase all care for patients from non-fundholding practices and cover emergency care and treatments that are not on the fundholding procedures list for *all* patients. Their budgets are reduced by the amount of money that goes to GP fundholders and, since fundholding budgets are protected by what is called a 'stop loss' provision, they cover the cost of individual patient care which currently exceeds £6,000. However, in the recent White Paper *The New NHS* (DoH, 1997) the Labour government has indicated that the role of health authorities will change once more. They will lose all but a very specialist purchasing role to more than 500 new primary care commissioning groups, consisting of local networks of GPs and community nurses, which will cover populations of around 100,000. Health authorities will be sub-regional strategic bodies responsible for overseeing primary care commissioning groups, and will act as led agencies in the development of three-year local Health Improvement Programmes (DoH, 1997). The development of primary care commissioning groups will take place in stages, with the possibility of evolving to primary care trust status over time. However, the distinction between fundholding and non-fundholding GPs will disappear in April 1998. (In Scotland, where GP fundholding was never widespread, primary care trusts, which will have a wide purchasing remit, including mental health services, will be implemented earlier in 1998.) *The New NHS* (DoH, 1997: 10) portrays the new commissioning process as a 'third way' between the 'old centralized command and control systems of the 1970s' and 'the divisive internal market system of the 1990s'. The move towards primary care groups would seem to be a logical extension of developments already under way, since increasingly practices are both joining together to form multifunds and developing joint commissioning projects with health authorities to offset risks to their savings or an overspend for particular expensive services.

The abolition of a dual structure in which some patients' care is paid for solely by health authorities, while that of others is paid for by their fundholding GPs, may help to address concerns of equity which have dominated discussion from the early days of the internal market. Since the introduction of the health service reforms included no provision for evaluation, research on issues of equity is, even now, woefully inadequate. Some, such as Coulter (quoted in Moore, 1996: 32), have concluded that 'there is very little evidence that fundholding, and indeed any of the reforms in general, have made any difference to patients'. Others pointed to disadvantages for patients of fundholders given that there may have been a perverse financial incentive to hold out on a referral to hospital until a condition became an emergency covered by the health authority rather than the GP budget. But more commonly, commentators were concerned about an emerging two-tier system where the patients of fundholders received preferential treatment. For example, 75 per cent of fundholders and 68 per cent of non-fundholders surveyed by Francome and Marks (1996) in 1994 felt that patients of fundholders were given priority in hospital referrals. This is echoed by a 1993 survey by the BMA (*BMJ*, 1994) which found that 40 per cent of short-stay hospital respondents said that patients of fundholders were treated more quickly than patients of non-fundholders in their hospitals. In the summer of 1997 the government announced that from April 1998 NHS hospital trusts will be required to operate common waiting-lists for non-urgent treatment, and that health authorities will be required to set maximum waiting-times which are common to all residents in their areas. Concerns about equity between patients of fundholders and non-fundholders were also linked to the practice of top-slicing of health authority budgets to cover fundholders in their districts. Specifically, remaining health authority money was likely to be taken up in providing emergency treatment, with little left to cover other aspects of care for patients of non-fundholders (Whitehead, 1994). Certainly, there was much in the media about health authorities running out of money before the end of the financial year, while the patients of fundholders, private patients and patients from outside the locality were treated, and beds lay empty. At the end of 1996, three-quarters of health authorities were in the red with a total deficit of £182 million – almost triple the sum for 1994–5 (*Health Service Journal*, 1 January, 1997). The Association of Community Health Councils for England and Wales (ACHC, 1996) reported that 15 per cent of purchasers asked providers to slow down admissions so that they could keep within their budget for 1995/6. While there is every reason to assume that patients are put under significant stress when they cannot get admissions to hospital for non-emergency care which could, of course, include treatment for quite serious conditions, it is telling that the wider views of patients on the health-care market are largely unknown. Even studies which have evaluated fundholding and quality of patient care (see for example, Glennerster et al., 1994) seem to reach their conclusions with little or no recourse to the patient's own view.

Providers: NHS trusts

By 1996 there were 492 hospital and community care trusts in the country covering almost 95 per cent of NHS activity (*Health Service Journal*, 1996); this represented a leap from only fifty-seven trusts in 1991. Hospital and community care trusts are self-governing units within the NHS. They are statutory corporations run by a board of directors, and are directly accountable to the Secretary of State for Health through the National Health Service Executive (NHSE) (the body within the Department of Health which is responsible for the operation and management of the NHS). In April 1996 the NHSE (which previously had a slightly different title) replaced the old regional health authorities (which had already been cut from fourteen to eight in 1993) with eight NHSE regional offices to monitor the growing number of trust hospitals and engage in strategic planning. Trusts are able to determine their own management structures, can employ their own staff and set their own terms and conditions of employment. The Department of Health imposes three financial duties on trusts: each year they must (1) earn a 6 per cent return on assets; (2) break even; and (3) stay within their external financing limit as set by government. Despite these statutory obligations, at the end of 1996 it was reported that thirty-six trust hospitals were in the red to the tune of £34 million (*Independent*, 4 November 1996). From April 1998, trusts will have the additional responsibility to publish details of their performance against six dimensions of a New National Performance Framework (DoH, 1997).

In theory, all hospital and community care trusts are in direct competition with each other as well as with the private sector. These providers currently (late 1997) seek contracts from GPs, health authorities (whose purchasing role is to be replaced by primary care commissioning groups) and from private patients who pay by insurance or out of pocket. Private health care has a significant place in the competitive market.

Private health care and the NHS

The reforms of the 1990s gave new momentum to long-standing debates about private provision within the NHS, resurrecting the pay-bed debate that dominated party politics during the 1970s (the abolition of pay-beds was part of the manifesto on which the Labour government of 1974 was elected). The 1988 Health and Medicines Act for the first time allowed NHS hospitals to charge commercial prices for services and to earn profits from private patients, rather than just to recover costs. Income from private work in NHS hospitals rose from £77.6 million in

1988/9 to £198.2 million in 1994/5 (Brindle, 1996). In fact, by 1996 the NHS was the largest provider of pay-beds with a 16.5 per cent share of the acute care market (Cervi, 1996). The issue of pay-beds cuts across the political divide, with the right and many hospital managers claiming that they generate income to plough back into services, and some on the left arguing that they are not properly costed for the use of NHS accommodation, staff and resources, and reduce the number of beds that are available to NHS patients.

The increase in pay-beds represents significant competition to the independent hospital sector which has experienced a slow-down in growth following the boom period of the early 1980s. Nonetheless, independent-sector medical and surgical beds increased from 7,035 in 1981 to 11,681 in 1995. In 1994, the overall UK private health-care market had an estimated worth of £2,064 million, a 9.5 per cent increase over 1993 figures (Bartlett and Phillips, 1996). But, the fortunes of the private sector notwithstanding, it is important to appreciate that the line between NHS and private provision is becoming increasingly blurred. Although the amount of work that the NHS contracts to the private sector is not yet large, Baggott (1994) reports that the NHS spent over £250 million treating NHS patients in private hospitals during the 1992/3 financial year (a 25 per cent increase over 1991/2), mostly in a bid to reduce its waiting-lists for elective (i.e. non-emergency) surgery. Research by Yates (1995a) suggests an invidious link between NHS waiting-lists and the private work undertaken by consultant surgeons. He argues it is no coincidence that NHS consultants in specialisms with the longest waiting-lists have the highest private sector earnings; that the private sector concentrates on conditions that have the longest waiting-times for treatment in the NHS; and that surgeons who do private practice have the longest waiting-lists. Consultants are able to hold very loose NHS contracts which allow them to forfeit part of their salary (currently one-eleventh) in return for permission to undertake what appears to be unlimited private work. Individual gross earnings from private practice averaged £33,000 in 1992, although this hides a wide range, with individuals earning from £20,000 right up to £200,000 (Higgins, 1995). In a study of two specialisms with some of the worst NHS waiting-lists – orthopaedics and ophthalmology – Yates (1995a, 1995b) found that the average NHS surgeon was spending three half-days per week in the private sector. In a report of the research on the Channel 4 television programme *Dispatches* (broadcast in January 1995) he suggested that some consultants deliberately build up long lists so that they can encourage patients (either directly or through their GPs) to pay for their services on a private basis.

The entrepreneurial spirit

As has been discussed in relation to the United States, there is no such thing as a truly non-profit-making hospital; profit is disguised administratively via salary increases and perks, and net earnings are used to expand and finance new services (Bartlett and Le Grand, 1994). There are incentives for profit maximization at all levels of service provision in Britain. For example, GPs can pay themselves to conduct a limited amount of minor surgery (just over three-quarters of all GPs were approved to undertake this work by late 1994) and in many hospitals individual clinical directorates can retain surpluses.

Joint ventures with the private sector received the full support of the Conservative government, and look set to continue under the current Labour government (DoH, 1997). Early in 1995 the Chancellor of the Exchequer pronounced the government's Private Finance Initiative (PFI), which was introduced in 1992, 'unstoppable' stating that private investment in health care was to take the place of public borrowing. Although the PFI has been bureaucratically cumbersome and slow to get off the ground, the alliance between private capital and the NHS seems set to reach unprecedented levels. Millar (1995: 14) reports that large construction companies 'appear to be taking the lead in private finance deals' as PFI is used to procure new general hospitals, and to redevelop existing sites. She quotes a director of John Laing Construction as saying 'we are as hungry as anyone . . . we have been active in the health service for a long time and now the NHS is beginning to respond positively'. Under this initiative NHS hospitals are built and maintained by private investors and then leased back to the NHS for a specified period. But the construction industry is not alone; companies which produce new technologies and equipment which is deemed to be more cost-effective (such as equipment for minimum-access or 'keyhole' surgery) are also aggressively marketing their products and services. Although the current Secretary of State for Health has given an assurance that *clinical* services will not be provided by the private sector, there is considerable confusion over how they are to be defined. These broad changes led Hunter (1995a: 21) to conclude that 'the PFI is slowly, and by stealth, beginning to transform the NHS into a private health service'.

But joint ventures in the more traditional areas of construction and clinical and clinical support services seem to pale when considered alongside the movement of new information and communication services into the NHS. Since a reliable, computerized information system has been lacking in many hospitals and general practices, and NHSE strategy is for every hospital to have an integrated system by the year 2000, computer companies have had virtually an open field during the 1990s. There are seemingly endless possibilities, ranging from the new open system called TotalCARE offered by AT&T, to the new computerized NHS numbers which everyone in Britain will soon have (a contract worth £2.5 million has gone to a computer service company to generate the new-format ten-digit numbers).

At the management level companies like Touche Ross merchandize the latest techniques such as business process re-engineering which, it is argued, will improve efficiency and profitability; others run seminars to help service providers develop their pitching skills to beat the competition when bidding for contracts, and courses are available to train general practice and hospital receptionists in 'customer care'. Panic over patient complaints and litigation (discussed below) creates a lucrative market for clinical risk-management systems which claim to create 'risk awareness' thereby helping a hospital to protect its assets by avoiding costly claims. Marketing companies organize expensive conferences which bring together managers of trusts and general practices with lawyers, private health-care companies, and the construction and retail sectors. One such company – International Communications for Management – advertised an event held in February 1995 in the following way:

> The Private Finance Initiative has opened the door for the NHS to embark on new capital projects and gives the opportunity to make creative use of under-utilised assets for securing deals with the private sector. From car parks to fast-food outlets, shopping malls to new hospitals there is endless scope for joint venture.

British sociologists have given only passing attention to these issues in recent discussions of the NHS, at a time when we can argue that McKinlay's thesis (1977) that formal health care is suffused by the activities of capital (see chapter 1) has never been more pertinent. The recent reforms have created a competitive market in which responsibility is driven down to the point of contact with consumers. For example, hospitals must be sensitive to purchasers such as GP commissioning groups; hospitals, health authorities and GPs must *all* be sensitive to their patients. In such a context it is not surprising to find the new information and communications structures, which are emblematic of the new forms of capital referred to earlier in this chapter, making inroads into health care. As has been emphasized, these structures are two-edged, being simultaneously a vehicle for reflexivity and choice, and a new forum for capitalist domination (Lash, 1994). This is a useful way to conceptualize the health service, which at one and the same time appears to offer new opportunities for health-care workers and patients (whom to merge with in purchasing consortia, where to place contracts, where to go for care), while also maintaining a strong sense of central control (by direction of the market through the Private Finance Initiative, Charter Standards in the provision of care, changes in primary health-care commissioning and so on). These tensions are equally apparent in the provision of community care.

Care in the community

The intention to develop a 'primary care-led' health service is the latest in a succession of attempts to fuse the historical division between health (NHS) and social care (local authorities) that has marked the NHS since its inception. Local authority social service departments became the lead agencies in the provision of social care in 1993. They currently (late 1997) act as purchasers in an analogous way to GPs, with whom they are encouraged to form joint purchasing arrangements, along with health authorities, for the combined provision of health *and* social care. In the summer of 1997 the Secretary of State for Health referred to breaking down the 'Berlin walls' between the range of agencies involved in health and social care, initially by setting up between ten and twenty 'Health Action Zones' in which health authorities, trusts, GPs, nurses, health visitors, dentists, opticians and others will co-operate in partnership with local authorities, community groups, the voluntary sector and local businesses in areas of pronounced deprivation and poor health.

The shift from the Department of Social Security to local authorities as lead agencies for social care grew out of the Griffiths inquiry into the funding of community care (Griffiths, 1988). During the 1980s, in a bid to promote the private provision of community care, the then government allowed the elderly to claim social security benefits to pay for residential care. As expenditure on social security rose from £20 million in 1980 to around £70 million by the end of the decade (Baggott, 1994), the government began to recognize that it had created a 'perverse incentive' in favour of residential rather than domiciliary care. By 1992 spending had reached £2,530 million (Klein, 1995). Griffiths reduced social security benefits for residential care to a basic level, with the balance or 'care element' paid by local authorities on a needs-assessed basis. If residential care is not necessary, the care element can be used to purchase 'care in the community'. At the time of writing local authorities have a statutory duty to make maximum use of the private (commercial and voluntary) sectors; they must use 85 per cent of their government funding to buy private sector (residential and domiciliary) care. This new rule fanned the fires of debate over the privatization of health and social care, with many commentators, such as Carpenter (1994: 75), contending that community care is undoubtedly 'stacked in favour of the private and voluntary sectors'. Although it is too soon to assess the direct impact of the move to local authority funding and the '85 per cent rule', there is sufficient evidence that while the private sector is blooming, the public sector is fading away. Indeed, private residential and nursing home provision has expanded at an even faster pace than the acute sector, with an estimated expenditure of £4,582 million in 1994, an 800 per cent increase over 1970 figures. In comparison, the number of long-stay NHS geriatric beds has dwindled from 52,000 to 34,700 over the same period (Bartlett and Phillips, 1996).

Like the NHS, community care policy is still evolving, moving away from mass institutionally based care (for example, large mental hospitals) towards a package of care that is tailored for the individual and, therefore, 'close to the client'. The double-edged nature of this change is thrown into particular relief in the case of informal or unpaid care in the home.

Informal carers

Research from the 1990 General Household Survey (GHS) shows that there are 3.4 million adults in Britain who are *sole* carers for relatives, friends and neighbours who are sick, handicapped, or elderly, either by looking after them in their own homes or by giving regular assistance in a different household. Although gender differences in the sample are relatively small – 17 per cent of women, compared to 14 per cent of men are carers – women are more likely to be sole carers than men (57 per cent versus 42 per cent) and to be involved in caring for more hours per week (Evandrou, 1996). Unfortunately even commentators who have pointed to the underside of the new economic order of late capitalism (see Jameson, 1984; Lash and Urry, 1994) have tended, if not to ignore, to gloss over the fact that the new economy is underpinned by social relations of gender. Feminists, however, have tackled these issues head on. As Graham (1993b: 463) writes, the 1980s was a decade 'in which informal care became the orthodoxy' as feminist research began a sustained critique of and challenge to government policy 'pointing to the ways in which the patterns of informal care reflected and reinforced gender divisions'.

Yet by the 1990s commentators had begun to argue that this literature had reached an impasse (Baldwin and Twigg, 1991). Part of the problem was that it looked increasingly out of step with developments in feminist theory, failing to engage with the debates that were already raging over 'unity and difference' between women that were discussed in chapter 3. Consequently, feminist research on caring has been subject to an important autocritique (Graham, 1993b), at the core of which is a challenge to the rather ingrained and limited conceptualization of caring as 'unpaid services for dependent close kin provided by women' (Thomas, 1993: 654). The problem is that, while on the one hand this definition might seem to strike at the heart of women's oppression, it can also have the ironic and unintended consequence of entrenching women *in* caring roles. Most simply put, feminists have tended to adopt the same vision of 'caring as women's work' that has suffused government community care policy in recent years. Of course feminism and government policy differ in that feminism is critical of the effects of the burden of care for women, while government often assumes women's 'caring role' to be natural and taken for granted. But, nonetheless, feminists have not really *challenged* the narrow definition of caring (Graham, 1991). A lot of women's activism has been focused on gaining individual rights before the law (for example, married women's entitlement to the Invalid Care Allowance in 1986). Although this can have the important consequence of extending benefits for some, as Finch writes (1990: 51), 'it does not represent any challenge to the traditional division of labour which ensures that many more women than men are actually doing caring work'. Indeed, as she goes on to state, 'it could be argued that policy changes which make family care practically and financially more bearable for women can have the effect of actually strengthening the underlying traditional division of labour' (1990: 52).

A further consequence of the overwhelming focus on women is that men's caring work has been made virtually invisible. The GHS data suggest that men make a larger contribution to caring than has traditionally been assumed. That is, caring is not unequivocally 'women's work'. However, it is not just men who have been cut out of debates on caring. The rather limited conceptualization of caring as unpaid services for kin provided by women often assumes a *generic female carer* who is young or in mid-life, 'white' and able-bodied. This ethnocentrism has led feminists to overlook the potential diversity in caring by ethnicity and social class. It has also marked out unrealistic divisions between women. For example, as Arber (1994) writes, feminists have neglected older women who are construed as the 'other', and as a burden from the perspective of younger women (especially daughters) when, in fact, elders often reciprocate with unpaid caring work such as baby-sitting, minding children after school, shopping and so on for the young (a similar argument can be made for men). Indeed, 28 per cent of all carers are aged 60 or over (Evandrou, 1996).

Clearly, feminist conceptualizations of unpaid caring work are undergoing considerable revision at the current time, mirroring broader debates within feminism that were discussed in chapter 3. Concern has been raised that if we focus just on *women's* experience and take it as a priori different to the experience of men, we can end up quite unintentionally reinforcing the idea that caring is women's work. Moreover, there is concern that feminist research on caring has tended to neglect differences between women. That is, it has been suggested that it has been led by a 'white', middle-class bias failing to appreciate the plurality and heterogeneity of women's (and also men's) experience. While these debates are important, they take nothing away from the fact that caring is gendered work, rather, they suggest that the reality may be more complex than it has hitherto been thought to be.

Whether referring to acute care in the hospital or care in the community, the discussion in this chapter so far has taken on an almost paradoxical quality: the notion of consumerism has been omnipresent, but the active, thinking patient (or potential patient) has been left out of the frame altogether. This neglect of the patient's view has been deliberate, intended to highlight the fact that while the reforms of the 1990s have been couched in the language of consumerism, to date the patient has been given a rather circumscribed role to play.

The patient reborn as consumer

Consumers are the motif of the health service reforms. Purchasers and providers have been required to take their views into account when developing services, facilitated by a number of formal mechanisms such as the Patient's Charter and local health needs assessment (Flynn et al., 1996). The concept of patient consumerism lends itself readily to a range of different meanings which can be construed not simply as existing side by side, but as multi-layered, one meaning shaded from view by another. Thus behind notions of the sovereign individual may lie a less palatable paternalism. This possibility is explored in this section, beginning with a consideration of policy initiatives which involve 'listening to patients' voices'.

Listening to local people

Since the early 1990s, health authorities have had a duty to give people an effective voice in shaping health services locally. Indeed, they are expected to assume a 'champion of the people role', involving local people in the assessment of health needs and the purchasing and evaluation of services (NHSME, 1992: 3). As the *Local Voices* initiative recognizes, this poses the significant methodological challenge of how to assess local views reliably, particularly 'silent voices' such as the housebound and disadvantaged who are not represented by voluntary organizations and consumer groups. Concerns of equity are raised when results of particular assessment exercises, perhaps inevitably, reveal preferences for one kind of service over another – such as a postal survey in Solihull which found that those who responded favoured investment in high-technology acute care rather than in access to basic services (Ham et al., 1994). In a similar vein, services for socially stigmatized conditions such as HIV and AIDS, or drug addiction, may be compromised when they are given a low priority by the public. Finally, whatever their priorities, local voices may be silenced by financial exigencies. For these reasons, to seek local views 'is not necessarily to hear them, and to hear is not readily equated with understanding, involvement or participation' (Popay and Williams, 1994a: 92). A study of commissioning for community health services by Flynn et al. (1996) found that health authorities were confused about whether they were consulting in order to give the public a major role in determining their contract decisions, or simply allowing their views to have a formative role. Their limited success in responding to needs is supported in research by Ham et al. (1994) who found that, although most health authorities felt that health needs assessment had had an impact, many were unable to give actual examples. Often health authorities fall back on consulting with ready-defined user-groups such as the elderly or those with mental illnesses, and certainly there is evidence of success in this regard, such as the 24-hour helpline for mental health crisis care set up by one authority, reported by Flynn et al. (1996). However, summarizing their analysis these authors found that, despite considerable willingness on the part of health authorities to involve local people, there were 'major uncertainties as to how this should be achieved in practical terms, and what implications it might have for the commissioning and contracting process, and indeed, what the ultimate purpose should be' (1996: 77). Although health authorities are to lose their major purchasing role from April 1998 (DoH, 1997), they will still be involved in local health needs assessment as lend agencies in the development of the new Health Improvement Programmes.

Health authorities are of course not the only voice for current and prospective patients. Community health councils (CHCs), which were established in the 1970s, are expected to monitor standards of health care from the consumer's point of view and to use this information to inform GP and health authority purchasing plans. Yet there is evidence that cash-strapped CHCs are increasingly preoccupied with rising numbers of patient complaints about the NHS to the relative neglect of their service-monitoring role (Barnes and Cox, 1997). Consequently, while CHCs have the statutory powers to challenge purchasers on behalf of patients, in reality it appears that they have inadequate resources to do so. Moreover, policies which seek to foster good working relations between CHCs and health authorities seem to prompt a corporatist agenda. Indeed, most of the CHCs surveyed by Barnes and Cox reported 'good' (40 per cent) or 'very good' (40 per cent) relations with health authorities, with only relatively few stating that relations were just 'okay' (12 per cent), or 'poor' (8 per cent). This raises the question of whether it may be more appropriate to conceive of CHCs as part of the policy community than a source of independent consumer power, since it is palpably evident that when they mount a direct challenge to a health authority's decisions they have little political clout.

While it would be inappropriate to denounce attempts that have been made to represent local views in the commissioning of local health services out of hand, the evidence seems to be stacked against any truly effective role. May (1996: 19) goes as far as to view consultation in the new NHS as 'little more than a charade' which inappropriately raises public expectations which cannot be met. It is in this context that surrogate or normative consumerism can quite easily take the place of the ideal typical individual consumer pursuing their own interests in the market (Walsh, 1994). The potential for GPs to become consumers on behalf of their patients was clearly laid out in *Working for Patients* (DoH, 1989: 36), which stated that 'offering choice to patients means involving general practitioners far more in key decisions'. Here, again, the purchaser is expected to somehow represent the interests of users through contracts with providers. Yet, as with health needs assessment, patient and GP preferences may not coincide. For example, in their study of surgical referrals Mahon et al. (1994) discovered that, while GPs clearly recognized the importance of patients' views, ultimately they took second place to their own judgements based on the convenience of the hospital and their knowledge of the consultant. It is questionable whether normative consumerism can ever work in a market in which economic competition rules the day. Seeming to underline this, the BMA has issued guidelines for GPs in response to fears that elderly and costly patients are being discriminated against (80,000 patients are struck off GP lists annually). This process, which is called cream-skimming, has been a concern since the inception of the internal market. Using data from a large fundholding practice Glennerster et al. (1994) found that only sixty-nine patients (4.5 per cent of the practice sample) incurred any expenditure for hospital in-patient services, with 1 per cent of patients requiring 44 per cent of all in-patient expenditure. Using the example of diabetes they demonstrate that cream-skimming is both technically feasible and financially profitable. Thus, if a practice with thirty-seven patients with diabetes receives £46.77 per patient as part of its budget formula (making just over £1,730 in total), and its records reveal that the *actual* costs exceeded this amount – say, £90.92 per patient, or £3,364 in total – the GPs could identify extra 'unreimbursed costs' of approximately £1,634. Although the authors found it very difficult to predict expenditures from a knowledge of factors like social class and health status in their research, this does not rule out the possibility that GPs themselves will feel that it is possible to do so. In summary, the internal market in health care may at best mean that there will be specific occasions when the doctor cannot act in the patient's interest (for example, in rationing very expensive treatments), and at worst it may continuously pit the interests of patient and practitioner against each other (as with cream-skimming).

This suggests that, while normative consumerism may not unequivocally benefit patients, it may serve as a cost containment mechanism, acting as a fetter to runaway costs. In the name of the patient and exercising fiscal constraint in the process, purchasers have an incentive to curb the spending power of hospital and community trust providers through the contracts that they place with them.

The activist individual

Patient–consumers are expected, incited even, to secure their rights under a contractual model of social relations in the NHS, not only through surrogates (i.e. purchasers), but also as individual actors. This can be seen in the rights and expectations listed in the Patient's Charter, as well as in the rising tide of complaints and litigation. Here, too, the language of the market is very evident with the route to quality framed in the language of formal, contractual obligations.

Introduced by the Conservative government in 1992 and revised in 1995, the Patient's Charter lists a series of rights and expectations based on the concept of the individual rights of the citizen as a consumer of public services. The rights, the legal enforceability of which has yet to be tested, are defined as 'services which all patients will receive all the time' (DoH, 1995b: 4). They are currently the right to:

- receive health care based on clinical need
- be registered with a GP (and to be able to change GP if desired)
- get emergency treatment at any time through a GP, ambulance service, and hospital Accident & Emergency departments
- be referred to an acceptable consultant
- choose whether or not to take part in medical research or medical student training
- have any treatment explained (including any risks) before giving consent
- have access to medical records
- have any complaint investigated and receive a quick and full response
- receive full information on local health services (including waiting-times)
- be guaranteed minimal waiting-times for treatment (from April 1995 patients had a right to admission within eighteen months).

These ten rights are accompanied by a series of expectations or 'standards of service which the NHS is aiming to achieve' but which 'exceptional circumstances may sometimes prevent' it meeting (DoH, 1995b: 4). From 1995 the wide-ranging list of expectations included: respect for privacy, dignity and religious beliefs; treatment within a year for coronary artery bypass grafts, hip or knee replacements and cataract operations; and the provision of single-sex washing and toilet facilities. The Labour government has announced that a new NHS Charter will be published in 1998. It is expected to be wider than the Patient's Charter, described above, and to give attention to outcomes of treatment and care (DoH, 1997).

If patients feel that their rights and expectations are not met, they are encouraged to complain to the relevant authority. The Health Service Commissioners' (or Ombudsman's) Report for 1993/4 showed a record 1,384 complaints for the period, a 13 per cent increase over 1992/3. Formal complaints about GP services have undergone a fairly modest rise in the UK as a whole since the early 1980s, while hospital complaints (clinical and non-clinical combined for England) have risen at a rate of 1,000–3,000 per year (with the exception of a 1,000 drop between 1987/8 and 1988/9), from 19,255 in 1983 to 32,996 in 1990/1. The most striking observation is the massive leap from this figure to 44,680 in

1991/2. Figures for Wales also show a large jump from 1,800 to 2,377 between the same two years (DoH, 1994b). (In Scotland and Northern Ireland data were not collected until 1992.)

In an environment in which the liberal values of individualism and competition are paramount, patient–consumers (or their surrogates) are increasingly defined as individually responsible for the quality of care that they receive and encouraged to hold health-care providers to account. In these terms complaints can be viewed as a virtue. This comes through in the NHS Complaints Review of 1994 (also known as the Wilson Report), which recommended that existing procedures, which were both cumbersome and fragmented, should be replaced with a common complaints system for primary care and hospital care, clinical and non-clinical grievances. Allsop (1995a), who was a member of the Review Committee, explains that a survey of private sector complaints handling commissioned by the Committee suggested that tracking user concerns helps to maintain customer loyalty. If the customer is both the patient *and* the patient's surrogates (i.e. GPs and health authorities), it is not surprising that trusts are increasingly concerned about complaints handling. As the Wilson Report (DoH, 1994b: 29) itself recognizes, for private companies customer retention is a major aim of complaints handling 'since it is cheaper to keep old customers than to win new ones . . . increasingly, however, parts of the public sector are open to competition, and with the advent of trusts and the consequences of recent reforms, the NHS is no exception'. Moreover, quick and efficient resolution of complaints is certainly seen as a means of deflecting legal action.

The number of medical malpractice cases has increased markedly over the last decade. Spending on awards for clinical negligence rose from an estimated £60 million in 1990/1 to £155 million in 1994/5 (DoH, 1996b), leading to growing fears that a trust could find itself unable to pay if faced with a number of major damages awards within a short period. These and other figures have created a moral panic (Dingwall, 1994) and the perception among health-care managers is that the NHS is under severe strain. After 1990 individual health authorities and trusts were individually responsible for claims against staff, footing the first £300,000 of any claim, with the DoH picking up the rest of the bill. In April 1995 the DoH set up a Special Health Authority to manage a new Central Fund for Clinical Negligence in England. This is a pooling arrangement open to all trusts which is based on a contribution formula with likely future incentives for good risk management and claims monitoring. Under the scheme members can apply for reimbursement for 80 per cent of the damages and legal costs for outgoings of over £10,000 and up to £5,000,000.

To a large degree consumerism is individual rather than collective in form. As Beck writes (1992: 99), 'the motor of individualization is going at full blast, and it is not at all clear how new and lasting social arrangements, comparable in depth of penetration to social classes can even be created'. However, political and social alliances *do* emerge, many being 'temporary coalitions between different groups' as 'different camps are formed and dissolved, depending on the *particular issue* at stake and on the *particular situation*' (Beck, 1992: 100). In this context consumers have collectively and successfully used 'lay' expertise to challenge 'expert' knowledge (Popay and Williams, 1994b). For example, the Bristol Survey Support Group (Stacey, 1994) contested 'scientific research' which had questioned the efficacy of the Bristol Cancer Self-Help Centre which uses alternative as well as conventional therapies in the treatment of breast cancer. Brown (1987) has used the term 'popular epidemiology' to refer to the challenges that lay persons can collectively make to public agencies, such as public health departments, which fail to do their job adequately – for example, in the case of environmental hazards.

Contracts: competition or co-operation?

Harrison and Lachmann (1996:1) contend that the current NHS is characterized by low-trust relationships in which 'everything must be defined, costed and documented and in which patients are merely a sort of currency for organisational transactions'. The *source* of this ethos is the misguided belief that health-care markets can operate much like retail markets; the *result* is secrecy and non-co-operation which undermines any aspirations to run the NHS in the public interest. Patients, who are construed as discrete disease episodes that are 'contracted for', literally become products in a market, caught up in a system which is mystifying and within which they can have little real say about what happens to them.

At the present time the NHS is a hybrid model which tries, unsuccessfully, to *combine* a public service with a market-based, commercial ethos. A clash of cultures develops where on the one hand, staff work within high-trust relationships with others characterized by diffuse patterns of tacit mutual obligations, and on the other in an environment in which everything must be defined and documented and placed in a quasi-contractual relationship – a situation which is anathema to the ethos of public service (Hunter, 1996). The problems that exist for those working in the system become clear in Flynn et al.'s (1996) study of contracting in community health services (CHS) which comprise, among other things, district nursing, health visiting, chiropody, community midwifery, and preventive services. For a number of reasons, CHS do not accommodate well to the quasi-market. First of all, CHS trusts are often more or less monopoly providers in an area, and purchasers (especially GP fundholders) want to retain local services and a close collaborative relationship with them. However, contracting for services takes place within an environment of cost constraints and a central push to build quality into contracts. Specifying cost and quality is far from easy in any area of health care, but is especially problematic in CHS. The nature of CHS is difficult to specify due to the heterogeneity of services provided, the relatively 'invisible' nature of the professional work undertaken (often one to one in people's homes), and the fact that the care delivered does not lend itself readily to the measurement of outcomes. This means that high-trust relationships are necessary. Not surprisingly difficulties arise because 'central strategic objectives create pressures for purchasers to increase the volume of activity while controlling (or reducing) providers' costs *and* assume that purchasers will cooperate in harmonious partnerships' (Flynn et al., 1996: 137). This can be seen in respondents' own words. Thus a purchaser director of finance related, 'There is a dilemma. We are pushed to show how we are buying more health gain, but we don't know what we are buying at the moment. So we can't demonstrate health gain.' Often purchasers were frustrated by what was seen as providers' recalcitrance in providing outcomes data to demonstrate the health benefits of CHS. But, as a trust manager stated, 'It's a great deal easier when you're producing nuts and washers, isn't it? When you're trying to improve somebody's well-being in the community, and improving their quality of life – these things are difficult to measure, there is no doubt about that.' Trusts' claims of under-resourcing tended to be met with scepticism when they were not accompanied by evidence. In the words of one purchaser chief executive, 'you expect us to trust you about the alleged underfunding, but you need to *show* us'. Their fieldwork leads Flynn et al. to conclude that, despite the fact that the very nature of CHS requires high-trust relations and the recognition of this by purchasers, trust was essentially eroded by contract negotiations. Negotiations over two contracting rounds revealed a difficult oscillation between assumptions of 'high-trust/high-discretion' relationships and 'low-trust/low-discretion' contracts in the internal market.

Low trust may also increasingly typify relations between patients and providers. While securing what is perceived to be the best health care that is available is likely to be the aim of both patient and health-care provider, their interests may not always coincide. The ethos of individualism that pervades health policy holds patients personally accountable for their own health, and health workers accountable for the care that they provide. There is an attempt to make actions far more visible through standard-setting and clinical and consumer audit, and, increasingly, staff must be able to provide demonstrable proof that they have carried out their work to a high standard. In chapter 8 (and also later in chapter 9) we will see that, while the aim to make staff accountable to patients may enhance the quality of some aspects of patient care, it might also generate a backlash as staff perceive patients to be more and more 'aware of their rights' and ready to complain and take legal action against them as individuals. Fearful of lack of support from colleagues (particularly hospital management), they may increasingly turn to defensive practices which are not in the interests of good patient care. Thus, if the flip side of reflexivity and choice is the assumption of individual responsibility, an unintended consequence of the new health service may be to pit not only purchasers against providers, and providers against other providers, but also providers and their 'clients' against each other.

The road ahead

Commentators now seem resigned to the continued existence of the health-care market, even though it may be tempered by more evidently collaborative relationships. Indeed, leading commentators on the NHS have begun to argue that a split between those who fund health care and those who provide it does not *need* to involve competition. Ham (1996) recommends that the purchaser–provider split be retained since it helps to promote accountability of providers and to ensure that resources are used in patients' best interests, but maintains that this does not need to be competitive. As we have seen, the Labour government has said that it will put NHS purchasing solely in the hands of primary care commissioning groups which will buy virtually all aspects of care for all patients (DoH, 1997). Writing in the *Independent* newspaper before the 1997 election, the then shadow Health Secretary Chris Smith stated that the Labour Party wanted to 'retain the division of responsibility between those who order care and treatment for patients and those who deliver. That is a common sense division, but we would want it to lead to a system where doctors, hospitals and health authorities would sit down together and agree a forward programme of treatment for their patients' (Smith, 1996: 15). In mid-September 1997 the Health Secretary announced new guidance on the future of the NHS which emphasized the development of longer-term contracts (spanning at least three years) and greater financial openness between health authorities and trusts. This is spelt out in the White Paper, *The New NHS* (DoH, 1997). But here, as elsewhere, it is evident that the relationship between those who fund and those who provide health care will still involve what is called *contestability* so that provider interests do not prevail. Thus Harrison and Lachmann (1996) refer to those who fund health care, in the last resort and after due notice, withholding the renewal of contract with a trust whose services are not satisfactory.

Appleby (1992) likened the reforms of the 1990s to a super-liner which takes time to gain momentum when it first slips from its moorings, but soon begins to gather speed. In the minds of many, full speed ahead set the NHS on a collision course. It remains to be seen whether the ship can change direction and sail into the calmer waters of collaboration, rather than competition. Importantly, it remains to be seen whether any change in direction, as the NHS reaches its fiftieth anniversary in the summer of 1998, will benefit patients who, as we have seen, despite their ubiquity have had a rather ghostly presence in discussion of the provision of health care during the 1990s.

8

Professional Powers: The Formal Health-Care Division of Labour in Transition

*Anyone who has ever known doctors well enough to hear medical shop talked without reserve knows that they are full of stories about each other's blunders and errors, and that the theory of their **omniscience and omnipotence** no more holds good among themselves than it did with Molière and Napoleon. (Shaw, 1980 [1911]: 15; emphasis added)*

The theme of medical omniscience and omnipotence exceeds all else in twentieth-century discussions of the health-care division of labour. From the words of the Fabian playwright George Bernard Shaw, who referred to the professions as conspiracies against the laity, to a number of more recent critics of the self-serving character of medicine, writers on the professions have viewed medicine's power as *the* defining feature of contemporary health care.

But is all this set to change? Increased questioning of professional expertise by the public and attempts to undermine the expensive monopoly hold of doctors over the diagnosis and treatment of illness together constitute a forceful threat to the power of medicine. This has led to a radical shift of focus in the sociology of the medical profession: after a period of almost thirty years spent exploring the sources of medical *dominance*, sociologists are now turning their attention to professional *decline* (Annandale, 1989a). This chapter begins by considering recent theoretical debates on the powers of medicine in Britain and the United States. As the chapter unfolds attention turns increasingly towards the contemporary NHS and to what promises to be *the* significant debate of the new century, namely, the erasure of traditional clinical boundaries between medicine and nursing and the shifting intra-professional division of labour.

Current theoretical debates on the power of medicine

Eliot Freidson's concept of 'professional dominance' so successfully captured the collective imagination of a generation of sociologists that it continues to serve as the lens through which debates on the power of medicine are refracted.

In *The Profession of Medicine* (first published in 1970) he wrote that

> *the professional has gained a status which protects him [sic] more than other experts from outside scrutiny and criticism and which grants him extraordinary autonomy in controlling both the definition of the problems he works on and the way he performs his work. (Freidson, 1988 [1970]: 337)*

The monopoly right which medicine has been able to secure over the diagnosis and treatment of illness has afforded physicians a prominent place in the health-care division of labour:

> *organised autonomy is not merely freedom from the competition or regulation of other workers, but in the case of such a profession as medicine . . . it is also freedom to regulate other occupations. Where we find one occupation with organised autonomy in a division of labour, it dominates the others. Immune from legitimate regulation or evaluation by other occupations, it can itself legitimately evaluate and order the work of others. By its position in the division of labour we can designate it as a **dominant profession**. (Freidson, 1988: 369)*

For Freidson, then, medicine's power has two interrelated dimensions: *autonomy*, or the ability to control its own work activities, and *dominance*, or control over the work of others in the health-care division of labour. Taken together, dominance and autonomy 'are such as to give the professions a splendid isolation, indeed the opportunity to develop a protected insularity without peer among occupations lacking the same privileges' (Freidson, 1988: 369). Although professional self-regulation may seem quite straightforward, it has, in Wolinsky's (1993: 13) words, potentially staggering implications, since how can we trust the profession not to 'misuse its autonomy and abuse its clientele'? The medical profession has steadfastly stuck to the claim that the specialist nature of its knowledge must rule out external regulation – only other members of the profession can judge a physician's work. For Freidson (1988: 370) this is the 'critical flaw' of professional autonomy, for it encourages 'a self-deceiving view of the objectivity and reliability of its knowledge and of the virtues of its members'. Errors of practice go undetected, and alternative views of health and illness are ruled out of court. In the final chapter of *The Profession of Medicine* Freidson boldly stated that it was time for medicine's autonomy to be tempered. He outlined several means of achieving this, including changes in the way that physicians are trained and, most importantly for our discussion here, he recommended that individuals must be required to set up mechanisms whereby they review each other's work.

The changes that have taken place over the last decade have far surpassed those urged by Freidson when he wrote *The Profession of Medicine* now almost thirty years ago, prompting commentators to refer to the proletarianization and deprofessionalization of the medical profession.

Proletarianization theory

Proletarianization theory as it has been applied to health care was initially formulated in the 1970s and is most closely associated with the work of John McKinlay and his colleagues in the United States. In *The Communist Manifesto* Marx and Engels wrote that 'the bourgeoisie has stripped of its halo every occupation hitherto honoured and looked up to with reverent awe. It has converted the physician, the lawyer, the priest, the poet, the man of science, into its paid wage labourers' (1975 [1848]: 45). The logic of capitalist expansion is such that all workers, including professionals, will eventually be absorbed into the mass of workers and, by this process, stripped of their control over the terms and conditions of their work. In other words, they will very gradually be reduced to proletarian status.

As recently as forty years ago it was typical for physicians to work in small independent practices in the United States. But, with the state-sponsored encroachment of capitalist prerogatives into health care, larger-scale organizations have gradually developed to support new technologies, and increasingly complex organizational structures have been put in place to monitor the flow of work. Like craftworkers before them, as physicians are incorporated into large-scale bureaucracies they are gradually shorn of control over their work, which becomes increasingly subject to rationalization as it is divided into numerous specialist tasks, some of which can be undertaken by less qualified, cheaper workers (such as nurses). Physicians, it is argued, now work in the service of capital, selling their labour power on the market in much the same way as any other worker. McKinlay defines the proletarianization of physicians as, 'the process by which an occupational category is divested of control over certain prerogatives relating to the location, content, and essentiality of its task activities, thereby subordinating it to the broader requirements of production under advanced capitalism' (McKinlay and Stoeckle, 1988: 200). Although, of course, physicians' salaries are considerably higher than those of most workers, they are still subject to a similar process of exploitation. Hafferty and McKinlay (1993: 216) argue that we need to consider not the *amount* of money earned, but the *total value* that is created each year by the physician's labour for the employing organization: 'through the presence of sophisticated biotechnology, testing procedures, referrals, and other means, a physician can easily generate in excess of $1 million in value for an employer, thus rendering a $200,000 salary as less than a twenty per cent return on value created'. This 'rate of exploitation' has been increasing over time.

For many sociologists of the professions it takes a great leap of faith to define physicians as members of the proletariat. The physicians that most of us have had contact with may seem to bear little resemblance to Derber's (1982: 7) definition of the proletarianized worker as someone who first and foremost 'is powerless to shape the nature of his [*sic*] product or the process of his work'. Even other theorists from *within* the tradition of political economy have had problems with the thesis of proletarianization. Navarro (1988), for example, writes that, unlike physicians, truly proletarian labourers do not have the kinds of skills that need to be credentialled by the state, do not supervise others, and have control over neither the means nor the organization of production.

The process of proletarianization is evidently very much bound up with the move from self-employed to employee status and the lack of control that this is said to signify. But, really, as a number of commentators have pointed out in criticism of McKinlay, the shift to employee status is really too gross an indicator of proletarian status. More important are the consequences that being employed has for the independence of the professions and their capacity to control their own work. Self-employment does not necessarily confer autonomy when one is subject to the vagaries of a precarious market; similarly if your services are highly valued and in demand you can 'write your ticket' *as* an employee (Freidson, 1986). What counts, then, is the professional's relationship to the economic market. This means that proletarianization theory is embroiled in larger debates about the transformation of work alongside the economic and cultural shifts that have taken place in late capitalist/late modern society and the contentious issue of how we can signify the class location of professionals within Marxism.

Derber et al. have brought together a focus on structural changes in the capitalist economy and opinions and experiences of a number of professional groups, which includes physicians, in their research in the USA. For these authors 'intellectual property is becoming the coin of the realm, convertible into class power, privilege and status' (Derber et al., 1990: 55). Credentialled knowledge has thus become a unique form of power wielded by the professions over clients and other workers. This power was exhibited in its purest form in the imperial Chinese empire where, under Confucian logic, Mandarin scholars ruled as an aristocracy controlling all aspects of life. Current professionals, write Derber et al., 'are neither new mandarins nor new proletariat, but blend qualities of both'. They quote two American physicians: referring to his work in a hospital, one said 'we run our show here. We set this place up and run medicine our own way', while another remarked 'I don't have control over how my life works because I'm just an employee' (1990: 139). Neither of these positions fully tells the tale of the true nature of physicians' work: in reality, professionals *are* increasingly taking on employee status, but they have found ways to turn 'dependent employment into authority and privilege' (Derber et al., 1990: 122).

For Derber et al., the powers of the professions and capital are 'two intertwined systems of domination co-existing in relative harmony' (1990: 119). There are gains and losses for each side. For physicians the 'gain' is the expensive physical plant and equipment that they could otherwise not afford, for capital it is the ability to harness the productive resource of knowledge that no one else can provide. The loss, or 'trade-off' for the medical profession is having to accept new controls over their work imposed by management; for capital, it is professionals' inroads into and claims to steer the organization. Although this thesis would appear to pertain more readily to the American private health-care market, it is arguably also relevant to the British context with the emergence of a quasi-market in the NHS during the 1990s (as discussed in chapter 7 above). The relationship of physicians and management is an issue that we will take up in more detail later in this chapter.

The implication of Derber et al.'s work is that, even though professional wings can be severely clipped, full proletarianization is unlikely ever to occur because of the power that is invested in expertise. These authors place a great deal of weight on the success that physicians have had in securing a state-sponsored monopoly over what counts as legitimate knowledge and their ability to stave off or co-opt challenges from consumers and alternative practitioners of various kinds (Saks, 1994). Effectively, this is the basis of professional power. Other contributors to the debate on the power of medicine are far less sanguine in this regard.

Deprofessionalization theory

Like the theory of proletarianization, Haug's deprofessionalization thesis can be placed in the context of debates about the emergence of a new economic order. Her hypothesis on the future status of medicine was first developed in the early 1970s making her one of the first commentators to prophesy a decline in professional powers. Deprofessionalization is defined as 'a loss to professional occupations of their unique qualities, particularly their monopoly over knowledge, public belief in their service ethos and expectations of work autonomy and authority over clients' (Haug, 1973: 197). More specifically, Haug argues that professional authority is being undermined by the emergence of an increasingly educated and critical populace. She goes as far as to refer to a 'revolt of the client' which hits at the heart of professional claims to authority. Media messages which exhort patients to demand their rights, an increasingly educated public and the growing specialization of medical knowledge are said to lie behind this social movement. There is now *so much* knowledge to keep abreast of that medicine is finding it more and more of a challenge to keep one step ahead of the public in the knowledge stakes. Physicians have traditionally coped with this by dividing up the 'expertise pie so that each would master slices in depth'; thus maintaining monopoly through specialization (1973: 200). This becomes less viable with the advent of the computerization of knowledge and the possibility of codifying diagnostic and treatment regimens so that they can be accessed by less qualified persons. Furthermore, as individual physicians become progressively less able to grasp the whole corpus of medical knowledge, patients and their advocates may find themselves more and more able to present themselves as experts on a particular condition and its treatment.

Commentators on the deprofessionalization thesis have tended to conclude that, although consumerism no doubt has some impact on physicians' work patterns, it does not constitute a significant challenge to professional dominance (see Elston, 1991). Marie Haug's own most recent statement on the issue was published back in 1988. At that time she wrote that 'although there is considerable evidence favouring the hypothesis, the findings do not, to date, appear sufficient to retain it with ninety-five per cent confidence'. However, she went on to remark that 'there is no evidence favouring rejecting it either' (Haug, 1988: 54).

Even though Haug's thesis was developed to explain the American situation of the 1970s and 1980s, her work was in many ways ahead of its time in hypothesizing consumerism in health care, particularly in the British context (see chapter 7 above). Yet, despite its obvious topicality, the thesis of deprofessionalization is curiously out of tune with contemporary theoretical debates in sociology. In much the same way that McKinlay sticks quite resolutely to a rather unreflexive use of Marxist theory, failing to engage with complex disputes about the class structure in late capitalist society in his theory of proletarianization, Haug's work is outside recent theoretical debates about 'the self' in the 'late modern' age.

At this point it is useful to refer back briefly to the discussion of reflexivity that was outlined in chapter 1. Under conditions of what has variously been called late capitalism, high modernity or reflexive modernity, new and constantly shifting parameters of risk and uncertainty thread through everyday life, coaxing individuals into a continual process of making and re-making their lives (Beck et al., 1994). Under such conditions the populace must be constantly questioning – reflecting not only on the conditions of their own lives, but also on the authority of others. Lash contrasts the old 'bureaucratic' and new 'reflexive' welfare state in these terms:

> If simple modernization's totalising inversion of the social rights of the Enlightenment project is the impersonality of the bureaucratic welfare state, then its reflexive counterpart understands that welfare services are a client-centred co-production and advocates a decentralised citizen-empowering alternative set of welfare arrangements. (Lash, 1994: 113)

The 'empowerment of the individual', then, is at the heart of 'reflexive modernity'. But what does consumerism actually mean in the context of challenges to medicine? Theoretically it can be thought of as a corollary of reflexivity. Making choices necessarily involves a process of evaluation, of deciding which expert individual or expert system can best meet our needs and, when they fall short, it involves calling them to account. On the face of it, recent rises in medical malpractice litigation and formal complaints against health-care workers are important indicators of consumerism. Yet we know that plaintiffs rarely win their cases and that complaints are often evaded (Lloyd-Bostock, 1992). When we add to this the limited ability of patients really to exercise choice when registering with a GP or seeking a referral to hospital (see chapter 7), it becomes apparent that consumerism is not living up to its promise. The new ideology of consumerism in health care may have less to do with enhancing the power of consumers for the *sake* of consumers, and more to do with putting the consumer at the centre of a market-led system as a means of tempering the power of the medical profession by holding physicians to account for their actions in various ways. Viewed in this light, is reflexive modernity's empowered citizen really just a stick with which to beat the medical profession?

The particular terms in which the debate on consumerism and professional powers has been framed make it very difficult to answer this question. Its American progenitors tend to conceptualize 'reflexivity' and consumerism in cultural rather than political terms. This means that they overlook the possibility that, under current conditions, consumerism may be politically implicated. Thus, attempts to cut health-care costs by changing doctors' behaviour can be promoted in the name of the consumer. As Klein (1995: 137) writes, in the NHS reforms 'consumers were cast as the rank and file in the assault on provider power in the public services: the infantry who would follow up the ministerial artillery barrage. The strong state, in other words, would draw its power from mobilising the people, by-passing (and so undermining) the entrenched interests.'

Moving debates on the powers of medicine forward

Although the debate between the theories of professional dominance, proletarianization and deprofessionalization sensitizes us to a range of important issues, in the end it raises many more questions than it answers. As Freidson (1994: 149) himself has written more recently, the sociology of the professions is in 'an intellectual shambles'.

It is important to make clear that Freidson, Haug and McKinlay agree wholeheartedly that medicine's autonomy and dominance is being challenged. They all appreciate that physicians now work in increasingly complex organizational structures; that medical work is increasingly rationalized (through new technologies and management prerogatives which curtail discretion); that other practitioners and patients are making inroads into what were once exclusively medical enclaves; and that, as a profession, medicine is increasingly subject to hierarchical divisions (Hafferty and Wolinsky, 1991). They part company, however, in their interpretation of (1) *why* these changes are taking place, and (2) *what they portend* for the future. To recap, for McKinlay the inroads of capital into medicine are leading to proletarianization of the medical profession (i.e. a fall to proletarian status), while for Haug the challenge of consumers means that medicine is gradually losing its cultural legitimacy. For both of these theorists the power of medicine is on a downward slide. However, as we will see in the next section, Freidson predicts that, despite significant challenges, medicine will have little difficulty maintaining its position of dominance as we enter the twenty-first century.

It is clear that the concepts of professional dominance and autonomy have been defined in different ways by different theorists, leading to a great deal of confusion over just *when* the powers of medicine can be said to be in decline. Theoretical differences notwithstanding, there is a lack of testable hypotheses in the positions that we have considered. This means that it is far from clear what evidence is necessary for the outcome of proletarianization or deprofessionalization (Wolinsky, 1993). That is, how will we know it when we see it? The same indicators can be read in different ways – for example, do various attempts by the professions to protect their interests tell us that medicine can still successfully maintain its status? Or, does the very existence of challenges indicate that the powers of medicine are on the decline (Hafferty and Wolinsky, 1991; Harrison and Pollitt, 1994)?

Added to this, there is confusion over what professional dominance and professional autonomy themselves consist of (Levine, 1993). Before we can move forward, then, it is important to clarify the different dimensions of professional power. As we saw at the beginning of this chapter, sociologists of the medical profession have largely adopted Freidson's (1988) view that the power of medicine rests on its autonomy and dominance. It is important to maintain the distinction between these terms, which are often used interchangeably in the literature. As we saw earlier, as originally defined, *autonomy* refers to the ability of medicine to control its own work activities. Medical *dominance* refers to medicine's control over the work of others in the health-care division of labour. The concept of medical autonomy rightly comes in for considerable criticism; it is all very well to refer to autonomy as control over the content of work, but what this entails is never made clear in a consistent manner (Coburn, 1992). In Elston's (1991) opinion, we can think of autonomy in three dimensions: (1) *economic autonomy* (the right to determine remuneration); (2) *political autonomy* (the ability to influence health policies); (3) *clinical/technical autonomy* (the right of the profession to set its own standards and to monitor its own performance).

A second issue that we must make clear is the level of analysis that we are referring to when we consider the professional powers of medicine. Sometimes commentators refer to the clinical practitioner, sometimes the corporate body of medicine. More often than not, they do not make the level they are referring to clear at all. This is particularly problematic since, as we will see, we can come to quite different conclusions about whether professional autonomy and dominance are declining depending on the level of analysis that we employ. This point is particularly important to Freidson in his recent writing on professional powers.

Professional dominance revisited

Like Haug and McKinlay, Freidson is well aware of the significant changes that have taken place in health care over the 1980s and 1990s. But, unlike them, he does not feel that they are likely to have a big impact on the powers of medicine. However, when he makes this statement, Freidson is referring to the medical profession as a *collective* or corporate body, not to the work of *individual* practitioners. The crucial point to grasp from Freidson's recent work on the professions is his thesis that *divisions within medicine* are intensifying. He argues that this very process of stratification helps to maintain the powers of medicine as a corporate body, but significantly undermines the autonomy of some segments of the profession. Let us look at this argument in a little more detail.

Of course the medical profession has *always* been stratified. But whereas in the past physicians in different specialisms and at different ranks in the hierarchy acted as 'presumptive peers', the various divisions are now heightened, far more visible and 'up front.' In Freidson's own words, 'what is new today is the magnification and formalisation of . . . relationships into a considerably more overt and consequential system of stratification within the profession which can no longer be protected by the face-saving norms of traditional professional etiquette' (1994: 144). There has been a loss of internal cohesion within the profession as it has increasingly divided into a *rank and file* on the one hand and a tripartite disciplinary, educational and administrative *elite* of physicians on the other (Freidson, 1989). This process of internal stratification is itself an adaptive response to attempts by the state and other agencies (such as insurance companies and employers in the USA) to cut costs by curbing the discretion that physicians have traditionally enjoyed in diagnosis and treatment. Quite simply put, the medical profession is dividing and policing itself in order to keep external control at bay.

At the collective or corporate level, physicians are still firmly in control of the key factors that confer autonomy: control over *credentialling* (training and the right to practice) and over the monitoring of *practice standards*. It is the rank and file, that is the vast majority of doctors working with patients in the community and in hospitals, who bear the brunt of these changes. Freidson writes that the elites 'subject everyday practitioners to unprecedented surveillance and evaluation . . . they are empowered to impose concrete economic sanctions, in some cases so severe as suspending their license to practice' (Freidson, 1989: 216). Physicians are now expected to use formal evaluation alongside the traditionally informal methods (see Atkinson, 1981) in monitoring the work of juniors and peers. An interesting indicator of this is what Freidson (1994) calls the restructuring of formal criticism of colleagues since physicians must now judge each other not only informally as in the past, but formally and often in public. The General Medical Council (GMC) – the body which controls registration of competence to practise in Britain – for example, has been pushed increasingly towards the monitoring of clinical skills and, after a long period of resistance, has recently told registered practitioners that they now have a duty to inform on a colleague 'whose behaviour may have raised a question about serious professional misconduct' (GMC quoted in Stacey, 1992: 234). This move was given added bite by the Secretary of State for Health's announcement (in August 1995) that doctors are under a contractual obligation to report colleagues whose work they believe to be incompetent. It is also evident that physicians are now far more willing to act as expert witnesses in malpractice cases heard in court.

As we have seen, McKinlay talks of the proletarianization of the medical profession *as a whole*. From our discussion so far, it would appear that Freidson is referring to the polarization of the profession and proletarianization of one segment of it. However, this is not, in fact, the tenor of his argument. He still maintains that even the rank and file have infinitely more discretion in their daily tasks than most other workers. To be sure, he argues, the formal rules of the elite 'establish a basis for evaluating, even if not closely monitoring, the work of the rank and file' (Freidson, 1986: 215), but medicine is characterized by contested knowledge and contingencies of practice. This means that the rank and file will typically enjoy a legitimate discretion in their work in spite of budgeting and the burgeoning mechanisms of quality audit and peer review.

Freidson's recent work suggests that concepts like professional dominance, proletarianization and deprofessionalization are far too sweeping and over-generalized. Rather than talking in terms of opposites such as whether physicians are dominant/not dominant, professionalized/deprofessionalized and so on, we need to appreciate the medical profession as a body which is subject to a series of *countervailing pressures* for change, some of which may undermine and some of which may enhance professional powers. He consistently affirms that the key to understanding the professions is through the *work that they do* (Freidson, 1994). In other words, we need to bring the debate on the powers of medicine down to earth by placing it more firmly in the context of the health-care division of labour as it is played out each and every day in the work that occupies doctors, managers, nurses and other carers.

Professions in the health-care division of labour

The concept of countervailing powers is a very useful corrective to theories which see the medical profession as dominant/not dominant, proletarianized/not proletarianized. It asks us to consider the powers of medicine in terms of a series of moves and countermoves between a number of key actors, which include the state, health-care managers, and nurses. The idea of countervailing powers, which goes back to the work of Montesquieu in the eighteenth century, has recently been brought into the sociology of the professions by Light and others. Donald Light argues that the concept of countervailing powers

> *focuses attention on the interactions of powerful actors in a field where they are inherently interdependent yet distinct. If one party is dominant, as the . . . medical profession has long been, its dominance is contextual and eventually. elicits counter-moves by other powerful actors, not to destroy it but to redress an imbalance of power. (1995: 26)*

In other words, the medical profession and other actors undergo cyclical 'phases of harmony and discord in which countervailing actions take place' (Light, 1995: 27). In these terms, dominance has ironic consequences since 'a profession's power to shape its domain in its own image leads to excesses that prompt counter-actions' from other groups in the division of labour (1995: 25). The cycle continues as physicians and others respond by changing *their* behaviour in order to circumvent the controls that are placed on their actions by others.

This suggests that it is far more appropriate to envisage power in the contemporary health-care arena in terms of a number of groups jockeying for position; as a game of move and countermove, rather than as a trajectory towards a propositional endpoint (such as proletarianization). There are copious illustrations of this. For example, the fact that contemporary British psychiatry retains a medical orientation at the core of a rather eclectic belief system both shores up what is presented as a rather unique knowledge base, but also renders it vulnerable to jurisdictional claims from a range of alternative providers in the move away from the hospital to community care (Samson, 1995). While on the one hand, like other medical specialisms, psychiatry is exposed to loss of control and de-skilling in response to managerial concerns with cost efficiency and outcomes measurement, on the other its flexible knowledge base means that it is also able to co-opt these discourses to its own ends (for example in the current vogue for evaluation and appraisal within psychiatry) and to 're-direct thinking back to the advantages of the mental hospital – biomedical knowledge, legal custody, and "safety"' at a time when 'community care has begun to lose its glow' as concerns about social order come increasingly to the fore (1995: 265).

The relative power of any one occupation can, then, only be fully understood through an examination of the intricate web of interactions with other occupations. Both *inter-* and *intra*-professional interactions are becoming enormously complex at the present time, a move which, in Britain, has been driven in large part by concerns about medical staffing patterns within the Department of Health which, interestingly, although declaring that 'it is clearly time for some changes in the structure and pattern of working arrangements in the health service', has also stated that 'the direction, extent and mechanisms of such changes are not certain' (DoH, 1995c: 57). The boundaries between medicine, nursing and management, in particular, are currently in a state of flux; new roles such as the physician–manager and advanced nurse practitioner cut across traditional professional jurisdictions, raising vexed questions of allegiance. With whom does the new physician–manager identify – with physicians or with management colleagues? The recent reduction in the hours that junior doctors should work, as well as concurrent changes in medical education which require extra dedicated time for supervised medical training in Britain, mean that an elite cadre of nurses is beginning to take on 'doctors work': might they find themselves with more in common with junior doctors than with nurses? Following on from this, what are the implications of the blur-

Table 8.1   Strategies for managing clinical activity

Continuum of management intervention		
Minimal_____Maximal		
Strategy 1	Strategy 2	Strategy 3
Raising professional standards	*Involving doctors in management*	*External management control*
• Medical audit	• Budgets for doctors	• Managing medical work
• Standards & guidelines	• Resource management	• Changing doctors' contracts
	• Doctor–managers	• Extending provider competition

Source: adapted from C. Ham and D. Hunter (1988), *Managing Clinical Activity in the NHS* (London: King's Fund), Briefing Paper 8. Reproduced by permission.

ring of roles for intra-professional solidarity – is, as Freidson's work implies, the power of one segment of the medical profession and one segment of the nursing profession being bought at the cost of a worsened position for the more numerous rank-and-file doctors and nurses?

Physicians and management: better the devil you know?

As we saw in chapter 7, one of the explicit agendas of the NHS and Community Care Act of 1990 was to get a grip on clinical freedom and hold doctors accountable for expenditure (Hunter, 1994). Management was to be the conduit for a sea-change in the culture of the NHS. As Harrison and Pollitt (1994) discuss, there are two principal ways in which physicians' work can be managed: by *direct attack* and by *incorporation*. It is useful to think of these as ideal types on the end of a continuum of management control of physicians. Ham and Hunter (1988) provide us with a useful typology of management strategies which range from minimal to maximal in form (as outlined in table 8.1).

Maximal control via external monitoring – which can be thought of as a form of direct attack, rather than incorporation – has been relatively rare to date in Britain, although the new GP and consultant contracts of the 1990s might be thought of as one example. For example, the Audit Commission (1996a: 4) reports that, although most consultants work long hours, many fail to provide the job plans setting out their day-to-day work that are required as a condition of contract. The Commission recommends that all trusts should ensure that these plans are completed for all consultants, specifying all their duties and responsibilities, and that they be regularly monitored. External monitoring has been far more common in the USA to date, where attempts by buyers of health care (such as the government, employers and insurance companies) to cut costs have generated a new industry of physician 'utilization management' systems which aim to monitor doctors' behaviour according to a range of pre-set and costed criteria. Light (1993) writes that one major medical centre, the Mayo Clinic, now deals with 1,000 clinical review plans which are tailored to meet the needs of various buyers; the large average hospital, he reports, deals with 100–200 plans. Control over the implementation (if not the design) of these plans is often external to the medical profession, with *nurses* evaluating physicians' clinical practices and determining the reimbursement that they will receive from buyers (Wolinsky, 1993).

In Britain, medicine's elite governing bodies such as the Royal Colleges have lobbied for minimalist intervention. The 1989 White Paper *Working for Patients* (see chapter 7) appeared to endorse medicine's control of its own standards of work when it stated that 'quality of medical work can only be reviewed by a doctor's peers' (quoted in Harrison and Pollitt, 1994: 97) and affirmed that results of such reviews would be confidential. Harrison and Pollitt conclude that we have 'a version of audit which is kept as a non-threatening activity carried out only by doctors and rigorously protected from the public gaze' (1994: 101). In short, up to now doctors have largely been able to keep clinical audit (which was made mandatory in 1990) off the management brief. Medicine's political autonomy notwithstanding, the problems of measuring medicine's efficacy, and health outcomes, alongside the acceptance of variations in clinical practice, make it difficult to judge professional competence. However, it is interesting to note the expectation that around fifteen new clinical indicators will soon be added to hospital performance league tables providing data on mortality, infection, and readmission rates (for example: deaths in hospital within thirty days of surgery; emergency readmissions within twenty-eight days of previous discharge; and wound infection in hospital following a surgical procedure) (Healy, 1997). This suggests that even quite gross and highly controversial indicators may be used to monitor clinical performance in the near future.

While the maximalist strategy may come more to the fore in the future, the NHS is more aptly characterized by *incorporation* of physicians (through management strategies 1 and 2 – see table 8.1) than by direct attack on doctors by management (through control strategy 3). Physician–managers, in fact, occupy a range of positions in the health service (Hunter, 1992). First of all, there is the physician who takes on the role of general manager of a unit or who becomes the chief executive of a trust. At this level they would effectively do the same job as the non-physician–manager. Since these jobs typically involve a full-time commitment, leaving little or no time for clinical work, there are very few physician–managers at this level. Far more typical is the second type: the part-time managers of departments and clinical directorates. The clinical directorate structure effectively sets up a number of semi-independent units in a hospital, each of which contains a number of medical specialisms. Each directorate usually has a directorate manager (often in a joint clinician–management role) who holds a budget and acts as a corporate manager, supported by a business manager and, sometimes, a nurse manager. This model incorporates a cadre of doctors into management on a part-time basis, effectively controlling colleagues and subordinates and building on the fear that, if physicians do not manage themselves, others will do it for them. The third type of manager referred to by Hunter (1992) is the individual who runs an area such as a clinical laboratory managing a large team of technical and clerical staff.

How do we read the incorporation of physicians into management? Should it be thought of as the co-optation of physicians by government? Or, alternatively, is it a shrewd move to take control on the part of physicians themselves? There are several reasons for supporting the co-optation thesis. For example, we might see the involvement of an elite cadre of doctors in management as a form of corporatism, where physician–managers sell cost-cutting and the control of clinical work to the rank and file on the behalf of the state. In similar terms quality-control measures and audit might be seen as

> the state tightening its grip on most health care workers . . . while
> continuing to allow the medical elite just enough autonomy to ensure
> that they, and not the politicians, continue to carry most of the
> responsibility for painful micro-rationing decisions on exactly which
> patients to treat. (Harrison and Pollitt, 1994: 110)

If physicians manage themselves, they remain effectively in control of politically contentious rationing decisions. As Harrison and Pollitt (1994:

28) remark, 'it is one thing ... to be aware that ... access to renal dialysis is in practice governed by an age cut-off, but quite something else to announce it as government policy'. Indeed, the current Labour government has like its Conservative predecessor stressed that it will not take a lead in rationing. Managers and doctors-as-managers can diffuse blame and decentralize responsibility.

In support of the 'shrewd move' hypothesis is the proposition that when doctors are involved in management they will make their decisions based on what is best for *physicians* (Harrison et al., 1992; Hunter, 1994).

Physician–managers notwithstanding, there are a number of other reasons why physicians might find themselves able to retain control over what Elston (1991) has called their clinical/technical autonomy, i.e. the right to set their own standards and to monitor their own performance. Even when managers (medical and non-medical) attempt to intervene, they can be blocked as the countervailing powers of individual physicians come into play.

A zone of discretion

Despite the possibility for the increased routinization of practice through scientific advances such as computer software programmes (Harrison and Pollitt, 1994), the stress on evidence-based practice and the use of clinical protocols, it seems unlikely that it will ever be possible fully to standardize diagnostic and treatment decisions. Freidson (1994: 42) refers to physicians' enjoyment of a 'zone of discretion' which is intrinsic to medical work. This is micro-level power; it is the power to resist, to non-comply, that is bound up with a monopoly over skills and the uncertainty and risk (feigned or real) that still pervades clinical practice (see chapter 9). The presence of discretionary countervailing powers raises the possibility that attempts to undermine clinical autonomy will be met with a backlash. As Hunter (1991: 446) puts it, attempts to encroach on doctors' territory 'risk creating a range of perverse behaviours' and 'the circumvention of controls and regulations imposed by management'. In the absence of ethnographic research, we know very little about the form that these 'perverse behaviours' might take in Britain. However, US research provides a number of examples, such as physicians' evasion of the constraints of the diagnostic-related group (DRG) system, which pays a fixed amount for the treatment and length of stay for specific diagnosed conditions (Notman et al., 1987). Physicians engage in what Hafferty and McKinlay (1993) call clinical charades such as 'discharging' a patient and then 'readmitting' them under a different diagnosis in order to keep them in hospital. Physicians also shift diagnoses to high-cost groups and/or record complications to collect higher fees – a phenomenon known as 'DRG creep'. A further instance of manipulation follows from the rise in malpractice litigation and complaints (in both the USA and UK). Fearful of a court case or disciplinary action, physicians may engage in 'defensive practices', undertaking certain expensive procedures (such as electrical foetal monitoring, and diagnostic tests) for legal rather than clinical reasons (Annandale, 1989b; Summerton, 1995).

Unfortunately, the abstract nature of the debate on professional powers has meant that we have very little information both on the way that physicians have responded to attempts to curb their clinical autonomy, and also on the impact that their behaviours may have on patients (Hafferty and Light, 1995). This is ironic to say the least, given that sociologists have traditionally drawn a strong association between high levels of professional dominance, clinical autonomy and poor-quality care. Levine quite correctly writes that 'it is not completely clear whether writers in this field are bemoaning the decrease in autonomy that the physician is experiencing or whether they think some form of justice is being served' (1993: 201). As we saw earlier, Freidson (1988) referred to self-regulation as the critical flaw of the medical profession. We might, therefore, expect him to welcome the fact that most physicians now find themselves subject to evaluation by others. But his answer is only a qualified 'yes': monitoring that is *internal* to the profession is acceptable; *external* control is not. The professions, he claims, should not be driven by managerial bureaucracy. This is unacceptable because it standardizes practice and reduces patients to 'formally defined categories', thereby undermining 'the flexible discretionary judgement that is necessary to adapt services to individual needs' (Freidson, 1994: 193) and, we might add, may also generate the 'perverse behaviours' and 'clinical charades' that have just been referred to.

Divisions within medicine

At the most general level, we are led to conclude that, to date, clinical autonomy has not been *significantly* undermined by government-led attempts to use managers to control physicians' practice in Britain. As we have seen, medicine's move into management is likely to tip the control of clinical practice in the favour of physicians as a collective body, and even the rank and file, who bear the brunt of regulation, may be able to find ways of evading control over clinical practice.

But restratification of the profession clearly has winners and losers.

There are opportunities for the elites who now, more than ever before, police the work of their colleagues. There may also be opportunities for general practitioners (GPs). GPs have historically enjoyed less power and status than senior hospital doctors, although their relative isolation has tended to afford them a fairly high degree of clinical autonomy (Light, 1995). With the development of fundholding and the move towards primary care commissioning (DoH, 1997) as well as the shift towards preventive care, GPs have greater economic leverage over their hospital colleagues (Allsop, 1995b; Glennerster et al., 1994). For the first time they are in a position to 'take their business elsewhere' and to exact a financial penalty on providing hospitals if they do not meet the terms of their contracts (Harrison and Pollitt, 1994: 124). Klein (1995: 241) writes of the shifting balance of power between GPs and hospital doctors as 'a revolution (no less a word will do) whose full effects have still to work themselves through, but which clearly represents a new era in the history of the NHS'. But this apparent growth in professional dominance might be offset by increased management control, since the new GP contract of 1991 calls, among other things, for data on practice activity to be provided to health authorities; for GPs to prescribe drugs within an indicative budget; and for practices to meet targets for vaccination, immunization and cervical cytology. The late 1990s have seen a recruitment shortage of doctors into general practice, reflecting perceptions of a stressful and poorly remunerated occupation. In early 1997 the BMA's general medical services committee was calling for a £60,000 basic rate of pay for GPs – effectively a more than 50 per cent rise for most. Apparently, then, 'GPs' power and autonomy are being simultaneously circumscribed and enhanced' (Elston, 1993: 45).

Alongside practitioners who might enhance their autonomy and dominance through the restratification of medicine, there are those whose position of relative weakness is likely to be exacerbated. Divisions by 'race' and gender are of utmost importance in this regard. There is every likelihood that the developments that we have discussed in this chapter will heighten the 'race'- and gender-based inequalities that have historically characterized medicine. The glittering prizes of the new power positions such as clinical directorships and other managerial posts are likely to be white male preserves, while women and minority ethnic groups are coaxed onto a different track as they work in non-consultant positions and in less prestigious specialities.

Women make up only 23 per cent of hospital doctors and 20 per cent of GPs. Only 17 per cent of consultants are women (DoH, 1994a), and these are concentrated in particular areas such as paediatrics, anaesthesiology, and radiology. In 1990 there were only twelve female general surgeons and four cardio-thoracic surgeons in England and Wales (Elston, 1993). Lorber (1991: 31) writes that women are likely to end up in the lower echelons 'where they do not control budgets, allocate resources, or determine the overall direction of the organizations for which they work'. Only 10.8 per cent of general managers at the health authority level, for example, are women (Doyal, 1994b). My own analysis of the gender of senior managers (taken from listings in the Health Service Journal's *Directory of the NHS* for 1994) shows that just over 12 per cent of chief executives of hospitals and approximately 25 per cent of chief executives of community units are female; women made up about 8 per cent of hospital medical directors and 19 per cent of community unit directors/advisers. In contrast, 87 per cent of nurse directors/advisers in hospitals and 68 per cent in the community were women (it should be noted that the Department of Health is a member of the business campaign Opportunity 2000 which aims to increase women's participation in the workforce).

Figures for the ethnic status of physicians is very difficult to come by. Department of Health data (for 1993), which use the unsatisfactory categorization of 'white' and 'non-white' (see chapter 6 above), show that of all EC-qualified consultants, only 6 per cent were self-defined as 'non white' (compared to 79 per cent as 'white' and 14 per cent who did not state their ethnic origin). The largest cluster of 'non-white' physicians at 19 per cent is in the senior house officer grade (78 per cent 'white', 3 per cent not stated). Recent research points in the direction of systematic discrimination in the admission of candidates to UK medical schools and in hospital-based appointments. Thus McManus et al. (1995) found that applicants to medical school from minority ethnic groups were 1.46 times less likely to be accepted (controlling for 'A' level examination results and a range of other factors). Research by the Commission for Racial Equality (CRE, 1996: 8) on consultant and senior registrar appointments between October 1991 and March 1992 shows that 'while the chances of appointment for white applicants increased in the successive stages of the selection process, the reverse was true for ethnic minority applicants'. For example, 147 of the 418 consultant vacancies (in general medicine, general surgery, obstetrics and gynaecology, psychiatry, and geriatrics) attracted minority ethnic group applicants. A total of 42 per cent of the total applicant pool, which consisted of 56 per cent of 'white', but only 28 per cent of the minority ethnic candidates, was shortlisted for interview.

The important point to appreciate from the foregoing discussion, then, is that increased stratification within medicine is likely to affect women and minority ethnic physicians disproportionately. This factor has been totally neglected by the theorists that we considered in the first part of this chapter.

Contested domains: medicine and nursing in the new NHS

So far we have been looking at the clinical autonomy of medicine by reference to the growing *intra*-professional divisions that have been prompted by reforms in the health service. Medicine has also tradition- ally ruled supreme in the *inter*-occupational health-care division of labour, but, for reasons that we will now go on to discuss, this is changing and with this change may come a new set of challenges for medicine, nursing and other health occupations.

Nursing has not traditionally appeared in debates on medical power. As Walby et al. (1994: 141) explain, 'most accounts of medicine in the NHS presume that they are dealing with two groups – doctors and managers'. Why has nursing been neglected? Part of our answer lies in the gender-blind nature of research on professional powers, referred to above. Nurses are the largest group of health service workers constitut- ing 50.9 per cent of the workforce (405,280 full-time equivalent posts in 1991; Alaszewski, 1995). In fact, approximately one in forty of all em- ployed persons in Britain works as a nurse (Robinson, 1992) and the vast majority (90 per cent) of these are women. Around 15 per cent of male, and 6 per cent of female, nurses are from minority ethnic groups (Beishon et al., 1995).

The gender- and 'race'-blind nature of research on the professions is, of course, consonant with nursing's traditional lack of power in the health-care arena. Although it has long been recognized that nurses and midwives are often able to exercise autonomy and exert a fair degree of control (especially over junior doctors) at the level of individual interac- tion with physicians (Hughes, 1988), structural conditions such as legal and professional proscriptions on the kind of work that they can under- take have meant that commentators have largely taken medical domi- nance as given. But is all this set to change?

The stimulus for a shift in the boundaries between medical and nursing work derives from three broad structural factors. First, non- physician providers can sometimes deliver a comparable service at lower cost. This is fostered by specialization which permits knowledge to be broken down into smaller tasks which can be undertaken by less skilled workers. The second factor precipitating change is the statutory reduction in junior doctors' hours of work as part of the 'new deal for junior doctors' in Britain. A government task force found that most juniors were actually working for seventy-two hours a week, and spent an average of 104 hours a week on duty (NHSME, 1991). The new deal stipulated that by April 1993 doctors should be spending no more than sixty hours actually working each week, to be reduced to fifty-six hours by December 1994. It is interesting to note that long hours on duty were explicitly linked to 'costly mishaps', and that the policy to reduce hours coincided with the Department of Health's assumption of liability for medical malpractice. The removal of a body of relatively cheap junior doctors from hospital wards and casualty departments has precipitated an ongoing staffing crisis in many British hospitals (places for 390 new junior doctors were announced in September 1997). A window of opportunity opened up for nurses and midwives: the possibility of taking on enhanced and advanced nurse practitioner (ANP) roles.

A change in the nature of nurses' and midwives' work, then, seems an obvious solution to the ambition both to cut costs and to reduce doctors' hours of work. These agendas also sit well with the third factor precipitating boundary changes between nursing and medicine: nursing's own professionalization strategy. The last few years have seen major changes in nurse training as it has moved out of hospitals and into higher education (Davies, 1995). New 'nursing models' have been developed, such as 'primary nursing', which aims to enhance practice autonomy by putting the nurse at the centre of the health-care division of labour as the key carer of a particular patient, whose care is approached in a holistic manner (Salvage, 1992). A second, and arguably contrasting, professionalizing strategy has been to develop a cadre of highly technically oriented clinical nurse specialists. The development of the new ANP role has been caught on the horns of a dilemma between these two roles. My own observation of the meetings of senior nurses and consultants in one (then) regional health authority during 1994 as it sought to implement the new deal revealed that, although nurses initially worried about the loss of what was seen as nursing's distinctive 'caring role' or ability to see the patient in a holistic manner, the new roles that were eventually developed were very task-oriented. Debate centred around the ability and willingness of *nurses* to undertake procedures (such as venepuncture and suturing minor wounds) and the willingness of *physicians* to relinquish these tasks and to take responsibility for overseeing nurses' performance.

The boundary between medicine and nursing is currently a great source of tension and change. The traditional distinction between nursing work as *care* and medical work as *treatment* is blurring for the reasons that have been outlined. In different circumstances, nurses and physicians may embrace or reject this redefinition of their role. A number of scenarios present themselves. First of all, there are occasions when nurses may be happy to take on what were once physicians' tasks, and physicians are willing to let them. For example intensive care nurses may take on diagnostic work such as making decisions about the level of sedation that a patient needs. Or, in the context of rapid discharge from hospital and the rise in day surgery, some community nurses may prescribe from an agreed formulary, and some practice nurses may take blood samples. A second, and contrasting, scenario involves situations where the care–treatment boundary is confused and contested, such as in wound management or the appropriate care for dying patients (Walby et al., 1994). A third scenario emerges when nurses are reluctant to take on responsibility for work that doctors do not want to do. Nurses feel especially vulnerable to complaints, as they work on the front-line of patient care, and to discipline from management if they make a mistake. They also feel that physicians may 'pass the buck' if something goes wrong. In these terms they may fear taking on tasks under verbal instruction (such as giving out drugs in the night that have not been 'written up') and be concerned about new responsibilities such as administering potent drugs which can have serious side-effects. Roles can also be entrenched for political reasons when resources are tight. Based on their own empirical research, Walby et al. (1994) report a series of tensions when doctors want to keep theatre lists low, or admit patients from casualty, but nurses are reluctant to cover the theatre or take the patient onto the ward when staffing levels are low and patient care may be compromised, and the nurse rendered vulnerable as a result.

Divisions within nursing

As Carpenter (1993: 124) explains, in most instances nursing 'will involve less of a direct challenge to medical power than an attempt to reform it, a re-negotiation of traditional patterns of subordination and a claim for "responsible autonomy" within it'. Some nurses stand to gain more from this process than others. Freidson's (1994) thesis that the medical profession staves off threats to its dominance and autonomy by a process of internal restratification pertains equally, if not more, to nursing – although in this case it is arguably as much about attaining professional status as it is about preventing it being taken away. Though not making reference to Freidson, Witz writes that

> the paradoxical situation where nurses' rhetoric of professionalization
> seems to be winning through in spite of a more general attack on
> professional monopoly, particularly that of the medical profession,

> *may well have more to do with the cost-cutting potential of a nursing service – at the core of which are a small number of highly educated 'knowledgeable doers' surrounded by a peripheral workforce of cheaper care assistants – than a successful re-negotiation of occupational boundaries between doctors and nurses, or a significant challenge on the part of nurses to the traditional dominance of doctors over nursing. (Witz, 1994: 40)*

With student nurses no longer supernumerary on the wards, and hospital management ever more concerned to cut the expensive nursing budget, we are seeing the increased employment of a large peripheral workforce of vocationally qualified health-care assistants whose work is organized by a small elite of highly qualified graduates and diplomates. In addition, there has been a trend towards more fixed-term and part-time contracts in recent years. Cohen (1995) reports that in some hospital trusts a third of all nurses are on fixed-term contracts, and one in six is on a bank or agency contract. This has been linked, by managers, to uncertainties about contracts and service levels in the internal market (although government has indicated that 'endless part-time contracts' should end) (*Health Service Journal*, 1997). The contrast between Fordist and post-Fordist work organization that was referred to in chapter 7 can help us to understand this division and its implications for the experience of nurses (and physicians). As was noted in the previous chapter, social scientists have only very recently begun to apply concepts of Fordism and post-Fordism to health and welfare services (see Burrows and Loader, 1994; Walby et al., 1994). Harrison et al.'s explanation of the two contradictory faces of post-Fordism is worth quoting at length here:

> *on the one hand it is frequently portrayed as a liberating force for the employee. The dead hand of bureaucracy will be removed. Innovation will be encouraged. Flexibility will be at a premium. Performance will be rewarded. The appropriate culture for such an organisation will surely be open, positive, valuing of staff creativity and productivity.*
>
> *   Yet there is a dark-side to post-Fordism . . . 'human resource management' requires from employees not merely the compliance of the old Fordist, bureaucratic regimes, but positive commitment and enthusiasm . . . the nine-to-five mentality is no longer enough. Staff are now expected to 'go the extra mile', and not to gripe about union rules or late homecomings. In so far as top management believes that it can re-fashion organisational culture (. . .) it may do so in a way which erodes employee protections and punishes the doubting and disaffected. The vision of NHS staff rising early to gather and sing the*

hospital song before tramping happily off to work is not a reassuring one. (Harrison et al., 1992: 16–17)

The NHS of the 1990s has been an odd mixture of Fordist and post-Fordist styles. The various inroads into physician autonomy that we have discussed suggest that, taken as a group, physicians are, in fact, shifting away from a post-Fordist to a Fordist style, while this is reversed for nurses (Walby et al., 1994). Yet, as has been emphasized throughout this chapter, in discussions of professional powers it is not always appropriate to think of nurses and doctors in collective terms. Viewed in the Fordist/post-Fordist framework, it is more appropriate to think about intra-professional change in the manner of Lash (1994: 120), who, in the context of the restructuring of the wider economy, refers to reflexivity's 'winners' and 'losers' and, in Freidson's terms, to envision the winners getting ahead *at the cost of* the losers.

As we have seen, in the context of medicine, restratification means that medical elites increasingly police the rank and file of their colleagues. In nursing, clinical nurse specialists, advanced nurse practitioners, and nurse managers may experience enhanced autonomy in their work. The majority of lower-grade sisters, staff nurses, and health-care assistants/auxiliaries, however, are being asked to take on added responsibilities with limited resources making them, to paraphrase Witz (1994), the model flexible workers of the dark side of post-Fordist work organization.

The loss of the nursing hierarchy with the Griffiths reforms of the mid-1980s (Strong and Robinson, 1990) and the delegation of budgets, responsibility for outcomes and quality assurance to ward level mean that individual nurses are now very much working on the 'front line' (Alaszewski, 1995). Managers of clinical directorates stress nurses' individual accountability for every aspect of their work. While, on the one hand, this might be said to enhance professional autonomy, it may also have generated a climate of fear. Nurses and midwives fear reprisals, such as disciplinary action, for what they see as any minor error (drugs errors are of particular concern). They report a need to 'watch your back' or, as one sister more graphically put it, to 'cover your arse' all the time by making sure that any concern about patient care, patient progress, or any patient complaint, however minor, is documented and reported to others so that nurses can show that they have followed correct procedures. Nurses and midwives now persistently remark on patients' (and, perhaps more importantly, relatives') 'awareness of their rights' and increased propensity to complain and to blame nurses (who are their most visible and accessible carers) for things that go wrong, both major and minor. In the words of one staff nurse, with the advent of the Patients' Charter, 'Joe public goes to bat.' Nurses, then, feel increasingly vulnerable (Annandale, 1996a).

We have seen, then, that the blurring of the boundaries between medical and nursing work is likely to have mixed effects for the powers of nursing: some may benefit, some may not. In similar terms, it is questionable whether increased personal accountability (at least as it is currently construed as individual responsibility) is unequivocally in the interests of nurses. A number of question marks hang over nursing's current professionalizing project. Davies (1995), in particular, cautions nurses against embracing the model of profession that characterizes modern medicine and health-care management. This model, she remarks, is imbued with the mark of masculinity, the very characteristics of which (i.e. emotional distance, impartiality, individual autonomy) have themselves forced nursing into its adjunct status. How, she asks, can nursing aspire 'to be a profession when the concept expresses a gendered vision that is a denial of the feminine values of nurturing that nursing seeks to espouse'? If nursing opts into this project, she continues, it will surely be 'wrongfooted, stymied by the very terms we employ to discuss the issue' (1995: 62, 63).

Conclusion

The 1980s saw the emergence of what has turned into a protracted theoretical debate on the contemporary status of the medical profession as the theories of proletarianization and deprofessionalization sought to contest Freidson's theory of professional dominance. While each of these theoretical positions helps to sensitize us to important changes in the powers of medicine, their over-generalized nature, and their lack of sensitivity to issues of gender and 'race', mean that they fail to come to grips with the complex realities of the changing health-care division of labour and their implications for professional powers.

Sociologists of the professions have taken far too simplistic a view of the corporate structure of health care, assuming that one doctor, nurse, midwife, or other health-care worker is much the same as any other as far as professional powers are concerned. In reality, there are significant internal divisions within medicine and nursing in particular, and these divisions may be intensifying in response to health service reforms. In this chapter we have been able to explore the intra-professional differences within medicine and within nursing and the changing nature of interactions between medicine and nursing, and to speculate

on their implications for changes in professional autonomy and dominance.

There has been relatively little empirical research on these issues, but
leading commentators conclude that medicine still retains significant
powers in the face of invading forces. For example, Hunter (1994: 17)
remarks that

> *suggestions that medicine is under siege by numerous hostile forces
> arranged against it in the shape of assertive managers and policy
> makers are almost certainly premature. The odd skirmish may afford a
> victory or two for the invading forces but the real issue is one of
> sustainability and the successful engineering of a new balance of
> power in medicine that gives managers a dominant role.*

Medicine may, then, still have the upper hand at present but, to continue the war metaphor, the battle is still being waged. This makes it far
more appropriate to conceptualize the field in terms of a series of
countervailing powers than it is to think in terms of a predetermined
trajectory of decline.

One of the most interesting questions to be explored is whether the
countervailing power of a 'zone of discretion' in individual clinical
decision-making might co-exist uneasily with a form of corporatism
whereby medical and nursing elites are co-opted into management and,
through this, into the control of the rest of the profession. In these terms,
does medicine triumph at the cost of a strategy of divide and rule? In
the spirit of Freidson's thesis on the internal stratification of medicine,
Hunter (1992) remarks that medicine's move into management may
lead to increased control of the front line by those above. This is likely to
tip the control of clinical practice in favour of physicians as a corporate
body, although it may not always serve the interests of the rank-and-file
of physicians. We have seen that a similar process may occur as part of
a professionalizing strategy in nursing.

This is one area that calls out for detailed empirical research. Another
is the impact of countervailing powers – the series of moves and countermoves between physicians, nurses, other health-care occupations,
management and the state – upon *patient care*. As was noted earlier, this
has been the sorely neglected side of the contemporary debate on
professional powers. With patients in mind Stacey (1992) warns against
the view that the *political autonomy* of medicine should be dismantled.
She is particularly concerned that government deregulation has sys-
tematically tamed structures that have historically posed an effective
voice of opposition, such as trade unions, the universities and local

government. She argues that, despite its self-interested nature, the organized medical profession has, on significant occasions, been an effective public ally, voicing opposition to government policies over issues such as nuclear waste, listeriosis, and restrictive abortion laws. In her view, then, the medical profession of the future should not be organized around external control, but through effective internal policing and the rediscovery of its old service ethic. In similar terms, Freidson (1994) has argued against attacks upon physicians' *clinical autonomy*, claiming that the standardization that it implies reduces their ability to respond to individual patient need. In rather speculative, and perhaps unduly optimistic, terms for the current climate of health care, Davies (1995) refers to an emerging revaluation of the masculine ethos of managerialism and revitalization of collectivist values through a gendered dialogue about caring. The final chapter of this book draws on our knowledge of the structure and function of the health service, and the place of physicians and nurses and other carers within it, to explore dimensions of the experience of health, illness and health care.

9

The Experience of Illness and Health Care in Contemporary Society

The screen is black and white and we hear the faint sound of what seems to be snoring. A white rectangle of light suddenly silhouettes the form of a woman who has just opened a door. A man is revealed, dressed in medical scrubs and lying on a gurney. It is Dr Mark Greene, dead asleep at five a.m., being awakened to care for his first patient of the day. The patient turns out to be his friend and co-worker, Dr Doug Ross, who has just reeled into the hospital, quite drunk, and is in immediate need of chemically induced sobering. Greene reluctantly gets up. It is another long and very full day in the ER. (Pourroy, 1996: 7)

So begins twenty-four hours in the life of a Chicago Hospital Emergency Department as portrayed by writer, executive producer and ex-medical student Michael Crichton in the US top-rated television drama series *ER*. As the day unfolds, the script reveals

a scaffolding that collapses, injuring twelve; an eight-year-old with a bleeding ulcer; a thirteen-year-old with an ectopic pregnancy; a nurse who has taken an overdose of drugs; and more than a dozen other major and minor crises. In between these emergencies fall the everyday routines of filling out paper work and having lunch with a spouse. Chaos is juxtaposed with calm; sunshine gives way to snowfall, which gives way to rain, and lengthy scenes keep tempo alongside the merest glimpses of plot and character. (Pourroy, 1996: 7)

The Baudrillardian nightmare, it seems, is replacing the reassuring face of medicine of yesteryear, as images of patients transported around the country in search of a bed, rationing of care, staffing crises, vulnerable doctors and incompetent practice dominate both our cinema and television screens as well as the print media.

Yet perhaps not so much has changed. Consider, for example, another drama from an altogether different time and place. In the *Doctor's Dilemma*, George Bernard Shaw (1980 [1911]) paints a picture of medical practice at the turn of the century well before the inception of the modern health service. As the play opens, Dr Ridgeon, a well-known Harley Street doctor, has just received a knighthood having discovered that tuberculosis, a mortal illness at the time, can be cured by buttering the disease germs with Opsonin. Opsonin is vitally sensitive to the phase of the disease: when the patient is in the negative phase you kill; when he or she is in the positive phase you cure. The drama unfolds as Ridgeon's colleagues debate the latest trumpery cures and the careers that can be made through the discovery of new fashionable surgeries, particularly by giving one doctor the competitive edge over others in the market. Medicine's moral failings, explicitly linked by Shaw to the existence of private practice, dominate the plot as the doctors are forced to make a decision about whom to treat with the drug, since only ten people can be saved. Sensitive to the pleadings of a pretty young wife for her artist husband, they put him on the list in preference to another, believing that he is a 'worthy case'. The twist in the tale comes, however, when they find out that the artist is not only a bigamist, but has also swindled each of the doctors out of a sum of money. Realizing not only this, but that one of their own, an impoverished GP, also needs 'the cure', they pass the artist on to another doctor, who kills him in the course of treatment.

The concerns of Shaw's drama reflect the issues that dominate contemporary medical practice in a quite uncanny way: clinical uncertainty, medical negligence, the profit motive, and the issue of rationing care are as high on the agenda today as they were over ninety years ago. Obdurate as these concerns may be, however, the new century that dawns will be far removed in experience from Shaw's early twentieth-century Britain, providing us with unprecedented questions. Many of these questions can be approached in terms of a tension between, on the one hand, the premium that is increasingly placed on reflexivity and personal choice (over issues as wide-ranging as the treatment options for a particular disease and how to 'keep oneself healthy') and, on the other hand, the moral responsibility to actually make these choices and the constraints that surround decision-making for both patients and health-care providers. Within the confines of this chapter we will have the opportunity to discuss only a limited number of ways in which this tension impacts on the experience of health, illness and health care. The first section focuses on illness, beginning with a discussion of contemporary approaches to death and dying. We then explore social representations of health and illness, paying particular attention to the search for meaning, and the insight that this provides into the contemporary social condition. In the second part of the chapter, we turn to today's medical practice, principally in the acute hospital setting. Here it will become apparent that the modern hospital is undergoing a transformation; no longer easily typified by patients lying in beds in the ward setting, the hospital has diversified into an array of practices (fast-tracking of patients, performance guides, high-technology surgery) with significant implications for the delivery of care to patients.

The experience of health and illness

Death, so it would seem, has been sequestered from modern experience. Unable to contemplate the end, we have, in the words of Bauman, 'fought death tooth and nail'. While never quite believing in the end of death, we have pushed it back tiny bit by tiny bit, making it an event without a cause as we diffuse the 'perennial horror of mortality' (Bauman, 1993: 28, 29) by deconstructing it into an infinite chain of particular preventable causes (i.e. certain diseases) which can be conquered, and, on an individual level, by avoiding various 'unhealthy' practices. Engaged in 'excessively time-consuming' body projects in a bid to stave off anxiety about death, it seems that we have 'no time to think about death itself' (Mellor and Shilling, 1993: 425). When death is pushed to the margins of life, life itself begins to lose meaning. Prometheus, in the Greek tragedy of the same name, took away knowledge of the 'hour of our death' and, with it, removed the will to live. For we can only have a future when we are aware of its end, only exercise reason in the need to avoid the ultimate threat. This argument has a ring of truth, for certainly we speak of never being so aware of the value of life as when it might soon be taken from us (perhaps, for example, when anticipating bad news from a diagnostic test result or a brush with death in a near accident, for ourselves or a loved one). Moreover, when actually facing death it is not uncommon for individuals to find new meaning in life, or to experience 'living life to the full' for the very first time (although this is not something that can be generalized). Yet, as Walter (1994) points out so well, surely the magnification of debate about the sequestration of death itself in recent years – witnessed, for example, in the work of Aries (1981) and Elias (1985), as well as by a growing number of sociologists of health and illness – points to a paradox: we deny death, yet talk (and write) increasingly about it. Walter contends that we are witnessing a revolution in death and dying, powered by the new authority of the self. 'In a culture of individualism that values a unique life', he writes, 'the requirement that I live my life my own way is increasingly being extended to a requirement that I die and mourn my own way' too (1994: 2). Walter's thesis is that the modern 'revival of death' is an attempt to resolve the contradiction of the visible public side of death (the insurance industry, funeral business, stylized media display) with its private side (that is, the grief that is increasingly hidden away in late modern society). A resolution is achieved by making the public side of death more personal, something which is exceedingly important to us because the rational bureaucratic approach to death (hospital-based, under medical control, a relatively impersonal funeral service) can no longer be tolerated in a Western world that puts such a premium on the unique individual.

The revival of death, however, contains a subtle blend of individual choice and manipulation. The choices may be ours, but we are not alone in making them, guided as we are, not by a taboo on death, but by 'a babel of voices proclaiming various good deaths', leaving us with an open question, but nonetheless one which must be answered: 'what are we to make of our own death when it looms over the horizon?' (Walter, 1994: 2, 122). How are we to know what to do? Surrounding the individual, whether dying or in grief, is an array of professional and semi-professional helpers – counsellors, self-help groups, and gurus such as Elisabeth Kübler-Ross (1970) – helping to construct appropriate feeling states for those concerned. In sum, the fragmentation of public discourse by private experience is manipulated by expert knowledges of various kinds, and the individual is faced with a paradox of control and dependence.

This brief discussion of death and dying raises wider issues for us. On the face of it, the experience of dying, and of serious illness too, would seem to be very personal, nowhere more so, it would seem, than in contemporary society with its stress upon the authority of the self amid competing ideas about how illness should be understood and treated. Yet, alongside this, there are strong normalizing forces structuring our experience of illness in various ways – the imperative to make one's own choice being a rather ironic illustration of this. Out of these multiple realities people fashion their own understandings as 'clever weavers of stories', moment by moment making 'sense of their world amid the cacophony' of competing voices (Stainton Rogers, 1991: 10). We turn now to consider this process.

Social representations of health and illness

'Acting like a sponge, illness soaks up personal and social significance from the world of the sick person.' This quotation, which comes from Kleinman's (1988: 31) study of illness narratives, draws our attention to two things. First of all, it reveals that to make sense of illness is simultaneously to make sense of the wider social world around us. Secondly, it discloses the highly metaphorical nature of sense-making, which, as the quotation demonstrates, is of as much importance to the doctor's or the social scientist's understanding as it is to the individual's search for meaning in everyday life.

Metaphor takes on a unique role in illness, shaping our understandings, extending meaning and creating new ideas (Lupton, 1994). The body itself, of course, is a potent metaphorical site as seen, for example, in our representations of it as a 'machine', a 'fortress', and a 'temple'. Our modern knowledge of the association of illness with the introduction of certain organisms ('invaders'), the mobilization of immunological 'defenses' and the 'aggressive' use of medicine (for example, in most chemotherapies) makes the military metaphor a stalwart in the search for meaning at the present time. Sontag makes us particularly aware of the dangers of these associations for, as she recounts, with the war metaphor 'particularly dreaded diseases are envisaged as an alien "other", as enemies are in modern war' (1988: 11). From this, she argues, 'the move from the demonization of illness to the attribution of fault to the patient is an inevitable one'. Undoubtedly the characterological predispositions often attributed to cancer sufferers (for example, inexpressive, repressed, hypersensitive etc.) do untold damage, and the potential to link affliction to lifestyle (for example, diet) lays the ground open to fictions of unsurpassed personal responsibility, drawing attention away from environmental and other causes in the process. Audre Lorde made this clear in recounting her own experience of breast cancer:

> Last week I read a letter from a doctor in a medical magazine which said that no truly happy person ever gets cancer. Despite my knowing better, and despite my having dealt with this blame-the-victim thinking for years, for a moment this letter hit my guilt button. Had I really been guilty of the crime of not being happy in this best of all possible infernos? . . . The happiest person in this country cannot help breathing in smokers' cigarette fumes, auto exhaust, and airborne chemical dust . . . (Lorde, 1980: 66–7)

In cancer, it seems, people have found a sense of guilt and shame, although this seems now to be changing with the emergence of a new candour and a wider discourse of hope (Sontag, 1988). AIDS, Sontag (1988: 24) contends, has now replaced cancer as 'the generic rebuke to life and hope'. Here shame is forcefully linked to the attribution of guilt since 'AIDS is not a mysterious affliction that seems to strike at random. Indeed, to get AIDS is precisely to be revealed, in the majority of cases so far, as a member of a certain "risk group", a community of pariahs' (1988: 25).

With AIDS, an identity is 'flushed out' (Sontag, 1988) with significant implications for the personal experience of the sufferer. A number of research studies have made this clear. Carricaburu and Pierret (1995), for example, employ Bury's (1982) concept of biographical disruption to recount the experience of a sample of HIV positive Parisian men (defined as homosexuals and haemophiliacs by the researchers). Although not yet subject to symptoms of ill health, they had to manage their apparently healthy lives in conditions of uncertainty, and to do so in a very public arena where moral discourses about AIDS are virtually impossible to ignore. AIDS is a language not just of personal identity, but of social relationships with others, and all of the men in this study (although to varying degrees) felt a need to 'manage the secret'. This involved not only concealment in work and social contexts (often in fear of discrimination), but also reconstructing their own biography. For many of the haemophiliacs, there was a tragic continuity: they had been forced to live with illness and the monitoring of the body in the past and this was reinforced in the present (now overlain, of course, with the failure of medical science, since HIV had been transmitted during treatment). For others who in the same circumstances had worked to normalize haemophilia, there was a keen sense of disruption, as the threat of AIDS no longer permitted this. Disruption was also felt by all of the homosexual men.

This literature points to the potency of metaphorical discourses which cannot be easily ignored, yet also serves to highlight the reflexive character of responses to illness as personal meaning and a way to cope are actively sought by individuals. The concept of *illness narratives* encapsulates this process. As the preponderance of illness changed from acute to chronic in form, a new status, that of the sick person, was born. With illness no longer swiftly followed by death in most cases, individuals need to make sense of their experience; to learn from it in order to move forward and, importantly, to 'tell their stories' to others. Sociologist Arthur Frank (see 1993, 1995), who has written extensively on illness narratives, insists that stories do not just *describe* the experience of illness; rather, stories *are* repair work, creating a new self out of the wreckage that illness inflicts on a life story. In earlier work, Williams developed the concept of narrative reconstruction to refer to the attempts that people make to 'reconstitute and repair ruptures between body, self, and world by linking up and interpreting different aspects of biography in order to realign present and past and self within society' (1984: 197). Narratives seem to have a natural affinity with a social world which is seen as increasingly fragmented and polycentric (see chapter 2); therefore it is not surprising that they have become exceedingly popular within academia and popular writing in recent years (for a decade review of research on illness narrative, see Hydén, 1997). Frank (1995) argues that in modern times the medical narrative, with its emphasis on technical expertise, has colonized the experience of illness. However, living within the 'remission society', cured but with the ever-present possibility of a return to the world of the sick, people give their bodies over to medicine in treatment, but refuse narrative surrender, wishing instead to hold on to their own stories. Hence, a new, *post*modern, experience of illness begins when people recognize that there is more to their experiences than medicine can tell. Crucially, 'the post-colonial ill person, living with illness for the long term, wants her own suffering recognised in its *individual particularity*' (Frank, 1995: 11; my emphasis).

Reflexivity lies at the heart of illness stories. While it may be an injustice to their variety and complexity, social scientists have found it useful to refer to ideal typical genres. Frank (1995), for example, writes of three narrative types: restitution, chaos and quest. Restitution narratives, those preferred by modern medicine with its expectation that for every suffering there is a remedy, has the plot of: 'I was healthy, I am sick, I will be healthy again.' For the story-teller, there is an effort to fix what was wrong and return to the beginning 'as good as new'. Problems can occur when the narrative of survival becomes impossible to sustain. Chaos narratives, in contrast, imagine a life that will never get better. They are more aptly described as an anti-narrative, as the life of illness cannot be told, only lived. Words fail the body in an experience of 'time without sequence, telling without mediation and speaking about oneself without being fully able to reflect on oneself' (Frank, 1995: 98). Finally, there are quest stories of self-transformation and the offering of help to others through illness.

Through his own experience of illness (a heart attack and cancer while in his forties) and the telling of it to others, Frank (1991b, 1995) cultivates the quest story, fostering in the process acceptance of illness as part of living, and encouraging people to talk about suffering as a route to renewal. This quest, however, will never be easy in a society which views health as a moral virtue and illness as a 'fall from grace'. In such a context illness calls for a good deal of work on the part of the individual to reclaim their place of worth in the world. The nature of this work and its significance is seen in Gareth Williams' (1995) study of rheumatoid arthritis sufferers. He presents the account of a 62-year-old woman, at the centre of whose narration of illness and how she copes is a desire not to be a burden on others. Bound up with this is her need to show that she is a responsible rather than a careless person, able, for example, to pay her debts such as utility bills. She also wishes to make clear that, while she is aware that others may attribute any failings that they see to moral weakness rather than to 'the illness', she can work to avert this. For example, others may imply that she is 'letting herself go' or not keeping a clean and tidy house, but she can plan ahead and get things such as housework done 'now rather than later', mindful that she can never be sure when her illness will flare up. Williams concludes that this pursuit of moral virtue reveals her view of society and her place within it.

Social representations of health and illness have an enduring quality and, as such, require some degree of attention from the individual on an ongoing basis even though, since the experience of chronic illness is extremely wide-ranging (influenced, among a great many other things, by gender, 'race', age, marital status, and material circumstances), there is likely to be significant individual variation. Although the subtlety of this needs to be borne in mind, the current literature stresses the need for individuals to make sense of bodily disruptions by attending to the relationship between mind and body. Simon Williams stresses the vicissitudes of embodiment across the illness trajectory, referring to an ideal typical movement from a sense of 'embodiment' to 'dys-embodiment', eventually to reach a sense of 're-alignment' of body and self. In health, the body is taken for granted, an absent presence as we 'both feel and are embodied' (Williams, 1996: 25). When illness strikes, be this suddenly or through an insidious onset, this sense of unity is disrupted. The body then confronts us as an alien presence and a perception of mind/body dualism often takes precedence in our experience.

A range of illness narratives makes this point. Here we will look at just one in some detail. In Bloom's (1992) account, Sandy, an American woman who was in her late forties, narrates her experience of kidney disease and cancer. Sandy's story of illness begins in high school, during a period of her life which she describes as extremely pressured by the need to succeed, both academically and in her other pursuits such as music. These circumstances help to explain why, paradoxical though it may seem, Sandy was personally relieved to be diagnosed with kidney disease. In her own words, 'it was just the first time that I had really gotten in touch with myself, my reflective self' (1992: 322). The pressure to achieve in school was off and she was glad of a period of time in hospital when no one bothered her. Here, then, the self used the body to gain incapacity. Later, when Sandy undergoes a kidney transplant at the age of 32, her body is objectified in perhaps one of the most forceful ways imaginable. She recounts the experience of coming around after surgery aware that her physicians and nurses were talking of the kidney's rejection by her body. At that point, as she puts it herself, 'everything in my mind went into the effort to make my body accept that kidney. And the only words I can put on it are just, it was sort of like, you know, "welcome" to this new kidney. You know; "welcome kidney, this is your body. This is your home"' (1992: 323). Her mind, then, kept her kidney in the body, something which Sandy herself believed in intensely as 'mind control'.

Bloom's analysis alerts us to a new relationship between mind and body as it has moved from a simple state of opposition (i.e. the body as constraint on the self) towards a new form of transcendence of the dualism. By this she appears to interject an explicit transitional stage between the 'dys-embodied self' and eventual 're-alignment'. In this stage the body and self are still distinct and far away from the unity of the healthy state, but they are not in base opposition. Rather, the self masters the body, but enables it nonetheless to 'cultivate new abilities' which will ultimately result in a 'heightened harmony between body and self' (1992: 318). Growing out of this is the final stage during which the body at last begins to emerge as a being in its own right – it becomes what Bloom (drawing on Gadow, 1982) refers to as the 'subject body'. As a subject, the body makes clear its own needs which are respected, in this case in the experience of skin cancer, even though, as I read it, this would seem to be far from effortless (a hallmark of the embodied state of health) since Sandy refers to the effort of making her mind and body work together in a 'finely-tuned harmony' to help her to resist cancer. Perhaps, as Simon Williams (1996) relates, any 'negotiated settlement' can be precarious, fragile and in need of constant repair work, reminding us of a point made earlier: that our relationships to our bodies, be this in health or in illness, are unlikely ever to be static. As the authors recognize, even to suggest processual stages in the relationship between mind and body in chronic illness imposes significant order on what is likely to be a far more ambiguous and fraught experience.

Individual accounts of illness often seem to express a privileging of mind over body, something which itself is invested with strong moral force. Metaphorically speaking, one is expected to fight illness and not to give in to it, a perspective which seems common to many kinds of therapies (for example, in cancer). Pollock (1995) gives a vivid sense of 'mind' over 'matter' in her interview-based study of families in the Nottingham area of England who either had no serious illness, or had a member suffering from multiple sclerosis or schizophrenia. While all of those interviewed felt that there was a reciprocal relationship between mind and body, they placed considerably more emphasis on the 'power of the mind to influence bodily processes and determine the individual's state of health than the converse' (1995: 51). Indeed, 87 per cent of respondents referred to the power of 'mind' over 'matter', a belief which for 25 per cent of these individuals was held very strongly (interestingly, half of the latter were multiple sclerosis sufferers or their spouses). Generally, the mind was felt to be the most vital aspect of the person, while the 'body, as "mere matter", was relegated to a position of secondary significance' (Pollock, 1995: 52). Attitude of mind was felt to have no real role in the prevention of serious illness, but it could be important for more minor conditions. As one respondent said, 'you can make yourself healthy or you can make yourself unhealthy. You can work for or against health. It's in the mind.' Mind over matter was crucial, however, in all recoveries, even from serious illness: 'I imagine it's up to the person . . . I mean, if you let yourself sort of . . . suffer, I suppose you'll suffer more than if you say "Oh, I'm not having this, I'm going to shake it off." Some people are stronger-minded than others' (respondents quoted in Pollock, 1995: 53–4). Mental illness, in particular, was seen as a condition that could be overcome through an act of will, but for some respondents, even with physical illness, there was a striking belief that, in certain circumstances at least, people can literally will themselves to live or die.

Such beliefs may provide determination and cultivate hope. But they also carry problems in their wake. Several commentators have criticized the fostering of disability as a personal problem that needs to be overcome through efforts of will on the part of the disabled. Oliver, for example, refers to the body fascism of ambulist culture which views disability as a personal tragedy to be surmounted by the individual, rather than as the 'failure of society to remove its disability barriers and social restrictions' (1996: 129). Hillyer (1993) mounts a forceful attack on both academic and popular feminism in these terms. She writes of caring for her daughter Jennifer, who has both physical and mental disabilities. Jennifer's body, she writes, is not reliable. Feminism has too easily assumed that the unreliability of the body in illness and disability is a condition all of us should be able to overcome with the exercise of willpower. But how can Jennifer do this? She can't, and because she can't feminism fails to account for her experience.

It should be clear, then, that the privileged status of the mind in illness can be disempowering as well as empowering, irrespective of whether it is a view held by health professionals in their work or by individuals in their everyday accounts. There can also be a denial of physical pain and emotional suffering, and a failure to validate what can be a wretched experience. However, Frank (1991b, 1995) contends that the struggle that is chronic illness embodies an ethic. Following Ricoeur (1991: 26), who stresses that 'the significance of a narrative stems from the intersection of the world of the text and the world of the reader' – or, we might add, listener – Frank argues that the moral genius of storytelling is as much for another as it is for oneself, as teller and listener both enter into the space of the story *for* the other. There is, then, an ethic of solidarity and commitment and of inspiration in many stories, especially where they are told in the public arena – for example, in the swelling number of published biographies. Frank argues that postmodern testimony speaks not in grand narratives, but in bits and pieces, for these are all that the overwhelmed consciousness can deal with as events happen so fast that they fail to fit easily into existing frames of reference. But 'what the story teaches is that there is always another story, and other stories have always been possible' (Frank, 1995: 16). At the heart of life in the postmodern world it is not an end-point that is held in mind, but a self that is discovered and *made available to others* in the *process* of telling the story. It was, as Ricoeur (1991) relates, Aristotle who said that every well-told story teaches us something about the universal aspects of the human condition. Although he is conscious of romanticizing suffering, Frank's concluding words in *The Wounded Storyteller* are proselytizing: 'the wounded storyteller is a moral witness', he writes, 're-enchanting a disenchanted world . . . postmodern times may be pandemonium, but they are not a void. Illness stories provide a glimpse of the perfection' (1995: 185). The morality of illness in the truths that it can speak is expressed by Frank in his autobiographical account: 'The ultimate value of illness is that it teaches us the value of being alive; this is why the ill are not just charity cases, but a presence to be valued. Illness and, ultimately, death remind us of living' (1991b: 120). However, significant questions remain about the extent to which a culture which values health, control and personal responsibility can accommodate the ethic which Frank sees as embedded in the quest story.

Conceptualizing health

It is a sociological commonplace to point out that we seem to know health only as a lack, as the absence of disease. Along with Gadamer, who reflects on the enigma of health in a collection of essays, we can wonder: 'is it not an extraordinary thing that the lack of something, although we do not know precisely what it is that is lacking, can reveal the miraculous existence of health?' (1996: 74). As he continues, you can try to define health by standard values, but all you will end up doing is making the person ill, since at least some degree of deviation from whatever values you impose is likely to occur for most people. To further compound the problem, research has consistently shown that definitions of 'health' can themselves accommodate a fair amount of discomfort and disability (see the discussion of Cornwell's (1984) work in chapter 1). Health and illness are not polar opposites and it is not uncommon for people to report that they are in good health while simultaneously referring to a number of often quite severe functional limitations. Since health seems able to embrace significant deviation, it obviously cannot be thought of as the absence of illness in any stand-ardizable manner. Health, like illness, it would seem, needs to be ap-proached from the reference point of the individual concerned; for each of us, with different biographies living in different social circumstances, health is indeed likely to be known when it is unsettled, but what this means for each of us is likely to vary considerably.

Even with this point in mind, it is notoriously difficult to access concepts of health (rather than illness). For example, Blaxter (1990: 19) found that over 10 per cent of respondents in the British Health and Lifestyle Survey could not answer the open-ended question 'what is it like when you are healthy?' For a minority, more often the elderly, this was because 'I am never healthy so I don't know', but more frequently health was quite simply the 'ordinary'; a norm that is difficult to de-scribe (Blaxter, 1990: 19–20). As one woman struggled to articulate, 'I don't really know. Sometimes I do feel less healthy, but I can't say that I feel what it is to be healthy at other times' (1990: 20). In-depth qualita-tive studies have been able to group social representations of health in a number of ways. For example, in a well-known study published in the 1970s, Herzlich's (1973) middle-class French respondents referred to three dimensions of health: 'health in a vacuum', i.e. health as the simple absence of disease; a 'reserve' of health (stressing the individ-ual's capacity to maintain good health); and health as a positive state of well-being or personal 'equilibrium'. Very broadly speaking, other stud-ies have tended to confirm these patterns. For example, Pierret (1995), reporting research undertaken in France in 1980, found that her re-spondents referred to four kinds of health 'register': 'health-illness' (health as not being sick); 'health-tool' (health as capital or reserve which can be worn down); 'health-product' (health as a product of various factors, often external to the individual, but over which one has some control); and 'health-institution' (health as a collective good, often affected by societal politics). In each of these registers Pierret points to a tension. For 'health-illness' this is between 'not being sick' and 'being well'; for 'health-tool' between possessing health, but needing to use it or 'wear it down' in the course of life and work; for 'health-product' between the search for pleasure and the control of risks; and for 'health-institution' between the state and other institutions as benevolent and as agencies of force. In each context, then, the individual's concept of health is placed within a wider moral universe, in much the same way that the researchers that we considered earlier in the chapter stressed the need to understand the reflexive nature of personal accounts of illness and their connection to wider social discourses (and here again we see the use of metaphorical thinking in the course of analysis).

It is evident that accounts of illness and of health are deeply embed-ded in the wider social context. But as social analysts we need to be alert to the ever-present danger of imposing a rather smooth conceptual order on experiences that may be craggy and ever-changing. As postmodern perspectives remind us, the very process of interpreting individual narratives involves constructing a certain kind of subject. Fox, for example, contends that there are various readings of health and illness – from medicine, psychology, sociology, and health promotion, for example, each of which should be seen as internally fragmented – trying to 'persuade us to a particular perspective on the person who is healthy or ill' (1993a: 139). From such a vantage-point there is little to be gained by trying to establish an authentic account. But, perhaps, para-doxically, this very indeterminacy itself reflects a new social formation which has ambiguity at its core. In the second part of the chapter we move on to consider social transformation in the experience of health care.

Modern medical practice

The character of medical knowledge and the conduct of medical prac-tice has been of great fascination to the sociology of health and medicine since its inception. Indeed, as we saw in chapter 1, it was attempts by early medical sociologists to separate out their own activities from those of biomedicine that laid the foundations for the distinctly social approach that characterizes the field. It will be remembered that Freidson (1988 [1970]: 211) proposed that sociology's interest should lie in the social reality of illness, not in the testing and refinement of medical concepts of illness and treatment, which were seen as the doctor's job. In Atkinson's opinion, the legacy of this distinction has had the most adverse of effects upon sociological research as 'medical sociology's taken-for-granted assumptions concerning what is self-evidently social' (1995: 31) lead it to tread a very narrow path through the complexities of medical work. Typically its domicile has been within the rather limited confines of the doctor–patient relationship. From Atkinson's vantage-point this is not surprising, since this is precisely where we can see the social context of illness played out. Although he seems to overstate the degree to which the study of medical work has been ring-fenced by this focus, his basic point holds true: all too often the complex division of labour in medical work (which of course interfaces with all other categories of 'lay' and 'professional' healers including patients themselves) is 'imploded into this one microcosm', rendering great tracts of work, such as the interactions of health-care providers, invisible (Atkinson, 1995: 34). The conceptual landscapes of the sociology of health and illness, then, appear to have set limits upon the empirical research domain. The unfortunate consequence of this is that we currently lack a detailed contemporary insight into the conduct of medical work in formal settings such as the hospital and general practice. The ethnographic work that is now undertaken tends to be restricted in scope, limited in space to a particular clinic, ward or treatment setting, and in time to short periods of observation and/or a small number of in-depth interviews. Although there is a greater willingness of award-making bodies to fund ethnographic work nowadays, the imperatives of immediate policy needs mean that the research is often limited in scope.

As we have seen in chapters 7 and 8, the provision of health care (in both formal and informal settings) and the work of those involved are changing at a dizzying pace. While, for the reasons that have been discussed here, it is difficult to get a thorough sociological grip on the impact that this has upon the experience of health providers and patients, the key issues are clear enough. Patients and their relatives are increasingly being made aware that medical practitioners (and other healers) do not deal in certainties; rather, there are often hard choices to be made and someone must make them. But *who* is to decide and *how* are they to do this? This is the thread that will run through the discussion in this final part of the chapter. We begin by sketching the social transformation of the modern hospital and its technologies of care. This is then followed by a consideration of the new risks and responsibilities that are emerging, and the dilemmas of choice that accompany them.

The modern hospital

There is every indication that the hospital as it has traditionally been conceived is undergoing a major transformation. Since it has been in the nature of health-care systems to evoke crisis imagery, commentators are being driven to new descriptive heights in their attempts to capture the contemporary scene. Shortell et al., referring to the United States, for example, write of a 'state of hyperturbulence' (1995: 131). The hospital, they contend, is at the epicentre of an earthquake in the health-care system, facing the lack of control and the anxiety that goes along with this. Quite simply, 'the institution is being shaken at its core foundations, and institutional legitimacy is at stake' (1995: 131). During the period between 1980 and 1993 a total of 949 hospitals closed in the United States; between 1984 and 1992 there was an 11 per cent absolute decline in admissions from 38 million to 33.5 million. 'Downsizing' of staff follows. Writers, most with the United States in mind, are referring to the emergence of the 'bedless hospital'. The countervailing forces behind this change are new technologies and the rise of ambulatory care and preventive medicine. Stoeckle pinpoints the following factors as important: the substitution of quick diagnostic tests for in-bed observations; a decline in the use of bed-rest as therapy; and the pressure from the 'corporate press to increase profits and reduce costs' (Stoeckle, 1995: 11).

Some predictions for the future seem almost apocalyptic. Take for example the following description from Jolly and Gerbaud (1992). The hospital of the year 2000, they prophesy, will 'no longer consist of hospital wards, attached to which are a radiology unit, laboratory and outpatient clinic, but the opposite. The total number of "conventional" hospital admissions will decrease substantially and some hospitals will close.' There will be no more 1,500-bed tower-block hospitals; 'instead, there will be horizontal 300–400-bed hospitals, more accessible to the outside world, with various shops, cinema and video room . . .' (1992: 51). Hospitals will have good-quality hotels attached for patients who are not sufficiently ill that they need to stay in overnight. Flexibility will be the order of the day as far as infrastructure is concerned, since

we do not know yet what the future technologies will be, just as in 1970 we knew nothing of the advent of the scanner, MRI, or the

> *lithotriptor. Since hospitals are built of concrete, the whole of the inside will need to be made suitable for extensive modification, for example, siting all the piping and cables alongside the outside walls or above fake ceilings. (Jolly and Gerbaud, 1992: 51–2)*

This account is particularly intriguing, since it does not come from the pens of postmodern fantasy, but is published under the auspices of the World Health Organization. Writing in the *Milbank Quarterly*, Robinson (1994: 259) refers to the hospital of the future as a 'health care centre without walls' as it diversifies into ambulatory diagnostic and surgical centres. The total institution (Goffman, 1961), it would seem, is falling down.

These accounts may seem rather fantastical in the British context where, when most citizens think of the hospital, it is not this new, flexible, multi-tier unit, but more often the crumbling Victorian edifice which comes to mind. However, the bedless hospital certainly has an edge of truth, if perhaps not wholly in terms intended by the authors referred to above. The 1990s have witnessed a wave of hospital mergers as well as well-publicized closures. In total, 245 hospitals closed and twenty-one opened between 1990 and 1995 (Francome and Marks, 1996). The emptying out of mental hospitals set the trend earlier in the 1970s and 1980s (as in the United States), to be followed more recently by the planned closure of cottage and specialist hospitals, and the cessation of particular services within hospitals (for example, Accident & Emergency departments). Additionally, we have seen contentious exchanges in Parliament over the future of London's teaching hospitals (Klein, 1995: 207–9; Tomlinson, 1992). The closure of inner-city public hospitals in the United States has led to the 'turfing' of patients from emergency room to emergency room; in Britain the recent rise in emergency admissions (Audit Commission, 1996b) alongside declining numbers of in-patient beds, has led to fraught searches for beds for patients country-wide. Parallels are also found in the internal climate of the hospital. Britain has seen the gradual emergence of day-care services and bed reductions. In 1994 the then Secretary of State for Health, Virginia Bottomley, heralded a 'high-technology revolution' in health care, announcing that 50,000 beds, that is, 40 per cent of the national total, would be cut, providing in the process day surgery to 60 per cent of patients, most of whom would be expected to leave hospital within hours (Rogers, 1994). In the US, 50 per cent of surgery already takes place in surgicentres – many away from the traditional hospital complex (Stoeckle, 1995) – and in Britain over half of all elective operations were carried out as day cases in 1994/5 (DoH, 1996b). Changes that are coming to pass in the United States, then, have parallels in Britain as well as in other developed countries, even though the pace of change has been less rapid to date.

These trends notwithstanding, the wide diversity of sites and their internal differentiation mean that the experience of patients and those who work in hospitals defies easy summary. Medical knowledge itself is incredibly complex and, as noted in earlier chapters, can no longer readily be captured under the rubric of the 'biomedical model'. Zussman (1993: 180) contends that the social transformation of the hospital 're-casts the intellectual and research agenda for hospital life'. In-depth ethnographic studies of collective in-patient culture such as Roth's (1963) *Timetables* (a study of the way in which patients negotiate bench-marks in the treatment of tuberculosis – see chapter 1) and Coser's (1962) *Life on the Ward* have disappeared from the scene along with the long-term patients who populated them. The individual patient, recon-structed as a decision-maker, is now at the centre of medical and research culture. Self-evidently, this trend is bound up with the shifting nature of medical work which, in the hospital context and beyond, is increasingly marked by technological testing and treatment.

Medical technology and decision-making: panacea or chimera?

Medical technology is the 'apotheosis of medical magic' (Lupton, 1994: 53), simultaneously the symbol of hope and of tragedy. Medicine, Beck contends, is a golden goose as the 'spiral of medical formation and decision-making' is 'twisted deeper and deeper in the . . . reality of the risk society', able to 'profit from self-produced risks and hazardous conditions and to extend its own area of activity continually through related techno-therapeutic innovations' (Beck, 1992: 211). Critical ac-counts of the use of technology in health care, of course, have a long history in the social sciences. Those writing from political economy and feminist perspectives have, for example, raised significant concerns about the profit motive in procurement, and the control of physicians over patients (see chapters 1 and 3). In the context of childbirth, for instance, feminists have questioned the way that control is wrested from women when birth is orchestrated by technologies such as electri-cal foetal monitoring (see Rich, 1992).

Now, more than ever, we place a premium on the possession of information, believing that by acting on it we can reduce risks to our health. Yet how true is this? Research has shown that 'preventive' technologies, epitomized in health screening – for example, mammography for breast cancer, blood tests for prostate cancer, amniocentesis for foetal chromosomal abnormalities, and genetic screening for a range of diseases – not only close off risk but may sometimes increase it. Tests which, on the face of it, provide us with the 'gift of knowing' (Kenen, 1996) and hold out the hope of a cure for a disease that might be detected, carry their own problematics. Firstly, there is the creation of a new 'at-risk' status. Screening tests reach into the previously hidden and unimaginable interiors of the body, creating diseases-in-waiting in their wake (Kenen, 1996). Potential patients are put into a liminal state where the 'integrity of their bodies is questioned and left dangling while they await their test results', and 'where the notion of a mysterious disease, which has silently invaded the body and lies in wait, is engendered' (Lupton, 1994: 99). Personal agency can be undermined rather than enhanced in this context, particularly when the result that follows holds out little hope in the way of therapy. While 'knowing' can be a personal benefit for some, for others it can foster guilt and a sense of hopelessness.

A second problematic of screening, then, relates to the medical interventions that can follow testing. For example, prophylactic surgeries such as mastectomy and prostatectomy can result not from having cancer, but from being at potential risk of it. Scientists' claims that they are close to detecting a gene for familial breast cancer (Brown, 1993) heralds formidable 'choices' for women. What, for example, should a young woman at 'high risk' do? While, on the one hand, we might claim that she has the knowledge before her to prevent an untimely death, she will never really know in any absolute sense that this was her fate. She is, then, caught between the proverbial 'rock and a hard place': she could decide to 'wait and see', but, then, she can hardly rely upon conventional surgery and treatment to offer her the hope of a cure; or, instead, she could opt for prophylactic mastectomy and perhaps also oophorectomy (removal of the ovaries) with all of the longer-term consequences'that this will have for her reproductive capacity and personal well-being. Other 'choices' will likely accompany this decision, such as whether or not to take hormone replacement therapy (HRT), which carries its own putative risks to health (see below). 'Choices' spiral ever forward in time. Whatever happens, the point is that she is impelled to decide: the option of not being tested at all carrying the sanction of abdication of personal responsibility (and maybe also lack of fortitude). For, after all, don't we 'want to know'?

Widespread prophylactic mastectomy on the basis of genetic screening is some time away, although there are instances of women with strong maternal-line breast cancer opting for this major surgery at the current time. Recurrent debates over the efficacy of mammography, however, exemplify a range of pertinent contemporary concerns on a wider scale. National breast screening, which, as Foster (1995: 111) states, 'can only be described as a mass experiment', was introduced to Britain just before the 1987 general election. Far from epitomizing the reassuring and scientific image of its uptake publicity, in the minds of many it has the dubious consequence of turning symptomless well women into 'patients' in the absence of a guaranteed cure, generating profound psychological stress in the process (Foster, 1995). Breast cancer is, of course, a prevalent disease affecting one in twelve women in Britain, and the leading cause of death among women aged 45–64 (Wilkinson and Kitzinger, 1995). For this reason alone, it is not surprising that there is an imperative to try and 'do something'. Maureen Roberts, who was clinical director of the Edinburgh Breast Screening Project up until the time of her own death from breast cancer in 1989, raised a range of concerns in the *British Medical Journal*. She asked the simple but fundamental question: is it worth it? In her own words: 'we know that mammography is an unsuitable screening test: it is technologically difficult to perform, the pictures are difficult to interpret, it has a high false positive rate, and we don't know how often to carry it out' (Roberts, 1989: 1153). There are some telling figures in respect of these comments from the twenty-six health authorities which had accumulated sufficient data to draw together a picture of the results from the British screening programme by 1989. Research by Richards, summarized here by Foster, provides the following figures:

> *Of those screened 7.4 per cent had been recalled for further assessment and 1.3 per cent underwent a biopsy. Of those biopsies approximately half resulted in a diagnosis of breast cancer. In absolute numbers this meant that over 8,000 women out of 164,000 had suffered the trauma of being recalled for further investigation. 1,410 had suffered the further trauma of undergoing a biopsy but only 733 women were ultimately diagnosed as having early breast cancer.*
> *(Foster, 1995: 121)*

Moreover, as Roberts (1989) reports, clinical trials do not point with any certainty to a reduction in mortality as a result of the information provided from this screening programme.

No doubt the debates about breast cancer screening will continue. When we reflect on the danger of false negatives and false positives that result from human error and lack of specificity (for example, recent well-publicized errors in cervical cytology and HIV antibody testing in

Britain), the aggregate picture that emerges for many screening technologies is not especially reassuring. We might well be forgiven for concluding that what we have before us is not a panacea, but a chimera.

The realm of medical technology is, of course, wide. Screening techniques appear almost outdated when we consider recent developments such as virtual surgery. In this technology, computer-generated representations can be imported from MRI (magnetic resonance imaging) and CAT scans to surgeons or surgeons in training so that they can experience the anatomical structures that previously required a cadaver (Meire et al., 1995). Most virtual reality applications are currently in the area of telepresence surgery (i.e. surgeon in one site, patient in another) and the minimally invasive operative procedures (endoscopic or so-called 'keyhole surgery') that characterize day surgery, and neurosurgery. For training, the 'virtual clinic' is a system which

> *uses tracking devices attached to actual surgical instruments which are inserted through trocars [sharp-pointed rods which fit inside hollow tubes used to withdraw fluid from the body] into a fibreglass mould of the body. Graphic representations of the body change as the instruments are moved, and interaction is visible on a high resolution computer located at the head of the virtual patients. Data produced by computed tomography and magnetic resonance imaging are used to recreate the anatomy of an actual patient. Computer manipulation allows the virtual surgical instruments to interact with the virtual tissues in a way that resembles what happens in real life. New images are created as tissues are dissected. (McGovern, 1994: 1054)*

The interface of body and machine and the empowerment and disempowerment that this affords takes on new dimensions as human and machine become less distinct in cyber-medicine. Much is being made at present of cyberbodies; that is, human–machine hybrids in which machine parts are integrated into the body, replacing or acting as 'supplements to the organism to enhance the body's power potential' (Featherstone and Burrows, 1995: 2). In effect, many of the medical practices towards which cyber-imagery directs our attention are already part of popular currency, such as joint replacements (e.g. prosthetic hips), cosmetic surgeries, and organ replacements. But if the reimplantation of severed limbs, and the implantation of donor organs are a media – though hopefully not personal – commonplace to us, tissue engineering, which involves the actual fabrication of organs, is altogether less familiar. Advances in cell biology and plastics manufacture are increasingly making it possible to construct artificial tissues which look and function like their natural counterparts. As explained by Langer and Vacanti (1995: 101), tissue engineering depends on the manipulation of ultra-pure, biodegradable plastics or polymers which are suitable for use as substrates (surfaces) for cell culture and implantation. Computer-aided design (CAD) is used to shape plastics into 'intricate scaffolding beds that mimic the structure and function of specific tissues and even organs'. Treated with compounds, the cells adhere, multiply and mimic natural tissue as the three-dimensional mesh structure degrades. In late 1995, the BBC television programme *Tomorrow's World* reported on experimental work at the Massachusetts Institute of Technology in Boston, USA, where scientists have developed an ear grown out of cartilage cells on the back of a mouse (bred to be without an immune system) and tissue-engineered heart valves seeded with cells from natural heart tissue. Such developments are, of course, some way off from being part of everyday medical practice since, at the time of writing, there have been no clinical trials on humans. They are, however, ripe for exploitation and a number of question marks hang over them in terms of safety: for example, will the engineered tissues continue to grow in the body or be absorbed by it? Will the new tissue turn malignant?

Treatment choices

All new treatments are to varying degrees experimental, and history reminds us of many dreadful failures, such as the quest for the mechanical heart (Bernstein, 1990), and the consequences of the use of drugs such as Diethylstilboestrol (DES) (a hormonal treatment for threatened miscarriage which has put female offspring at increased risk of vaginal cancer) and Thalidomide. Such concerns, of course, are not new to our age. As we saw earlier, for example, Shaw (1980 [1911]) pronounced on the perils of inoculation at the turn of the century. The important question, whatever the time and place, is: how do we deal with the choices that confront us? When our health is at risk – whether this be from a diagnosed condition in the present, or from the prospect of future illness – we need to weigh up the risks of various actions (which might, of course, include inaction) – not sometime down the line, but *now*. This is not easily done when, as is often the case in medicine, the knowledge before us is uncertain and contested. More and more it would seem, it is we alone who must decide. As has been stressed throughout this chapter, medical culture increasingly places the patient at the centre of decision-making (Zussman, 1993).

High technology, the epitome of the 'biomedical model', increasingly lives side by side with a plethora of other kinds of therapy, many of which might be considered 'complementary' to conventional practice. Charlton speculates: what would a thoroughly postmodern medicine look like? He paints the following picture:

> Medicine would quietly abandon science as altogether too crude and inflexible to encompass the plurality of human pleasure and prefer-ence. Choosing a doctor would become like choosing a pair of shoes. We would expect 'alternative' therapies to be abundant, competitive and aggressively marketed like films and books – promising to en-hance the consumer's life-style and sense of worth. Professional ethics and medical morality would dissolve into the commercial arena – you could select the doctor (or 'healer') with the ethical and spiritual outlook that suited you. However, caveat emptor – let the purchaser beware – you could buy 'health' at your own risk; because whether or not the healer's promises were fulfilled would not depend upon ra-tional constraints. (Charlton, 1993: 498)

Considering the combined use of biomedicine and other therapies, Walter points to the double coding in oncology treatment in a London out-patient clinic: 'as the chemotherapy cocktail is infused into them, patients are offered massage and aromatherapy, to be followed if de-sired by counselling and spiritual healing'. Like postmodern buildings, he continues, 'this kind of mix is both becoming part of the mainstream and is consumer friendly' (Walter, 1994: 43). Of course, competing paradigms are far from new. Pelling and Webster (1979), for example, have demonstrated the interdigitation of medicine with a wide range of other trades in sixteenth-century Britain. But the limitations of local knowledge and access to care in the past meant that sick people would not have had the choices that prevail today. As with screening, with treatment options come choices, none of which are easily made, espe-cially when knowledge is uncertain and contested. The examples that can be given are legion. Take, for example, the controversy in the early 1990s over the efficacy of alternative (often adjunct) therapies for the treatment of breast cancer at the Bristol Cancer Self-Help Centre in England (Stacey, 1994). A second example can be taken from the use of HRT post-menopause. As Hunt (1995) discusses, widely oscillating opinions and polarized debate about the risks and benefits of HRT over the last twenty years have created a climate of heightened anxiety for women making choices. Thus, during the mid-1970s concerns were raised about the risk of endometrial cancer (cancer within the womb); while in the 1980s and 1990s the elevated risk of breast cancer has been to the fore. These worries are counterpoised by evidence of protection from osteoporosis (brittle bone disease) and cardio-vascular disease.

The impression from the discussion so far is that any decision to be made is the prerogative of the patient or potential patient. In reality, of course, this is far from being the case. This has been brought home with some force in recent years in the debate over the rationing of health care.

Health-care rationing

Annas (1995) accentuates many of the controversies that surround rationing in his fable of health-care regulation in twenty-first-century America. In this future time, if people want to buy an artificial heart they need a permit from the 'US National Health Agency' which picks people at random from a computer-generated list (i.e. it is a lottery). Annas's tale debates this method as it is challenged by a thoracic surgeon and two of her patients – one who is in need but does not qualify, being only 15 years old, and the other, who qualifies, but has not yet been picked. The plaintiffs argue through the courts that the allocation mechanism is not rational since it is not related to need and also that it violates the Fifth Amendment right to equal protection. A study of the data collected during the year 2018 reveals that 50 per cent of applicants have been rejected by the Agency. Of these rejections, 90 per cent are on the basis of being 'incapable of ten additional years of life' or because of chronic alcoholism or drug addiction. In addition, 98 per cent of applicants whose IQ is less than 80 have been rejected, as have 80 per cent of those with a history of mental illness, 75 per cent of applicants with a criminal record, 80 per cent of indigents, and 70 per cent of applicants who are unemployed.

These dilemmas of the future are with us already in the present, albeit in less sensational terms. In recent years a number of high-profile cases of rationing of care have come to the fore, most notably the experience of the late Jaymee Bowen, a child who was denied expensive 'experimental' treatment on the NHS for relapsed leukaemia by Cambridge and Huntingdon Health Authority. In wider terms, there is, according to many sources, a growing recognition that some form of rationing is unavoidable given the mismatch of demand and resources in the national health service. Three questions are posed: what treatments are to be rationed, who should get what is available, and who should make the decisions about both of these (New and Le Grand, 1996)?

On the question of what should be rationed, we saw the exclusion of a number of treatments by health authority purchasers in the mid to late

1990s. These include *inter alia* the removal of non-malignant lumps and bumps, the excision of varicose veins, cosmetic surgery, tattoo removal, and IVF treatment for infertility. But such exclusion lists do nothing to solve the problem of who should receive the expensive treatments that are available. Needs-based criteria are typically referred to, but how do you determine need, particularly when it is high-cost, scarce 'rescue' medicine that is at issue? Do we try to assess the amount of pain and distress that a patient is experiencing? Is it the person closest to death who should come first? Or, is it the person who is most likely to experience long-term health benefits (however these might be defined)? Should we take account of patient characteristics such as age, gender, or some criteria of 'moral worth'; as New and Le Grand (1996) put it, a decision between Tiny Tim and Scrooge? Might we, for example, feel the need to choose between 'the unrepentant militant smoker versus the ex-smoker who succeeds in giving up after an immense personal struggle? The Nobel Prize-winner versus the serial killer' (1996: 61)? The 'choices', of course, are unlikely ever to be this stark, which, if we work on the premise that some choice needs to be made (which can itself be contested), makes things even more difficult.

Yet moral evaluations are made and we have known for some time that they impact on quality of patient care. For example, back in the 1950s Howard Becker (1993) found that physicians in training disliked 'crocks', that is, patients with nebulous complaints who take up time. The large body of research on doctor–patient interaction has ably demonstrated the way in which the personal judgements of physicians (and to a lesser extent other practitioners) impact significantly upon their decision-making. Issues of gender (moral evaluations of appropriate femininity for example), social class, 'race', and age all influence clinical decision-making (see Clark et al., 1991). Silverman (1987), for example, shows how physicians engage in a discourse of wellness to prepare the ground for a non-medical outcome, dissuading parents from surgical intervention for congenital heart disease among infants with Down's Syndrome. Although not directed towards rationing as such, this wider body of research is important because it establishes the fact that clinical decision-making is strongly marked by moral discourse, as well as pointing to the tendency of power to remain with the doctor. Yet it is unclear at present whether physicians will want rationing decisions to remain implicit, camouflaged as they currently are by clinical discretion. The politics of rationing is 'messy and treacherous' (Hunter, 1995b) and there is a growing indication that physicians are less willing to tolerate this. As successive governments appear to renege on unspoken bargains to uphold clinical autonomy, physicians may be increasingly willing to make at least some aspects of what is in strict terms non-clinical decision-making clear (Klein et al., 1995). Patients, on the other hand, who have not been fully aware of implicit rationing, may, as New and Le Grand (1996) relate, view a shift towards a more open policy as an outrage.

This was made quite clear in 1993 when stories broke in the British media about the refusal of some surgeons to operate on patients who smoke cigarettes. Writing in the *British Medical Journal*, Underwood and Bailey (1993) highlighted the exacerbation of post-surgery complications such as vein graft failure, sternal and mediastinal infections after coronary bypass surgery in patients who smoke, all precipitating prolonged and costly in-patient stays. In the authors' view, in an era of waiting-lists and resource constraints, patients who smoke deprive those who have never smoked and those who have given up smoking of efficient and effective surgery. Others, such as Shiu, a general practitioner, see this as setting a very dangerous precedent. How far do we go? There are, he cites, other complications of coronary artery surgery such as hypertension, diabetes, obesity, and hypercholesterolaemia. 'Diabetic patients are operated on', he writes, ' – even the ones who cannot stay on a strict diet. Will patients be refused surgery because they cannot stick to a cholesterol-lowering diet?' (Shiu, 1993: 1048). And, as he continues, the costs of not operating on such patients may be higher than doing so if a patient becomes unemployable and in need of benefits, expensive medicines, and repeated hospital visits for chest pain.

There have been few sociological studies as yet of how rationing operates in practice. Therefore, Hughes and Griffiths' (1996) analysis of talk in eighteen conferences on cardiac catheterization (covering 130 patients) in one large British teaching hospital during 1989/90 is of particular interest. In these conferences, cardiologists present cases to the cardiac surgeon who will make the judgement of whether to take the patient on for surgery or angioplasty. Of particular interest to Hughes and Griffiths was the tension that can arise when physicians move between a more technical discourse related to the coronary anatomy and feasibility of surgery and a social discourse which refers to age, lifestyle and other social structural factors. It is through this dialogue that physicians engage with a wider rationing debate that draws on notions of deservingness. The physicians concerned stressed that technical suitability was their main concern, and, indeed, Hughes and Griffiths found that this was to the fore as patient histories were presented. As angiograms were reviewed, attention was directed towards the extent of narrowing of the coronary arteries, the state of the heart muscle supplied by the diseased artery, and whether the artery was suitable for grafting. But technical feasibility did not mean that the surgery would necessarily take place since longer-term risks and prognosis also came into play. This was where correlates of risk such as age could be drawn upon, even if implicitly. There was, for example, evidence that the surgeon prioritized younger patients, since the average age for those designated 'urgent' on the waiting-list was 48.2, while for those who were designated 'routine' it was 59.7, and for those 'on hold', 61.5.

With so-called lifestyle factors such as cigarette-smoking the explicit talk was about health risks rather than morality. Ultimately the physicians refer back to the patients, putting the ball in their court and intimating that they must change their lifestyle in order to qualify for treatment. As Hughes and Griffiths (1996: 187) explain, 'the seductiveness of this approach lies in the way it allows doctors to side-step responsibility. They do not need to ration care, rather, patients are seen to rule themselves out by their own wilful decisions. By attributing choice to patients, doctors avoid hard choices of their own.' 'Pressures now affecting medical practice' they explain, are leading practitioners to 'pay more attention to the characteristics that differentiate patients' with an attendant push to 'move beyond technical calculations of risk to consider deservingness and an associated moral agenda' (1996: 193).

Clearly, then, the 'pressure to choose' on the part of the patient is significantly tempered by the political milieux that engulf clinical practice. Yet the same sociological concerns pertain: as was stressed in the introduction to this chapter, choices need to be made, none of which are easy, surrounded as they are by quite forceful moral imperatives and a profusion of competing interests. In the final part of the chapter we continue the theme introduced through Hughes and Griffiths' study, and consider the way in which physicians' perceptions of patients can engender defensive practice in an era of increasing concern about complaints and medical malpractice.

Medical malpractice and clinical decision-making

In contrast to the United States where it has been a feature of the medical scene for many years, medical malpractice is of relatively recent concern to British practitioners. A signal that malpractice might need to be taken seriously came in the 1980s when the medical defence organizations (which insure physicians) became alarmed at the escalating cost of out-of-court settlements, rising legal fees and court awards. Obstetrics in particular saw a notable rise in litigation. For example, the

Medical Protection Society found that the largest share of paid claims came from this specialism (amounting to £7.6 million) between 1985 and 1988. The Medical Defence Union reported that 23.7 per cent of claims settled in hospital practice came from obstetrics and gynaecology in 1989 (see Annandale, 1996b). Concern was heightened in the early 1990s when it was reported that fully 85 per cent of British obstetricians had had at least one claim against them, and that 65 per cent had had two (Brahams, 1991). Currently, individual trusts are responsible for claims against staff following the introduction of NHS indemnity (for hospital staff only) in 1990. As was noted in chapter 7, health authority spending on awards rose from £53 million in 1990/1 to an estimated £155 million in 1994/5 (DoH, 1996b). The new Central Fund for Clinical Negligence (which spreads the risk for an individual hospital in a pooling arrangement for those who pay to join) was set up by the Department of Health in 1995 with the intention of defraying the possibility that any one trust could face a serious cost crisis if it experienced a major legal suit.

In this context, physicians, midwives, nurses and other providers of formal health care are being made increasingly aware of the risks that patients pose to their personal well-being (see also chapter 8). Considerable anxiety can be created by the downward push upon staff from the dual threat of patient complaints or litigation from management and the upward push from patients who, in the eyes of many, are ever more 'aware of their rights'. Confidence can be undermined in the process: as one midwife put it in research carried out in two hospitals, 'although at the time you feel you have done the right thing, often people, mainly relatives, interfere and question if you have given the right treatment in an attempt to intimidate you by suggesting that they will take further action' (Annandale, 1996a: 424). A sense of risk emanating from the dual authority of management and patients (or their relatives) is in the background; it is an atmosphere: it is always there. As one staff nurse explained, 'it is always in your mind that you may be held responsible in a legal dispute for actions and words'. Or, in the words of one sister, 'litigation is the "bogey man" that stands behind my shoulder as I practise as a midwife' (1996a: 420). To date nurses and midwives have little direct experience of litigation against them (actual figures are not publicly available). However, there is some evidence that even a sense of threat can generate high anxiety. For example, they spoke of a wariness about particular patients who can be spotted as the types who might complain or sue. While these patients were not easily typified by socio-demographic characteristics (except perhaps a hint of a need to be wary of lawyers, doctors and their families!), they seemed to stand out and be readily identifiable to the practitioner concerned. For example, one senior sister remarked,

> *It's just a manner that they approach you with and they try, I suppose they try and pin you down. You're trying to be evasive because that's the way you deal with something you're not quite sure of, but they are sort of ferreting away at it and they're ferreting away at you and they're just waiting for a little something to go wrong and they've got you. (Annandale, 1996a: 433)*

The nurse and midwife respondents in the study reported a number of effects that followed on from this: for example, greater vigilance with regard to patients (arguably a positive effect); excessive attention to documentation (taking time away from direct patient care); and avoiding getting into discussions about a patient's condition (passing the buck to physicians).

For physicians this picture is amplified many times over. While it has been appropriately suggested that the sense of 'crisis' might best be seen as a moral panic (Dingwall, 1994), there are indications that physicians are changing their practice in response to the threat of patients who they think might complain. Evidence for this comes from Summerton's (1995) study of British general practice. He found that fully 98 per cent of his national sample said that they had made some practice change as a result of the possibility of a complaint. Among other things, 25 per cent said that if there seemed to be the likelihood of a complaint they would consider removing patients from their list; 29 per cent would prescribe unnecessary drugs; 42 per cent would avoid treating certain conditions in their practice; 60 per cent would generally increase diagnostic testing; 90 per cent felt it likely that they would engage in more detailed note-taking; and 87 per cent would give more detailed explanations to patients. Summerton found that the extent of 'worry' about a complaint (which 52 per cent said they did 'sometimes' and 32 per cent 'often') was highly correlated with defensive practices of the kind described. Of course, the actions that they might take, as listed here, could have both negative and positive effects upon patient care.

A larger literature referring to the USA suggests that the doctor–patient relationship is a major site for litigation reduction. Physicians (and nurses too) are exhorted that a good relationship with a patient can help to preclude the bringing of a malpractice suit when negligence occurs. Honesty is said to be the best policy, since patients are then likely to be more forgiving (Annandale, 1989b). Such exhortations are also appearing in Britain. For example, a commentary in the *British Journal of Obstetrics and Gynaecology* reads, 'the real answer to the question of "How to avoid medico-legal problems in obstetrics and gynaecology" is good practice and communication. Whilst the former will provide a perfect defence to litigation, the latter (irrespective of the standard of care) will often obviate it' (Clements, 1991). A study conducted in the Oxford region (Mulcahy, 1996) found that consultants strongly implicated the patient's disease in the bringing of a complaint. Being aggrieved then became an offshoot of the disease which made the patient behave irrationally in a way that contrasted with the rational science of medicine. This mirrors Millman's (1977) research in the USA, which vividly recounts the ways in which physicians shift the blame for diagnostic mistakes onto patients.

In the USA notions of the suit-prone patient have been associated less with socio-demographic characteristics, where data are equivocal (about whether blue- or white-collar patients are a risk, for example), than with certain personalities. It actually seems difficult to escape some form of typification on the patient's part since a whole gamut appears in the literature. For example, physicians are told to be wary of the 'dependent', the 'unco-operative', the 'hostile', the 'self-styled experts', the 'flatterers', the 'subservient', the 'demanding', the 'untrusting', and the 'emotionally disturbed' patient, to name but a few (Annandale, 1989b). This kind of discourse has not taken hold in Britain, although I did hear a speaker at a gathering for final-year medical students remark that when considering litigation and practice 'it is not what you do, but who you do it to!' The same speaker also stressed to the students that 'if you communicate well and are empathetic and sympathetic you can literally get away with murder'.

Conclusion

The chapter began by drawing attention to a tension between the premium that is increasingly placed on reflexivity and choice and the moral imperative to make choices in health care. This theme has threaded through the chapter as we have considered both the 'care of self' in illness and care by others in the formal health-care context. We have seen that there is a compulsion to make sense of illness in terms of one's own place in the world that is to a considerable extent marked with an ethos of personal control and responsibility. This is reflected, for example, in the principle of 'mind over matter' in coping with chronic illness. While complicity with this ethos can cultivate a sense of empowerment, its chiasmus is the sense of alienation that can result from the inability to actually do anything to alter one's circumstances, or the backlash that can accompany actions that are taken. Thus we have seen that the drive to present oneself as healthy in the face of sometimes quite severe illness can be disempowering for the individual. Far from cultivating a sense of agency, the result can be despair. In the health-care context there is an impulsion to seek information and to make choices. Yet the ability of the patient to do this is very much circumscribed by the highly politicized nature of the health-care milieu. Actions provoke counter-actions, as in the case of defensive medicine. Of course, the degree to which these tensions are felt by any one individual will vary enormously according to the illness concerned and personal circumstances involved. The concerns that we have discussed are not new to this age, simply more tenacious and biting in their impact. For this reason, the tension between reflexivity and the imperative of choice in illness might be viewed as a trope for the contemporary social condition.

Notes

Chapter 1

1 The term late modernity has been used here as an umbrella term since the authors considered refer variously to late modernity, high modernity, reflexive modernization and late capitalism. Moreover although the work of Beck, Giddens and Lash and Urry is drawn together under this umbrella, there are in fact some significant differences between them. A useful discussion can be found in Beck et al. (1994).

Chapter 4

1 The standardized mortality ratio (SMR) is the percentage ratio of the number of deaths observed in a specific group to the number expected from the age-specific death rates of the standard population. The SMR of the standard population is 100, so mortality is lower than expected when it is below 100, and higher than expected when it is above 100.

Chapter 6

1 While the Labour Force Surveys use a self-classification of ethnic status, the categories differ from those employed in the 1991 Census. The Labour Force Survey which gives a figure of 4.9 per cent (2.67 million) for 1989–91, seems to have underestimated the percentage of the total population from minority ethnic groups, since the 1991 Census gives a figure of 5.5 per cent (3.01 million) (Skellington, 1996: 56–7). In fact, following improvements in methodology after 1992, the Labour Force Survey estimated that in 1992–3 minority ethnic groups constituted 5.8 per cent of the population (Owen, 1996).

2 It should be recognized that even to separate out 'black' and 'Asian' poses dilemmas, since as Sheldon and Parker (1992) relate, the umbrella term 'Asian' contains a heterogeneity of experience (e.g. of country of origin, culture, religion) that makes it virtually meaningless.

3 It should be noted that, although the census captures experiences in 1991, the long process of validation and preparation for general use means that data have only recently become available. In this section of the chapter the language of ethnic categorization is taken from the literature that is drawn upon. In light of difficult debates that are implicated in deciding which terms should be taken at face value and which not, inverted commas are often not used. However, it is very important to bear the problematic nature of many of these classifications in mind.

References

ACHC (Association of Community Health Councils) (1996) *The Financial Health of the NHS*. London: ACHC.

Ahmad, W. (1993) Making black people sick: 'race' and health in health research. In W. Ahmad (ed.), *'Race' and Health in Contemporary Britain*, Buckingham: Open University Press, 11–33.

—— (1996) The trouble with culture. In D. Kelleher and S. Hillier (eds), *Researching Cultural Differences in Health*, London: Routledge, 190–219.

Alaszewski, A. (1995) Restructuring health and welfare professions in the United Kingdom: the impact of internal markets on the medical, nursing and social work professions. In T. Johnson, G. Larkin and M. Saks (eds), *Health Professions and the State in Europe*, London: Routledge, 55–87.

Allen, J. (1992) Post-industrialism and post-Fordism. In S. Hall, D. Held and T. McGrew (eds), *Modernity and its Futures*, Oxford: Polity/Open University Press, 170–220.

Allsop, J. (1995a) The NHS complaints review: opportunities for working and the contribution of research. *Medical Sociology News*, 20, 27–32.

—— (1995b) Shifting spheres of opportunity: the professional powers of general practitioners within the British National Health Service. In T. Johnson, G. Larkin and M. Saks (eds), *Health Professions and the State in Europe*, London: Routledge, 75–85.

Andrews, A. and Jewson, N. (1993) Ethnicity and infant deaths: the implications of recent statistical evidence for materialist explanations. *Sociology of Health & Illness*, 15, 137–56.

Annandale, E. (1989a) Proletarianisation or restratification of the medical profession? The case of obstetrics. *International Journal of Health Services*, 19, 611–34.

—— (1989b) The malpractice crisis and the doctor–patient relationship. *Sociology of Health & Illness*, 11, 1–23.

—— (1996a) Working on the front-line: risk culture and nursing in the new NHS. *Sociological Review*, 44, 416–51.

—— (1996b) Professional defenses: medical students' perceptions of medical malpractice. *International Journal of Health Services*, 26, 751–75.

—— (1998) Health, illness and the politics of gender. In D. Field and S. Taylor (eds), *Sociological Perspectives on Health, Illness and Health Care*, Oxford: Blackwell Scientific, 115–33.

Annandale, E. and Clark, J. (1996) What is gender? Feminist theory and the sociology of human reproduction. *Sociology of Health & Illness*, 18, 17–44.

—— + —— (1997) A reply to Rona Campbell and Sam Porter. *Sociology of Health & Illness*, 19, 521–32. See also Erratum 19, 680–1.

Annandale, E. and Hunt, K. (1990) Masculinity, femininity and sex: an exploration of their relative contribution to explaining gender differences in health. *Sociology of Health & Illness*, 12, 24–46.

Annas, G. (1995) Minerva v. National Health Agency. In C. Hables Gray with H. Figueroa-Sarriera and S. Mentor (eds), *The Cyborg Handbook*, London: Routledge, 169–81.

Appleby, J. (1992) *Financing Health Care in the 1990s*. Buckingham: Open University Press.

Arber, S. (1994) Gender, health and ageing. *Medical Sociology News*, 20, 14–22.

Arber, S., Gilbert, N. and Dale, A. (1985) Paid employment and women's health: a benefit or a source of role strain? *Sociology of Health & Illness*, 7, 375–99.

Aries, P. (1981) *The Hour of Our Death*. London: Allen Lane.

Arms, S. (1975) *Immaculate Deception*. New York: Simon and Schuster.

Armstrong, D. (1983) *The Political Anatomy of the Body*. Cambridge: Cambridge University Press.

—— (1985) Review essay. The subject and the social in medicine: an appreciation of Michel Foucault. *Sociology of Health & Illness*, 7, 108–17.

—— (1987a) Bodies of knowledge: Foucault and the problem of human anatomy. In G. Scambler (ed.), *Sociological Theory and Medical Sociology*, London: Tavistock, 59–76.

—— (1987b) Theoretical trends in biopsychosocial medicine. *Social Science and Medicine*, 25, 1213–18.

Arney, W. R. and Bergen, B. J. (1983) The anomaly, the chronic patient and the play of medical power. *Sociology of Health & Illness*, 5, 1–24.

—— + —— (1984) *Medicine and the Management of Living*. London: University of Chicago Press.

Atkinson, P. (1981) *The Clinical Experience*. Farnborough: Gower.

—— (1995) *Medical Talk and Medical Work*. London: Sage.

Atkinson, P. and Heath, C. (1981) *Medical Work: Realities and Routines*. London: Gower.

Audit Commission (1996a) *The Doctors' Tale Continued: The Audits of Hospital Medical Staffing*. London: HMSO.

—— (1996b) *By Accident or Design: Improving A&E Services in England and Wales*. London: HMSO.

BMA (British Medical Association) (1989) *Special Report on the Government's White Paper 'Working for Patients'*. London: BMA.

BMJ (1994) Fundholders' patients are treated quicker, says BMA. *British Medical Journal*, 308, 11.

Baggott, R. (1994) *Health and Health Care in Britain*. Basingstoke: Macmillan.

Baker, R. and Woodrow, S. (1984) The clean, light image of the electronics industry: miracle or mirage? In W. Chavkin (ed.), *Double Exposure: Women's Health Hazards on the Job and at Home*, New York: Monthly Review Press, 21–37.

Balarajan, R. and Bulusu, L. (1990) Mortality among immigrants in England and Wales. In M. Britton (ed.), *Mortality and Geography: A Review in the Mid-1980s*, London: OPCS, series DS, No. 9.

Balarajan, R. and Raleigh, V. (1990) Variations in perinatal, neonatal and post-neonatal and infant mortality by mother's country of birth. In M. Britton (ed.), *Mortality and Geography: A Review in the Mid-1980s* (London: OPCS), series DS, No. 9.

Baldwin, S. and Twigg, J. (1991) Women and community care. In M. Maclean and D. Groves (eds), *Women's Issues in Social Policy*, London: Routledge, 117–35.

Barnes, C. and Cox, D. (1997) Patients, power and policy: NHS management reforms and consumer empowerment. In K. Isaac-Henry, C. Painter and C. Barnes (eds), *Management in the Public Sector: Challenge and Change* (2nd edition), Andover: Thompson's Business Press, 182–215.

Barrett, M. (1991) *The Politics of Truth*. Cambridge: Polity Press.

—— (1992) Words and things: materialism and method in contemporary feminist analysis. In M. Barrett and A. Phillips (eds), *Destabilising Theory*, Cambridge: Polity Press, 201–19.

Bartlett, H. and Phillips, D. (1996) Policy issues in the private health sector: examples from long-term care in the U.K. *Social Science and Medicine*, 43, 731–7.

Bartlett, W. and Le Grand, J. (eds) (1994) *Evaluating the NHS Reforms*. London: King's Fund Institute.

Bartley, M., Carpenter, L., Dunnell, K. and Fitzpatrick, R. (1996) Measuring inequalities in health: an analysis of mortality patterns using two social classifications. *Sociology of Health & Illness*, 18, 455–74.

Bartley, M., Popay, J. and Plewis, I. (1992) Domestic conditions, paid employment and women's experience of ill-health. *Sociology of Health & Illness*, 14, 314–43.

Baudrillard, J. (1983) *Simulations*. New York: Semiotext(e).

—— (1987) *Forget Foucault*. New York: Semiotext(e).

Bauman, Z. (1987) *Legislators and Interpreters: On Modernity, Postmodernity and Intellectuals*. Cambridge: Polity Press.

—— (1988) Sociology and postmodernity. *Sociological Review*, 36, 790–873.

—— (1993) The sweet scent of decomposition. In C. Rojek and B. Turner (eds), *Forget Baudrillard?*, London: Routledge, 22–46.

Beck, U. (1992) *Risk Society*. London: Sage.

Beck, U., Giddens. A. and Lash, S. (1994) *Reflexive Modernization*. Cambridge: Polity Press.

Becker, H. (1993) How I learned what a crock was. *Journal of Contemporary Ethnography*, 22, 28–35.

Beishon, S., Virdee, S. and Hagell, A. (1995) *Nursing in a Multi-ethnic NHS.* London: Policy Studies Institute.

Bell, D. and Klein, R. (1996) *Radically Speaking: Feminism Reconsidered.* London: Zed Books.

Bem, S. (1974) The measurement of psychological androgyny. *Journal of Consulting and Clinical Psychology*, 42, 155–62.

Ben-Shlomo, Y., White, I. and Marmot, M. (1996) Does the variation in the socio-economic characteristics of an area affect mortality? *British Medical Journal*, 312, 1013–14.

Benzeval, M. and Webb, S. (1995) Family poverty and poor health. In M. Benzeval, K. Judge and M. Whitehead (eds), *Tackling Inequalities in Health*, London: King's Fund, 69–81.

Bernstein, B. (1990) The misguided quest for the artificial heart. In P. Conrad and R. Kern (eds), *The Sociology of Health and Illness* (3rd edition), New York: St Martin's Press, 351–7.

Best, S. and Kellner, D. (1991) *Postmodern Theory.* New York: Guildford Press.

Bhatti, N., Law, M. R., Morris, J. K., Halliday, R. and Moore-Gillon, J. (1995) Increasing incidence of tuberculosis in England and Wales: a study of the likely causes. *British Medical Journal*, 310, 967–9.

Blane, D. (1985) An assessment of the Black Report's explanation of health inequalities. *Sociology of Health & Illness*, 7, 423–45.

Blaxter, M. (1987) Health and social class: evidence on inequality and health from a national survey. *Lancet*, 4 July, 30–3.

—— (1990) *Health and Lifestyles.* London: Tavistock/Routledge.

Bloom, L. R. (1992) How can we know the dancer from the dance? Discourses of the self-body. *Human Studies*, 15, 313–34.

Bloor, M., Samphier, M. and Prior, L. (1987) Artefact explanations of inequalities in health: an assessment of the evidence. *Sociology of Health & Illness*, 9, 231–64.

Blumer, H. (1969) *Symbolic Interactionism: Perspective and Method.* Englewood Cliffs, NJ: Prentice-Hall.

Bordo, S. (1993a) Feminism, Foucault and the politics of the body. In C. Ramazanoglu (ed.), *Up Against Foucault*, London: Routledge, 180–202.

—— (1993b) *Unbearable Weight: Feminism, Western Culture and the Body.* London: University of California Press.

Boston Women's Health Book Collective (1973). *Our Bodies, Ourselves.* New York: Simon & Schuster.

Bourdieu, P. (1984) *Distinctions.* London: Routledge.

Bowler, I. (1993) 'They're not the same as us': midwives' stereotypes of South Asian descent patients. *Sociology of Health & Illness*, 15, 157–78.

Bradby, H. (1995) Ethnicity: not a black and white issue. *Sociology of Health & Illness*, 17, 405–17.

Brahams, D. (1991) Worried obstetricians. *Lancet*, 337, 1597.

Brindle, D. (1996) NHS to sell private care plans. *Guardian*, 25 March.

Britton, M. (1989) Mortality and geography. *Population Trends*, 56 (summer), 15–23.

—— (1990) *Mortality and Geography: A Review in the Mid-1980s*. London: OPCS, series DS, No. 9.

Brody, M. (1992) The liberation of Mary Wollstonecraft: life and writings. Introduction to M. Wollstonecraft, *A Vindication of the Rights of Woman* (1792). London: Penguin Books, 1–20.

Brown, Phil (1987) Popular epidemiology: community response to toxic waste-induced disease in Woburn, Massachusetts. *Science Technology and Human Values*, 12, 78–85.

—— (ed.) (1989) *Perspectives in Medical Sociology*. Belmont, Calif.: Wadsworth.

Brown, Phyllida (1993) Breast cancer: a lethal inheritance. *New Scientist*, 18 September, 34–7.

Bryan, B., Dadzie, S. and Scafe, S. (1985) *The Heart of the Race*. London: Virago.

Bunton, R. and Burrows, R. (1995) Consumption and health in the 'epidemiological clinic' of late modern medicine. In R. Bunton, S. Nettleton and R. Burrows (eds), *The Sociology of Health Promotion*, London: Routledge, 206–22.

Burns, T. (1992) *Erving Goffman*. London: Routledge.

Burrows, R. and Loader, B. (1994) *Towards a post-Fordist Welfare State*. London: Routledge.

Bury, M. (1982) Chronic illness as biographical disruption. *Sociology of Health & Illness*, 4, 167–82.

—— (1986) Social constructionism and the development of medical sociology. *Sociology of Health & Illness*, 8, 137–69.

Butler, J. (1994) Origins and Development. In R. Robinson and J. Le Grand (eds), *Evaluating the NHS Reforms*, London: King's Fund Institute, 1–12.

CRE (Commission for Racial Equality) (1996) *Appointing NHS Consultants and Senior Registrars*. London: CRE.

CSO (Central Statistical Office) (1995a) *Social Trends 1995 Edition*. London: HMSO.

—— (1995b) *Social Focus on Women*. London: HMSO.

—— (1996) *Social Trends 1996 Edition*. London: HMSO.

Callari, A., Cullenberg, S. and Biewener, C. (1995) Marxism in the new world order. In A. Callari, S. Cullenberg and C. Biewener (eds), *Marxism in the Postmodern Age*, London: Guildford Press, 1–10.

Calloway, H. (1993) The most essentially female function of all: giving birth. In S. Ardener (ed.), *Defining Females: The Nature of Women in Society*, Oxford: Berg, 146–67.

Carpenter, M. (1993) The subordination of nurses in health care: towards a social divisions approach. In E. Riska and K. Wegar (eds), *Gender, Work and Medicine*, London: Sage, 95–130.

—— (1994) *Normality is Hard Work: Trade Unions and the Politics of Community Care*. London: Lawrence & Wishart/Unison.

Carricaburu, D. and Pierret, J. (1995) From biographical disruption to biographical reinforcement: the case of HIV-positive men. *Sociology of Health & Illness*, 17, 65–88.

Carrigan, T., Connell, B. and Lee, J. (1987) Hard and heavy: toward a new sociology of masculinity. In M. Kaufman (ed.), *Beyond Patriarchy*, New York: Oxford University Press, 139–92.

Cervi, B. (1996) Tax payers 'subsidise' NHS pay beds. *Health Service Journal*, 3 October, 5.

Chadda, D. (1996) New focus. *Health Service Journal*, 7 March, 11.

Charlton, B. (1993) Medicine and post-modernity. *Journal of the Royal Society of Medicine*, 86, 497–9

Charlton, J., Wallace, M. and White, I. (1994) Long-term illness: results from the 1991 Census. *Population Trends*, 75, 18–25.

Chesler, P. (1990) *The Sacred Bond: Motherhood Under Siege*. London: Virago.

Chollat-Traquet, C. (1992) *Women and Tobacco*. Geneva: World Health Organization.

Clark, J., Potter, D. and McKinlay, J. (1991) Bringing social structure back into clinical decision making. *Social Science and Medicine*, 32, 853–66.

Clarke, J. (1983) Sexism, feminism and medicalism: a decade review of literature on gender and illness. *Sociology of Health & Illness*, 5, 62–82.

Clements, R. (1991) Litigation in obstetrics and gynaecology. *British Journal of Obstetrics and Gynaecology*, 98, 423–6.

Coburn, D. (1992) Freidson then and now: an 'internalist' critique of Freidson's past and present views of the medical profession. *International Journal of Health Services*, 22, 497–512.

Cohen, P. (1995) Flexible foe. *Health Service Journal*, 9 February, 17.

Cole, M. (1993) 'Black and ethnic minority' or 'Asian, Black and Other minority ethnic': a further note on nomenclature. *Sociology*, 27, 671–4.

Coleman, D. and Salt, J. (1996) The ethnic group question in the 1991 Census: a new landmark in British social statistics. In D. Coleman and J. Salt (eds), *Ethnicity in the 1991 Census*, Vol 1. London: HMSO, 1–32.

Coleman, L. and Dickinson, C. (1984) The risks of healing: the hazards of the nursing profession. In W. Chavkin (ed.), *Double Exposure: Women's Health Hazards on the Job and at Home*, New York: Monthly Review Press, 37–66.

Collins, P. (1990) *Black Feminist Thought*. London: HarperCollins Academic.

Connell, R. (1987) *Gender and Power*. Cambridge: Polity Press.

—— (1995) *Masculinities*. Cambridge: Polity Press.

Cooley, C. (1981) Self as sentiment and reflection. In G. Stone and H. Faberman (eds), *Social Psychology through Symbolic Interactionism*, New York: Wiley, 377–82.

Corea, G. (1985) *The Mother Machine: Reproductive Technologies from Artificial Insemination to Artificial Wombs*. London: The Women's Press.

Cornwell, J. (1984) *Hard Earned Lives*. London: Tavistock.

Coser, R. (1962) *Life on the Ward*. East Lansing, Mich.: Michigan State University Press.

Craib, I. (1995) Some comments on the sociology of the emotions. *Sociology*, 19, 151–8.

Crawford, R. (1984) A cultural account of 'health': control, release, and the social body. In J. McKinlay (ed.), *Issues in the Political Economy of Health Care*, London: Tavistock, 60–103.

Crompton, R. (1993) *Class and Stratification: An Introduction to Current Debates.* Cambridge: Polity Press.

—— (1996) Consumption and class analysis. In S. Edgell, K. Hetherington and A. Warde (eds) *Consumption Matters,* Oxford: Blackwell, 113–32.

Crompton, R. and Mann, M. (1994) *Gender and Stratification.* Cambridge: Polity Press.

DHSS (Department of Health and Social Security) (1983) *NHS Management Enquiry Report* (Griffiths Report). London: DHSS.

DoH (Department of Health) (1989) *Working for Patients.* London: HMSO, Cmnd 555.

—— (1994a) *Hospital, Public Health Medicine and Community Health Service Medical Service and Dental Staff in England 1983–1993.* Statistical Bulletin 1994/10.

—— (1994b) *Being Heard: The Report of a Review Committee on NHS Complaints Procedures* (Wilson Report). Leeds: DoH.

—— (1995a) *Fit for the Future: Second Progress Report on the Health of the Nation.* London: DoH.

—— (1995b) *The Patient's Charter and You.* London: HMSO.

—— (1995c) *Planning the Medical Workforce.* Medical Workforce Standing Advisory Committee: Second Report. Leeds: DoH.

—— (1996) *Expenditure Plans 1996–97 to 1998–99.*

—— (1996a) *Health Survey for England 1994,* vol 1. London: HMSO.

—— (1997) *The New NHS. Modern, Dependable.* London: The Stationery Office, Cmnd 3807.

DSS (1995) *Households Below Average Income: A Statistical Analysis 1979–1992/93.* London: HMSO.

Daly, M. (1973) *Beyond God the Father: Towards a Philosophy of Women's Liberation.* Boston: Beacon Press.

—— (1984) *Pure Lust: Elemental Feminist Philosophy.* London: The Women's Press.

—— (1990 [1978]) *Gyn/ecology: The Metaethics of Radical Feminism.* Boston: Beacon Press.

Davey Smith, G. (1996) Income inequality and mortality: why are they related? *British Medical Journal,* 312, 987–8.

Davey Smith, G., Bartley, M. and Blane, D. (1990) The Black Report on socioeconomic inequalities in health 10 years on. *British Medical Journal,* 301, 373–7.

Davies, C. (1995) *Gender and the Professional Predicament in Nursing.* London: Open University Press.

Davis, K. (1995) *Reshaping the Female Body: The Dilemma of Cosmetic Surgery.* London: Routledge.

Davis, M. A. (1981) Sex differences in reporting osteoarthritis symptoms: a sociomedical approach. *Journal of Health and Social Behaviour,* 22, 298–310.

Day, R. and Day, J. (1977) A review of the current state of negotiated order theory: an appreciation and a critique. *Sociological Quarterly,* 18, 126–42.

Derber, C. (1982) *Professionals as Workers: Mental Labor in Advanced Capitalism.* Boston, Mass.: G. K. Hall.

Derber, C., Schwartz, W. and Magrass, Y. (1990) *Power in the Highest Degree:*

Professionals and the Rise of the New Mandarin Order. Oxford: Oxford University Press.

Derrida, J. (1982) *Margins of Philosophy.* Hemel Hempstead: Harvester.

Di Stefano, C. (1990) Dilemma of difference: feminism, modernity and postmodernism. In L. Nicholson (ed.), *Feminism/Postmodernism*, London: Routledge, 63–82.

Dingwall, R. (1976) *Aspects of Illness.* London: Martin Robertson.

—— (1994) Litigation and the threat to medicine. In J. Gabe, D. Kelleher and G. Williams (eds), *Challenging Medicine*, London: Routledge, 46–64.

Donovan, J. (1988) *We Don't Buy Sickness, It Just Comes.* Aldershot: Gower.

Doyal, L. (1979) *The Political Economy of Health.* Boston: South End Press.

—— (1994a) Waged work and well-being. In S. Wilkinson and C. Kitzinger (eds), *Women and Health*, London: Taylor and Francis, 65–84.

—— (1994b) Changing medicine? Gender and the politics of health care. In J. Gabe, D. Kelleher and G. Williams (eds), *Challenging Medicine*, London: Routledge, 140–59.

—— (1995) *What Makes Women Sick?* London: Macmillan.

Dreifus, C. (1978) *Seizing Our Bodies: The Politics of Women's Health.* New York: Vintage Books.

Dubos, R. (1960) *Mirage of Health.* London: George Allen and Unwin.

Dundas Todd, A. (1989) *Intimate Adversaries.* Philadelphia: University of Pennsylvania Press.

Dworkin, A. (1988) Dangerous and deadly. *Trouble and Strife*, 14, 42–5.

Ebert, T. (1996) The crisis of (ludic) socialist feminism. In C. Siegel and A. Kibbey (eds), *Forming and Reforming Identity*. London: New York University Press, 339–69.

Ehrenreich, B. and English, D. (1973) *Witches, Midwives, and Nurses: A History of Women Healers.* New York: Feminist Press.

—— (1978) The 'sick' women of the upper classes. In J. Ehrenreich (ed.), *The Cultural Crisis of Modern Medicine*, New York: Monthly Review Press, 123–43.

Eisenstein, Z. (1988) *The Female Body and the Law.* London: University of California Press.

—— (1993) *The Radical Future of Liberal Feminism.* Boston: Northeastern University Press.

—— (1994) Writing hatred on the body. *New Political Science*, 30/31, 15–22.

Elias, N. (1985) *The Loneliness of the Dying.* Oxford: Blackwell.

Elstad, J. I. (1996) How large are the differences really? Self-reported long-standing illness among working-class and middle-class men. *Sociology of Health & Illness*, 18, 475–98.

Elston, M. A. (1991) The politics of professional power: medicine in a changing health service. In J. Gabe, M. Calnan, and M. Bury (eds), *The Sociology of the Health Service*, London: Routledge, 58–88.

—— (1993) Women doctors in a changing profession: the case of Britain. In E. Riska and K. Wegar (eds), *Gender, Work and Medicine*, London: Sage, 27–91.

Engels, F. (1993 [1845]) *The Condition of the Working Class in England.* Oxford: Oxford University Press.

Esping-Anderson, G. (1993) Post-industrial class structures: an analytical frame-work. In G. Esping-Anderson (ed.), *Changing Classes*, London: Sage, 7–31.

Evandrou, M. (1996) Unpaid work, carers and health. In D. Blane, E. Brunner and R. Wilkinson (eds), *Health and Social Organisation*, London: Routledge, 204–31.

Everton, J. (1993) Single homelessness and social policy. In K. Fisher and J. Collins (eds), *Homelessness, Health Care and Welfare*, London: Routledge, 12–31.

Faberman, H. (1989) The sociology of emotions: feedback on the cognitive and a-structural biases of symbolic interactionism. In D. D. Frank and E. D. McCarthy (eds), *The Sociology of Emotions*, Greenwich, Conn.: JAI Press, 271–88.

Featherstone, M. and Burrows, R. (1995) Cultures of technological embodiment: an introduction. In M. Featherstone and R. Burrows (eds), *Cyberspace/Cyberbodies/Cyberpunk*, London: Sage, 1–19.

Fee, E. (1975) Women and health care: a comparison of theories. *International Journal of Health Services*, 5, 397–415.

Fenton, S., Hughes, A. and Hine, C. (1995) Self-assessed health, economic status and ethnic origin. *New Community*, 21, 55–68.

Figlio, K. (1987) The lost subject of medical sociology. In G. Scambler (ed.), *Sociological Theory and Medical Sociology*, London: Tavistock, 77–109.

Finch, J. (1990) The politics of community care in Britain. In C. Ungerson (ed.), *Gender and Caring: Work and Welfare in Britain and Scandinavia*, London: Wheatsheaf, 34–58.

Fine, G. (1993) The sad demise, mysterious disappearance, and glorious triumph of symbolic interactionism. *Annual Review of Sociology*, 19, 61–87.

Firestone, S. (1970) *The Dialectic of Sex*. New York: Bantam Books.

Fisher, S. and Dundas Todd, A. (1986) *Discourse and Institutional Authority: Medicine, Education and Law*. Norwood, NJ: Ablex.

Flax, J. (1990a) *Thinking Fragments*. Oxford: University of California Press.

—— (1990b) Postmodernism and gender relations in feminist theory. In L. Nicholson (ed.), *Feminism/Postmodernism*, London: Routledge, 39–82.

Flynn, R., Williams, G. and Pickard S. (1996) *Markets and Networks*. Buckingham: Open University Press.

Ford, G., Ecob, R., Hunt, K., Macintyre, S. and West, P. (1994) Patterns of class inequality in health through the lifespan: class gradients at 15, 35 and 55 years in the West of Scotland. *Social Science and Medicine*, 39, 1037–50.

Foster, P. (1995) *Women and the Health Care Industry*. Buckingham: Open University Press.

Foucault, M. (1977) *Language Counter-Memory Practice*. Ithaca: Cornell University Press.

—— (1979) *Discipline and Punish*. New York: Vintage Books.

—— (1980) *Michel Foucault: Power/Knowledge*, ed. C. Gordon. Brighton: Harvester.

—— (1982) The subject of power. *Critical Inquiry*, 8, 777–95.

—— (1985) *The Use of Pleasure*. Harmondsworth: Penguin.

—— (1986) *The Care of the Self*. Harmondsworth: Penguin.

—— (1988) Technologies of the self. In M. Luther, M. Martin, H. Gutman and P. H. Hutton (eds), *Technologies of the Self*, Amherst, Mass.: University of Massachusetts Press, 16–49.

—— (1989) *The Birth of the Clinic*. London: Routledge.

Fox, J. and Benzeval, M. (1995) Perspectives on social variations in health. In M. Benzeval, K. Judge and M. Whitehead (eds), *Tackling Inequalities in Health*. London: King's Fund, 10–21.

Fox, J., Goldblatt, P. and Jones, D. (1990) Social class mortality differentials: artifact, selection or life circumstances?' In P. Goldblatt, (ed.), *Longitudinal Study: Mortality and Social Organisation 1971–1981*, London: HMSO.

Fox, N. (1992) *The Social Meaning of Surgery*. Buckingham: Open University Press.

—— (1993) *Postmodernism Sociology and Health*. Buckingham: Open University Press.

—— (1994) Anaesthetists, the discourse on patient fitness and the organisation of surgery. *Sociology of Health & Illness*, 16,1–18.

Francome, C. and Marks, D. (1996) *Improving the Health of the Nation*. London: Middlesex University Press.

Frank, A. (1991a) From sick role to health role: deconstructing Parsons. In R. Robertson and B. Turner (eds), *Talcott Parsons: Theorist of Modernity*, London: Sage, 205–16.

—— (1991b) *At the Will of the Body*. London: Houghton Mifflin.

—— (1992) Twin nightmares of the medical simulacrum: Jean Baudrillard and David Cronenberg. In W. Stearns and W. Chaloupka (eds), *Jean Baudrillard: The Disappearance of Art and Politics*, London: Macmillan, 82–97.

—— (1993) The rhetoric of self-change: illness experience as narrative. *The Sociological Quarterly*, 34, 39–52.

—— (1995) *The Wounded Storyteller: Body, Illness, and Ethics*. London: University of Chicago Press.

—— (1996) Reconciliatory alchemy: bodies, narratives and power. *Body and Society*, 2, 53–71.

Frankenberg, Ronald (1974) Functionalism and after? Theory and developments in social sciences applied to the health field. *International Journal of Health Services*, 4, 411–27.

Frankenberg, Ruth (1993) *White Women, Race Matters: The Social Construction of Whiteness*. London: Routledge.

Freidson, E. (1986) *Professional Powers*. Chicago: University of Chicago Press.

—— (1988 [1970]) *Profession of Medicine*. London: University of Chicago Press.

—— (1989) *Medical Work in America*. London: Yale University Press.

—— (1994) *Professionalism Reborn*. Cambridge: Polity Press.

Freund, P. (1988) Bringing society into the body. *Theory and Society*, 17, 839–64.

—— (1990) The expressive body: a common ground for the sociology of emotions and health and illness. *Sociology of Health & Illness*, 12, 451–77.

Freund, P. and McGuire, M. (1995) *Health, Illness and the Social Body*. Englewood Cliffs, NJ: Prentice-Hall.

Friedan, B. (1963) *The Feminine Mystique*. New York: Dell.

Fuchs Epstein, C. (1988) *Deceptive Distinctions: Sex, Gender and the Social Order.* London: Yale University Press.

Fuss, D. (1989) *Essentially Speaking.* London: Routledge.

Gadamer, H.-G. (1996) *The Enigma of Health.* Cambridge: Polity Press.

Gadow, S. (1982) Body and self: a dialectic. In V. Kestenbaum (ed.), *The Humanity of the Ill: Phenomenological Perspectives.* Knoxville: University of Tennessee Press, 86–100.

Gallagher, E. (1976) Lines of reconstruction and extension in the Parsonsian sociology of illness. *Social Science and Medicine*, 10, 207–18.

Gallie, D. (1994) Are the unemployed an underclass? Some evidence from the social change and economic life initiative. *Sociology*, 28, 737–57.

Garfinkel, H. (1967) *Studies in Ethnomethodology.* Englewood Cliffs, NJ: Prentice-Hall.

Gatens, M. (1983) A critique of the sex/gender distinction. In J. Allen and P. Patton (eds), *Beyond Marxism*, Leichhardt: Intervention Publishing, 143–60.

—— (1992) Power, bodies and difference. In M. Barrett and A. Phillips (eds), *Destabilising Theory*, Cambridge: Polity Press, 120–37.

Gerhardt, U. (1989) *Ideas about Illness.* Basingstoke: Macmillan.

Giddens, A. (1987) *Social Theory and Modern Sociology.* Cambridge: Polity Press.

—— (1991) *Modernity and Self Identity.* Cambridge: Polity Press.

—— (1992) *The Transformation of Intimacy.* Cambridge: Polity Press.

—— (1994) *Beyond Left and Right: The Future of Radical Politics.* Cambridge: Polity Press.

Gilman, S. (1991) *The Jew's Body.* London: Routledge.

Gilroy, P. (1990) One nation under a groove: the cultural politics of 'race' and racism in Britain. In D. Goldberg (ed.), *Anatomy of Racism*, Minneapolis: University of Minnesota Press, 263–82.

Glaser, B. and Strauss, A. (1965) *Awareness of Dying.* Chicago: Aldine.

Glassner, B. (1989) Fitness and the postmodern self. *Journal of Health and Social Behavior*, 30, 181–91.

Glennerster, H., Matsaganis, M., Owens, P. and Hancock, S. (1994) *Implementing GP Fundholding.* Buckingham: Open University Press.

Goffman, E. (1961) *Asylums.* Harmondsworth: Penguin.

—— (1967) *Interaction Ritual.* New York: Doubleday/Anchor Books.

—— (1969) *Strategic Interaction.* Philadelphia. University of Pennsylvania Press.

Goldberg, D. (1990) The social formation of racist discourse. In D. Goldberg (ed.), *Anatomy of Racism*, Minneapolis: University of Minnesota Press, 295–318.

Goldblatt, P. (1990a) *Longitudinal Study: Mortality and Social Organisation 1971–1981.* London: HMSO.

—— (1990b) Mortality and alternative social classification. In P. Goldblatt, (ed.), *Longitudinal Study: Mortality and Social Organisation 1971–1981*, London: HMSO, 163–91.

Goldthorpe, J. (1983) Women and class analysis. *Sociology*, 17, 483–8.

Goldthorpe, J., Lockwood, D., Bechhofer, F. and Platt, J. (1969) *The Affluent*

Worker in the Class Structure. Cambridge: Cambridge University Press.

Gordon, Deborah (1988) Tenacious assumptions in Western biomedicine. In M. Lock and D. R. Gordon (eds), *Biomedicine Examined*, London: Kulwer Academic Publishers, 19–56.

Gordon, D. F. (1995) Testicular cancer and masculinity. In D. Sabo and D. Gordon (eds), *Men's Health and Illness: Gender, Power and the Body*, London: Sage, 246–65.

Gouldner, A. (1970) *The Coming Crisis of Western Sociology.* New York: Equinox Books.

Graham, H. (1987) Women's smoking and family health. *Social Science and Medicine*, 25, 47–56.

—— (1991) The concept of caring in feminist research: the case of domestic service. *Sociology*, 25, 61–78.

—— (1993a) *Hardship and Health in Women's Lives.* London: Harvester Wheatsheaf.

—— (1993b) Social divisions in caring. *Women's Studies International Forum*, 16, 461–70.

—— (1994) Surviving by smoking. In S. Wilkinson and C. Kitzinger (eds), *Women and Health*, London: Taylor and Francis, 102–23.

—— (1995) Cigarette smoking: a light on gender and class inequality in Britain? *Journal of Social Policy*, 24, 509–27.

Graham, H. and Oakley, A. (1986) Competing ideologies of reproduction: medical and maternal perceptions of pregnancy. In C. Currer and M. Stacey (eds), *Concepts of Health, Illness and Disease*, L'Spa: Berg, 97–115.

Griffiths, R. (1988) *Community Care: Agenda for Action.* London: HMSO.

Grimsley, M. and Bhat, A. (1988) Health. In A. Bhat, R. Carr-Hill and S. Ohri, (eds), *Britain's Black Population* (2nd edition), Aldershot: Gower, 177–207.

Grosz, E. (1990a) Contemporary theories of power and subjectivity. In S. Gunew (ed.), *Feminist Knowledge: Critique and Construct*, London: Routledge, 59–120.

—— (1990b) Conclusion: a note on essentialism and difference. In S. Gunew (ed.), *Feminist Knowledge: Critique and Construct*, London: Routledge, 332–44.

—— (1994) *Volatile Bodies.* Bloomington and Indianapolis: Indiana University Press.

HEA (Health Education Authority) (1994) *Health and Lifestyles: Black and Minority Ethnic Groups in England.* London: HEA.

Hafferty, F. and Light, D. (1995) Professional dynamics and the changing nature of medical work. *Journal of Health and Social Behavior* (extra issue), 132–53.

Hafferty, F. and McKinlay, J. (1993) Conclusion: cross-cultural perspectives on the dynamics of medicine as a profession. In F. Hafferty and J. McKinlay, (eds), *The Changing Character of the Medical Profession*, Oxford: Oxford University Press, 210–26.

Hafferty, F. and Wolinsky, F. (1991) Conflicting characterisations of professional dominance. *Current Research on Occupations and Professions*, 6, 225–49.

Hall, E. (1989) Gender, work control and stress: a theoretical discussion and empirical test. *International Journal of Health Services*, 19, 29–35.

Hall, S. (1992) New ethnicities. In J. Donald and A. Rattansi (eds), *'Race', Culture and Difference*, London: Sage, 252–9.

Ham, C. (1996) Dividing the spoils. *Health Service Journal*, 28 November, 28–9.

Ham, C., Honigsbaum, F. and Thompson D. (1994) Priority setting for health gain. In A. Oakley and A. S. Williams (eds), *The Politics of the Welfare State*, London: UCL Press, 98–126.

Ham, C. and Hunter, D. (1988) *Managing Clinical Activity in the NHS*. London: King's Fund Institute, Briefing Paper 8.

Hammersley, M. (1992) *What's Wrong with Ethnography?* London: Routledge.

Hanmer, J. (1990) Men, power and the exploitation of women. In J. Hearn and D. Morgan (eds), *Men, Masculinities and Social Theory*, London: Unwin Hyman, 21–42.

Haraway, D. (1989) The biopolitics of postmodern bodies: determination of self in immune system discourse. *Differences*, 1, 3–43.

Harding, S. (1995) Social class differences in mortality of men: recent evidence from the OPCS Longitudinal Study. *Population Trends*, 80, 31–7.

Harris, L. (1993) Postmodernism and utopia: an unholy alliance. In M. Cross and M. Keith (eds), *Racism, the City and the State*, London: Routledge, 31–44.

Harrison, G., Owens, D., Holton, A., Neilson, D. and Boot, D. (1988) A prospective study of severe mental disorder in Afro-Caribbean patients. *Psychological Medicine*, 18, 643–57.

Harrison, S., Hunter, D., Marnoch, G. and Pollitt, C. (1992) *Just Managing: Power and Culture in the National Health Service*. London: Macmillan.

Harrison, S. and Lachmann, P. (1996) *Towards a High-Trust NHS*. London: Institute for Policy Research.

Harrison, S. and Pollitt, C. (1994) *Controlling Health Professionals*. Buckingham: Open University Press.

Hart, N. (1982) Is capitalism bad for your health? *British Journal of Sociology*, 33, 435–43.

—— (1985) *The Sociology of Health and Medicine*. Ormskirk, Lancs.: Causeway Books.

—— (1989) Sex, gender and survival: inequalities of life chances between European men and women. In J. Fox (ed.), *Health Inequalities in European Countries*, Aldershot: Gower, 109–41.

Hartmann, H. (1981) The unhappy marriage of Marxism and feminism: toward a more progressive union. In L. Sargent (ed.), *Women and Revolution: A Discussion of the Unhappy Marriage of Marxism and Feminism*, Montreal: Black Rose Books, 363–73.

Haug, M. (1973) Deprofessionalization: an alternative hypothesis for the future. *Sociological Review Monograph*, 2, 195–211.

—— (1988) A re-examination of the hypothesis of physician deprofessionalization. *Milbank Memorial Fund Quarterly*, 66 (supplement 2), 48–56.

Health Service Journal (1996) *What's Happening in the National Health Service?* (3rd edition). London: Macmillan.

—— (1997). Dobson pledges 'new deal', and first-wave HAZs by April 1. *Health Service Journal*, 2 October, 3.

Healy, P. (1997) Jay spells out significance of new clinical indicators. *Health Service Journal*, 17 July, 10.

Hearn, J. (1996) Is masculinity dead? A critique of the concept of masculinity/ masculinities. In M. Mac an Ghaill (ed.), *Understanding Masculinities*, Buckingham: Open University Press, 202–17.

Helgeson, V. S. (1990) The role of masculinity in a prognostic predictor of heart attack severity. *Sex Roles*, 22, 755–74.

—— (1995) Masculinity, men's roles, and coronary heart disease. In D. Sabo and D. Gordon (eds), *Men's Health and Illness: Gender, Power and the Body*, London: Sage, 68–103.

Helmore, E. (1994) The new cutting edge. *Sunday Times*, 26 June, Section 9, 14–15.

Herzlich, C. (1973) *Health and Illness: A Social Psychological Analysis*. London: Academic Press.

Higgins, J. (1995) Gold rush. *Health Service Journal*, 23 November, 24–6.

Hillier, S. (1991a) Women as patients and providers. In G. Scambler (ed.), *Sociology as Applied to Medicine* (3rd edition), London: Ballière Tindall, 129–45.

—— (1991b) The health and health care of ethnic minority groups. In G. Scambler (ed.), *Sociology as Applied to Medicine* (3rd edition), London: Ballière Tindall, 146–59.

Hillyer, B. (1993) *Feminism and Disability*. London: University of Oklahoma Press.

Hochschild, A. R. (1979) Emotion work, feeling rules, and social structure. *American Journal of Sociology*, 85, 551–75.

—— (1983) *The Managed Heart*. London: University of California Press.

Hoggett, P. (1994) The politics of the modernisation of the UK welfare state. In R. Burrows and B. Loader (eds), *Towards a Post-Fordist Welfare State?*, London: Routledge, 38–48.

Holton, R. and Turner, B. (1989) *Max Weber on Economy and Society*. London: Routledge.

Hood-Williams, J. (1996) Goodbye to sex and gender. *Sociological Review*, 44, 1–16.

hooks, b. (1984) *Feminist Theory: From Margin to Centre*. Boston: South End Press.

—— (1991) *Yearning: Race, Gender, and Cultural Politics*. London: Turnaround.

Horobin, G. (1985) Medical sociology in Britain: true confessions of an empiricist. *Sociology of Health & Illness*, 7, 94–107.

Hughes D. (1988) When nurse knows best: some aspects of nurse/doctor interaction in a casualty department. *Sociology of Health & Illness*, 10, 1–22.

Hughes D. and Griffiths, L. (1996) 'But if you look at the coronary anatomy . . .': risk and rationing in cardiac surgery. *Sociology of Health & Illness*, 18, 172–97.

Hunt, K. (1995) A 'cure for all ills'? Constructions of the menopause and the chequered fortunes of hormone replacement therapy. In S. Wilkinson and C. Kitzinger (eds), *Women and Health*, London: Taylor and Francis, 141–65.

Hunt, K. and Annandale, E. (1993) Just the job? Is the relationship between health and domestic work and paid work gender-specific? *Sociology of Health & Illness*, 15, 632–64.

Hunter, D. (1991) Managing medicine: a response to the 'crisis'. *Social Science and Medicine*, 32, 441–9.

—— (1992) Doctors as managers: poachers turned gamekeepers? *Social Science and Medicine*, 35, 557–66.

—— (1994) From tribalism to corporatism: the managerial challenge to medical dominance. In J. Gabe, D. Kelleher and G. Williams (eds), *Challenging Medicine*, London: Routledge, 1–22.

—— (1995a) Making a virtue out of chaos. *Health Service Journal*, 23 March, 23.

—— (1995b) Rationing in health care: the political perspective. *British Medical Bulletin*, 51 (special issue on health care rationing), 876–84.

—— (1996) The changing roles of health care personnel in health and health care management. *Social Science and Medicine*, 43, 799–808.

Hydén, L.-C. (1997) Illness and narrative. *Sociology of Health & Illness*, 19, 48–69.

Illsley, R. (1955) Social class selection and class differences in relation to still-births and infant deaths. *British Medical Journal*, 24 December, 1520–5.

Jaggar, A. (1983) *Feminist Politics and Human Nature*. Totowa, NJ: Rowman and Littlefield.

Jaggar, A. and Rothenberg, P. (1993) *Feminist Frameworks: Alternative Theoretical Accounts of the Relations between Men and Women*. New York: McGraw-Hill.

James, N. (1989) Emotional labour: skill and work in the social regulation of feelings. *Sociological Review*, 37, 15–42.

—— (1992) Care = organisation + physical labour + emotional labour. *Sociology of Health & Illness*, 14, 488–509.

Jameson, F. (1984) Postmodernism, or the cultural logic of late capitalism. *New Left Review*, 146, 53–93.

Jarvie, I. C. (1983) Rationality and relativism. *British Journal of Sociology*, 34, 44–60.

Jeffrey, R. (1979) Normal rubbish: deviant patients in the casualty department. *Sociology of Health & Illness*, 1, 90–108.

Jenny, H. (1994) *Silicone-gate: Exposing the Breast Implant Scandal*. Palm Springs: Siliconegate.

Jewson, N. (1976) The disappearance of the sick-man from medical cosmology, 1770–1870. *Sociology*, 10, 225–44.

Johansson, S. R. (1977) Sex and death in Victorian England. In M. Vicinus (ed.), *A Widening Sphere: Changing Roles for Victorian Women*, London: Indiana University Press, 163–71.

—— (1996) Excess female mortality: constructing survival during development in Meiji Japan and Victorian England. In A. Digby and J. Stewart (eds), *Gender, Health and Welfare*, London: Routledge, 32–66.

Johnson, M. (1993) Equal opportunities in service delivery: responses to a changing population? In W. Ahmad (ed.), *'Race' and Health in Contemporary Britain*, Buckingham: Open University Press, 183–98.

Jolly, D. and Gerbaud, I. (1992) *The Hospital of Tomorrow*, Current Concerns SHS Paper No. 5. Geneva: World Health Organization.

Kandrack, M., Grant, K. and Segall, A. (1991) Gender differences in health-related behaviour: some unanswered questions. *Social Science and Medicine*, 32, 579–90.

Kane, P. (1994) *Women's Health: From Womb to Tomb* (2nd edition). London: Macmillan.

Katz Rothman, B. (1988) *The Tentative Pregnancy*. London: Pandora.

Kelleher, D. (1996) A defense of the use of the terms 'ethnicity' and 'culture'. In D. Kelleher and S. Hillier (eds), *Researching Cultural Differences in Health*, London: Routledge, 69–90.

Kelleher, D. and Hillier, S. (1996) The health of the Irish in England. In D. Kelleher and S. Hillier (eds), *Researching Cultural Differences in Health*, London: Routledge, 103–23.

Kellner, D. (1989) *Jean Baudrillard: From Marxism to Postmodernism and Beyond*. Cambridge: Polity Press.

Kelly, M. (1992a) Self, identity and radical surgery. *Sociology of Health & Illness*, 14, 390–415.

—— (1992b) *Colitis.* London: Routledge.

Kelly, M. and Charlton, B. (1995) The modern and the postmodern in health promotion. In R. Bunton, S. Nettleton and R. Burrows (eds), *The Sociology of Health Promotion*, London: Routledge, 78–90.

Kelly, M. and Field, D. (1994) Comments on the rejection of the biomedical model in sociological discourse. *Medical Sociology News*, 19, 34–7.

Kenen, R. (1996) The at-risk health status and technology: a diagnostic invitation and the 'gift' of knowing. *Social Science and Medicine*, 42, 1545–53.

Kimmel, M. (1990) After fifteen years: the impact of the sociology of masculinity on the masculinity of sociology. In J. Hearn and D. Morgan (eds), *Men, Masculinities and Social Theory*, London: Unwin Hyman, 93–109.

Kimmel, M. and Levine, M. (1992) Men and AIDS. In M. Kimmel and M. Messner (eds), *Men's Lives* (2nd edition), New York: Macmillan, 318–27.

Klein, R. (1995) *The New Politics of the NHS* (3rd edition). London: Longman.

Klein, R., Day, P. and Redmayne, S. (1995) Rationing in the NHS: the dance of the seven veils – in reverse. *British Medical Bulletin*, 51 (special issue on health-care rationing), 769–80.

Kleinman, A. (1988) *The Illness Narratives*. New York: Basic Books.

Koenig, M. and D'Souza, S. (1986) Sex differences in childhood mortality in rural Bangladesh. *Social Science and Medicine*, 22, 15–22.

Krieger, N. (1987) Shades of difference: theoretical underpinnings of the medical controversy on black/white differences in the United States, 1830–1870. *International Journal of Health Services*, 17, 259–78.

Kroker, A. and Kroker, M. (1988) *Body Invaders*. London: Macmillan.

Kübler-Ross, E. (1970) *On Death and Dying*. London: Tavistock.

Landry, D. and MacLean, G. (1993) *Materialist Feminisms*. Oxford: Blackwell.

Langer, R. and Vacanti, J. (1995) Artificial organs. *Scientific American*, September, 100–3.

Laqueur, T. (1990) *Making Sex*. London: Harvard University Press.

Lash, S. (1994) Reflexivity and its doubles: structure, aesthetics, community. In U. Beck, A. Giddens and S. Lash, *Reflexive Modernization*, Cambridge: Polity Press, 110–73.

Lash, S. and Urry, J. (1994) *Economies of Signs and Space*. London: Sage.

Lather, P. (1991) *Getting Smart: Feminist Research and Pedagogy With/in the Postmodern*. London: Routledge.

Levin, D. M. and Solomon, G. F. (1990) The discursive formation of the body in the history of medicine. *Journal of Medicine and Philosophy*, 15, 515–37.

Levine, S. (1993) Some problematic aspects of medicine's changing status. In F. Hafferty and J. McKinlay (eds), *The Changing Character of the Medical Profession*, Oxford: Oxford University Press, 197–201.

Levy, R. (1994) Silicone litigation. *Solicitors Journal*, 25 November, 1214–15.

Light, D. (1993) Countervailing powers: the changing character of the medical profession in the United States. In F. Hafferty and J. McKinlay (eds), *The Changing Character of the Medical Profession*, Oxford: Oxford University Press, 69–80.

—— (1995) Countervailing powers: a framework for professions in transition. In T. Johnson, G. Larkin and M. Saks (eds), *Health Professions and the State in Europe*, London: Routledge, 25–41.

Lindesmith, A. R. and Strauss, A. (1969) *Readings in Social Psychology*, London: Holt, Rinehart and Winston.

Lip, G., Luscombe, C., McCarry, M., Malik, I. and Beevers, G. (1996) Ethnic differences in public health awareness, health perceptions and physical exercise: implications for heart disease prevention. *Ethnicity and Health*, 1 (1), 47–54.

Lipshitz, S. (1978) *Tearing the Veil: Essays on Femininity*. London: RKP.

Lloyd-Bostock, S. (1992) Attributes and apologies in letters of complaint to hospitals and letters of response. In J. Harvey, T. Orbuch, and A. Weber (eds), *Attributions, Accounts and Close Relationships*, New York: Springer-Verlag, 209–20.

Lorber, J. (1991) Can women physicians ever be true equals in the American medical profession? *Current Research on Occupations and Professions*, 6, 25–37.

Lorde, A. (1980) *The Cancer Journals*. London: Sheba Feminist Publishers.

—— (1984) *Sister Outsider*. New York: Crossing Press.

Lupton, D. (1994) *Medicine as Culture*. London: Sage.

Lyotard, J. (1986) *The Postmodern Condition: A Report on Knowledge*. Manchester: Manchester University Press.

McCarthy E. D. (1989) Emotions are social things: an essay in the sociology of emotions. In D. D. Frank and E. D. McCarthy (eds), *The Sociology of Emotions: Original Essays and Research Papers*, Greenwich, Conn.: JAI Press, 51–72.

MacCormack, C. (1988) Health and the social power of women. *Social Science and Medicine*, 26, 677–83.

McGovern, K. (1994) Applications of virtual reality to surgery. *British Medical Journal*, 308, 1054–5.

Macintyre, S. (1986) The social patterning of health by social position in contemporary Britain: directions for sociological research. *Social Science and Medicine*, 23, 393–415.

—— (1993) Gender differences in the perceptions of common cold symptoms. *Social Science and Medicine*, 26, 15–20.

—— (1997) The Black Report and beyond: what are the issues? *Social Science and Medicine*, 44, 723–45.

Macintyre, S., Hunt, K. and Sweeting, H. (1996) Gender differences in health: are things as simple as they seem? *Social Science and Medicine*, 42, 617–24.

Macintyre, S. and West, P. (1991) Lack of class variation in health in adolescence: an artefact of an occupational measure of social class? *Social Science and Medicine*, 32, 395–402.

McKinlay, J. (1977) The business of good doctoring or doctoring as good business: reflections on Freidson's view of the medical game. *International Journal of Health Services*, 7, 459–83.

—— (ed.) (1984) *Issues in the Political Economy of Health Care*. London: Tavistock.

—— (1988) Introduction. *Milbank Memorial Fund Quarterly*, 66 (supplement 2: special issue on the changing character of the medical profession), 1–9.

McKinlay, J. and Stoeckle, J. (1988) Corporatisation and the social transformation of doctoring. *International Journal of Health Services*, 18, 191–205.

McLoone, P. and Boddy, F. (1994) Deprivation and mortality in Scotland, 1981 and 1991. *British Medical Journal*, 309, 1465–70.

McManus, I., Richards, P., Winder, B., Sproston, K. and Styles, V. (1995) Medical school applicants from ethnic minority groups: identifying if and when they are disadvantaged. *British Medical Journal*, 310, 496–500.

McNay, L. (1992) *Foucault and Feminism*. Cambridge: Polity Press.

Mahon, A., Wilkin, D. and Whitehouse C. (1994) Choice of hospitals for elective surgery referrals: GPs' and patients' views. In R. Robinson and J. Le Grand (eds), *Evaluating the NHS Reforms*, London: King's Fund Institute, 108–29.

Makdisi, S., Caserino, C. and Kark, R. (1996) Preface and Introduction. Marxism, communism and history: a reintroduction. In S. Makdisi, C. Caserino, and R. Kark (eds), *Marxism Beyond Marxism*. London: Routledge, ix–x, 1–13.

Marmot, M., (1986) Social inequalities in mortality: the social environment. In R. Wilkinson (ed.), *Class and Health*, London: Tavistock, 21–33.

—— (1996) The social pattern of health and disease. In D. Blane, E. Brunner and R. Wilkinson (eds), *Health and Social Organisation*, London: Routledge, 42–67.

Marshall, H. (1996) Our bodies ourselves: why we should add old-fashioned phenomenology to the new theories of the body? *Women's Studies International Forum*, 19, 253–65.

Martin, E. (1987) *The Woman in the Body*. Milton Keynes: Open University Press.

Marx, K. and Engels, F. (1975 [1848]) *The Manifesto of the Communist Party*. Moscow: Progress Publishers.

Mason, D. (1995) *Race and Ethnicity in Modern Britain*. Oxford: Oxford University Press.

Mason, M.-C. (1993) *Male Infertility: Men Talking*. London: Routledge.

May, A. (1996) The public must be told. *Health Service Journal*, 26 September, 19.

Maynard, M. (1990) The re-shaping of sociology? Trends in the study of gender. *Sociology*, 24, 269–90.

Mead, G. H. (1972) *Mind, Self, and Society* (ed. C. W. Morris). London: University of Chicago Press.

Meire, H., Darzi, A. and Lee, N. (1995) Digital imaging. *British Medical Journal*, 311, 1218–21.

Mellor, P. and Shilling, C. (1993) Modernity, self-identity and the sequestration of death. *Sociology*, 27, 411–31.

Merleau-Ponty, M. (1962) *Phenomenology of Perception*. London: RKP.

Miles, A. (1991) *Women, Health and Medicine*. Milton Keynes: Open University Press.

Miles, R. (1994) *Racism After 'Race Relations'*. London: Routledge.

Millar, B. (1995) The big push. *Health Service Journal*, 2 February, 14.

Millett, K. (1991) *Sex and Politics*. London: Virago.

Millman, M. (1977) *The Unkindest Cut: Life in the Backrooms of Medicine*. New York: Morrow Quill.

Mishler, E. (1989) Critical perspectives on the biomedical model. In P. Brown (ed.), *Perspectives in Medical Sociology*, Belmont, Calif.: Wadsworth, 153–66.

Mohan, J. (1995) *A National Health Service?* London: Macmillan.

Moore, W. (1996) And how are we feeling today? *Health Service Journal*, 28 March, 30–2.

Morris, L. (1994) *Dangerous Classes: The Underclass and Social Citizenship*. London: Routledge.

Mouzelis, N. (1993) The poverty of sociological theory. *Sociology*, 27, 675–95.

Mulcahy, L. (1996) From fear to fraternity: doctors' construction of accounts of complaints. *Journal of Social Welfare and Family Law*, 18, 397–412.

Muller-Hill, B. (1988) *Murderous Science*. Oxford: Oxford University Press.

Murcott, A. (1977) Blind alleys and blinkers: the scope of medical sociology. *Scottish Journal of Sociology*, 1, 155–71.

Murray, C. (1990) *The Emerging British Underclass*. London: IEA Health and Welfare Unit.

NHSME (National Health Service Management Executive) (1991) *Junior Doctors: The New Deal*. London: NHSME.

—— (1992) *Local Voices*. Leeds: NHSME.

Nagel, J. (1994) Constructing ethnicity: creating and recreating ethnic identity and culture. *Social Problems*, 41, 152–69.

Nathanson, C. (1980) Social roles and health status among women: the significance of employment. *Social Science and Medicine*, 14a, 463–71.

Navarro, V. (1985a) US Marxist scholarship in the analysis of health and medicine. *Social Science and Medicine*, 15, 525–45.

—— (1985b) Double standards in the analysis of Marxist scholarship: a reply to Reidy's critique of my work. *Social Science and Medicine*, 20, 441–51.

—— (1986) *Crisis, Health and Medicine*. London: Tavistock.

—— (1988) Professional dominance or proletarianisation? Neither. *Milbank Memorial Fund Quarterly*, 66 (supplement 2), 57–75.

—— (1989) Race *or* class, or race *and* class. *International Journal of Health Services*, 19, 311–14.

—— (1994) *The Politics of Health Policy: The US Reforms 1980–1994*. Oxford: Blackwell.

Nettleton, S. (1992) *Power, Pain and Dentistry*. Buckingham: Open University Press.

New, B. and Le Grand, J. (1996) *Rationing in the NHS: Principles and Pragmatism*. London: King's Fund.

Norman, D., Henriques, F. and Slaughter, C. (1969) *Coal is Our Life*. London: Tavistock.

Notman, M., Howe, K. R., Rittenberg, W., Bridgham, R., Holmes, M. M. and Rovner, D. R. (1987) Social policy and professional self-interest: physician responses to DRGs. *Social Science and Medicine*, 25, 1259–67.

ONS (Office of National Statistics) (1996) *Population and Health Monitor*, London: HMSO, DH2 96/1 & 2.

OPCS (1991) *Explanation of the Occupational Classification Scheme*. London: HMSO.

—— (1992) *1841–1990 Mortality Statistics, Serial Tables. England and Wales*. London: HMSO Series DH1, No. 25.

—— (1993a) *The General Household Survey*. London: HMSO, Series GHS, No. 24.

—— (1993b) *1991 Mortality Statistics, General: England and Wales*. London: HMSO, Series DH1, No. 26.

—— (1994a) *1989 Cancer Statistics: Registrations*. London: HMSO, Series MB1, No. 22.

—— (1994b) *1992 Mortality Statistics: Serial Tables*. London: HMSO, Series DHI, No. 27.

—— (1995a) *Occupational Health: Decennial Supplement*, ed. F. Drever. London: HMSO, Series DS, No. 10.

—— (1995b) *Morbidity Statistics from General Practice: Fourth National Study 1991–2*. London: HMSO.

—— (1995c) *Living in Britain: Results from the 1994 General Household Survey*. London: HMSO.

Oakley, A. (1974) *The Sociology of Housework*. Oxford: Blackwell.

—— (1984) *The Captured Womb*. Oxford: Blackwell.

O'Connor, J. (1973) *The Fiscal Crisis of the State*. New York: St Martin's Press.

Offe, C. (1984) *Contradictions of the Welfare State*. London: Hutchinson.

Olesen, V. (1990) The neglected emotions: a challenge to medical sociology. *Medical Sociology News*, 16, 11–22.

Oliver, M. (1996) *Understanding Disability: From Theory to Practice*. London: Macmillan.

Orr, J. (1990) Theory on the market: panic, incorporating. *Social Problems*, 37, 460–83.

Owen, D. (1996) Size, structure and growth of the ethnic minority population. In D. Coleman and J. Salt (eds), *Ethnicity in the 1991 Census*, Vol. 1, London: HMSO, 80–123.

Pakulski, J. and Waters, M. (1996) *The Death of Class*. London: Sage.

Parsons, T. (1951) *The Social System*. New York: Free Press.

—— (1975) The sick role and the role of the physician reconsidered. *Milbank Memorial Fund Quarterly*, summer, 257–78.

Patton, C. (1992) From nation to family: containing African AIDS. In A. Parker, M. Russo, D. Sommer and P. Yaeger (eds), *Nationalisms and Sexualities*, London: Routledge, 218–34.

Payne, S. (1991) *Women, Health and Poverty: An Introduction*. London: Harvester Wheatsheaf.

Pelling, M. and Webster, C. (1979) Medical practitioners. In C. Webster (ed.),

Health, Medicine and Mortality in the Sixteenth Century, Cambridge: Cambridge University Press, 167–235.

Petchey, R. (1995) General practitioner fundholding: weighing the evidence. *Lancet*, 346, 1139–42.

Pfeffer, N. (1985) The hidden pathology of the male reproductive system. In H. Homans (ed.), *The Sexual Politics of Reproduction*, Aldershot: Gower, 30–44.

Phillimore, P., Beattie, A. and Townsend, P. (1994) Widening inequality of health in northern England, 1981–1991. *British Medical Journal*, 308, 1125–8.

Pierce, M. and Armstrong, D. (1996) Afro-Caribbean lay beliefs about diabetes: an exploratory study. In D. Kelleher and S. Hillier (eds), *Researching Cultural Differences in Health*, London: Routledge, 91–102.

Pierret, J. (1995) Constructing discourses about health and their social determinants. In A. Radley (ed.), *Worlds of Illness*, London: Routledge, 9–26.

Pilgrim, D. and Rogers, A. (1993) *A Sociology of Mental Health and Illness*. Buckingham: Open University Press.

Piore, M. and Sabel, C. (1984) *The Second Industrial Divide*. New York: Basic Books.

Pollock, K. (1995) Attitude of mind as a means of resisting illness. In A. Radley (ed.), *Worlds of Illness*. London: Routledge, 49–70.

Popay, J. (1992) 'My health is all right, but I'm just tired all the time.' Women's experience of ill health. In H. Roberts (ed.), *Women's Health Matters*, London: Routledge, 99–120.

Popay, J., Bartley, M., and Owen, C. (1993) Gender inequalities in health: social position, affective disorders and minor physical morbidity. *Social Science and Medicine*, 36, 21–32.

Popay, J. and Williams, G. (1994a) Local voices in the NHS: needs effectiveness and sufficiency. In A. Oakley and A. S. Williams (eds), *The Politics of the Welfare State*. London: UCL Press, 75–97.

—— + —— (1994b) Lay knowledge and the privilege of experience. In J. Gabe, D. Kelleher and G. Williams (eds), *Challenging Medicine*, London: Routledge, 118–39.

Poster, M. (1988) *Jean Baudrillard: Selected Writings*. Cambridge: Polity Press.

Pourroy, J. (1996) *Behind the Scenes at ER*. London: Ebury Press.

Pugh, H. and Moser, K. (1990) Measuring women's mortality differences. In H. Roberts (ed.), *Women's Health Counts*, London: Routledge, 93–112.

Pulkingham, J. (1992) Employment restructuring in the health service: efficiency initiatives, working patterns and workforce composition. *Work, Employment and Society*, 6, 307–421.

Ramazanoglu, C. (1989) *Feminism and the Contradictions of Oppression*. London: Routledge.

—— (1992) What can you do with a man? Feminism and the critical appraisal of masculinity. *Women's Studies International Forum*, 15, 339–50.

Rattansi, A. (1994) 'Western' racisms, ethnicities and identities in a 'postmodern' frame. In A. Rattansi and S. Westwood (eds), *Racism, Modernity and Identity*, Cambridge: Polity Press, 15–86.

Rattansi, A. and Westwood, S. (1994) Modern racisms, racialized identities. In

A. Rattansi and S. Westwood (eds), *Racism, Modernity and Identity*, Cambridge: Polity Press, 1–12.

Reidy, A. (1984) Marxist functionalism in medicine: a critique of the work of Vicente Navarro on health and medicine. *Social Science and Medicine*, 19, 897–910.

Rich, A. (1992) *Of Woman Born*. London: Virago.

Ricoeur, P. (1991) Life in quest of narrative. In D. Wood (ed.), *On Paul Ricoeur: Narrative and Interpretation*, London: Routledge.

Roberts, M. (1989) Breast screening: time for a rethink? *British Medical Journal*, 299, 1153–5.

Robinson, J. (1994) The changing boundaries of the American hospital. *Milbank Quarterly*, 72, 259–75.

Robinson, K. (1992) The nursing workforce: aspects of inequality. In J. Robinson, A. Gray and R. Elkan (eds), *Policy Issues in Nursing*, Milton Keynes: Open University Press, 24–37.

Rogers, L. (1994) Future of NHS seen through a keyhole. *Sunday Times*, 26 June, 8.

Rose, D. (1995) *A Report on Phase 1 of the ESRC Review of OPCS Social Classifications*. Swindon: ESRC.

Roth, J. (1963) *Timetables*. New York: Bobbs-Merrill.

Rowland, R. (1992) *Living Laboratories*. London: Lime Tree.

Rowland, R. and Klein, R. D. (1990) Radical feminism: critique and construct. In S. Gunew (ed.), *Feminist Knowledge: Critique and Construct*, London: Routledge, 271–303.

Ruzek, S. (1980) *The Women's Health Movement: Feminist Alternatives to Medical Control*. London: Praeger.

Sabo, D. and Gordon, D. (1995) Rethinking men's health and illness. In D. Sabo and D. Gordon (eds), *Men's Health and Illness: Gender, Power and the Body*, London: Sage, 1–21.

Saks, M. (1994) The alternatives to medicine. In J. Gabe, D. Kelleher and G. Williams (eds), *Challenging Medicine*, London: Routledge, 84–103.

Salvage, J. (1992) The new nursing: empowering patients or empowering nurses? In J. Robinson, A. Gray and R. Elkan (eds), *Policy Issues in Nursing*, Milton Keynes: Open University Press, 9–23.

Samson, C. (1995) The fracturing of medical dominance in British psychiatry? *Sociology of Health & Illness*, 17, 245–68.

Sarup, M. (1993) *Post-structuralism and Postmodernism*. London: Harvester Wheatsheaf.

Savage, M., Barlow, J., Dickens, P. and Fielding, T. (1992) *Property, Bureaucracy and Culture*. London: Routledge.

Savage, M. and Miles, A. (1994) *The Remaking of the British Working Class*. London: Routledge.

Sawicki, J. (1991) *Disciplining Foucault: Feminism, Power and the Body*. London: Routledge.

Schacter, S. and Singer, J. E. (1962) Cognitive, social and physiological determinants of emotional state. *Psychological Review*, 69, 379–99.

Scott, J. (1991) *Who Rules Britain?* Cambridge: Polity Press.

Scott, S. and Morgan, D. (1993) *Body Matters*. London: Falmer Press.

Segal, L. (1992) *Slow Motion: Changing Masculinities, Changing Men*. London: Virago.

Seidler, V. (1994) *Unreasonable Men*. London: Routledge.

Shaar, K., McCarthy, N. and Meshefedjian, G. (1994) Disadvantage in physically disabled adults: an assessment of the causation and selection hypotheses. *Social Science and Medicine*, 39, 407–13.

Shaw, G. B. (1980 [1911]) *The Doctor's Dilemma*. New York: Penguin.

Sheldon, T. and Parker, H. (1992) The use of 'ethnicity' and 'race' in health research: a cautionary note. In W. Ahmad (ed.), *The Politics of 'Race' and Health*, Bradford: Race Relations Unit, University of Bradford, 55–80.

Shilling, C. (1993) *The Body and Social Theory*. London: Sage.

Shiu, M. (1993) Refusing to treat smokers is unethical and a dangerous precedent. *British Medical Journal*, 306, 1048–9.

Shortell, S., Gillies R., and Devers, K. (1995) Reinventing the American hospital. *Milbank Quarterly*, 73, 131–60.

Shorter, E. (1982) *A History of Women's Bodies*. London: Allen Lane.

Shott, S. (1979) Emotion and social life: a symbolic interactionist analysis. *American Journal of Sociology*, 84, 1317–34.

Silverman, D. (1987) *Communication and Medical Practice: Social Relations in the Clinic*. London: Sage.

Simon, R. W. (1995) Gender, multiple roles, role meaning, and mental illness. *Journal of Health and Social Behaviour*, 36, 182–94.

Skellington, R. (1996) *'Race' in Britain Today* (2nd edition). London: Open University Press/Sage.

Smaje, C. (1995) *Health, 'Race' and Ethnicity*. London: King's Fund Institute.

—— (1996) The ethnic patterning of health: new directions for theory and research. *Sociology of Health & Illness*, 18, 139–71.

Smart, C. (1989) *Feminism and the Power of Law*. London: Routledge.

—— (1990) Feminist approaches to criminology, or postmodern woman meets atavistic man. In L. Gelsthorpe and A. Morris (eds), *Feminist Perspectives in Criminology*, Buckingham: Open University Press, 70–84.

Smith, C. (1996) Blair's fresh prescription. *Independent*, 4 November, 15.

Smith, S. (1993) Residential segregation and the politics of racialisation. In M. Cross and M. Keith (eds), *Racism, the City and the State*, London: Routledge, 128–43.

Solomos, J. and Back, L. (1994) Conceptualizing racisms: social theory, politics and research. *Sociology*, 28, 143–61.

Sontag, S. (1988) *AIDS and its Metaphors*. London: Penguin.

Sorensen, G. and Verbrugge, L. (1987) Women, work and health. *Annual Review of Public Health*, 8, 235–51.

Stacey, J. (1993) Untangling feminist theory. In D. Richardson and V. Robinson (eds), *Introducing Women's Studies*, London: Macmillan, 49–73.

Stacey, M. (1981) The division of labour revisited, or overcoming the two Adams. In P. Abrams, R. Deem, J. Finch and P. Rock (eds), *Practice and*

Progress: British Sociology 1950–1980, London: Allen and Unwin, 172–90.

—— (1988) *The Sociology of Health and Healing*. London: Unwin Hyman.

—— (1992) *Regulating British Medicine: The General Medical Council*. Chichester: John Wiley and Sons.

—— (1994) The power of lay knowledge: a personal view. In J. Popay and G. Williams (eds), *Researching the People's Health*, London: Routledge, 85–98.

Stainton Rogers, W. (1991) *Explaining Health and Illness*. London: Harvester Wheatsheaf.

Stillion, J. (1995) Premature death among males. In D. Sabo and D. Gordon (eds), *Men's Health and Illness: Gender, Power and the Body*, London: Sage, 46–67.

Stoeckle, J. (1995) The citadel cannot hold: technologies go outside the hospital, patients and doctors go too. *Milbank Quarterly*, 73, 3–17.

Strauss, A., Fagerhaugh, S., Suczeck, B. and Weiner, B. (1985) *The Social Organisation of Medical Work*. Chicago: Chicago University Press.

Strauss, A., Schatzman, L., Ehrlich, D., Bucher, R. and Sabshin, M. (1963) The hospital and its negotiated order. In E. Freidson (ed.), *The Hospital in Modern Society*, London: Free Press, 147–69.

Strong, P. (1979) *The Ceremonial Order of the Clinic*. London: RKP.

Strong, P. and Robinson, J. (1990) *The NHS: Under New Management*. Milton Keynes: Open University Press.

Stubbs, P. (1993) 'Ethnically sensitive' or 'anti-racist'? Models for health research and delivery. In W. Ahmad (ed.), *'Race' and Health in Contemporary Britain*, Buckingham: Open University Press, 34–47.

Summerton, N. (1995) Positive and negative factors in defensive medicine: a questionnaire study of general practitioners. *British Medical Journal*, 310, 27–9.

Sweeting, H. (1995) Reversals of fortune? Sex differences in health in childhood and adolescence. *Social Science and Medicine*, 40, 77–90.

Thomas, C. (1993) De-constructing concepts of care. *Sociology*, 27, 649–69.

Tickle, L. (1996) Mortality trends in the United Kingdom, 1982 to 1992. *Population Trends*, 86, 21–8.

Tomlinson, B. (1992) *Inquiry into London's Health Services, Medical Education and Research*. London: HMSO.

Tong, R. (1992) *Feminist Thought*. London: Routledge.

Townsend, P. (1993) Underclass and overclass: the widening gulf between social classes in Britain in the 1980s. In G. Payne and M. Cross (eds), *Sociology in Action*, London: Macmillan, 91–118.

Townsend, P. and Davidson, N. (1982) *Inequalities in Health: The Black Report*. London: Penguin.

Tran, M. (1995) Breast implant firm files for bankruptcy. *Guardian*, 16 May, 3.

Turner, B. (1992) *Regulating Bodies*. London: Routledge.

Underwood, M. and Bailey, J. (1993) Should smokers be offered coronary bypass surgery? *British Medical Journal*, 306, 1047–8.

Vallin, J. (1993) Social change and mortality decline: women's advantage achieved or regained? In N. Federici, K. Oppenheim Mason and S. Sogner (eds), *Women's Position and Demographic Change*, Oxford: Clarendon Press, 120–212.

Verbrugge, L. (1985) Gender and health: an update on hypotheses and evidence. *Journal of Health and Social Behavior*, 26, 156–82.

—— (1988) Unveiling higher morbidity for men. In M. White Riley (ed.), *Social Structures and Human Lives*, London: Sage, 138–60.

Victor, C. (1989) Health inequality in later life: age, gender or class? In C. Martin and D. McQueen (eds), *Readings for the New Public Health*, 75–88.

—— (1991) *Health and Health Care in Later Life*. Buckingham: Open University Press.

WMRHA (West Midlands Regional Health Authority) (1994) *Agenda for Health: Report of the Regional Director of Public Health 1994*. Birmingham.

Wadsworth, M. (1986) Serious illness in childhood and its association with later-life achievement. In R. Wilkinson (ed.), *Class and Health*, London: Tavistock, 50–74.

Waitzkin, H. (1991) *The Politics of Medical Encounters*. New Haven: Yale University Press.

Walby, S. and Greenwell, J., with L. Mackay and K. Soothill (1994) *Medicine and Nursing*. London: Sage.

Waldby, C. (1996) *AIDS and the Body Politic*. London: Routledge.

Waldron, I. (1983) Sex differences in human mortality: the role of genetic factors. *Social Science and Medicine*, 17, 321–33.

—— (1995) Contribution of changing gender differences in behaviour and social roles to changing gender differences in mortality. In D. Sabo and D. Gordon (eds), *Men's Health and Illness: Gender, Power and the Body*, London: Sage, 22–45.

Walker, A. (1990) Blaming the victims: response to C. Murray. In C. Murray, *The Emerging British Underclass*, London: IEA Health and Welfare Unit, 49–65.

Wallen, J., Waitzkin, H. and Stoeckle, J. D. (1979) Physician stereotypes about female health and illness. *Women and Health*, 4, 135–46.

Walsh, K. (1994) Citizens, charters and contracts. In R. Keat, N. Whiteley and N. Abercrombie (eds), *The Authority of the Consumer*, London: Routledge, 189–206.

Walter, T. (1994) *The Revival of Death*. London: Routledge.

Ward, L. (1993) Race equality and employment in the national health service. In W. Ahmad (ed.), *'Race' and Health in Contemporary Britain*, Buckingham: Open University Press, 167–82.

Watson, J., Cunningham-Burley, S. and Watson, N. (1995) Lay theorising about the body and health. Paper presented at the BSA Medical Sociology Conference, 1995. York University, UK.

Weedon, C. (1987) *Feminist Practice and Poststructuralist Theory*. Oxford: Blackwell.

West, P. (1991) Rethinking the health selection explanation for health inequalities. *Social Science and Medicine*, 32, 373–84.

West, P., Macintyre, S., Annandale, E. and Hunt, K. (1990) Social class and health in youth: findings from the West of Scotland Twenty-07 Study. *Social Science and Medicine*, 30, 665–73.

Westergaard, J. (1995) *'Who gets what?' The Hardening of Class Inequality in the Late Twentieth Century*. Cambridge: Polity Press.

Westwood, S. (1994) Racism, mental illness and the politics of identity. In A. Rattansi and S. Westwood (eds), *Racism, Modernity and Identity*, Cambridge: Polity Press, 247–65.

White, K. (1991) *The Sociology of Health and Illness. Current Sociology* 39 (2): whole issue.

Whitehead, M. (1994) Is it fair? Evaluating the equity implications of the NHS reforms. In R. Robinson and J. Le Grand (eds), *Evaluating the NHS Reforms*, London: King's Fund Institute, 208–42.

Widgery, D. (1991) *Some Lives: A GP's East End*. London: Sinclair-Stevenson.

Wilkinson, R. (1986) Socio-economic differences in mortality: interpreting the data on size and trends. In R. Wilkinson (ed.), *Class and Health*, London: Tavistock, 1–33.

—— (1996) *Unhealthy Societies*. London: Routledge.

Wilkinson, S. and Kitzinger, C. (1995) Towards a feminist approach to breast cancer. In S. Wilkinson and C. Kitzinger (eds), *Women and Health*, London: Taylor and Francis, 124–40.

Williams, F. (1994) Social relations, welfare and the post-Fordist debate. In R. Burrows and B. Loader (eds), *Towards a Post-Fordist Welfare State?*, London: Routledge, 49–73.

Williams, G. (1984) The genesis of chronic illness: narrative re-construction. *Sociology of Health & Illness*, 6, 175–200.

—— (1995) Chronic illness and the pursuit of virtue in everyday life. In A. Radley (ed.), *Worlds of Illness*, London: Routledge, 92–108.

Williams, S. (1996) The vicissitudes of embodiment across the chronic illness trajectory. *Body and Society*, 2, 23–47.

Witz, A. (1994) The challenge of nursing. In J. Gabe, D. Kelleher and G. Williams (eds), *Challenging Medicine*, London: Routledge, 23–45.

Wolf, N. (1991) *The Beauty Myth*. London: Vintage Books.

—— (1994) *Fire with Fire*. London: Vintage Books.

Wolinsky, F. (1993) The professional dominance, deprofessionalization, proletarianization, and corporatization perspectives: an overview and synthesis. In F. Hafferty and J. McKinlay (eds), *The Changing Character of the Medical Profession*, Oxford: Oxford University Press, 11–24.

Yates, J. (1995a) *Serving Two Masters: Consultants, the National Health Service and Private Medicine*. London: Channel 4 Television.

—— (1995b) *Private Eye, Heart and Hip*. London: Churchill Livingstone.

Young, I. (1981) Beyond the unhappy marriage: a critique of dual-systems theory. In L. Sargent (ed.), *Women and Revolution: A Discussion of the Unhappy Marriage of Marxism and Feminism*, Montreal: Black Rose Books, 43–69.

Zalewski, M. (1990) Logical contradictions in feminist health care: a rejoinder to Peggy Foster. *Journal of Social Policy*, 19, 235–44.

Zussman, R. (1993) Life in the hospital: a review. *Milbank Quarterly*, 71, 167–85.

Index